STALINGRAD

MEMORIES AND REASSESSMENTS

JOACHIM WIEDER AND
HEINRICH GRAF VON EINSIEDEL

CASSELL

Cassell
Wellington House, 125 Strand
London WC2R 0BB

Originally published in German in 1962
This revised edition first published in German in 1993
by F. A. Herbig Verlagsbuchhandlung GmbH, Munich, as
Stalingrad und die Verandwortung des Soldaten

First published in Great Britain by Arms and Armour 1995
This Cassell Military Paperbacks edition 2002

British Library Cataloguing-in-Publication Data
A catalogue record for this book is available from the
British Library

ISBN 0-304-36338-3

Designed and edited by DAG Publications Ltd

Printed and bound in Great Britain by
Cox & Wyman Ltd., Reading, Berks.

CONTENTS

PREFACE

This book was first published in Germany thirty years ago, and received a surprising response both at home and abroad. For this was the first book dealing with Stalingrad in which the author not only placed the purely military problems of the battle in the background, but fundamentally questioned the political and moral responsibility of the military leadership.

Within a short time, it had been published in Spain, Italy and Hungary, and became the first West German book on Stalingrad to be published in the Soviet Union. Twenty years later, the French discovered it as well, and published it with great success.

Many competent critics consider it to be the most profound analysis of the tragedy that took place on the Volga fifty years ago.

Sadly, Joachim Wieder did not live to see the new German edition. He died on 18 October 1992 after a long and difficult illness. Because of this illness, he asked me, his comrade and friend of fifty years, to help him with the new edition. However, this assistance was restricted to purely technical matters, to the detailed study of the literature on Stalingrad published in the meantime, and to discussions about alterations, additions and abridgements, which he considered necessary after thirty years.

Basically, the only reason these changes and additions were required was because Manfred Kehrig's book *Stalingrad, Analysis and Documentation of a Battle*, which was published in 1974 by the Research Institute for Military History in Freiburg as Volume 15 of their *Contributions to Military and War History*, brought to light facts which the author could not have known in 1962.

The fundamental statements in his book remain unaltered. Nevertheless, Wieder felt duty bound to revise, to a limited extent, his judgements on the purely military responsibility for this dramatic defeat of the Wehrmacht, to bring out more clearly the pivotal role played by Field Marshal von Manstein, famed for his operational genius, and, by so doing, protect the commander of Sixth Army, Field Marshal Paulus, from von Manstein's reproaches.

Ten years ago, Wieder wrote in the concluding passages of the French edition of his book: 'From the very beginning, Hitler's war was a crime against humanity. But even if the whole war were a monstrosity that compromised all soldierly values from the very outset, the events of Stalingrad still represent an exemplary singularity within the framework of this suicidal madness.

'This applies not only to the military problems, but primarily to the questions of psychology and morality. The fact that the Army Command did not act on its own responsibility, even in the very last phase of the battle, alone proves the degree to which the soldierly ethic had been eroded of its true content. Every military leader has a responsibility not only to his superiors, but also to his soldiers. What took place at the end of this battle, however, was simply inhuman. The generals responsible despicably betrayed their obligation of loyalty towards the men entrusted to them.'

Heinrich Graf von Einsiedel
Munich, December 1992

INTRODUCTION

From the notes of a survivor of Stalingrad has grown a book that goes beyond the mere recounting of memories. Armed with these memories, it surveys the humanly frightful and historically far-reaching events of this battle, and examines the statements of those who participated in it in positions of leadership. The path of the author leads from the freezing steppe on the banks of the Volga, through prisoner-of-war camps in the Soviet Union (we met in one of these camps, and I gained the friendship of a man whose incorruptibility enmeshed him in grave dangers there), back to his native land and to a leading position in the German library system. He did not attempt to rid himself of what lay behind him by forgetting. He felt that the dead who stayed behind, and the fate he was required to endure, put him under an obligation. In the name of the dead as well as the living, and of those who would come after, he sought to determine what might be learned from these events. So too he also asks those who held any sort of position of command back then, what they have to say today about those events. He does not ask this as a judge; that would be at odds with the humility of his nature, but rather as a participant, as someone who escaped, and in the name of those who were sacrificed. However, prompted neither from resentment nor from a need of revenge, and without wishing it though unable to prevent it, his questioning becomes a tribunal. Not the Day of Judgement towards which we are all going and which none of us can anticipate, but the sort of preliminary tribunal that can and must take place here below among us human beings; accusation, indictment, examination, defence, attempts to put the blame on others, evaluation of the arguments of prosecution and defence; and finally the verdict. Still a preliminary verdict, a human verdict that does not irrevocably condemn those whose actions and omissions are on trial here. It takes the entanglements between human endeavour and overpowering circumstances into consideration just as readily as the human weakness and short-sightedness to which we are all prone. It dissects the pleas of defence and self-defence, judges the arguments presented, and asks the participants if they really believe that they will get by with nothing better than this. Get by before the tribunal of history, get by in the face of the dead, get by in the accounting before the Ultimate Judge; and whether they should not be saying something altogether different; confession of guilt and plea for absolution, and only then, and in that context, asking for the correction of false accusations and the granting of mitigating circumstances.

'The *leitmotiv* of this book', writes the author in his final statement, 'is the question of responsibility'. Because, since any chain of circumstances and the overpowering march of history do not change the fact that history is the result of the actions of human beings, therefore history must become the inquisition of past actions. The fact that much of it is not subjectable to human judgement does not mean that the terms 'guilt' and 'responsibility' are misplaced here, their use forbidden by the alleged immunity from influence enjoyed by the historic powers. He who deliberately attempts to exclude the moral question by appealing to this kind of fatalism promulgates an inhuman concept of history, at the end of which stand inhuman practices. While the history of mankind has not yet reached the Day of Judgement, history cannot be recorded without the question of the responsibility and guilt of individuals and entire groups being raised. Whether he wants to or not, the historian must become involved in the pleas of prosecution and defence, as must, even more deeply, the historian who is not merely recording history for its own sake, but to lend his voice to the victims, in an endeavour to prevent the present from forgetting and repeating the past.

What do we mean here by responsibility? 'I alone carry the responsibility for Stalingrad', we hear Hitler say. Had he been put on trial after the tragedy, had the leading generals nailed him to these words and called him to account, the statement might have become more than just empty words. In the absence of the court, in the face of which responsibility becomes concrete, words such as these only create the backdrop for the general lack of responsibility; the recipients of orders transfer the responsibility to him who gave them, and step by step it is passed upwards. The chief solemnly accepts it, but only to evade, together with those below him, any court of accounting – by suicide if there is no other way. The whole charade, totally without consequences, therefore without real meaning, is played out in the form of solemn declamations, and only serves to make responsibility become intangible. With feelings of relief, the immediate subordinates seize upon the readily given assurance of the superior, hold him to his purely verbal acceptance of responsibility, declare themselves to be 'soldierly decent', and are pleased with the exoneration so easily obtained; as von Manstein's report so clearly demonstrates. Therefore, to become real, responsibility must be legally recoverable. The whole idea behind God's Day of Judgement is that there is no escape from a final accounting, which every one of us must render. It does not abrogate the requirement, however, that an accounting must also be rendered between human beings. Without the willingness to do so, the appeal to a higher court, be it God's or that of history, becomes a cheap and empty phrase.

Another aspect of responsibility is that it can only be shunted off to a limited degree. The relationship between leader and follower is not a National Socialist invention, but a universal social phenomenon. It can happen anywhere and at any time, even outside the military sphere, that a leader accepts the responsibility for an action he has ordered, that the subordinate suppresses his misgivings and carries it out, and that because of this only the superior can be held accountable. The body of precedent and codified law in today's world shows clearly that the possibilities of transferring and accepting responsibility have their limitations; as for example, in the penal code. But there are also other limitations outside the legal sphere. The closer a person stands to the top of the leadership pyramid and the higher he rises above the mass of ordinary people, the more he becomes an active element in the decision-making process, the more will he be held accountable for it, and the less does his responsibility become transferable. The higher one stands, the less one can escape into passivity, or into the claim of passivity (as merely a recipient of orders). One must become active, not only downwards, but if necessary, upwards as well. One cannot claim the privileges and honours of the higher rank, without also accepting this increasing non-transferability of responsibility. A military leader in a high position, who consoles and defends himself by saying that he is not sufficiently aware of the overall situation, and that the supreme commander accepts the full responsibility, is reducing himself to the level of a non-commissioned officer, and revealing that he intends to enjoy the dignity of his rank, without accepting its burden.

These limitations also encompass those of the possible victim. Again, and not only in warfare, it may become necessary to sacrifice a group of people in order to save others. Whole armies may be lost. But is it permissible for an army to be put into a hopeless situation and deliberately sacrificed for the sake of a strategic objective? He who answers in the affirmative with cold military objectivity must realise that he is sundering the bond of trust between leadership and troops. Troops that are thus regarded as mere human *matériel* have their moral ties destroyed. In tomorrow's war of total destruction, this will become a commonplace problem, one that will prove that in such a war, any and all ethics have long become empty phrases. The pleas of self-defence of military leaders in the last war already enable us to anticipate with horror today, what the troops and the civilian population can expect from their military leadership in a future conflict.

A final element of responsibility is that with increasing rank and position the possibility of pleading mitigating circumstances decreases more and more. Weakness becomes guilt and no longer serves as an excuse. Human compassion for the heavy burden of the decisions required, as is made apparent in this report, cannot be denied. He who imagines himself to be in the situation, will no longer be able to condemn out of hand in cold blood. He who failed in these decisions, may plead for forgiveness. He cannot justify himself with his weakness.

For good reason therefore, in his closing remarks the author uses the term 'unwillingness to repent'. This phrase joins the sphere of ethics to that of religion. It reminds us that while there is no escape from guilt for us as actors, this does not exonerate us. All of us are always too weak for the demands put upon us, but we cannot excuse ourselves with our weakness and therefore must ever and ever be prepared to repent our failure and to shoulder the verdict this failure entails. Only where this is so, may the prosecution fall silent and the guilt be forgiven. Only then do we gain the possibility to learn for the future. Only its candid admission banishes the after-effects of guilt and opens the way into the future. Today's representatives of the military, of politics, of the Church, compete with one another in adhering to the 'unwillingness to repent'. That is why we make no progress and continually enmesh ourselves in new dilemmas. Only a 'willingness to repent' can clear the air. Self-righteousness and cynicism are twins and make politics unreal. The spirit of repentance is the Good Angel of those who carry responsibility. The bitter review which constitutes this book is intended to serve it, and thereby open the way into a living future.

Helmut Gollwitzer

OVERVIEW OF THE CAMPAIGN OF 1942

At about the turn of the year 1941–2, the momentous setbacks of the Wehrmacht before the gates of Moscow had led to a serious crisis and made it clear that the Blitzkrieg against the Soviet Union had failed. However, after these experiences, so bitter for him, Hitler was imbued with the fanatical wish, in particular when looking back to the victorious pocket battles of the preceding summer, to make up for everything that had remained unachieved, and by a new and decisive operation finally destroy the Bolshevik enemy whose ability to resist he no longer considered to be very substantial. The ultimate objective was to eradicate Bolshevism, to carve up and economically exploit the territories of the Soviet Union, and thereby to create the conditions for eliminating Great Britain and establishing German hegemony over Europe in the form of a 'Greater Germanic Reich'. Time was running out and victory on the eastern front had to be achieved the more quickly, since Hitler had declared war on the United States in December 1941, and an invasion in the west or the south was to be expected sooner or later. In that same month incidentally, after dismissing Field Marshal von Brauchitsch, he took over Supreme Command of the army. This enabled him gradually to erode the powers of the Army General Staff, which he viewed with increasing suspicion and contempt, and fatally to reduce the Chief of the Army General Staff's share of responsibility.

The plan of operations for the big summer offensive was set down in his directive No. 41 of 5 April 1942. Its objective was 'to finally destroy the active fighting strength remaining to the Soviets and to take away as far as possible their most important resources of war'. First, however, it was important to 'unite all available forces in the southern sector, with the objective of annihilating the enemy forward of the Don, and then gain the oil fields in the Caucasus region and the passage over the Caucasus itself'. In preparation for the main offensive, it was mandatory to 'clean up and stabilise the whole eastern front and its rearward areas'. In the south, the immediate objectives in the Crimea included taking the Kerch peninsula and the fortified port of Sevastopol, which was bitterly defended by the Soviets.

The summer offensive was intended to be carried out in four successive phases. After the capture of Voronezh, an important keystone in the whole advance, and the destruction of enemy forces between the Donetz and the Don, the third phase called for a concentric pincer movement by all available forces, in particular the armoured corps of the Army Group, in order to 'reach Stalingrad itself or at least to bring it into range of our heavy weapons, so as to eliminate it as a further centre of war production and logistics'. This subsidiary offensive planned against the city on the Volga was therefore originally only viewed as an absolutely necessary protection of the flanks, and as a screen for the main offensive against the Caucasus, which the German attack forces were to carry out in phase four.

Incidentally, the Führer Directive of early April had already ordered the establishment of a defensive front on the Don, as soon as operations were completed, in order to protect the increasingly longer flanks. This front was to be established with the help of our allies. The Hungarians were to be deployed in the north, the Italians in the centre and the Roumanians farther south, each as a national unit and grouped as a separate army. This measure was later to have a disastrous impact on the pocket battle of Stalingrad, because the satellite forces were poorly equipped and had little battle experience; their men and officers were often badly trained and therefore, understandably, of low fighting morale. As flank protection for advanced German offensive forces, they must naturally have appeared as an advantageous and tempting starting point for Soviet attacks.

The German summer offensive under the code-name Operation 'Blue' did not begin until 28 June. After a fluid advance, it reached the objectives of the first two phases of the operation in barely one month, but without capturing the expected new masses of prisoners. The Soviets conducted an orderly retreat and used space as a weapon, but their situation progressively came under increasing threat. The Germans had advanced to the middle Don; Voronezh, Millerovo and Rostov were in German hands. In addition, the Soviets had suffered exceptionally heavy defeats in the Crimea and near Kharkov. Eleventh Army under Colonel General von Manstein had taken Kerch on 15 May and Sevastopol on 1 July. These spectacular victories gained this outstanding strategist his Field Marshal's baton.

The daring and initially successful pincer movement by which Soviet Marshal Timoshenko intended to retake Kharkov and anticipate the German offensive, had broken down into a total fiasco, as a consequence of the encircling counter-offensive impressively carried out by Army Group South under Field Marshal von Bock, using the fast armoured forces already positioned for the main offensive. Towards the end of spring, therefore, the Red Army had again suffered very heavy losses – approximately half a million men and 300 guns and tanks. These military events could not fail to have an impact on the spirited beginning of the German offensive. Already in early July, the sizeable extension of the total front and the various operations set in motion had led to a regrouping of Army Group South. From it emerged the northerly Army Group B under Colonel General von Weichs, comprising Second and Third Armies, Fourth Panzer Army and Hungarian Second Army, and the southerly Army Group A under Field Marshal von List, consisting of Seventeenth Army, First Panzer Army and Roumanian Third Army.

For the continuation of the summer offensive, Operation 'Blue', which had been redesignated Operation 'Brunswick', the Führer issued directive No. 45 of 23 July 1942. This order contained a decision that was to have a momentous effect on later military developments. Instead of the former plan of operations that was to have been carried out in stages, now a simultaneous attack against Stalingrad and the Caucasus on two eccentrically diverging lines of movement were ordered. Army Group B was to destroy enemy forces in the Don–Volga sector, take the city and then advance along the river to Astrakhan, in order to cut the Volga completely as far as its mouth on the Caspian Sea. Army Group A was given the task of destroying the forces that had escaped over the Don south of Rostov in pocket battles, and subsequently advanced over the western Caucasus to occupy the whole of the eastern coast of the Black Sea. Various smaller forces and fast mobile units were to take the oil fields of Maikop and Grozny, cut the ancient military roads through the passes over the eastern Caucasus, to advance to the Baku area on the Caspian Sea and, in the south, to Batum on the Black Sea. Hitler's directive already hinted at plans for further operations in the future; an offensive through Transcaucasia to Iran and Iraq.

The boundlessness of such planning and the measures ordered for its execution stood in contradiction to the classic principles of war. They ignored the decisive factors of space and time, available *matériel* and human capacity. When Hitler's directive was issued at the end of July,

German forces already had a front of 1,200 kilometres to defend, in other words 400 kilometres more than at the beginning of the summer offensive. Had the set objectives all been reached by late autumn, the front that would then have had to be held from Voronezh through Stalingrad and Astrakhan to the southern Caucasus would have extended over roughly 4,000 kilometres. The advances into the limitless space of Soviet Russia were bound to lead to serious consequences; a continual over-taxing of the troops, continual crises of reinforcement and supply and most grave strategic implications, arising from the growing threat to the ever extending flanks. The fighting armies had no reserves worth mentioning. The entire plan only made sense if one could count on an early and complete collapse of the enemy.

When Hitler imposed his strategy of 'all or nothing', he was obviously under pressure for time and obsessed by the threat, which he himself had courted, of an approaching war on two fronts. He disregarded the warnings of 28 June from the department of Foreign Armies East of the General Staff, which spoke of a resurgence of Soviet fighting ability and declared the military collapse of the purposefully led Red Army to be highly unlikely. He repeatedly and confusingly interfered in operations, ordered tactical regroupings, designated new command structures, and changed the direction of movement of fast mobile formations. In the midst of the offensive, he ordered the re-deployment of two particularly combat-proven divisions to the western front in France and even the removal of Eleventh Army, with its numerous troops and powerful artillery element, to the northern front. This Crimean army was to take part in the capture of Leningrad that had been ordered to be accomplished in early September according to directive No. 25 of 23 July. Its deployment in the centre of the 1942 summer offensive, namely the southern sector of the eastern front, would have been to far greater effect.

Naturally, this method of leadership and the unilateral decisions by the 'Supreme War Lord' were strongly opposed and heavily criticised by his closest advisers, first and foremost by the Chief of the Army General Staff, Colonel General Halder. But Halder was not successful in weaning Hitler away from his false appreciation of the enemy, his delusions of victory and his belief in his own infallibility. The generals at the highest level of command were no longer able to assert themselves against the Führer. For the most part they had already been degraded to mere executors of the will of the dictator. On 23 July 1942 Halder wrote the following bitter, almost desperate, passage in his diary: 'The under-estimation of the enemy's abilities, which has been going on for a long time, has now reached grotesque proportions and is becoming danger-ous. Things are becoming increasingly more unbearable. One can no longer speak of serious work being done. Pathologically reacting to momentary impressions and a complete misapprehension in the evalua-tion of the leadership structure and its possibilities, is what characterises this so-called *leadership*.'

Hitler's strategic concept of, and operational objectives for, the major German offensive of 1942 on the southern sector of the eastern front, as they emerge from the directives of the OKW (Oberkommando der Wehrmacht = Supreme Military Command), already contain the germ of the military and human catastrophe of Stalingrad. We must therefore pay particular attention here to the assumptions on which the advances of Army Groups A and B were based. Over many months they moved ever farther apart at almost a right angle, while their respective fates still remained inter-connected in many ways. Let us therefore look at the operations themselves; briefly at the advance to the Caucasus, in more detail at the battle for Stalingrad, which began in the middle of July in the big bend of the Don, became the centre of action, and lasted more than six months!

The advance to the Caucasus remained fluid until the end of August, but the hoped-for encircling operations with masses of prisoners failed to come about. By adroit manoeuvring, the Soviets, who had learned a lesson from the first year of the war, succeeded in withdrawing their troops southward, where they were received by the forces of Mar-shal Budenny's newly formed army groups of the North Caucasian Front. Army Group A under Field Marshal von List occupied the oil fields of Maikop and Piatigorsk, which the Soviets had destroyed, and took the cities of Elista and Mosdok. On 21 August the Reichs War Flag was hoisted on the 5,633-metres-high Elbrus, the highest peak of the Caucasus and the most southerly point reached. While this was certainly a mountaineering feat of great skill, it was of no strategic importance. On the Black Sea, only the Kuban bridgehead and Novorossisk were gained. Because of stiffening Soviet resistance and the insurmountable transportation problems along the 900-kilometres supply line, the offensive faltered at the beginning of September. Neither the passes over the Caucasus nor the oil fields of Grozny, so important to the war effort, had been gained. Hitler, who was highly displeased and nervous about the lack of success, made Field Marshal von List the scape-goat. He dismissed him on 10 September and took over command of Army Group A himself. In this context, a long and serious crisis developed in the Führer Headquarters and in the OKH (Oberkommando des Heeres = Supreme Command of the Army), mainly because General Jodl, Chief of the Military Command Staff, defended List, and the disagreements between Hitler and the critical Chief of Staff Halder became increasingly more violent. A rupture appeared to be unavoidable. The disgraced Jodl quickly submitted and from then on became a yes-man. This situation, but above all Hitler's unadmitted realisation that the offensive in the Caucasus was doomed to fail and could not produce the decisive turning point of the campaign, was bound to have a disastrous effect on future decisions during the battle for Stalingrad. This was the time when the 'Supreme Commander' of Germany's armed forces became obdurately convinced that final victory depended mainly on the fanatical will to hold on to all positions at whatever cost and never to consider retreat. From then on, all his opinions and decisions were based on the unconditionally rigid dogma of holding on.

Within the context of the offensive of Army Group B into the Don–Volga area and towards Stalingrad, from the end of July the situation became increasingly more disquieting for the Soviets. The intention was to take Stalingrad by a vast pincer movement, with Sixth Army under General Paulus advancing from the west and Fourth Panzer Army under General Hoth coming up from the south. From the beginning of August, the Red Army offered the heaviest kind of resistance in all areas, particularly in the bridgeheads it was defending on the Don and in the extensive forward terrain of the city on the Volga. In a final major field battle during the second week in August, Sixth Army, with XIV and XXIV Panzer Corps, succeeded in eliminating the strong Russian bridgehead near Kalach, where the greater part of two Soviet armies was destroyed. A total of 35,000 prisoners was taken and the enemy lost 560 guns and 270 tanks. The Russians also suffered heavy losses in the other battles in the big bend of the Don, particularly in the north, in the bitterly and successfully defended bridgeheads near Kremenskaya, Kletskaya and Serafimovitsh. These could not be wrested from the Soviets, and on 19 November were to serve as the jump-off bases for their big counter-offensive.

Already in mid July and early August, the advance of Sixth Army had been checked for a time, because of a serious supply problem and the heavy fighting in the big bend of the Don. The extremely uneasy Soviet General Staff Headquarters in Moscow, the Stavka, used this breathing space to reorganise their forces in the area between the Don and the Volga and, by providing strong reserves, to prepare a planned defence of Stalingrad. The 700-kilometres-long Stalingrad Front of Marshal Timoshenko was divided into two Fronts, that is to say Army Groups, consisting of a new Stalingrad Front in the north and a South-eastern Front covering the approaches to the city and the particularly endangered southern flank down to the Kalmyk steppe. In this area, the newly appointed Commander-in-Chief, Colonel General Yeremenko, played an outstanding role up to the end of the battle. As early as the end of July Stalin had announced a national state of emergency with the order 'not one step back'. The loss of Rostov had contributed much to this desperate situation. Now the issue was the saving of Stalingrad, which both sides saw as a bulwark of Communism and, with its important factories, an indispensable centre of arms production for the entire Soviet south. On 19 August General Paulus gave his Sixth Army (with its seventeen divisions, it was the strongest major military formation on the entire eastern front) the order to attack and take Stalingrad. The daring advance jumped off from a bridgehead on the Don that had been taken against strong Soviet opposition, and the fast mobile forces of XIV Panzer Corps reached the Volga north of the city at Rynok on 23 August. Forming the other half of the pincer operation, Fourth Panzer Army under Colonel General Hoth, advancing in the face of sustained stiff resistance and heavy losses, did not reach the Volga directly south of the city until 10 September. Advancing on a broad front and constantly engaged in heavy fighting, the infantry forces slowly moved from the suburbs towards the city proper, the centre of which had been reduced to a gigantic ruin by devastating German bombing attacks on 23 August and successive days. The destruction, with its continuous conflagrations, allegedly cost 40,000 lives. Up to the end of October the Germans enjoyed air supremacy. Half the German air fleet on the eastern front was engaged at Stalingrad, and at the height of the attack VIII Air Corps supported the ground troops with an average of 1,000 sorties a day.

For approximately two and a half months, from the beginning of September to post mid November 1942, one of the most gigantic battles of *matériel* and attrition in military history raged in the city on the Volga, with its largely destroyed factories, silos, railway stations and workers' quarters extending for fifty kilometres along the western bank of the Volga. Occasionally and quite unjustly, the dimensions and strategic importance of this battle are over-shadowed by the pocket battle of Stalingrad, which followed immediately after and lasted just as long. Both sides fought for each street, each house, each apartment building, each cellar; for stairwells, trenches and piles of debris, with a ferocity that knew no pity. The destruction caused by aircraft and artillery offered the doggedly fighting and counter-attacking defenders an almost ideal terrain. The storm troops of General Chuikov forced the German soldiers into the much feared hand-to-hand combat. And this required the troops to give their very all. Losses on both sides were appallingly high. From 21 August to 16 October alone, Sixth Army lost 38,943 men and 1,068 officers.

In about mid-month of both September and October, particularly dramatic and costly fighting took place. On 13 September began the vicious fight for the Mamai–Kurgan, the blood-soaked hill of latter-day fame in the city centre, that was to change hands so often in the future. Following this, the Germans took the area of the main railway station and even a sector of the bank of the Volga near the main ferry. This put General Chuikov's 62nd Army which, together with units of General Shumilov's 64th Army, formed the backbone and heart of the defence of Stalingrad, into a very precarious position. It was saved by the 10,000 men of General Rodimzev's 13th Guard Division which, sent by Stalin personally, crossed the Volga during the night of 14/15 September and immediately successfully engaged in the fighting. But the unit sustained such heavy losses that it had to be temporarily withdrawn. In the last week of September Sixth Army again took the offensive with exchanged divisions newly brought in from the northern defensive front. This was directed against the northern sector of the city with its large factory complexes and slowly pushed back the Soviet line. The main effort, however, did not begin until 14 October, and it quickly led to the most serious crisis in the Soviet defence of Stalingrad. The advance of the four German divisions, supported by armoured forces and a handful of engineer battalions that had been air-lifted in and were trained for bunker fighting, aimed at the industrial complex with the tractor factory and the artillery production plant 'Red Barricade'. The fighting was extremely bitter and both sides suffered frightfully high losses. The combat power of the exhausted German units was no longer sufficient to take the whole industrial complex, despite extensive local gains, nor to destroy 62nd Army, which the German advance had split in two. It was no longer possible to reach the banks of the Volga and thereby eliminate the highly manœuvrable and courageous Soviet Volga Flotilla, and cut the constant flow of replacements in men and *matériel* from the eastern bank of the river. In September and October alone, six freshly arrived infantry divisions, including two Guard divisions and some Siberian troops, contributed effectively in helping General Chuikov and his self-sacrificing 62nd Army prevent the total capture of the city, despite the dramatically desperate situation they were in. That was precisely Chuikov's assignment. Simultaneously, he was to wear down his opponent in a months-long battle of attrition, by means of an unremittingly active defence, and offensive skirmishing for every square metre of ground. By the end of October his battle groups were left defending only a tenth of the city area: the Mamai–Kurgan, a handful of factory buildings, a relatively narrow strip of the high bank of the river and several strategically important bridgeheads. Led by boundless energy and single-minded determination, General Chuikov's 62nd Army, whose unique steadfastness will go down in the annals of military history, had by this time already achieved one of the decisive pre-conditions for the preparation and success of the approaching major Soviet offensive.

On the German side, the frontal positional fighting which had continued for more than two months had exhausted the attacking power of the troops and the effective strength of most of the companies in 40 per cent of Sixth Army's battalions had been melted down to between thirty and forty men. Together with the units of Fourth Panzer Army assigned to it, it disposed of only 180 tanks by the beginning of November. And these sacrifices had had to be made, after the Volga had already been cut and Stalingrad eliminated as a centre of arms production and logistics. To this were added the increasing anxieties of the leadership in the east, caused by over-extended and therefore dangerous flanks, the lack of replacements for the momentously heavy losses in men and *matériel,* and the disquieting experiences and information being received in respect of the enemy's combat power. As early as the end of September, the Commander of Army Group B had requested permission of the OKH to break off the costly attack in Stalingrad and, by giving up the city, withdraw the forces involved to a shortened line. This Hitler refused even to consider. Shortly before, he had rid himself of what he saw as an increasingly unpleasant Chief of Staff, Halder. Caught up in unendurable tensions with the pig-headed and incorrigible Führer, Halder was no longer able or willing to carry the responsibility. On 24 September Halder had been dismissed in disgrace. From his hand-picked successor, General Zeitzler, Hitler hoped for what was more important to him than professional judgement, namely blind obedience and a 'fanatical belief in the idea of National Socialism'. Under the new Chief of Staff, the dictator's possibilities of directly influencing the operations of the eastern forces were increased.

That Hitler held to the very end his determination to conquer Stalingrad was also due to weighty reasons of personal prestige. In two public propaganda speeches on 30 September in Berlin and on 8 November in Munich he had committed himself to taking the city connected with the name of his most bitter opponent and never again giving it up. In a situation briefing at Führer Headquarters on 2 October, the minutes of which have come down to us, he admitted that the conquest of Stalingrad was no longer vitally necessary for 'operational reasons', but rather for psychological reasons of 'world opinion and the morale of our allies'. After Sixth Army, marshalling seriously weakened troops from nine divisions and their last reserves of strength, had made a desperate advance to the Volga on 11–12 November over the devastated terrain of the artillery plant 'Red October', a direct Führer Order of 17 November demanded the storming of the remaining sectors of the city still defended by the Soviets. With obedient zeal, General Paulus passed this order, together with a personal word of encouragement, on to the commanders of his bled-out forces. If Hitler at that point brutally willed the subjugation of fate at all cost, risking everything on the turn of a single card, this assuredly had much to do with bad news from other theatres of his war. An offensive by Montgomery and Rommel's retreat in North Africa, and the Anglo–American landings with strong forces in Algiers and Morocco, were pointing to a military reversal.

On 19 November the major Russian offensive and the rapid encirclement of Sixth Army brought about this decisive reversal on the eastern front. The encircling pincer operation of remarkable dimensions, carrying the code-name 'Uranus', had been under preparation by Moscow Supreme Command with extreme care and secrecy since early September. Stalin sent his closest military advisers, initially Colonel Generals Zhukov and Vassilevski, as Stavka advisers to the Fronts on the Don and the Volga. Here, they carried out the offensive planning on site, in the observation posts and command headquarters of the jump-off positions of the various armies chosen for the major attacks. Time and again they flew back and forth between Moscow and the southern war theatre. The Commanders of the three army groups in the Don–Volga area took an active part, but it was not until October that their higher staffs were included in the planning, which otherwise was still kept top secret. Meanwhile a final regrouping of the major formations in the area had taken place. To Colonel General Yeremenko's Stalingrad Front in the south, and General Rokossovski's Don Front, extending to the northwest of it, had been added the strong new South-west Front of General Vatutin, extending to the latter's west in the Don area. During the final briefings of commanders in November, a third representative of the Stavka appeared, Colonel General Voronov, Commander of Artillery of the Red Army.

The total Soviet strength concentrated against German Army Group B, including the forces already deployed, numbered more than one million men, who disposed of 13,500 guns and mortars, as well as 100 rocket-launcher batteries, the dreaded 'Stalin Organs'. It included four tank corps and fourteen tank brigades, with approximately 900 tanks. Behind this total of nine armies, several air fleets, comprising 1,200 aircraft, were deployed. The number of men massed in this force roughly equated to that of the formations fighting on the German side, but the Red Army was markedly superior in artillery and tanks. The organisation of this gigantic deployment, with all the necessary troop movements, re-alignments and cantonments, required incredible effort and resourcefulness; all in the face of difficulties of road transport caused by the autumn mud period, and flood waters on the rivers. All movements were efficiently camouflaged. Large troop movements were carried out at night and strict radio silence was ordered. In this, the Soviets produced an extraordinary organisational achievement, together with a highly effective deceptive manoeuvre.

In spite of this, the German staffs continued to receive information about Soviet troop movements and possible attack preparations which gave cause for concern. It hinted at the dangers that threatened the vulnerable flanks of Sixth Army from the strong enemy bridgeheads on the Don, where the poorly equipped allied troops of low fighting quality, the Roumanians, Italians and Hungarians, were deployed on a 300-kilometre front towards the north-west. The alarming information intensified during the last week before the start of the Soviet offensive, and it came from 4th Air Fleet and the department of Foreign Armies East. In the meantime, the only existing reserve, the completely under-equipped XXXXVIII Panzer Corps, had been deployed in the area in which the danger appeared to be most acute, the sector of Roumanian Third Army, whose commander had already asked for help and protection. One thing however is certain; due to the adroit Soviet deception manoeuvres, the German leadership was taken completely by surprise at the tremendous power and purposefulness of the encircling offensive. A danger to the southern flank at Stalingrad seems not to have been thought of at all.

The Supreme Command of the Red Army was excellently informed as to the weaknesses, difficulties and problems of an enemy in such an exposed position. It had recognised that the time had sufficiently ripened for it to undertake the decisive counter-offensive, which the Germans' strategic mistakes had actually provoked. The issue was to exploit the situation created by the enemy's boundless and reckless advance to the Volga in any way possible. The two attack wedges of the pincer operation were applied at the most sensitive points: the units adjacent to Sixth Army in the south and west, in other words, the Roumanian Third and Fourth Armies, whose poor combat strength and low morale were well known. It was there, at the main focal points, that the grip could be applied with an overwhelming superiority in men and weapons. However, the key factor that decided the entire 'Uranus' operation and the ensuing follow-up offensives leading to the large-scale collapse of the southern sector of the German eastern front was not only numerical superiority, but rather the daring, flexibility and imagination of the Soviet leadership.

This book deals extensively with the pocket battle of Stalingrad, which lasted from 19 November 1942 until 2 February 1943, with the tragedy of Sixth Army, with the suffering and death of its brave soldiers, inhumanly sacrificed in the end, with the momentous decisions and omissions of its higher command, and with the inner conflicts between obedience to orders and duty of conscience, into which a fatal entanglement of guilt and destiny enmeshed it. At the close of this overview of the road and the reasons that had led Hitler's armies to the Volga, we therefore need only briefly to sketch the overall framework of the battle of destruction, the various phases of the operations, and their impact on the larger events of the southern sector of the eastern front.

The first phase of the Soviet offensive, Operation 'Saturn', lasted from 19 to 24 November. Already on the 23rd, the encircling ring around twenty German and two Roumanian divisions, totalling about 280,000 men, had been closed at Kalach on the Don and then continually reinforced. On 24 November Hitler's rigid order to 'hold on' was issued, together with his promise of adequate supply by air until relief could arrive. The next phase, from 25 November to 12 December, stood under the sign of defending 'Fortress Stalingrad' and the failure of the air lift.

In the third phase of the battle, the dramatic days from 12–23 December, the relief operation 'Winter Storm' took place. According to the plans of Field Marshal von Manstein, who had taken over command of the newly formed Army Group Don on the badly damaged front, this was to be followed by Operation 'Thunderclap', the break-out from Stalingrad by Sixth Army. The relief action failed because, in the face of extremely heavy enemy opposition, Army Group Hoth's armoured spearheads were unable to get closer than fifty kilometres to the edge of the pocket. Colonel General Paulus felt that he could not take the responsibility for breaking the encircling ring. The high risks involved, not the least of which was due to lack of fuel, and also the fact that he never received the final order for 'Thunderclap' from his superior command authority, made it impossible for him to reach a decision during the decisive period (19–22 December). Behind the relief army, hundreds of trucks, tractors and buses with 3,000 tonnes of supplies ear-marked for the troops in Stalingrad waited in vain.

Any hope of relieving Sixth Army finally disappeared when von Manstein was forced to withdraw strong armoured forces from the relief column and deploy them elsewhere, and then to discontinue the advance on 23 December. The left flank of his Army Group Don, which was seriously threatened by a strong new offensive by the Red Army, had to be protected. Directed by Zhukov and Vassilevski, Operations 'Saturn' and 'Little Saturn', advancing on Rostov out of Voronezh and the middle Don area, had already destroyed the Italian Eighth Army, and threatened to bring about a 'super Stalingrad' for the entire German southern front. At Christmas, the Soviets overran Sixth Army's most important supply centre, the Tatsinskaya air base, where numerous aircraft were destroyed in scenes of catastrophic confusion. Interconnected to the main offensive 'Saturn' on the Voronezh and South-west Fronts, were Rokossovski's operations on the Don Front and those of Yeremenko on the Stalingrad Front. Here, the decisive successes against von Manstein's relief attempts were brought about in no small degree by the deployment, on Stalin's orders, of General Malinovski's particularly combat-worthy 2nd Guards Army. By the end of the year, not only had Army Group Hoth's armoured units been driven back 100–150 kilometres from their jump-off area north of Kotelnikovo, but the Soviets had also succeeded in smashing a 350-kilometre-wide gap in the German defensive front south of the middle Don, thus creating a serious danger for all three southern army groups, particularly for the large formations in the Caucasus. Within the framework of this overall picture, the hopelessly encircled Sixth Army, continuing its defence in all directions despite the catastrophic consequences of a totally inadequate air lift, still played an important strategic role for a short period. In the penultimate phase of the battle, from 25 December to mid January 1943, it tied down seven Soviet armies in front of its 60- by 30-kilometre pocket. These could otherwise have been employed in other centres of operations, such as the Caucasus or against Rostov in the south-west. From January onwards the German forces were retreating from the Caucasus. On 28 December, after many futile attempts, Chief of Staff Zeitzler had finally succeeded in wresting an order permitting this from the fanatically pig-headed 'Supreme War Lord' and dictator.

The final phase of the battle of Stalingrad lasted from 10 January to 2 February 1943. Code-named Operation 'Ring', this consisted of the liquidation of the pocket, the planning and execution of which was entrusted to the Don Front and its seven armies under Rokossovski and General of Artillery Voronov, representing the Stavka. Supported by overwhelming artillery superiority, the offensive aimed at total destruction went ahead after the Soviet proposals for surrender had been rejected. In the end, it encountered only masses of starving, freezing and dying soldiers, mostly immobilised and unable to defend themselves. On 26 January the pocket was split in two, and a week later both segments in the central and northern city sectors were liquidated.

Sixth Army had already lost approximately 80,000 men in December 1942, and now a further 100,000 human beings were destroyed in the final phase of the battle. To the very end, Hitler forbade any surrender and repeatedly ordered resistance to the last bullet. Even in this situation, with few exceptions his higher commanders remained his obedient executive organs.

From mid January on, the concept of holding out had lost any strategic purpose. The order to continue fighting was a senseless sacrifice. It ended in an irresponsible and, yes, a criminal abuse of the best of soldiery.

Stalingrad
Memories and
Reassessments

PART I

MEMORIES OF A SURVIVOR

The Creator's hand slips away runs high-handedly
Nonform of lead and steel • strut and barrel;
Himself laughs grimly when false talk of heroes
Sounds earlier who saw as mash and clod
His brother fall • who burrowed like a worm
In dreadful churned up earth.
The ancient God of battles is no more.

Stefan George
From 'The War', 1928

The Army of Stalingrad is encircled

The nineteenth of November will live in my memory as a day of black disaster. At the break of dawn on this gloomy, foggy day in late autumn, during which lashing snowstorms were soon to appear, there began, simultaneously with the onset of an extraordinarily hard eastern winter, the catastrophe on the most rashly advanced sector of our German front in the east that had been feared and anxiously anticipated by many. With devastating force, the Russian offensive first struck the neighbouring Roumanian formations on the left flank of the army of Stalingrad. This took place in the big bend of the Don south of Kremenskaya.

After a longer period of deployment, of which most of our higher staffs were aware despite their being screened by wooded terrain and misty autumn weather, and after meticulous preparations of gigantic proportions, the Russians, with their overwhelmingly superior armour and cavalry forces attacking like lightning from the north and the following day from the east, pressed our entire Sixth Army into an iron vice. Within three days the encircling ring was closed at Kalach on the Don and constantly reinforced.

Stunned, we stared at our situation maps, on which menacing thick red lines of encirclement and arrows showed the enemy attacks, penetrations and directions of advance. We had never imagined a catastrophe of such proportions to be possible!

The abstract map pictures soon gained life and colour from the reports and stories of many men on the run from the north and west, who flooded into our erstwhile so quiet ravine in the steppe of Peskovatka, bringing with them tales of disaster. They came from Kalach, where on 21 November the sudden materialisation of Soviet tanks had created such a panic in the peaceful quiet of the rear echelons that even the strategically important bridge over the Don had fallen into enemy hands. Soon too, totally exhausted, run down and with haggard, dirty faces, they began to arrive from our immediate neighbour to the left, XI Corps, whose rearmost divisions in the big bend of the Don were in danger of being overrun from their own rear.

The smashing overture to the enemy's whirlwind attack had been played between Kletskaya and Serafimovitsh by an hours-long artillery bombardment by hundreds of guns. In the ensuing maelstrom, the entire

Roumanian army on our extreme left flank had been overrun and scattered. Not only for their attack from the Don bridgehead, but also south of Stalingrad on the bend of the Volga, the Russians had skilfully selected the weak points on the north-westerly and south-easterly front of our army; our boundaries with the neighbouring Roumanian formations, whose fighting power was limited, not only because of a lack of combat experience, but more importantly, from a lack of heavy guns and armour-piercing weapons. There were no reserves worth mentioning anywhere. The Luftwaffe was unable to intervene because of the bad weather. The mighty wedges of the Russian armoured columns could not be stopped, and a myriad of highly mobile cavalry troops increased the muddle and confusion in the rear of the bloodily rent front of the army.

The situation soon became unequivocally clear. Our Sixth Army and parts of Fourth Panzer Army, with twenty excellent German divisions belonging to four army corps and one armoured corps had been encircled. The gigantic pocket also included an anti-aircraft division and other important formations of the Luftwaffe, strong allotments of field artillery, two each of armoured gun detachments and mortar regiments, about a dozen engineer battalions, construction units, medical services, transport units, units of the Reichs Labour Services, military police, and secret military police. Added to these were the remnant of a Roumanian infantry division, parts of a Roumanian cavalry division, and a Croat infantry regiment attached to a German Jäger Division. Finally, there were thousands of Russian *Hilfswillige* (so-called 'voluntary helpers') and prisoners of war. The total count of human beings now thrown together for good or ill must have been as high as 300,000.

We only realised much later that the encirclement of our army was only one part of a Russian encircling offensive, planned and executed according to the proven German model. Included within the pincer arm attacking from the north were particularly combat-worthy Soviet storm troops and specially provided élite divisions from the south-western front, that had previously been deployed against our army's left-hand neighbour. So the enemy, about whom our official propaganda had repeatedly claimed that he was at the end of his reserves and capabilities, had suddenly attacked! And the fact that in the meantime his strategy and tactics had become so flexible and that he had seized the initiative filled us with deep concern.

We were not completely taken by surprise by the strength of the Russian grip and the numbers of new formations and élite troops provided for the attack. For weeks we had been able to observe that there was a highly threatening storm brewing against us in the wooded terrain across the Volga and above all in the northern bend of the Don. As an orderly officer in Enemy Intelligence (Ic) on the staff of VIII Army Corps, it was my job to evaluate the manifold reports and information on the enemy, his strength, organisation, weapons and morale, and to enter them on the enemy situation map. Since the spring I had noticed a very interesting but increasingly more menacing development.

The Russians had first begun to deploy larger armoured formations against us operationally in May 1942. Yet once again the Red Supreme Command had had to learn a costly lesson when attempting an encirclement according to the German model. In the sector south-east of Kharkov the attacking Russian Sixth Army, having almost achieved the planned penetration of our front, was annihilated in what was an almost classic pocket battle. Far more than 200,000 men, with more than 3,000 guns and tanks, fell into our hands. Their despairing Commander committed suicide.

After the battle, several captured Soviet generals passed through the hands of our staff. Their statements left a lasting impression, particularly those about the growing enemy production of tanks in the arms factories relocated behind the sheltering wall of the Urals, with which our own production was in no way able to keep pace.

During the summer, our massive advance from the Donetz, over the Oskol, into the big bend of the Don and on to the Volga had taken place.

For a short time, this advance had made us feel optimistic. Our rapid gains obviously caused considerable confusion among the constantly withdrawing Russian forces as the motley mass of prisoners proved. This was also confirmed by a Russian general, the commander of a division captured in the woods, who had wrapped his Lenin Medal in his spats and concealed it in his boot. Major parts of the 62nd Siberian Army had been destroyed, and the badly hit Russian First Tank Army had withdrawn over the Don after having lost the bulk of its equipment in a pocket battle to the north-west of Kalach. In overall total, however, remarkably few men, weapons or heavy equipment had fallen into our hands. The enemy appeared to be systematically evading our blows and to be withdrawing into the depths of Russia .

Our suspicions were confirmed by a number of captured documents, including a map with highly revealing entries. In colour, this map laid down the withdrawal of a major force in terms of time and space in exact detail and, taken as a whole, was a masterpiece of general staff thinking.

Today, I am convinced that those withdrawals of Russian forces during the summer of 1942 were an outstanding enactment of traditional Russian war tactics. While they brought the country to the brink of deadly danger, in the end they fulfilled their purpose. I also believe that the execution of this withdrawal plan was greatly influenced and made easier by an occurrence which took place shortly before our offensive to the Volga began and which was fatal for us. Only a small circle knew about this unlucky event that caused Army Command in Kharkov and the staff of our corps in the town of Volchansk days of feverish agitation, and confronted the OKH with grave decisions. This is what had happened shortly after the middle of June.

Our forces were in the process of occupying their jump-off positions in the bloodily gained bridgehead on the Donetz in preparation for the offensive scheduled for 28 June when a young major, the Ia of a division, flew to a meeting with the staff of a neighbouring division in a Fieseler Storch. For the discussion he was carrying secret orders and information. In the misty weather, the aircraft apparently wandered over the enemy lines and was lost. Our inquiries quickly led to a painful result. The Storch had been shot down and was lying in no man's land between the lines; gutted and plundered clean. There was no trace of the major. His briefcase had contained a number of secret Command and Supreme Command documents. Had these fallen into the hands of the Russians?

For days, high priority 'phone calls between the OKH, Army Command and our corps staff went back and forth. Since the incident had taken place in our sector, we were ordered to investigate the matter and to find the answers to the pressing questions. Numerous patrols supported by heavy weapons were carried out and prisoners were taken from the opposing enemy sector. From the mass of initially contradicting information gathered, we were slowly able to gain a picture that appeared to be believable. The plane had been shot at and had gone down between the lines. An officer with red stripes on his trousers had either been shot in the plane, or while trying to get away. A commissar had taken the briefcase. In a final patrol, a captured Red Army soldier showed us the spot where the German officer had been buried. Digging revealed the body of the major.

With this, our worst fears were confirmed. The Russians had learned the timing, the strength, the direction, and the objective of our major offensive that Sixth and Second Armies were to begin at the end of June out of the Kharkov–Kursk area towards the east and the southeast. We had also unwittingly betrayed to him our staging areas and the details of our battle order. The air attacks which soon began and were also directed at our own staff hampered our deployments, cost us losses everywhere and left no room for doubt. Nor did the regroupings which the enemy carried out on his own fronts.

It was too late for the German OKH to change the dispositions made. The commencement of our advance on Stalingrad was already standing under an evil star.

What then took place during late summer and autumn on the Don and the Volga, and the change in the overall appearance of the enemy were reason enough for grave anxieties and apprehensions. From August onwards we were faced with a tenacious spirit of resistance. That Russian withdrawals were at an end was brought home to us by a captured Russian order which spoke of deadly danger to the state and gave out the Red Army's watchword from now on – 'victory or death!'

While our divisions were bleeding to death in the bitter fighting against the forces of the resurgent Russian 62nd Army, which staunchly defended every metre of ground in the streets and houses, ferocious relief attacks and penetration attempts against our northern defence positions between the Volga and the Don began in September. In these our brave Potsdam Division, which wore the old Prussian grenadier helmet as a tactical emblem, had to deal with newly arrived Soviet élite forces. The masses of tanks lost on the approaches, the appearance of numbers of fresh, well-equipped forces, the tactical innovations in combat formations, and the frequent troop re-alignments, all spoke of the vitality of the enemy, of his frightening growth in *matériel* supply, and of his seemingly endless reserves of manpower.

Recent events on the northern front on the bend of the Don had suggested ever more clearly that we were threatened by a most grave danger from a mighty strategic reserve at the Russians' disposal. Opposing our Sixth Army on the front between Stalingrad and the bend of the Don were no less than seven Russian armies including strong tank and cavalry forces. There could be no doubt that a major attack was being prepared.

Our radio surveillance in particular gave us frightening insights into the continuing deployment of the enemy's attack forces all the way down to their tactical dispositions, their armament and their supply. And even if a Soviet army only had the fighting strength equivalent to a full-strength German army corps, the enemy's numerical superiority was still awesome. We were probably dealing with odds of three to one.

For many weeks I had dutifully evaluated and passed on the increasingly serious reports from the lines, from air reconnaissance and radio surveillance, as well as key statements by prisoners coming in from the extended fronts and from neighbouring army corps as well. Army, which shared our anxieties most sympathetically, had not failed to pass warnings, serious remonstrations, yes, even entreaties, up to Army Group. There was nothing Army itself could do for us directly. The only thing that could have been of any help would have been an effective reinforcement of the forces wearing themselves away in Stalingrad, and of the exceedingly thinly manned defensive line running deep into the bend of the Don. Failing that, the timely withdrawal and shortening of the dangerously extended front, which by its configuration was tempting the enemy into dealing us the decisive blow. We did not know what measures Army Group and the Supreme Command were taking to counter the approaching danger, about which we had been warning them for weeks.

We were aware that new Roumanian forces had taken over the protection of our endangered flanks. But these allied armies were badly equipped and of poor fighting quality. Available reserves were nowhere in evidence, and we were afraid that nothing effective was being done to improve the inner and outer situation of our vast frontal area.

In the depth of enemy space and in our extremely exposed position it was therefore inevitable that catastrophe was about to overwhelm us. Had the Russians, who had systematically avoided any decision during the summer, only led us into a trap in order to be able to smash us during the freezing eastern winter?

Thoughts and fears such as these had often entered my mind in the past. The last time had been on a grey day in October when I was required to drive for miles through the burned-out, monotonous Don steppe to Army Staff in Golubinskaya. Lost in a space devoid of all human beings, which appeared to be pregnant with evils and unfathomable dangers, I was suddenly overcome by a tormenting vision. I saw the Russian tanks running down on us through a driving snowstorm, and on the big situation map which immediately appeared before my mind's eye, the merciless claws of a gigantic iron vice gripping our forces as if caught in a trap.

It had not just been a spawn of my fear of the Russian winter that we all knew to be the enemy's most dangerous ally. It had now come to pass. We were actually caught in a trap. How were we to get out? Serious as the situation in the pocket was from the very outset, in our bunker there was still an atmosphere of confidence and a certain feeling of superiority. Our thoughts now ranged around the forthcoming break-out which we all expected as a matter of course. It would demonstrate that we were not prepared to have the initiative taken away from us.

Admittedly, an eerie memory arose within me and intensified my apprehensive unrest with each passing day. It was the memory of several fanatical statements that Hitler had recently made in public speeches. The German soldier, he had said, now stood on the Volga and no power on earth could make him leave. The 'Supreme War Lord' had emphatically committed himself, he had prophesied, and demanded that Stalingrad be 'relentlessly attacked and taken'. Shortly before the Russian offensive began, he had spoken about the economical importance of this 'gigantic trans-shipment centre' on the Volga, where the vital supply line for thirty million tonnes of wheat, manganese ore and oil could be cut. In presumptuous terms, he had even sworn 'before God and history' never again to relinquish this conquest, presenting it as already achieved.

With such an attitude as this on the part of the 'Supreme War Lord', was giving up the Volga and retreating conceivable at all? Perhaps our Stalingrad army would not only have to fight for its very life, but in addition, for political and military prestige trumpeted to the world. Hitler had tied his fame as a military leader to this city, which bore the name of his greatest opponent. All too soon a feeling was to arise and grow ever stronger in all of us; the Volga and Stalingrad were to be our inevitable and inescapable fate.

Fateful decisions are taken

Already during the opening days of the pocket battle, this uneasy feeling inside me grew stronger. I had been temporarily assigned to the operations department (Ia) and there was a huge amount of work to be done.

In the course of the necessary regrouping of our encircled forces our staff had become responsible for two additional army corps, XIV Panzer Corps and XI Corps, thereby putting our Commander temporarily in charge of the whole northern group of the army. This enabled me to gain a revealing insight into our overall situation and the decisive measures that were finally taken near Rastenburg in East Prussia, seat of the OKH and Führer Headquarters, 2,000 kilometres distant from the pocket. The fate of more than a quarter of a million human beings was decided over such a distance! From there, Hitler repeatedly addressed orders and appeals directly to the Stalingrad army, which had been removed from under the command of Army Group B and re-assigned to the newly formed Army Group Don.

Events were moving thick and fast and tension and excitement in our Ia department was at its height. There was a coming and going as in a disturbed beehive. Telephones rang incessantly, orderlies and liaison officers came and went. Orders were received and passed on. Commanders of all ranks and services constantly came in to report, to orientate themselves, and to receive new orders. The front was moving inexorably down from the north to the area between the Don and the Volga, and it was clear to us that the Russians would soon be occupying our bunker. In the meantime, Army headquarters in the Cossack village of Golubinskaya had already been evacuated helter-skelter, shortly before the Russian tanks appeared on the neighbouring Don heights.

A few fleeing officers from the Command Staff made it to our staff in the evening of 22 November, a freezing All Souls night. They were filled with anxious unrest and panic, and reported on the sorry events in the rearward area that had suddenly become the front. The Commander-in-Chief, together with his Chief of Staff, had flown to

Nizhne–Chirskaya, the prepared Army winter headquarters farther to the west, and for a time had been outside the pocket. Later on he had flown back with his Chief to rejoin the mass of his encircled army in Stalingrad and established his new headquarters near Gumrak.

The staff officers of our corps were confronted by extremely difficult problems. Our new Chief of Staff had only been transferred to us at the front a few weeks ago from the OKW where he had served in the department of Foreign Armies East. I had picked up this robust colonel with the red stripes from Army headquarters in a *Kübelwagen* and driven him through the barren, treeless steppe to our luxurious winter quarters at Peskovatka. Here he was immediately forced to plunge head over heels into his new area of responsibility. Furthermore, our new Deputy Chief of Staff, coming from the liaison staff with the Italian Eighth Army, had joined us just before the onset of the Russian offensive. Now he not only had to prepare the normal corps orders, but also to become involved in the responsibility for the highly dangerous and difficult withdrawal movement of a substantial army grouping. The immediate task was to lead the retreating forces out of the bend of the Don where, hard-pressed and repeatedly encircled by the advancing enemy, they were forced to destroy their heavy weapons and equipment in great haste, and to bring them eastwards across the two bridges over the Don so as to be able to rally and regroup them on the neck of land between the Don and the Volga.

Simultaneously, a new defensive front had to be established to the west and south in the completely denuded rear of the army. This was a vital task which was largely made possible by the exemplary conduct of the rear echelon service and supply units who kept their heads in the general confusion and fought to maintain contact to the east, thereby averting the threatening danger of the front being rolled up from its rear.

Therefore, even on the large scale, the general retreat made necessary by the Russian encirclement did not move towards the west, where the connection to the sundered German front could have been made, but rather to the east. Its purpose was to regroup the whole of Sixth Army to the west and north of Stalingrad and to re-deploy it for the rescuing break-out across the Don to the south-west.

The tensions and expectations among our staff grew from day to day. The only thing we talked about was the plan for the forthcoming break-out. We younger officers in particular were avid to hear the details of the rescue operation. We realised that in view of the rapidly diminishing food and fuel stocks time was of the essence, and swift action was necessary to arrest the stiffening and reinforcement of the enemy front that was taking place.

Naturally we were also aware of the precariousness of our situation and of the heavy fighting that lay ahead, which could lead to the loss of substantial elements of our army and much equipment. But the mass of so many divisions would fight hard to get home and would surely succeed in breaking through. Our army still disposed of about 130 combat-ready tanks, and about the same number of armoured scout cars and other armoured vehicles, in other words, we still had powerful motorised units available. And when I had to carry out several assignments at the bridge over the Don at Peskovatka, I was able to learn at first hand that the mood of the soldiers, even in those units that had been hard hit, was confident. The heavy weapons of XIV Panzer Corps, whose columns were passing through the general retreat in the opposite direction towards the west, created new confidence and hopeful trust. Everywhere people were waiting for the relieving signal for the break-out. With fluttering hearts we followed the preparations that were taking place mainly in the westward sector of the army.

In anticipation of the expected operation, the order had been given to destroy all superfluous *matériel*. Everywhere, damaged guns, tanks and trucks, useless communications and engineering equipment, huge amounts of clothing, files and paper, even food, were being consigned to the flames. In our neighbourhood a gigantic mountain of valuable equipment was put to the torch and at this stage passing troops were still able to salvage anything they desperately needed.

According to the decision by Army Command, the retreat from Stalingrad was to begin on 26 November. A powerful wedge of tanks reinforced by motorised troops was to open the road for the break-out of the army to the south-west, smash through the enemy ring, and provide flank coverage. The mass of the infantry divisions was to follow without any preliminary bombardment.

This plan, it was rumoured among our staff, had been passed on via Army Group. We did not entertain the slightest doubt that the Supreme Command must be convinced of its necessity. We counted firmly on its being carried out. With strong hearts, we believed in its success and hoped it would save us. We talked of nothing save the forthcoming big event. In it we saw our chance for salvation, and so the bowstring of our expectations was drawn to breaking point.

I will never forget how stunned we all were, the agitation, yes, the petrifying horror that befell us, especially among the higher ranks of our staff, when on 24 November the message came in from Army that Hitler had forbidden the planned break-out and finally ordered the Stalingrad army to 'temporarily take up a position of all-round defence'. Shortly before, I had overheard a dramatic telephone conversation between the Commander of Sixth Army, General of Panzer Forces Paulus, and my own Commander, General of Artillery Heitz. While listening to this conversation, in which there was talk of never recurring opportunities, of the possible loss of the last hope, and of pending disaster with regard to the air lift, my breath caught in my throat. In his very sceptical and for me disquieting statements, my commander had spoken of 2,000 aircraft that would quickly have to be made available from outside the theatre in order to maintain the fighting strength of the encircled divisions.

And now, on this 24th day of November, the fatal radio message from the distant Führer Headquarters had come like a stroke of lightning, forbidding the planned withdrawal of our northern front, the detachment of our forces from Stalingrad and thereby, the hoped for break-out.

This decision by the Supreme Command was just as heavy a blow for the staff at Army, as it was for us. We were unable to satisfy ourselves as to why all the reports, admonitions and requests of our responsible higher staffs, who were best able to judge the events and all the dangers they entailed, had not been successful. When the encirclement of his forces by the attacking enemy formations had made the danger of our situation clear, our Commander-in-Chief had already suggested to his superior Army Group that he withdraw his army to a tangential line in the Don–Chir area. And after orders had arrived from the OKH that Stalingrad and the Volga Front had to be held at all costs, he had repeatedly asked for freedom of action. The last time had been on 23 November, when General Paulus addressed himself directly to Hitler with a very serious and responsible evaluation of the situation.

In this momentous radio message, he had adamantly stressed the fact that all his senior Commanding Generals shared his conviction that, because it would be impossible adequately to supply the army in time, it would shortly be destroyed unless a concentration of all available forces were to succeed in decisively beating the enemy attacking from the west and south. In order to achieve this, however, a break-out towards the south-west, after withdrawal of all of the divisions from Stalingrad, was necessary.

Now the Führer and Supreme Commander of the Armed Forces had intervened directly, by-passing the Army Group responsible, and forbidding the desired freedom of action. His radio message ended with an appeal to the brave Sixth Army and its Commander. Hitler's promise to provide adequate supplies and a timely relief of the beleaguered forces henceforward formed the basis for all further measures undertaken by the army. But this hardly consoled our staff in the general disappointment and feeling of despair.

The situation had now become critical. Nothing like this had ever happened before! A complete army had withdrawn from the rest of the front towards the east into a highly dangerous defensive situation, in order to entrench itself in a position of all-round defence and there to await developments, while being completely encircled! My dashing general, whose grumbling manner concealed a heart of gold that beat warmly for his soldiers, shook with irritation and the thick, bushy eyebrows in his gruff features drew together like a thundercloud. He had declared earlier that he had no intention of passively dying a miserable death. It would be much better to get out with a few divisions, than to go under with the whole army. Had he ever before been in a comparable situation during the whole of his forty years of service in the army?

Even though he had left no doubt that in his view the only decision promising salvation lay in an immediate break-out, in the end he too submitted and obeyed. For him an order was an order, in spite of everything! All that remained to us was to hope for a rescue operation from outside.

The promised rescue operation could not be expected for several weeks. That meant losing precious time, continual reinforcement of the fresh Russian attacking forces, the erosion of the fighting strength of the encircled army which was desperately defending itself under conditions of extreme psychological pressure, and the dissipation of its last reserves. The fate of roughly 300,000 human beings now mainly depended on an adequate air lift. Would the available transport space be sufficient, would Russian air superiority and the difficult winter weather in the Don steppe permit several hundred aircraft daily to fly into the pocket?

Not only had the decision that Sixth Army was to form an all-round defence been taken by the highest authority over the heads of its Commander-in-Chief and Army Group, even the main line of resistance, in other words, the configuration of the line that had to be held all round the perimeter of the pocket, had been decided from above. For dozens of kilometres, this line ran over the empty steppe without any natural defensive features, any protection, any backup. There, the retreating troops simply had to dig-in in the snow and frozen earth and defend themselves. Later on, any changes to this line could only be made in situations of emergency and with the permission of Führer Headquarters, in other words, only with great difficulty.

If one excepted the extensive pile of ruins that was Stalingrad, which made up only a relatively small sector of the total front, and a few advantageous stretches of river, one could not speak of a 'fortification' anywhere. The term 'Fortress Stalingrad', that appeared in one of the earliest orders from OKH, must have sounded like pure irony, if not bloody sarcasm, to the encircled troops.

General von Seydlitz remonstrates

There was one general among the higher ranks of the encircled army who was not prepared to accept the fatal measures ordered, dooming twenty-two endangered divisions, for the most part the best troops in the German army, to an exhaustingly passive defence. He wanted to act, to break out as quickly as possible and to save whatever could be saved. This man was the commander of LI Corps, General of Artillery von Seydlitz. His reputation was that of a capable, efficient and extremely experienced commander, and he had long been decorated with the oak leaf cluster to the Knight's Cross. He could also be considered an authority on exactly the kind of situation that had to be dealt with here. In the spring, on another sector of the eastern front near Demjansk, he had contributed decisively to the relief of another, albeit smaller, pocket. He clearly saw the dangers that must lead to the destruction of the whole army. The fate of more than a quarter of a million German soldiers was at stake. To avert this he showed himself prepared to go to any extreme.

The general and his staff officers were firmly convinced that the only way to save the endangered forces on the Volga was to do what Army Command had adamantly recommended, that is, to break out to the south-west in the direction of Kotelnikovo. This was what everyone was feverishly awaiting. The preparatory orders from Army had been particularly well executed by the men of his command. When it was time to jettison superfluous ballast the general personally set an example. Except for the uniform he was wearing, he had all his baggage, papers and personal keepsakes thrown into the fire.

A real orgy of destruction, similar to that in other units of the army, had also taken place in his corps. He told the assembled General Staff officers of his eight divisions that the army had only the choice between a Cannae or a 'Brczeziny', alluding to a famous break-out near Lodz in 1914, in which he himself had been involved.

In order to lighten the coming tasks for his bled-out formations, which were required to defend a perimeter 70 kilometres in length, he found himself forced to withdraw a sector of his northern front to a shorter defensive arc. The measure had become necessary due to the withdrawal of XIV Panzer Corps, which had left a 25-kilometre-wide gap that could not be effectively closed and defended by the burned-out divisions moving in. His had been an independent decision taken during those early turbulent days when Army Staff was still on the other side of the Don and which the general had felt to be justified in view of the impending break-out. He had to believe that the shortening of the front initiated thereby was in the best interests of the decisions to be expected from Army Command and would be to the advantage of the expected break-out. He could not assume that a break-out would not be attempted.

It thus came about that the result of his daring action was just as damaging as was the destruction of valuable material ordered by Army in preparation for the break-out. This would only have made sense if the original plan to break out had been carried through. The shortening of the front, even though forced by circumstances, caused the troops additional suffering and danger by depriving them of their well-prepared winter positions. The infantry formations of one completely exhausted and decimated division were destroyed during the withdrawal by the hard-pressing Russians.

It must have seemed an irony of fate when this same General von Seydlitz, who from the very beginning had pressed his Army Command to act without further requests for permission and to break out with the army, received a special order from Hitler charging him with personal responsibility for holding the northern and eastern perimeters of the pocket. This order was brought to him personally by Commander-in-Chief Paulus together with the shattering news that the break-out had been forbidden and thereby any freedom of action as well.

Initially, General von Seydlitz was dumbfounded. Stunned, he accepted the order, but in his heart he rejected it, particularly since he was painfully aware that his own hands were tied. There was only one person who could act and that was the Commander of the 'Fortress'. Not until the following day, 25 November 1942, did General von Seydlitz react to Hitler's orders, and his reaction was as much filled with a sense of responsibility as it was temperamental. Addressed to Army Command, it took the form of a detailed evaluation of the situation that the Corps Commander had had his Chief of Staff prepare. It summarised once again all the arguments against the Stalingrad army digging-in and urged the breaking out of the ring immediately. Based on his particular experiences gained during the relief of the Demjansk pocket, the clear-sighted and realistically evaluating general warned against dangerously false conclusions being drawn from a comparison with what had then been a totally different set of circumstances. A sober analysis of the situation, assumptions about the probable conduct of the enemy, and an estimation of the chances for success of a relief operation, led to clear and unambiguous conclusions. In the emergency situation intensified by the OKH, General von Seydlitz demanded from the Commander-in-Chief of the Army that he act immediately against orders, in other words, against Hitler. He declared it to be an imperative duty to the army and the German people to obey the dictates of conscience and to seize the freedom of action that had been forbidden, in order to prevent the threatening catastrophe.

The memo was passed on by Army Command, but had no effect whatever. It was the fatal tragedy of its authors, the Commanding General and his Chief of Staff, that they, like all the other knowing or unknowing, doubting or trustfully hoping members of the Stalingrad army, were caught up in a disastrous event, whose course towards catastrophe they could foresee, but could not prevent. And so they had to suffer the additional pain that in the final analysis they could but give in and fulfil the bitter soldierly duty to obey against their own better insight.

Even so, later on General von Seydlitz would still not keep silent. Wherever his slim, erect figure with its grey-streaked red hair appeared, hope was kindled, particularly in the breasts of many younger officers for whom the waiting became intolerable as time went on. Time and again during the course of the battle, thoughts and plans for break-out attempts haunted the minds, not only of individuals, but of groups and whole formations. This went on even after it was far too late. The German front had recoiled for hundreds of kilometres and any attempt to reach it in the freezing winter weather would only have led to the certain death of the exhausted warriors of Stalingrad.

The break-out remained forbidden. The Army leadership continued to trust firmly in the promised relief from outside, obviously convinced that from Stalingrad, they could not see the overall picture, nor judge the possibilities of success of the relief operations they had requested and which had been promised from above. Almost to the last, save for the final inglorious end itself, the orders coming in from the highest authority served as guidelines for all actions. In their resolute execution, the Commander-in-Chief of the Army was strongly supported by his Chief of Staff, Major General Schmidt, who was seen to be a hard-nosed and uncompromising proponent of the OKH's directives. The conduct of the Commander-in-Chief towards his Corps Commander, the energetically and daringly rebellious General von Seydlitz, was revealing in several ways. He did not undertake any actions against this critic and rebel, probably because he himself entertained misgivings about the measures ordered, measures that stood in such crass contradiction to everything that he had shortly before declared to be mandatory. A deep and painful conflict must have raged in the breasts of these two men who had become involved in such an unusual situation of catastrophe and on whom lay the burden of a well-nigh crushing and indescribable responsibility.

During the agitating days of the battle of Stalingrad we knew nothing at all of the events and dramatic conflicts taking place at Führer Headquarters where Hitler, acting against the advice of the experts, imposed on us his fatal decisions, trusting in the rash promise by Göring to assure the supply of the encircled army by air. None the less, we did have evil premonitions. In any case, we were all deeply disturbed and full of despair and, in our hearts, even outraged. What was being demanded of us not only contradicted all military experience, it went against every soldierly feeling and robbed us of any hope of being able to save ourselves by breaking out under our own power.

'Hold on! The Führer will get you out!'

In the last week of November, when the formations that had been heavily damaged during the initial retreat were hastily and with great difficulty establishing themselves on the new main line of resistance, Army issued a grave Order of the Day.

I can still remember the exact wording. It started: 'Sixth Army has been surrounded. This is not your fault. As always, you have fought bravely and tenaciously up to the moment the enemy had you by the neck.' It went on to point out the hard fighting, suffering and deprivations that would still be demanded of the troops and which they would have to endure for a time in hunger and frost, trusting in the help from outside that had so definitely been promised. Finally, mention was made of the relief operation to which Hitler had personally committed himself. Psychologically clever and calculating, the appeal ended with the encouraging words promising consolation and salvation: 'Hold on! The Führer will get you out!'

This final sentence, appealing so strongly to emotion, which injected a new tone into the previously factual and sober language of military orders, gave rise to discussions among our staff. It made me realise on top of all that had already happened, how great the sacrifice was going to be that would be demanded of the troops.

When after a daring advance without precedent our Sixth Army had reached the Volga and Stalingrad in late summer, only to be immediately involved in bloody attack and defensive fighting in what was virtually a war on two fronts, the troops were already in need of a major degree of rest and recuperation. A large number of the soldiers had been in constant and exhausting action in the front line for two years without leave, without having been home to see their loved ones.

'   The summer offensive out of the hotly contested Kharkov area had led to months of strenuous advances fraught with deprivations, and the constant strain had overtaxed the physical strength of the men. In my mind's eye, I again saw the exhausted columns dragging themselves through the thick dust clouds of the endless steppe under the burning summer heat during the day, and at night through kilometres of suddenly flaring fires. I remembered the agonising lack of water, the village wells scooped dry to the last drop, the unbalanced, sketchy diet because the supply columns were no longer able to keep up, and the clouds of disgusting flies which we had to suffer in their millions. Next had come all kinds of fevers and intestinal infections, then malaria, and finally even jaundice, which many secretly hoped to contract in order to reach a hospital at home before the onset of the dreaded Russian winter.

The fighting on the Volga and the Don had eroded the last physical reserves of the troops. From mid August to October a large part of the army had already been involved in a two months' bloody battle in the ruins of Stalingrad. From the distance, we could see eerie fires and dust clouds of destruction hovering for many days and nights, without being able to take the last bitterly contested strongholds of the Russians on this side of the Volga. And during September the formations of our corps had had to pay a high sacrifice in blood while beating back desperate penetration attempts by the enemy on the northern defensive front. The divisions engaged in the heaviest fighting were dangerously worn out, their companies for the most part melted down to thirty to forty men. Replacements had reached the front, but in totally inadequate numbers, so that in many units active strength was finally down to one-third or one-quarter of what it had originally been. The secret hope of the troops of being replaced after such a great performance and strain was dashed by the order to hold their positions over the winter. And in the end, the Russian offensive had destroyed the yearningly wished-for hope of Christmas leave and home. The weighty Army Order of the Day, which spoke of encirclement and holding out, left no more doubt about the gravity of the situation.

Naturally, the troops were not in a position to appreciate the full extent of the suffering and deprivations they were about to face. They knew nothing of the difficult problems of the overall supply situation. They had no inkling of the countless worries that lay so heavily and depressingly on the higher staffs. Nor, at first, were they aware that at one stroke, the encirclement had made it impossible to complete preparations for winter positions. Out there in the supply depots of the army at Morosovsk and Tatsinskaya, and even farther back, lay tens of thousands of fur coats, warm stockings, protective headgear and other items of winter clothing, which could now no longer reach the encircled forces. For the most part the men remained completely inadequately supplied with winter gear and exposed to the murderous frost.

Since the prepared break-out of our army to the south-west had not come about and the encircled forces had to prepare for a longer period of defence, certain re-alignments of troops and heavy weapons became necessary. Despite the serious difficulties the troops had to contend with due to lack of dugouts, building material and firewood, particularly those divisions lying in the open steppe to the west and south, the line of defence slowly firmed up. The pocket achieved its final shape, which was maintained until the second week in January. It was about fifty kilometres long and forty kilometres wide.

After the wild disorganisation of the front caused by the Russian penetration had solidified, we in Ic were again slowly able to gain a fairly comprehensive picture of the enemy's dispositions. The army was now strongly compressed, so that we could attempt to mark the enemy attack forces grouped around 'Fortress Stalingrad' on our situation maps.

Initially there were about sixty major formations facing our Sixth Army, mainly rifle divisions and tank brigades grouped into seven armies. In addition to these, there were reserve formations that were difficult to identify. The main strength of the enemy, particularly the artillery, was spotted along the western perimeter and was therefore facing our own corps sector. We were able to calculate that the enemy was holding the iron ring about us with a numerical superiority of three to one and a frightening concentration of heavy weapons.

After deduction of the losses sustained during the Russian penetrations, and addition of new forces and the Roumanians who had joined us as the result of events during the battle, we calculated that our own army, whose total strength before the encirclement had been about 330,000 men, now numbered about 280,000. These men, from almost all of Germany's provinces (we even had a corps from Vienna), now formed a large community tied together by fate and facing a precarious future. For all of them the order and the promise held true: 'Hold on! The Führer will get you out!'

And the troops did trust blindly in the promised salvation. For a long time their morale remained unbroken; in fact it was higher and more optimistic than that in the staff departments. This I was able to ascertain time and again. They saw their immediate difficulties as being only temporary, as one of those 'messes' that can always occur at the front, and for the successful cleaning up of which they could later expect a special decoration, a Stalingrad badge or some sort of pocket battle medal. Everyone expected an early relief as a matter of course. The unshakeable hope of the promised relief from outside gave the troops the strength to hold on and fight despite the conditions, to suffer and die while assailed by gnawing hunger and biting frost.

For weeks the defensive front was able to contain the overwhelming superiority of the Russian tanks and heavy weapons. Only in a few isolated spots was the predetermined line dented in bloody local fighting. The worst pressure was applied on the western perimeter of the pocket during the first weeks in December, against our forces and those of our western and south-western neighbour, XIV Panzer Corps. The Russian attempts to penetrate failed. Many acts of sacrifice, of heroism and loyalty, were performed in natural and silent obedience to duty. The official German war bulletins, however, only reported the occurrences in Stalingrad in terms of very summary allusions to the events in order to disguise the true fact that a complete army had been encircled and was bitterly fighting for its life.

We, the officers in the staff departments, also pinned all our hopes on the relief operation which was being prepared. No one even considered that Hitler would be ready to abandon the outstandingly proven Sixth Army on the Volga and throw it to the wolves. He was bound to find ways and means to rectify the devilish situation. There were even starry-eyed dreamers, not however among the older and more experienced, who maintained that the Führer would not only 'get us out', but had probably already conceived a plan to turn our apparent defeat into a glorious triumph by encircling all the enemy armies surrounding us.

None of these dreamers and believers in miracles who kept surfacing here and there until the very end had any clear idea of what was implied by the fact that German soldiers were simultaneously fighting on the North Cape and the Bay of Biscay, in front of Leningrad and Vyazma, in the Caucasus, in Crete, and in North Africa. That there were hot spots in many places, that the over-extended fronts meant a shortage of men everywhere, and that the Allies were mounting their big offensive in North Africa at this very moment. The air supply fleet was just as desperately needed in the Mediterranean theatre as in Stalingrad. Slowly doubts and anxiety began to grow, but we had no option save to wait with impatience for the longed-for moment of salvation that depended on the approach of von Manstein's forces.

Worry and anxiety at Pitomnik Air Base

Time was pressing, however. During the weeks of December the fighting strength of the army was deteriorating at a horrendous pace. The blame for this lay mainly in the inadequate air lift. Here a catastrophic picture was slowly emerging, and I regrettably had more than enough occasion to occupy myself with this depressing subject. During the entire month of December, I lay at Pitomnik airport with our corps staff's executive department. There I was given the temporary assignment of daily reporting the results of incoming flights to my general. In order to be able to do this, I regularly contacted the supply staff that was housed in a neighbouring bunker under the command of a very active and energetic colonel of Flak.

During the first weeks of encirclement, we were far more disturbed by the increasingly menacing overall supply situation than we were by the tactical situation on our sector of the front. In order to be able to maintain its ability to live and fight, our army had initially requested 750 tonnes of supplies per day, later reducing this to 500 tonnes per day. There were only two types of air carrier available for the Stalingrad air lift, namely the Ju 52 cargo aircraft with a 2-tonne load capacity, and the He 111 fighter-bomber whose bomb-bays held barely 1.5 tonnes. As the Commander-in-Chief had specified during the initial days, assured daily delivery of the requisite quantity of supplies would require 2,000 aircraft. This number took into account the inevitable wastage – aircraft shot down, break-downs, repairs and rest periods.

We all quickly learned that an air transport fleet of this size could not be counted on. The Luftwaffe quartermaster had made a highly sobering statement to our supply staff that the best that could be hoped for was to fly 300 tonnes a day into the Stalingrad pocket. But even this quantity, which represented the absolutely crucial minimum, was soon proved to have been set too high.

Depending on the requirements of changing conditions, the emphasis within the daily total tonnage of 300 would have to shift between food, fuel and ammunition. In order to bring in this amount, a minimum of 150 flights per day was required. I cannot recall that this number was regularly reached. It was rare that more than 100 flights were recorded which, when there were, occasioned a small celebration for us. But on average far too few planes came in. As a rule they only brought in 80 to 120 tonnes of the required supplies, in other words not more than one-fifth of the amount needed. Purely and simply, this meant a daily deficit of 10,000 kilograms of bread, and a fatal under-supply of desperately needed fuel and ammunition. In the long term this led to the immobilisation of guns and tanks, whose numbers were already being rapidly depleted, or to their being so sparingly used that they no longer fought effectively. And what was even worse, it meant increasing starvation. Already in December the daily ration on the line was 200 grams of bread and in the rear echelon services and staffs, 100 grams. Lucky were the units that still had horses! They at least had some additional meat.

We were particularly depressed and outraged every time we discovered that the precious cargo space had been ineffectively used or even misused. We could not understand how it was possible that occasionally completely superfluous or non-required supplies were flown in. Instead of the urgently needed bread or flour, several aircraft brought tens of thousands of old newspapers or leaflets from the Military Propaganda Department, candy, spices, neckties, tar paper, barbed wire, and other things that were of no conceivable use. Later on an officer of the General Staff was sent out to rectify these inadequacies and to assume responsibility for the proper loading of the aircraft. But by then the overall situation of the air lift had deteriorated catastrophically so that even the best of intentions and clever measures were no longer of much help.

Another undoing was that the supply situation of the encircled army had initially not permitted the flying-in of large amounts of space-saving flour and other concentrated foodstuffs instead of bulky bread. Unfortunately the deficit in food supply incurred before field bakeries could be set up was never recovered.

There were many reasons why the air lift fell short of the required minimum in such a disappointing manner. It was in no way the fault of the pilots who truly performed the unbelievable in their untiring efforts. In their brave and fearless battle against the many dangers caused by the weather and the superiority of the enemy air force, they often flew their machines back and forth several times a day. What was simply lacking was sufficient cargo space, because this was simultaneously also needed in the Mediterranean theatre and in North Africa, where a decisive battle was taking place. The aircraft for the Stalingrad air lift were gathered from the north, from France and from the Mediterranean front. Only relatively late in the day did I discover, besides the usual old Junkers transports (Ju 52) and the Heinkel He 111, aircraft of a new type that could carry eighty men, occasional mighty four-engined super transports, and a few giant gliders.

The unfavourable and very unpredictable early winter weather in the Don steppe and on the Volga near Stalingrad prevented a regular flight schedule. Time and again there were fatal intervals, and this filled us with anxiety and despair. At times, for example during the first week in December, all aircraft were grounded because of thick fog or the danger of icing during snowstorms. Furthermore, the superior Russian air force posed serious problems, particularly after both the 200-kilometres distant air bases of Morosovsk and Tatsinskaya were lost at about Christmas time.

The long approach, in the final days more than 300–400 kilometres, was itself fraught with danger. Over such long distances, fighter cover had to be dispensed with. Hundreds of aircraft were shot down or crashed for other reasons. The landings and take-offs at Pitomnik air base were particularly critical. The aircraft stayed down for the shortest possible time, just long enough to unload the precious supplies and to take on the badly sick and wounded who had been given a ticket to fly out. Bombing attacks, fog and icing always had to be reckoned with. Many an aircraft, fully loaded with victims of the battle, with human beings who hoped to escape from hell and fly to freedom, was shot down or suddenly crashed during an unsuccessful take-off, and remained as a pile of wreckage in the snowy desert.

The Russians knew only too well that the heart of the Stalingrad army was beating at Pitomnik which was the only really serviceable air base in the pocket although an auxiliary base had been established at Gumrak. This was where the vital food and supplies for men, weapons and machines were being landed. Here were located important command posts and communication centres, air traffic control, the supply staff and the supply administration with its bunkers, in which the treasures of bread, biscuits, meat, vegetables, drinks, and canned goods flown in were stored until they could be distributed. Here too, in the centre of the pocket, was a main dressing-station, to which the sick and wounded were brought from all sides in their thousands and later on, in their tens of thousands.

Nearby was an assembly point for soldiers who had lost contact with their units, where frightened, confused and desperate human beings from shattered formations all over the front gathered together. Here at Pitomnik there was a constant coming and going, a feverish hurrying and bustling, an incessant grinding of engines, constantly recurring firing and explosions of bombs, a never-ending worrying, fearing, hoping and despairing.

Small wonder that the Russians saw this air base as a particularly worthwhile target for air attack! Their bombers and fighters appeared here as regular guests, dropped their deadly freight, and attempted to destroy as many of the cumbersome cargo aircraft as possible on the ground and in the air. The enemy also tried to maximise the disruption of the air lift by various manœuvres and ruses. In foggy weather or during the hours of darkness, they frequently succeeded in leading the aircraft astray by setting off German flares. Having become confused, they lost altitude and were shot down. Occasionally they landed in front of the German lines in no man's land or behind the Russian lines, where they were stripped clean and destroyed before the horrified eyes of the helpless German soldiers who were held in check by the enemy's heavy weapons.

It was always a splendid sight when, on a clear day, several dozen of the heavy cargo aircraft landed at Pitomnik and then slowly circled up to gain altitude, finally grouping together for departure. In the beginning they were accompanied by watchful fighters – the fast Messerschmitts. In the sharp frost, their rhythmic thrumming, the grinding sound of their motors by day and night, pulsating through the crystal-clear winter air like a cutting jingle, was always a calming, consoling music to our ears.

But I knew only too well that the subsistence level for our army was in no way being secured. Even if after fatal intervals an especially large number of aircraft occasionally flew into the pocket, what they were bringing in was not enough. And underlying the numbers I had to report to my general was a shattering balance sheet of suffering, hunger and death.

Memories of dark weeks in December

When I think back to those dark weeks in December which I spent on, or rather under, Pitomnik air base, and when I re-read letters that I received in those days, I again seem to feel the draught of that icy atmosphere of bitter disappointment, hidden fear and mounting despair.

Our Ic department had settled down in a primitive, dirty wooden bunker. Six of us were jammed together, but being underground, at least we kept warm. For the time being the horrors taking place outside only crept in by way of the various bits of information we had to evaluate in order to obtain a picture of the enemy situation. The messages from Army, from the neighbouring corps, from the divisions, the statements of the by now only occasional Russian prisoners and enemy pilots shot down, reports from German prisoners sent back from the Russian lines for propaganda reasons, leaflets, foreign radio broadcasts, the experiences reported by soldiers back from leave and officers flown into the pocket, the results of radio surveillance; in those days all this enabled us still to maintain a fairly comprehensive enemy situation map. On it the thick red entries, the letters and numbers, the arcs and arrows grew alarmingly. This evil blood-red circle was obviously preparing itself to crush what it contained inside. And in our sector especially, all kinds of dangerous wedges and arrows twitched towards the heart of the army, towards Pitomnik air base.

We were kept in mind of this all too plainly by the bombs whistling down, playing their hellish concert around our bunker. Of course our experiences during the eastern campaign and the first weeks in the pocket had long ago made us grow a thick skin. When the bombs sometimes landed close by so that our bunks shook together with the entire dug-out and the clay flaked down from the ceiling, we remained unconcerned and detached, just like our contentedly purring cat, that lived with us in our quarters below ground and kept the mice in check.

We mainly feared for the safety of our much patched-up window pane which provided light during the day and also protected us from the cold.

When an air raid ended and circumstances permitted, we still occasionally sat together in a comradely group, and wrote to our loved ones at home, to whom our thoughts turned so fearfully and longingly in this season before Christmas. The mail service had not yet completely stopped even if letters from home arrived less and less frequently. Or a diverting discussion began. But these were mostly too self-conscious and remained tense in their obvious expediency. Occasionally, with gallows humour and in memory of a highly pleasing meal of horse stew, we sang the 'Song of the German Soldier in the East', '... he, who never in the pocket, ate his horse ...!' Our feelings and thoughts could no longer get away from our cruel routine, the fatal place we were tied to for life and death, from Stalingrad and the Volga.

Life and times at Pitomnik with its desolate steppe landscape did not lack a certain uncanny romanticism. Even if air raids and dog-fights had become routine, we were often enticed out of our dug-out. Then we hunkered down amidst the snow drifts and, disregarding the danger, followed with those strange, mixed feelings of curiosity, sensation-seeking, carefreeness, enjoyment and secret horror, the breath-taking spectacle being enacted high above our heads in a combination of grace and deadly intent. The heavy thumping of the Flak, the thrumming and screaming of the engines, provided an infernal accompanying music. The fighters circled among the small white clouds of exploding shells, chased and rolled over each other in vicious dog-fights until finally one went down, trailing a growing black cloud of smoke. At the beginning we still had four sleek fighters at Pitomnik, which the attacking Russians held in great respect. Occasionally a huge jet of flame erupted on the air base with an ear-splitting bang. That meant a transport, its belly crammed with fuel, had been hit after landing. Occasionally a stricken aircraft, trailing a terribly bright flame, screamed down out of the cold blue depths of the winter sky like a meteor and immediately after a huge mushrooming cloud of smoke bore witness to the end of a minute catastrophe that had devoured a man and his machine.

In the course of the weeks of December the shot-down wrecks of every conceivable type of aircraft piled up on the base at Pitomnik.

Peacefully they lay there, one next to another, from small Russian fighters to the lamed or destroyed big birds, many of which had crashed on take-off. There was even a Fieseler Storch that had frozen to the ground. But in this extensive graveyard of equipment life still pulsed feverishly even deep under the ground. The low snow walls and domes of the bunkers with their smoking chimney pipes, ineffectively camouflaged vehicles, radio stations with masts and antennas, communications trucks, occasional tents; all this gave the impression of a ghostly city where people swarmed like ants, sometimes above ground and sometimes below. And yet the place with its masses of people was lost in the never ending wilderness of snow.

It was probably the saddest and most desolate place I had laid eyes on in the east. A bare, naked, dead steppe landscape with not a bush or tree, not a village for miles around. A single trunk without branches stuck up five kilometres away in the little hamlet of Pitomnik, where a few houses were still standing, and served as a sign post. Near the hamlet were a number of *balkas*, deeply eroded, steep-banked rain gullies, that gave some protection. Occasionally an ice-grey mist from the Volga drifted over this desolate piece of ground and the wind, which cut through everything with its biting edge, blew unmercifully over the boundless snowy waste. The loneliness of the eastern expanses was depressing and this eerie feeling was increased by the early fall of darkness. We had maintained our time setting from home and this no longer fitted our sector of the front. The sun set soon after lunch and by 14.00 to 15.00 hours it was already dark, and every day this too reminded us, depressingly, here in the desolation of the snow-bound steppe, of the enormous distance that separated us from home.

Were we not all, the living and the dead, long buried in a gigantic mass grave? Thoughts like this occasionally befell me when I returned from various sectors of the front where in my role as liaison officer, I had been sent on specific assignments, or to gather urgently needed information. There, on the heights above the infamous Rossoshka valley, the men of our divisions lay in a desperate battle demanding bloody sacrifice. There in the trenches and fox-holes in the snow, the soldiers were dying of exhaustion and cold, because the steadily shrinking rations of bread and other food issued were no longer sufficient to provide the physical stamina needed to combat frost and sickness.

Only the crows swarming in the endless steppe, those horrible, greedy birds that always seemed to me to be the harbingers of doom, still found enough to eat. Yes, these croaking companions of death did very well for themselves. They rose slowly before one's feet from the frozen carcasses of the dead horses half hidden in the snow that formed a kind of trail and showed, by bloody red gashes, that hungry soldiers had cut out coveted chunks of meat with their knives or bayonets.

Whereas the air lift disappointed all expectations, the troops had to perform and suffer beyond human capacity day and night. And they did so to the extreme. The reports of losses grew more and more serious. It was as if the horsemen of the Apocalypse had ridden in, instead of the hoped for relief. The thoughts of the sufferings of our comrades, the agonies and dangers that might be ours tomorrow or the day after, never left us. If only their sacrifices were not to be in vain.

Why had we been forbidden to break-out in time with the forces and energies that were now slowly and inexorably being ground down? I often recall those conversations I had overheard at the beginning of the battle, when the fatal decision to have the army dig-in was taken. Had we then not looked into the future with grave concern and great anxiety? The air lift on which everything had originally depended was now clearly failing, and the fate of the army seemed to be taking its fatal course. But one great hope remained; the possibility of salvation from outside. A rapid and successful relief operation could still bring about the longed-for turning point for our desperately endangered army.

Manstein is coming

One day in the second week of December, the staffs first heard the news that Army Group Don under Field Marshal von Manstein had begun the long hoped-for relief operation.

Soon the good news had also reached the troops. The words that gave new impetus everywhere and particularly on the hard-pressed western perimeter of the pocket spread like lightning, 'Manstein is coming!' The already dying hopes burst forth anew. New courage, happy expectations, a new spirit of initiative, began to blossom. The sufferings and sacrifices to date had not been in vain after all! Salvation was now beckoning. What the Führer had promised, he was bound to deliver. And he would surely redeem his promise in a most generous manner. It was in hope of this that the troops had loyally held out according to orders. Now relief was coming from outside. 'The Führer will get us out!' Everyone counted on the fact that this could only mean a comprehensive relief operation, the success of which was as good as assured.

The fact that it was Field Marshal von Manstein who had been specially selected for the job of battling through to our Stalingrad army filled us with particular satisfaction. The outstanding strategic capabilities of this senior commander, of whom our staff spoke with the greatest respect, increased our confidence and seemed for us to guarantee the happy conclusion of the forthcoming operation from its outset.

In these exciting days, my 'phone rang without cease. One call chased the next. The divisions demanded information. They wanted to know all sorts of details that we ourselves knew nothing about in the beginning. They urgently needed good news about the approach of the armoured forces promising relief. Such news, they maintained, was now more important than the daily beggarly rations of bread and ammunition. It was the best tonic for the men in the front lines, who needed a psychological lift. And I was only too happy to pass on the good news we initially received about the relief operation that had been set in motion.

Despite the premonitions that had been subconsciously torturing me until then and despite my knowledge of the sorry condition of the encircled army, I also embraced the newly surging feeling of hope. How happy I was to let some of this positive feeling which was revitalising me creep into the lines I penned to my loved ones at home! This was a consoling Christmas greeting. If everything went well, the hour of our relief could just coincide with Christmas. That would really and truly be an equinox for the warriors of Stalingrad who were wasting away in darkness and suffering. Into the larger perspectives and expectations were mixed all of the more humble longings and personal wishes, which for the moment primarily had to do with the Christmas mail from home and the fat Christmas packages full of the wonderful things promised that were stockpiling somewhere outside the pocket.

From the south, Colonel General Hoth had jumped off on 12 December with Fourth Panzer Army and, according to the first happy reports, was approaching in rapid advances. The name of Hoth made me feel particularly confident. He was the first general I had ever met, back in a small Silesian garrison town. He had given us young recruits an hour-long lesson at a sand-table. And later I had seen him again during my studies in Breslau, where this scientifically interested man had given our history course a talk on military history. I very vividly remembered this agile, white-haired general, with his fiery temperament and glowing eyes. For me he seemed to be the very epitome of energy.

The motorised groups and strong tank units being led by Colonel General Hoth, elements of which had been brought in from France in great haste, had begun their relief offensive from the Kotelnikovo area about 200 kilometres south-west of Stalingrad. They were approaching our encircled army in daring advances, but by dint of increasingly heavy fighting. By 10 December they had covered far more than 100 kilometres and forced an important bridgehead north of the Mishkova. Some time ago, regular radio communications had been established with our Supreme Command at Gumrak, and from our western perimeter one could clearly hear the thunder of the guns. Hoth's spearhead tanks were only about fifty kilometres away. 'Hold on, we are coming', said one of the encouraging radio messages which spread like wildfire among the troops on the western edge of the pocket.

A big decision lay in the air. It could no longer be concealed that our break-out, our junction with the approaching army of relief, was now seriously being prepared and appeared to be imminent. The staffs quickly learned that behind the attacking tank forces were rolling long columns of trucks with several thousand tonnes of supplies for our Stalingrad army. With feverish haste we were ordered to collect empty vehicles to be provided as transport space for all kinds of formations.

The excitement and tension, particularly on the western perimeter of our pocket and among the staffs, reached its high point. Without any doubt the troops too were only waiting impatiently for the big moment in order to break the encircling ring towards the west, resolutely prepared to give and risk their all so as to seize this last beckoning chance for freedom and salvation.

As far as I can remember, our army corps did not receive any official orders to prepare for the break-out. We were, however, given some guide-lines. Army's break-out plan resembled the one conceived at the beginning of the pocket battle. But the situation during the past months had deteriorated catastrophically and the risks had grown enormously as a consequence of our reduced combat power. Three of the most battle-worthy divisions were to force a breach south-west of Karpovka and establish the link to the Panzer Army advancing across the steppe, but not until it had approached to within about thirty kilometres. We no longer had sufficient fuel to cover a longer distance. One wanted to be absolutely sure of the success of the operation and hold the risks down as far as possible. The various units in the pocket were only to leave their positions under certain conditions which minimised risks and, starting with the Volga Front, fall in successively in a south-westerly direction and follow behind the advance point. The army's approximately 100 remaining serviceable tanks were to provide flank protection.

Within our circle of comrades, we frequently spoke about the dangers we would face in connection with the relief operation, code-named 'Winter Storm'. These had increased alarmingly since the end of November. The encircling ring had been heavily reinforced and the physical strength of the troops had seriously declined. The mobility of our units was limited or no longer existed at all, thanks to the increasingly serious loss of horses, that had wandered into the cooking pots, but above all, because of the catastrophic shortage of fuel. This hampered the regrouping and movement of the remaining tanks and heavy weapons, or prevented them entirely. On top of this there was the icy frost which had sharpened. Would we despite all this succeed in fighting through to the approaching Panzer Army and beating back the enemy who was bound to attack us viciously in the open ground of the Don steppe? But whatever misgivings we might have had, we clearly knew that this time we would have to risk all on the turn of a single card. In the sure knowledge that before us was the last chance for our salvation, we feverishly awaited the decisive hour with a feeling of confidence. The orders we expected could not be delayed much longer.

But all too soon our hopes were to be bitterly disappointed. Alarming messages began to come in. Rapidly attacking Russian tank forces were embroiling the relieving army in heavy fighting, were slowing the advance and finally leading, in connection with Russian offensive operations west of the Don, to a serious crisis for the entire Army Group.

During the preceding weeks we had unsuccessfully tried to dupe the enemy by all sorts of measures and ruses on the radio, feigning an early break-out operation, in order to tie down as many of his forces as possible on the perimeters of the pocket. It had been to no avail. Russian formations with tanks and heavy weapons had streamed by without interruption in a westerly and southerly direction. The reports from the outer lines of the pocket, especially on the southern front, had alarmed us in the extreme. For long nights the noises and lights of such movements had been observed, and not only on our own corps' sector.

We gained the impression that the encircled army was already no longer the most important factor for the Russians. They obviously did not consider our manœuvrability and strength to be very serious. Beyond doubt they were now also withdrawing substantial elements of their forces in order to throw them against our approaching relief. And indeed, to the west and south of our army, the enemy was engaged in securing his triumph initiated at Stalingrad against all hazards, and in deepening the gaping wound on the German eastern front. One of the attacks hit Colonel General Hoth who was hastening towards us. In fearful tension and daily mounting agitation we read the messages we were receiving from the far distant German air reconnaissance and radio surveillance units. Soon these brought news of disaster.

At the beginning of the last week before Christmas fate had also struck from the big bend of the Don. There the Russians had launched a major offensive and torn a new, deep hole in the defensive front. In the course of this the Italian Eighth Army, including the Alpini Corps, mainly fighting in the region of Millerovo, was destroyed. The OKH had seen fit to withdraw this hardy force of Alpine Jägers from the Caucasus front, for which it had been provided, and to deploy it in the Don steppe under specific combat conditions for which it could not have been prepared. The situation was becoming desperate.

Russian spearheads also crossed the Chir to the west, tore deep gaps in the front and threatened the northern flank of our Army Group Don. The radio messages intercepted from the enemy showed us the advances and positions of the Russian tanks.

A glance at the map made the blood freeze in our veins. Our advanced air bases from which our untiring cargo aircraft took off, our supply bases at Morosovsk and Tatsinskaya where the food stores and the army sutlers lay and where our mail bags were by now piling up mountain high, had become battle grounds. On the base at Tatsinskaya, as an officer recently flown into the pocket reported, the sudden and unexpected appearance of Russian tanks had caused wild confusion. The huge food supply depot for our Sixth Army had gone up in flames. Many aircraft were destroyed, ammunition blew up in a gigantic fireworks display, an orgy of destruction and panic seized the rear echelon services, and aircraft hastily taking-off were even reported to have collided in the air.

The relief operation began to run down. Hoth's forces, in turn threatened with being surrounded, were finally forced to retreat. The front fell back for hundreds of kilometres, and the encircled Stalingrad army on the Volga was left to its fate.

It was just before Christmas when all our expectations and hopes tumbled down like a huge house of cards. After our originally pleasing bulletins spreading comfort and confidence had become fewer and fewer and finally ceased altogether, desperate calls and questions began to come in from the divisions. They wanted to know what progress the relief operation was making, when they could expect to be relieved, why they had not yet received their orders from Army for the final break-out preparations. The troops needed encouraging news. They were holding on in the belief that Hitler's promise to 'get them out' would now be redeemed in time for Christmas. Everywhere the word was still, 'Manstein is coming!' But in those same days of anxious waiting, hoping and confident trusting, the forces designated for the relief of Stalingrad, hard hit and without achieving their objective, had halted their advance and begun to retire.

Only much later was I to learn the tragic details of the events and circumstances that had sealed the fate of the encircled army at this point. I did not know then that Hitler was still in no way prepared to give up Stalingrad and the Volga, that for the second time and after dramatic conflicts, he had explicitly forbidden the break-out of Sixth Army against the will of his Chief of Staff and in opposition to the demands of Army Group Don. For its supply, relief and replacement, a corridor of sorts was to be formed that was to ensure the planned subsequent re-establishment of the overall situation.

Despite the fact that Field Marshal von Manstein, in clear appreciation of the necessities arising from the overall situation, gave the order for the break-out of Sixth Army and also envisaged the complete evacuation of the Stalingrad area, the Commander-in-Chief of Sixth Army and his Chief of Staff, who rejected any 'catastrophe solution', could not see their way clear to accepting the responsibility for the risks of the break-out demanded by von Manstein. They knew the situation of their forces engaged in defensive fighting and suffering from a shortage of fuel. The distances to the relieving forces were long. If Stalingrad was not to be given up, they held a break-out to be impossible. And so the last chance for the salvation of the encircled army which the days before Christmas had held out was irretrievably lost.

Deep depression and bitter disappointment made the rounds of our staff. The circumstances of the events outside the pocket were largely hidden from us. But we instinctively felt that our last visible chance for salvation was gone. Had we possibly failed yet again to put everything on one turn of the cards and to dare the break-out? Now it was for ever too late.

Christmas and New Year in the Stalingrad Pocket

Slowly the talk about the expected von Manstein died down on the front lines as well. We could no longer pass on any news concerning the relief operation. That was undesired, even forbidden. Furthermore, we had no clear picture of the overall situation. Evil daily routine with all its thousands of great and small sufferings, deprivations, anxieties and dangers, bitterly re-imposed itself with its crushing demands. Certainly, for some time to come all sorts of fantastic imaginings about an impending relief ghosted about in some people's heads. These were but all too understandable spawnings of desperate optimism, longing wishes, secret hopes, and feverishly sick fantasies. Occasionally they led to the most curious rumours. Some even believed they could hear, behind the Russians and coming from the other side of the Don, the sonorous growling of German guns and the distant rattling of German tanks hastening to the relief.

Among the circle of our closer comrades we no longer entertained any illusions about the bleakness of our situation. The German front had withdrawn a great distance away, and for the time being there could be no thought of a new relief operation. In the midst of the cruelly hard eastern winter the encircled army was on its own on the Volga and in the empty steppe of the Don, hundreds of kilometres away from the front, bleeding from many new wounds, and dependent on a totally inadequate air lift made even more difficult by recent events. Would it be able to hold out for several more weeks? It was hardly to be expected. Hunger, frost and sickness were cutting terribly into its waning strength, and death was reaping an uncanny harvest, and not only on the fire-spewing iron ring around the pocket. And even the conditions for a great saving break-out operation scarcely existed any longer. In such an event the army would only be able to remain mobile for a few kilometres because of the lack of fuel. And if Stalingrad were to be given up, what would happen to the growing army of wounded, sick and exhausted men? Did the OKH intend to give up the Volga at all? The measures ordered so far seemed to point the opposite way. Once again I was often forced to recall Hitler's fanatical words about the German soldier on the Volga, about Stalingrad, and each time an icy unease crept through my bones. Maybe, yes maybe, we were supposed to hold on to the bitter end, to stay put and fight to the last bullet? On the dark horizon the outlines of a terrible disaster began to emerge.

Into this dark time of deepest disappointment, growing hopelessness and anxious foreboding for many tens of thousands of unhappy human beings who had been separated from their families for many a year and were suffering inhumanly in the Stalingrad pocket, fell Christmas, the saddest Christmas of their lives. Christmas Eve approached. All the visible and invisible wounds which the cruel events had caused burned even more painfully on this night. The atmosphere was depressed. There was virtually nothing that reminded one of the usual brightness and inspiring enchantment of this much loved festival. The mail from home, doubly longed for on this day, had not come, and this was especially bitter. No one knew when, or if ever again, greetings from our loved ones would bring us cheer and comfort.

Faced with the ever darkening future, these weeks with no word at all tortured me ever more consciously as Christmas approached. Only once had an aircraft been able to bring in larger quantities of mail. The letters were dated from the first half of November. And during Advent, to my great surprise and delight, someone flown into the pocket on returning from leave had brought me a small package already wrapped for Christmas. It contained fragrant gingerbread from my mother. It was probably the only Christmas cake from home that had found its way to the Stalingrad army on the distant steppe of the Don. Now the mail seemed to have stopped altogether. It was as if the links to home and to the world of private life had been cut. Even the best of comradeship could not carry one over the anxiously growing feeling of isolation and being lost. We celebrated Christmas in the circle of comrades of our administrative staff of the corps staff. They had moved to a *balka* near the hamlet of Pitomnik, one of those long, narrow ravines in the steppe. Our general had had a wooden bunker village erected there in order to get away from the disturbances and bombing of the air base. When first viewing these quarters and bunkers, newly built in great haste by a large engineering unit, into which our department was also to move after the turn of the year, I experienced all sorts of feelings of shame. Given the sad, insecure situation all around and the deprived state of the front-line troops who lacked building material and the most primitive necessities of life, was this not too much, superfluous luxury? And for how much longer were we going to be able to sit there undisturbed?

The Christmas speech by our Commanding General was filled with reflective earnestness. He no longer seem to be pleased about the high decoration he had just been awarded, the oak leaf cluster to the Knight's Cross. In any case, it was hardly mentioned. Our gathering was not very cheerful. Even the Christmas decorations in the room, yellowish-green fir branches from the outskirts of Stalingrad, a few warmly burning lights and some tinsel painstakingly cut from the silver wrapping paper of cigarette packs, were not able to change this. Nor were the modest but none the less highly welcome extra allotments of tobacco, bread and horse-meat dumplings. Memories of former Christmas celebrations with their blissful shimmer only dimly illuminated our harsh reality as from a world long gone. The well-loved Christmas carols sounded in low, melancholy sadness. No one could escape from the anxious worries and difficulties of the present, and the deliberate jocularity felt contrived. What depressed us at Christmas far more than the deprivations and sufferings, were the inner tortures, the anxieties, the unrest, the knowledge of how things really stood.

In the hour when Christmas mass was being celebrated at home far away, I went out into the night in order to collect myself and to be alone with my thoughts. An icy blizzard blew across the steppe which appeared even more desolate and eerie than usual on this Christmas Eve. The darkness of night swallowed me. But the feeling of being lost and abandoned abated in me the more I was able to make myself realise the meaning of Christmas even in our sorrowful here and now, and to find myself joined with my loved ones in my mind. Innumerable longing thoughts, wishes, hopes, wandered far away and came back to cheer the lonesome me in the whirling snowstorm of this winter night.

Right now my father was probably standing at the altar and in the warm glow of the candles was announcing the age-old message of love and peace to the members of his Silesian village congregation. In my mind I saw myself removed for a time into the village church at home and heard the Christmas gospel word by word, only interrupted by the festive liturgy. I felt as if the joyful ringing of bells out of the darkness far away were entering my heart and with them the voice of my father who, as was his custom on Christmas Eve, was reading from the old collection of religious sayings and stories and expostulating more earnestly than ever on the universally and everlastingly valid sense and comfort of the Christmas message.

Suddenly I felt myself sheltered under the everlasting tree of light that had been lit for all of us in the sky. And even if it had temporarily been hidden from us here by dark threatening clouds, I knew that it was still shining over us in incomparable splendour as it was over our families at home.

Despite all the misfortunes, sufferings, hatreds, destruction and death, the Christmas festival, which was to be the last one of their lives for many thousands of the encircled soldiers, remained the festival of peace, of light and of love. Especially amid the insecurity, darkness and the proximity to death that the warriors of Stalingrad felt so torturingly, this festival assumed a curiously shimmering brightness which did not come from outside. Any romantic feeling was absent, but the essence of Christmas glowed brightly in the dark. How many of the lonely men sunk in despair in their fox-holes, trenches, bunkers, in the dressing-stations and field hospitals, must have felt this then and gratefully accepted it as a precious gift!

Does not the 'Christmas Madonna of Stalingrad', hanging today in a Hessian vicarage as a legacy of her maker who died in captivity, remain as a moving testimonial to such a true Christmas experience that turned many of us into children of light in the middle of the night? A doctor and priest with the encircled army drew her on the back of a Russian map for their comrades and dedicated to her the mystical words from the gospel of St John, 'Light, Life, Love'. In the midst of the peril and horror of a hopeless and pitiless train of events, side by side with death, this impressive drawing radiates the strength and comfort of a security not of this earth.

The New Year arrived. Jangling frost lay over the Stalingrad pocket and breathed its icy, deadly breath. The sharp wind blew through the joints of doors and windows in the bunkers, and from the floors the cold crept up to one's knees. The daily casualty reports from our divisions that increasingly reported losses other than by enemy action represented a shattering balance sheet of death. Again the Russians furiously attacked several sectors of our perimeter. What did we have left to oppose these powerful Russian élite troops who were protected from the frost and had a full stomach; not to mention their numerous tanks, guns, rocket-launchers and mortars? Only small numbers of heavy weapons with insufficient, strictly rationed ammunition. Only emaciated men, exhausted by hunger, among whom the fighting, the cold and the spreading diseases were daily taking a frightening toll.

What use was it any longer if we succeeded in learning in time of impending Russian attacks and tank advances and immediately alerted the threatened sector of the front? Often we were able to warn the lines by giving them details of the strength, place and timing of individual enemy attacks. Our observation of the enemy and the passing down of messages via the Ic communications network to regiment and battalion level on the front line still functioned like clock-work. Our radio surveillance units frequently picked up enemy radio messages which we were able to decode almost completely. If there were talk of six 'boxes', the code-name for tanks, that were to move to a specific hill in a specific area at such and such a time, we could quickly identify by the entries on our maps what this was all about and pass the message on like lightning. But how bitter and painful it was on such occasions to receive the answer, that there were no more reserves or other means of defence available at the front so that nothing could be done except to warn the men.

How much longer could the perimeter withstand the pressure? It did not escape our attention that the Russians appeared to be concentrating in front of our sector in preparation for a major blow. The last sad possibility grew ever clearer on the dark horizon; the fate of our destruction by a shattering offensive breaking over our heads.

A number of occurrences at the turn of the year reinforced my apprehensions and feelings about this inescapable fate facing us. An important meeting of the General Staff took place at our corps in the Pitomnik gulley, which the Commander-in-Chief of the Army, General Paulus, attended with his Chief of Staff. The serious, reserved expression of the tall figure with the head of a scientist reflected something of the burden of responsibility that pressed down tormentingly on the shoulders of this man. It was the last time I was to see our Army Commander in the pocket. As far as I can remember he never visited our corps again.

I soon learned of the outcome of the meeting and the grave words of our General Staff officers left no doubt about the consequences of the orders that had been issued in the meantime. They dealt with the mobilisation of the last reserves of Sixth Army. The encircled forces were to hold on and fight to the last. For this purpose the formation of 'fortress battalions' was to be prepared and executed as quickly as possible. All remaining reserves of able-bodied men were to be collected and used as infantry. Members of the Luftwaffe ground personnel and anti-aircraft troops, gunners who no longer had guns, panzer grenadiers, engineers, truck drivers, clerical staff, rear echelon and supply personnel were once again to be ruthlessly combed out. The order amounted to the virtual dissolution of the rear echelon services and clearly demonstrated that the immobilised army was doomed to stay put and fight to the last man and bullet.

On New Year's Eve, two hours before midnight, a long-drawn-out booming, rumbling and clattering which suddenly began drew me outside. An appallingly beautiful spectacle presented itself. The Russians were celebrating in their own way, and were letting us take part in their festivities. All around us, firing with everything they had, they were putting on a hellish concert for our benefit with a fantastic fireworks display. The tracers were drawing a gigantic circle in the sky above the outer perimeter of our pocket, and effectively demonstrating the immense superiority of firepower that awaited us. In anticipation of their assured triumph, they were allowing us a glimpse of the prison from which we were not going to escape. All around us we could see, extending into the air in lines of fire, what amounted to the iron bars of a circular cage into which we had been locked and where the fate of our army was to be played out.

On New Year's Day, in our closed circle of staff officers, the Commanding General read a personal radio message from Hitler to Army Command. The content was neither passed on nor commented upon. I do not remember the wording in detail, but I remember distinctly how this message, which spoke of our holding on as one of the greatest acts of glory in the whole of military history, depressed and shattered us. We felt that we had already been written-off by the higher ups, and all that remained for us was to perform a heroic if futile gesture to ensure the 'fulfilment of the historic mission' of the army of Stalingrad on the Volga. The troops were again given the cheering radio message which the Führer and 'Supreme War Lord' had sent at the turn of the year: 'Sixth Army has my promise that everything is being done to get it out', but we now viewed this not just with doubt but as downright deception.

The Russian surrender proposal is rejected

The New Year had begun with a pitiless frost that increased the manifold sufferings of the encircled troops. The bread ration was reduced to 50 grams per day. Ringing cold, gnawing hunger, creeping illness, enemy fire, combined in an indissoluble offensive pact. Dysentery and typhoid fever had appeared as uncanny guests and the plague of lice increased from day to day. Death danced his murderous rondo back and forth throughout the pocket. His headquarters were the numerous places of suffering and despair, the dressing-stations and field hospitals that filled to overflowing alarmingly, but he also felt at home on the lines by day and night.

During the fifty days that the pocket battle had lasted so far, he had already cleaned out horribly among the men of the army. About one-third of its manpower was gone. Of the more than 300,000 men who were present at the time of the Russian break-through, about 200,000 were probably still alive. A large number, it is true, but how tiny was the still healthy, combat-worthy core contained therein. And how many of these enduring and hoping, fighting and suffering human beings, had death not already marked as his own!

General Hube, the commander of our neighbouring Panzer Corps, had meanwhile been to Führer Headquarters where he had personally reported to Hitler on the catastrophic state of our army, in particular on the fatal failure of the air lift. The tank general was known to be a man with his heart in the right spot who was not afraid to speak a sharp, open word to his superiors. He must have banged his fist on the table and, who knows, perhaps even succeeded in pushing through effective measures for our salvation. We had awaited his return with tense expectation and rekindling hopes. Now he had flown back into the pocket and the result of his trip quickly made the rounds among the staffs. He had brought back nothing at all, no beacon of hope was to be seen. That he had been promised an increase in the air lift was of small comfort to us. Since Christmas, the air lift had reduced alarmingly. Only about thirty to forty aircraft were coming in per day.

However, the news that we could no longer count on any relief before spring was really shattering. There was nothing more to be done save to hang on and endure the horror. Was there really no other alternative? The tank general seemed to answer this question unequivocally by his words and actions. He talked about the necessity of forming an 'Alcazar', soon had a fox-hole dug for himself in the middle of his army corps sector and declared that this was where he was going to fight hand-to-hand among his men until the last moment and then go under. But for him this extreme situation did not arise. He was flown out of the pocket and assigned to other important duties, primarily the reorganisation of the air lift.

The second week in January had just begun when all of a sudden we received a surprise that threw us into a state of extreme excitement. To the piles of 'enemy documents' overflowing my desk; maps, reports, papers, appeals and other information and propaganda material, there was suddenly added a leaflet printed in good German, the contents of which almost bowled us over. Outside one could pick up copies of this leaflet by the bundle. They were blowing over the snow and here and there they were impaled on the blades of the stiffly frozen steppe grass. Soviet aircraft, probably the 'sewing-machines' that slowly trundled along over our heads by night and normally only dropped small bombs to annoy us, must have released them by the thousands.

It was a surrender proposal, sent to our encircled army by the Soviet Supreme Command. The document was addressed to Paulus, who had been promoted to Colonel General, and to all the officers and men of the German forces fighting at Stalingrad. It was signed by Colonel General of Artillery Voronov, Stavka's representative on the

Volga, and by the Commander-in-Chief of the forces of the Don Front, Lieutenant-General Rokossovski, who had now obviously been put in sole charge of all of the forces surrounding us.

The proposal began with a short, factual and largely correct evaluation of our situation. In particular, it stressed the catastrophic state of supply of our troops who were suffering from hunger, cold and sickness, lack of winter clothing, and terribly insanitary conditions. Realistic possibilities of breaking the encircling ring no longer existed. Any further resistance in such a hopeless situation had to be senseless. Therefore in order to avoid further unnecessary shedding of blood, the Red Army was proposing a number of terms.

For the main part these were a demand to cease all further resistance and to place the total human and *matériel* resources of the army under Soviet control in an orderly fashion. The surrendering soldiers were promised their lives and safety, immediate normal rations and medical treatment. The date given for the acceptance of the surrender proposal was 9 January 1943, at 10.00 hours Moscow time. The reply in writing was to be taken over at a specified point on the northern defensive front by a negotiator carrying a white flag. The document ended with a reference directed to the Commander-in-Chief of the Stalingrad army, pointing out that in the event of a refusal, the forces of the Red Army and Air Force would be obliged to destroy the pocket for which he, Colonel General Paulus, would bear the responsibility.

Naturally the proposal caused the greatest agitation. But this touchy subject was discussed with guarded reticence. In one's intimate circles, however, one spoke more freely and the criticism of the orders and measures coming from above and deciding our fate, slowly began to be debated more openly.

What would happen if we were to lay down our arms? We did not believe the Russians and were highly mistrustful of their promises. Would they be able to provide food and medical care immediately for such a gigantic mass of prisoners? Would not the ferocious hatred and the wild thirst for revenge that were deliberately being fostered in the Red Army, particularly by the Soviet leaflets written by Ilya Ehrenburg, vent themselves unchecked? I had an up-to-date collection of these, and they all spoke of the fascist beasts and monsters that had to be strangled. Would not the Russians abuse their prisoners and above all, kill all of the officers? The best we could expect was slave labour in Siberia! The inhuman conduct of the war in the east by both sides, and above all the angry, bitter struggle for Stalingrad, made us fear the worst.

Some of the phrases in the surrender proposal made us laugh. In pathetic words, the soldiers were not only guaranteed life and safety, but also later repatriation to Germany or to another country of their choice. The surrendering troops would be allowed to keep their uniforms, rank insignia, decorations and valuables, and the officers were to be left their 'swords'.

The questions arising from fear, doubt and mistrust were to be raised again and again until the army went under. At the same time, we constantly wondered whether in only expecting the worst, we were perhaps being too greatly influenced by our own propaganda. Maybe the Russians would let us live and treat us tolerably? Had we not recently learned all sorts of interesting things about this from captured German soldiers who, for propaganda reasons, had been sent back to us with bread and bacon? And were not many of the reports on the enemy sent to us from higher up obviously coloured by many deterring details, in order to prevent the troops entertaining thoughts of desertion or surrender?

Perhaps the Russian proposal offered an avenue of escape from our hopeless situation. In the end it could not be dishonourable to lay down our arms after having fought so bravely for so long, since our dying army no longer had enough food or ammunition. Had not even old Blücher once capitulated in a similar situation and not considered it to be dishonourable?

I well knew that our resistance was still tying down a number of strong Soviet armies which included élite forces and considerable masses of artillery. By our capitulation these forces of the Red Army would become available for deployment against other sectors of the fronts of our army groups which were endangered everywhere. Under these circumstances, was it appropriate and, from the point of view of soldierly honour, permissible even to think of surrender? There was no room for doubt that our resistance was completely futile in the long term. But maybe we still had an important role to play within an overall situation that we could not judge? Was there not talk of a withdrawal of our armies from the Caucasus region? Must not higher strategic-operational considerations and measures demand the stark requirement for us to keep on fighting? Therefore, could the certain hopelessness of our last desperate engagement be a justification for giving up? Or would such an attitude lay destructive hands on the foundations of traditional soldiery with its firmly established concepts of honour and duty? In my thoughts and considerations during these days I was tortured by the whole terrible problematic question of war. How much heavier must it seem to the men who were weighed down by the responsibility for our fate!

Much as contradictory imagining and brooding may have troubled me, one thing was clear in my mind; from now on, and in the face of immeasurable sufferings all around, my concepts of humanity and ethics made me increasingly more reluctant to accept strictly military points of view and strategic considerations. This may have been mainly a consequence of my most recent experiences and observations and of the reports coming in to our corps, which one only had to multiply in order to obtain the shattering overall picture of our army.

Was the gigantic sacrifice of human lives and human dignity that was being offered here in any way still responsibly related to any strategic needs and necessities? Military-strategic considerations and actions had in the final analysis to be reconcilable with humane-ethical responsibility. In secret I hoped that our Army Command would try to gain time by negotiations and obtain more dependable, detailed promises for the treatment of the sick and wounded, or at least more favourable surrender terms.

Army did not leave us long in doubt as to their view of the matter. We soon received various orders, directives and messages whose burden was that surrender was out of the question. The Commander-in-Chief had passed the Russian ultimatum on to Führer Headquarters and asked for freedom of action for all eventualities. In immediate reply Hitler had personally forbidden surrender, and on 9 November Paulus had rejected in writing the proposal of the Soviet Command. The troops were not to be informed in detail, but from now on they were ordered to fire without warning on flags of truce appearing near the front lines. This instruction from Army, which we received by radio, was especially revealing as to the intentions of the leadership. In our staff it was received with rejection and objection, because it was a clear breach of international law. The outrage and criticism, however, was not voiced aloud.

Official cognisance was therefore taken of the Russian surrender proposal, but it was rejected in a proud, even offensive, manner as being something dishonourable and unacceptable. One did not even consider negotiating with the enemy. In an appeal from Army the troops were admonished to reject propaganda attempts to undermine fighting morale and to place their firm trust in the promised relief.

I was again reminded of Hitler's high-sounding words about the invincibility of the German soldier for whom nothing must be seen to be impossible. The very thought of a capitulation must be irreconcilable with the prestige of the 'Supreme War Lord'. In his speech in Munich shortly before our encirclement, had he not solemnly sworn: 'You may rest assured, and I repeat this with full responsibility before God and history, that we shall never again leave Stalingrad.!' Never again ...

For life or death, we were committed to the cheerless Don steppe. Here our fate must come full turn. The most terrible weeks were still before us and during those icy days in January the fearful premonition of what was to come descended on us like a lead weight.

The Pocket is broken up

On the morning of 10 January 1943, exactly 24 hours after the ultimatum had expired, the Russian began the destruction of the pocket with a hellish artillery barrage.

A long-lasting, uncanny thundering and dull roaring filled the air. The earth trembled and our wooden bunker shook to its foundations. Before the lines of communications in all directions were cut, we had received several messages from our neighbouring units. From them we gained a first rough picture of the situation. The bombardment was taking place along the entire western half of the pocket, from the eastern approaches to the Rossoshka valley, at whose edge our worn-out, mostly burned-out divisions were fighting desperately, over the whole sector of the neighbouring Panzer Corps, to the 'Nose of Marinovka' sticking out towards the west. And even in the sector farther south all hell had broken loose. Over this huge area, totalling fifty kilometres of front, rolled the grinding, smashing waltz of iron and fire with which the Russians intended to open the road to Stalingrad.

And we ourselves belonged to the immediately threatened crew that was deployed on that spot on the constantly repaired dike, where the surging flood tide was shortly to break through unstoppably. The big Russian offensive had begun. It was the answer to the rejection of the surrender proposal.

The initial excitement was soon replaced by a deep gloom, especially since the destroyed wires and cables temporarily made any transmission of messages impossible. When I was sent to various sectors of the front to carry orders and collect situation reports I breathed a little more deeply in the vast, seemingly endless white space of the steppe with its polished encasing of ice and snow that was occasionally dirtily torn up by misdirected artillery and mortar fire.

Up front among the staffs on the line I again entered the atmosphere of tension, excitement, nervousness and despair. The situation was partially unclear and confused. Initial penetrations by the Russians had meanwhile taken place and everywhere the anxious questions were being raised: how were the holes to be plugged; from where could the missing men, weapons, ammunition and equipment be found? The catastrophe did indeed appear to be unavoidable.

Into this helpless situation orders from Army came in time and again. Defend! Hold! Clear up the situation! Fight to the last bullet!

From their desks, 2,000 kilometres away (!), the OKH together with the constantly interfering Führer Headquarters, forbade any independent withdrawal from endangered sectors of the perimeter. And Army, which had to meticulously justify itself for any change in the front line caused by the pressure of circumstances, obeyed. The army corps, divisions and regiments obeyed, often with bitter criticism, with open or hidden reservations, flaring up or knuckling under, but they obeyed. And the suffering and dying troops in the trenches and fox-holes in the icy steppe obeyed, giving their all in the natural fulfilment of their duty, or in apathy and silent despair.

The bloody defensive fighting in the former ring positions lasted for more than three days and cost several tens of thousands of human lives, until the western perimeter of the pocket was dented without hope of recovery and smashed. Before the rearward flight began, which was later to become unrestrained, praiseworthy deeds of valour and desperate actions of self-sacrifice and personal fortitude were enacted, as if in a last upsurging of wild resolution and dogged self-preservation. The higher leadership did not stint with recognition; promotions, decorations, and medals rained down *en masse* on the fighting, suffering, doomed men. But what purpose did this huge, this monstrous commitment and dedication of human beings serve?

In the face of the increasing military helplessness and the daily worsening human plight, I was becoming more and more depressed by the torturing question of the why of this sacrifice of most precious blood, this pitiless dying. Was it not only for the sake of a prestige that a military Supreme Command thousands of kilometres removed mercilessly wished to maintain, and for whom the price in many thousands of human lives did not appear to be too high? This question haunted me and would not leave me until the final sorrowful ending.

In the meantime the tragedy had run its course at our neighbouring units to the west. The advanced 'Nose of Marinovka', where a motorised division was deployed in relatively strong positions, could no longer be held. Originally it was probably intended to serve as a preparatory springboard for the break-out planned for December when von Manstein's relieving force had come close.

Since the sensible shortening of the pocket perimeter had not been carried out there after the failure of the break-out plans, the 'nose' was now in danger of being cut off by the Russian wedges advancing from the north and south. In this instance, Army gave one of its very few official orders to withdraw.

The Russians swiftly advanced into the pocket on the heels of the rapidly retreating troops who lost most of their valuable equipment, and soon set the whole western sector of the line in motion. One after another, they gained a number of important towns and bases such as Krovzov, Zybenko, Dmitrevka and Karpovka. That meant the dike had burst. The enemy flood surged in. Nothing could now hold it back for long.

The withdrawal of the troops finally turned into a full-fledged flight into which further formations and combat groups of various divisions were drawn. Whole units ceased to exist in this confusion. In the sector of our neighbour to our left this fate also put an end to a whole division that had long been under our command and in the end had burned-out like a slag-heap. This division had suffered frightfully since the beginning of the pocket battle. Back on 19 November, when the Russians had broken through the northern defensive position on the Don at Kletskaya, it had already been forced into the maelstrom of a panicky withdrawal. Later on it had suffered very heavy attacks when in December, the enemy had beaten against the northern perimeter of the pocket in an attempt to split it. And in the area of the death hill of Kasachi it had had to make a great sacrifice in blood. Small wonder that the Russians selected this hard-hit formation as a target for their propaganda tactics. They had bombarded them with leaflets in which, following the division's official designation 'V.D.' after the initials of its commander, they had been addressed variously as the *versoffene* (drunk), the *verlorene* (lost) or the *verbrecherische* (criminal) division. Now it no longer existed. Shortly afterwards I saw its distraught general, now a commander without troops, wandering around in a bunker, desperately seeking a new assignment.

Coming from the neighbouring Panzer Corps, disaster quickly reached menacingly into our sector. Near the Kasachi hill further high ground had been lost and the way into the Rossoshka valley now lay open to the Russians. The withdrawal and re-deployment of all the formations of the corps had become necessary. In some sectors the withdrawal of the troops, particularly on the hard-pressed left flank, took place in great haste and panic-stricken confusion.

And this desperate withdrawal was being carried out in icy cold weather and pitiless snowstorms. At thirty degrees (centigrade) below zero, the remnant of the regiments that had shrunk to combat groups and the suffering hordes of other shattered units moved over the empty white steppe dragging crowds of lost, lightly wounded and frost-bitten soldiers with them. How many of those that so far had been spared enemy fire succumbed there to exhaustion and over-exertion, to the strains of hunger, and to the cold! Innumerable men fell by the wayside and were soon mercifully covered by the snow.

And this was no longer an authorised withdrawal. The recoil of the front was now taking place despite standing orders to hold on and maintain position at all costs and despite the line of resistance laid down by OKH. Under the pressure of circumstances the exhausted troops simply reeled back, losing the greater part of their remaining heavy weapons and equipment in the process. They were long gone and at the end of their strength.

In spite of all this, for a short time, a sort of line of resistance was again successfully held for the protection of Pitomnik air base, which had already been temporarily evacuated due to panic among the supply and rear echelon services. The supply base in the centre of our army was not to be lost on any account. But after the former strong points of the original western and north-western perimeter of the pocket, from Bolshaya Rossoshka, through Baburkin to Novo Alexeyevka, had fallen into Russian hands, the air base could no longer be defended. The new, makeshift defensive ring established to close the broad gap torn into the perimeter of the pocket from the west existed more on the maps of the General Staff than it did in pitiful reality. It was only thinly and dubiously patched together. It consisted of exhausted formations that were melting away, that had not only been eroded by battle, but among whom death was daily reaping a frightening harvest. Effective heavy weapons and ammunition were lacking everywhere, as were all the conditions for a sensible continuation of the fight with any hope of success. The psychological ability of the troops to resist had now also been eroded.

In mid January, therefore, the heart of our army, the Pitomnik air base, was lost, and the pocket shrank to about half its original circumference. With this our fate was finally sealed. Later on Army Command tried to establish a final line of resistance along the ring railroad running through Voroponovo and to defend it with troops who were scarcely fit for further combat. But the remains of the beaten army flooded unceasingly and in growing dissolution towards the gigantic pile of rubble, sticking up for miles along the banks of the Volga, that was Stalingrad.

The tragedy approaches its climax

What took place in the second half of January 1943 in the desolate snowscape of the Don steppe was a tragedy of unimaginable proportions. It broke over the fortunes of 200,000 human beings who faced death daily in many forms and saw it approaching inescapably. In the final analysis it also hung like a dark shadow over the heads of innumerable families, who feared for their sons and fathers.

In the pocket, we too occasionally heard the news broadcasts on the radio. The news reports, at first contrived and obscuring or merely hinting at the true state of affairs, gradually became more blunt. From time to time the voice of the reporter was suddenly drowned out by the dreadful croaking of the ghostly voice of a Russian jamming transmitter speaking of the 'mass grave of Stalingrad' and calling attention to the downfall of Sixth Army.

There could indeed no longer be any doubt about our fate. The relief operation that could have brought the hoped-for salvation had failed. Army had rejected the Russian surrender proposal and the freedom of action it had requested had been denied. In its turn it had not acted on its own initiative to avert the impending disaster in time. After the enemy had begun his decisive attack bent on destruction and our dissolution was in full progress, it was too late for a last desperate attempt to break out to the west. Help from outside could no longer be considered.

More devastating even than the enemy's weapons were hunger, exhaustion, cold and illnesses of all kinds among the soldiers who had not been adequately fed for so many long weeks. With the advent of the indescribable strains of daily retreats, the situation had deteriorated catastrophically. We were lacking in food, weapons, rest, warmth, hope; in short, we were lacking in all the vital conditions for fighting. Since the rejection of the surrender proposal, the troops had again survived a long, terrible week of tenacious defensive fighting, retreat and flight, thereby tying down superior enemy forces in their area. Now after the loss of our life-support base, Pitomnik air field, on 16 January, the time really seemed to have come to stop fighting. The air lift temporarily ceased altogether. No more food and ammunition came in. The wounded and sick could no longer be flown out. Slowly but surely the temporarily cleared air field at Gumrak with its too short and narrow runway covered with ruins and snow drifts was coming dangerously within range of enemy fire.

By now, every day that the fighting was prolonged was costing thousands of human lives. There was no more time to be lost and we waited for something to happen. Like me, innumerable comrades and brothers in fate probably clung to the same secret hope. But nothing happened and the tragedy took its course.

The continuation of the 'defence' only meant a cruel prolongation of the dying that was becoming general. Was our army really still able to fulfil an assignment that ethically justified such a gigantic sacrifice? From day to day the battle was increasingly losing any sense or purpose. I do not remember any special orders and appeals to the troops that explained the need to keep on fighting in an appropriate manner. There was however still one argument that the OKH and Führer Headquarters insisted on raising to the very end, and which probably also affected the decisions of Army Command, namely the argument that by our holding on to the extreme, or better, by our self-sacrifice, we were buying time for the establishment of a new front. We had no clear picture of events within the overall framework of military operations on the southern sector of the eastern front. The fact was not hidden from us in the higher staffs that the overall situation of our Army Group was highly menaced and that in the south, the armies in the Caucasus were conducting a dangerous retreat. But our holding out and slow destruction could no longer really influence the course of events, particularly since the pocket was being compressed into a smaller and smaller area.

From now on the Russians were daily able to withdraw further forces that were no longer needed. Soon after mid January they probably made good use of this possibility. By using their storm troops during the initial days of the offensive, it would probably have been easy for them to make a further effort and liquidate the pocket relatively quickly. But they no longer needed to make such a highly costly attempt. Time was on their side.

By beating down our tenacious defence with a crushing attack, our enemy had won his penetration into the pocket. Now he was no longer in a hurry and no longer appeared to consider his victim to be very dangerous. The battle that had begun in the meantime was merely a question of finishing-off wounded game already marked for death. For some time already the Russians had dictated the course of events. The date of our final end depended on their will alone.

What was taking place here on the Volga could not be compared to one of the normal, sorrowful sacrifices that must be demanded in war from time to time under certain circumstances. The Stations of the Cross of an army of 200,000 soldiers, particularly because of the slow, helpless death of such a vast number of human beings, made anything seen before, with the exception of Verdun, pale by comparison. A part of the entire German nation was sentenced to death here, and by this, its vital substance was dangerously under attack. The moral effect of these events touched the whole nation. Could such a monstrous measure of human suffering, could a death agony so greatly prolonged, could the growing disregard of human dignity, serve to re-establish, maybe even in the long run only as an illusion, a strategic balance?

That the requirements and conditions for a meaningful or even humanly dignified continuation of the battle indeed no longer existed after the loss of Pitomnik air base, was already proved from mid January on by the horrifying increase in wounded and sick and the catastrophic inadequacy of their treatment. In the midst of the general destruction of the army, there were thousands of individual tragedies whose localities of horror were the numerous collection points for the sick and wounded; the main dressing-stations and field hospitals. After the Russians had begun to break the pocket apart these were the places where misery piled up. The collection points which had been established were rapidly no longer able to deal with the surging tide of sick, wounded. Medicine, dressings, tents, winter clothing, instruments, fire wood, fuel, trucks, and field kitchens were lacking everywhere. Since an Army order prohibited letting the wounded fall into the hands of the enemy, immediately after the western and northern perimeter of the pocket broke apart, the dressing-stations there with their many hundreds of badly wounded had had to be hastily evacuated. Whoever was still barely able to walk, hobbled, shuffled, dragged himself into motion, aided as much by his fear of the Russians as by the hope of finding shelter and salvation somewhere, or only some protection from the murderous cold.

And so whole convoys of mostly open trucks, overloaded with their pitiable freight of freezing, wounded, groaning sick and dying, moved deeper into the pocket from Karpovka, Dmitrevka, Novo-Alexeyevka, Baburkin and Bolshaya Rossoshka, places whose names still strike a chill in the hearts of Stalingrad survivors. Often enough trucks dropped out of the widely dispersed columns, because they could no longer advance through the snowstorms and drifts, or because their fuel had run out.

The objective of all of these columns of misery and despair was the army field hospital at Gumrak, parts of which were also temporarily located in the ruins of the railway station and in numerous freight cars standing on the tracks. Field hospitals like this were scattered all around Stalingrad, the largest of them being in the city itself.

All of them became places of horror, because death raged unrestrainedly among the wounded and half-frozen, the exhausted and emaciated, the sufferers from dysentery and fever. The offal pits of the surgeons filled with amputated limbs. Despite the high rate of death there were insufficient dressing material and shelter space for the living. As a rule the doctors, themselves exhausted and at the end of their resources, could only deal with those cases for whom there was still some hope. The rest had to be left to their fate as sure victims of death. In the evacuation of the wounded, terrible scenes of desperation and panic occurred towards the end around the aircraft taking-off for the flight to salvation. The number of wounded and sick that could no longer be cared for continued to rise by leaps and bounds from day to day; towards the end of January they probably numbered more than 50,000. Were these conditions not reason enough to give up on humane grounds the senseless struggle of our dying army? This question plagued me even more in the third week in January, when a comrade from our staff who had been sent to the field hospital at Gumrak some while ago because of a serious illness of the stomach, suddenly reappeared. He was our senior orderly officer, a lively captain who was certainly not unaccustomed to stress. But at Gumrak in the midst of the hell of terrible human misery he had not been able to stick it out. In his helplessness and despair, himself already a wreck, he had escaped and come back to us in order to die among his comrades. What he told us about Gumrak and the zone of death from which he had just escaped I would hardly have believed, had I not looked into the deathly pale face still marked by horror and the disturbed eyes of the unhappy man before me.

From the second half of January until the bitter end, the harsh suffering of the fighting soldiers continued by day and night. After eight evil weeks of indescribable torture and deprivations they were now plunged into a veritable hell of hopelessness and destruction. The way stations on the road of suffering were Pitomnik, Gumrak, Stalingradski, Stalingrad. Along this road of the misery of retreat leading to the pile of ruins on the Volga, the individual, sorry scenes of the unimaginable tragedy kept recurring in the same way. Time and again it was fight, resist, hold to the end, then disengage, withdraw, turn back and dig-in again for defence in the snow and stonily hard frozen earth. Time and again there were heavy losses, panic and flight and the never-ending, useless struggle against hunger and cold. Prepared positions, adequate shelter, barbed wire or field fortifications, sufficient fire wood, were nowhere to be found. Only here and there did the narrow ravines in the steppe, the *balkas*, as a rule crammed with the staffs and rear echelon services, offer temporary protection. Otherwise, the bare, snow-bound steppe without positions or cover was the stage for the tragedy.

Among the staffs there was unending tension, perplexity, despair and feverish activity. Leadership was still to be seen, From the higher commands came continual orders, directives, questions, admonitions, threats. Criticism, opposition and misgivings were not lacking at the lower levels, but for the time being the mechanisms of command still functioned. The staffs occupied themselves with the improvising of new lines of resistance, regroupings, the scratching together of combat-worthy men from the rear echelon units, the lightly wounded and the frostbitten, of collecting the many lost and miserable figures who wandered about in the steppe and could easily be gathered around a steaming field kitchen where, by dint of being given a watery soup, stringy horse meat and maybe 200 grams of bread, they were again made 'fit for combat'.

Even if here and there completely nonsensical hopes of the salvation so firmly promised by Hitler flared up, the numb feeling of approaching death still spread throughout the mass of the warriors of Stalingrad. In the midst of the general suffering and dying we helplessly watched the catastrophe of destruction approaching us, mercilessly and inexorably. The terrible human tragedy that was nearing its climax was finally commented upon by the war news broadcast at home, in the pretty and spirited words: 'In Stalingrad Sixth Army is attaching immortal honour to its banners by its heroic and self-sacrificing battle against crushing odds.'

Experiences and encounters on the run

Towards the end of the third week in January we and our staff were on the run. Temporarily we had found shelter in the well-built wooden bunkers on the auxiliary air base of Gumrak, which the Russians had constructed under ground and which had shortly before housed Army Command. Above the swarms of retreating vehicles and men, the Russian aircraft circled time and again. There were more than enough worthwhile targets for them. The peace in the bombproof underground rooms was more than welcome. I used the occasion to write my letters of farewell to home.

The last greetings from my wife dated from the end of December. For a long time now, no further air mail from home was expected. Many of my comrades had mentally written themselves off. Intentions to commit suicide were voiced with increasing frequency.

For some the sad hour was already past in which they had written a last message and consigned it to the more than dubious mail. Others had given their valuables and wedding rings to wounded being flown out. I myself had so far been at pains to prepare my relatives for the catastrophe by means of sparse hints. Now I felt the need to send home an open word of farewell and gratitude. The letter was hard to write. In my ears rang once more the last *auf wiedersehen* my wife had imploringly and beseechingly called down the telephone line to Kiev on a spring evening of last year, before the seemingly endless space of the Russian plains east of the Dnieper had swallowed me up. Now all would soon be over. And on our approaching second wedding anniversary feelings of doubt and sorrow would possibly for ever seize a heart that was at this moment still beating in fearful hope.

While death was stalking outside and the bombs were bursting all around us, as I was writing, I was suddenly filled with a wonderful confidence past understanding and comforting. It helped me in my task and through the sorrow of the lines I was writing there broke through an almost bright assurance that after a long, dark time of waiting, the hour of a happy life and reunion would strike once again.

But all too soon I was again overcome by the feeling of being lost and the knowledge pressed heavily on my heart, that I had been torn away from my loved ones at home, that I could not help them, that I must abandon them at a time when probably they would be most in need of me. And would my farewell greetings even reach them? When I sealed the letter I was gripped by especially deep despair. I felt as if I were suddenly looking into an abyss of suffering and hopelessness towards which our whole nation was reeling, as if the events of Stalingrad were the preview of an immeasurable disaster that was to break upon Germany.

During our flight we were destined to experience one further brief period of relative peacefulness. That was in a long, narrow gulley in the Gorodishche area. There we were given shelter in the village of wooden bunkers of a division from the Rhineland that had earlier repeatedly fought in the forces under our command.

On the north-eastern perimeter of the pocket the Russians had so far remained relatively quiet. Large parts of the divisions deployed there in their initial defensive positions had therefore been withdrawn and thrown into the north-western and western battle zones as 'fire-fighters'. The remaining formations in the north-east were still relatively well off. For months they had been sitting in their old camouflaged bunkers which were warm and comfortable. They even had furniture and equipment which they had dragged in from the ruins of the city in the autumn. At a time when the troops were forced to eat up their last reserves of food, here they were much better off, having succeeded before the encirclement took place in providentially stocking up on food. It thus came about that a few individual spots in the Stalingrad pocket had remained almost untouched by the terrible events that were now suddenly approaching with the remorseless impetus of an avalanche.

The division from the Rhineland, whose staff received us as guests, was one that had so far been spared the miseries and death of the catastrophe into which the other army formations had been plunged. But hunger had raged here as elsewhere and I was shocked when I laid eyes on the Ic, a reserve officer and states attorney from Westphalia, whom I had known earlier and who took me into his pleasantly furnished bunker. This big, strong man had shrivelled and his pessimism left me in no doubt that he harboured no illusions with regard to the threatening proximity of the final catastrophe. However, this realisation was not prevalent everywhere and least of all among the forces who were defending the perimeter along the Volga towards the east. There, quite optimistic perceptions of our situation and brave expectations still abounded. Even among the staff our reports initially met with an occasional lack of belief. They were thought to be exaggerated. But we reeked of an atmosphere of horror and flight. This could not be ignored.

When we first broke into the ravine of the staff quarters with our group of vehicles, there was great excitement. The numerous vehicles could hardly be camouflaged and, together with the sudden movements beginning in this sector, were bound to attract enemy aircraft. Soon the first bombs began to rain down. The comrades quite rightly apprehended that with us and our train misfortune had made its fatal entrance and that soon they too would be drawn into the general whirlpool of retreat and flight. In this gulley as well, insecurity and fear had long crept in. Our appearance and our reports caused great agitation and finally led to depression.

The general of this division had had a nervous breakdown and was no longer fit for command. His hopes of being flown out with the badly wounded and sick had not been fulfilled. He now had to share the fate of his soldiers to the bitter end. Since command of the division had been assigned to a younger general, there was nothing left for him to do. The sitting around to which he was now condemned must have left him prey to the most tortuous thoughts imaginable. To me he appeared to be the embodiment of disquieting unrest and fear in the uniform of a general. He wandered about in the gulley from quarters to quarters to talk about the situation and to hear the news. He even addressed himself to me, a vastly junior officer, with tired, timid glances. Because of my being assigned to a higher staff, he obviously hoped to gain dependable or maybe even consoling information from me. 'When will the Russians be here? How will they treat our captured soldiers? What do you think they will do to the officers?' This general, who a short time before as the commander of a division had carried the responsibility for many thousands of men, was once more a mere human being trembling for his life. And did his questions not reveal the same fear that secretly tormented all of us?

We experienced two more pensive evenings in the bunker of the Ic department. Our circle was enlarged by a Protestant pastor, a Catholic convent priest and a philosophically inclined orderly officer from the division's Ia department. After initial discussion of our situation during which bitter words and open criticism were voiced, the talk soon turned to more fundamental matters.

The catastrophe that was threatening to swallow us up unveiled itself to us in many ways as the natural conclusion of a long trail of errors from which our inner misgivings had not pulled us back. The mental roots of our misfortune arose before our eyes, as did the crisis of true soldiery which here in Stalingrad was degenerating into a soulless materialism with a misunderstood sense of duty and mechanistic concepts of honour, despite all the personal commitment and sacrifice of individual soldiers. What higher insights did these virtues serve, and for the achievement of which ethical objectives were they being employed? We reminded ourselves of the unchangeable, true ranking of values and of the respect for human dignity that appeared to have been buried long ago.

We made one another realise that the impending military cata-strophe was also a political catastrophe, the result of presumptuous beliefs and actions that had long shaken the healthy foundations of our intellectual, cultural and national life. Had the power that we served as citizens and soldiers bent its knee before the law that was rooted in the code of ethics? Or rather had not a new gospel of violence been pro-claimed and introduced that, in a fatal reversal of all values, had ceased to differentiate between right and wrong? We reminded ourselves of the imploring words with which, before the war, the poet Ernst Wiechert had branded this development on a descending incline, by speaking of the fame of gladiators and the ethics of boxers.

By means of a destructive battle against the universal educational and cultural powers of classic antiquity, humanism and Christianity, an anti-intellectual political religion of power had successively extracted the German people from the best of the commonly-held European body of human thought and thereby also out of any commitment to the objec-tive concepts of truth, compassion and justice. It was just these self-same supra-national cultural values and educational powers, however, that had always tamed and ennobled the dangerous forces and dynamic drives that slumbered in the Germanic–German character.

National Socialism had unleashed those fatal forces with their inborn drive towards excess. In despite of our possibly best personal beliefs and intentions, had we not since then all marched along a road leading into error? Were not the German armed forces the instrument of National Socialist power politics and had they not shared in the disregard for international treaties, foreign borders and the *lebensraum* of others ? All of us who wore a uniform were entangled in a fabric of developments and circumstances that we certainly had not sought or desired. We surely could not believe that our employment here in Stalingrad was part of a noble, legitimate battle for German interests. Painfully, we felt that the soldierly virtues of bravery, commitment, loyalty and obedience to duty in their objective sense, were being despicably misused. This deepened the tragedy of the cruel events in which we now would have to atone for much that we had never wanted.

The two priests read to us from Holy Scriptures. They spoke about divine justice before which the fate breaking in upon us would receive its ultimate sense of purpose. Would we have the strength truly to accept such a sense of purpose and submit to it with humility? In the proximity of death things appeared in their true light and proper order. In such a situation the Bible speaks to us with an insistence and clarity, the like of which we had never felt or understood before. In our circle we sat together not only as brothers in adversity over whom the same fate hung. We were also a small congregation, brought together by the need of true comfort and unambiguous support. The fear and misery at the edge of our existence had given us a religious experience whose strength-giving power bound us together.

A fair number of books had been my trusty companions through-out the war so far. They contained much of the wisdom of the world. In silent communication with some of the noblest of poets and thinkers, I had often found strength, comfort and inner freedom amidst the crush-ing and unfeeling reality of harsh, cruel, everyday life.

Among my favourite books in the little private library I had taken with me to the eastern front was a copy of Marcus Aurelius's self-obser-vations. The slim leather-bound volume dated from 1675, in other words from the time of Louis XIV. It was a French translation of the wise Stoic on the Roman imperial throne, dedicated to Queen Christina of Sweden in a spirited introduction. It contained the *ex libris* of a French general from the time of the great revolution and of Napoleon. What must this little book have witnessed in the way of fates over almost nine generations! And to how many long-forgotten human beings had it given peace and imperturbability in many of the storms and vicissitudes of life! I too had often found support and comfort in it. It had contributed markedly to completing my equipment for war, by serving me as a suit of armour that protected me from all too frequent woundings by events, and by giving me an inner equanimity.

Now this book too, like several others, had become meaningless. The wisdom of the world, with its merely human-temporal comfort, had failed. It did not penetrate into the ultimate and most profound, and could no longer stand firm in the terrible shock and helplessness at whose mercy I felt myself to be. In extreme distress, with the ground shaking underfoot and a menacing abyss of nothingness seeming to open before me, there was only one last support; the comforting strength of the Christian belief. In our small contemplative circle at Gorodishche, while faced with the hopelessness of our situation and in the heartrending feeling of being lost, we mutually tried to deepen one another's awareness of the existence of an ultimate shelter. This gave us comfort and supportive help against the heaviness and bitterness we still would have to face. Perhaps we could pass on some of this comfort and support to other comrades who, bewildered, were reeling towards the abyss.

In their desperation, faced with the destruction of a whole world of concepts, and in view of the senselessness of the catastrophe, many a soldier on the staffs as well as with the fighting troops, had reached for his pistol and put an end to his life. There was no way back and no escape. Others disguised their secret fear and inner feeling of emptiness behind a contrived soldierly stance, or even deliberately assumed the cast of mind of a *landsknecht*. If they themselves were doomed to go under, they would at least sell their skin dearly to the end, and take as many Russians as they could with them.

We agreed that suicide was out of the question for religious and ethical reasons. If within our own small area of responsibility, we were no longer to be enabled to take any saving action against the downfall ordered from above, we at least wanted to attempt to maintain the human being in the uniform of the soldier to the end.

We wished to labour against despair and to try to accept with silent dignity the extreme misery into which we were being led. We also wanted to try to influence other brothers in fate and to prevent them from simply throwing away their lives in their final despair. As normal, weak human beings, caught up in error and guilt, there was nothing left to us but to drink the cup of suffering to the last bitter dregs.

Dissolution of our Corps and the hour of farewell with our Commanding General

The situation of our army corps was catastrophic. We no longer had a clear picture of the exact extent of the front or the deployment and strength of our formations. Communications had been cut everywhere and new changes occurred hourly. The General Staff officers tried unsuccessfully to keep their maps in order, so as to still be able to provide leadership. Did what they were doing make any sense any more?

It was virtually impossible to obtain an overview of what was going on in the divisions under our command. Support could not be obtained. Orders and directives sent out were regularly outdated by events. The General Staff maps no longer gave a clear picture of the situation because the entries hardly bore any resemblance to the true facts. They did however paint a very unambiguous picture, namely the continuing dissolution and impending final collapse of the corps.

Our Ic department was as good as out of a job. Now we had to deal with the preparations for the local defence that had been ordered, so as to protect the perimeter of our headquarters, and finally – to fall with our weapons still in our hands. Already the Russians were intermittently shelling our area. Soon they would come and make an end. We at least hoped to be able to stay within the circle of old comrades that had formed over years of shared work and experiences, and to spend the last hard days shoulder to shoulder. Our Commanding General had no objections. He too wanted to assemble the older members of the corps staff around him and to celebrate the hour of farewell in an intimate circle. Together with a few other comrades, therefore, I received the order to report to him in his bunker one evening.

In the meantime, something unbelievable had happened and quickly made the rounds. Our Quartermaster, a still young general staff officer, had suddenly disappeared. His driver, who had taken him to Gumrak air base in his *Kübelwagen*, had waited in vain for his return. The lieutenant-colonel was missing. He had silently left the Stalingrad pocket, the zone of death and destruction, on his own initiative. Probably it was a mixture of nerves, fear, cowardice and the vain hope that in the general confusion he might be able to fly out and save his life, that had tempted him to desert. The Commanding General had made inquiries by radio. The deserting staff officer had shown up at Army Group, claiming to have flown out on an official assignment from corps on matters of supply. Our General was wild with indignation and rage. He declared that he would have the criminal flown back into the pocket and shot before our eyes. We were all deeply depressed and anticipated with horror the terrible scene that had been announced and which we were spared to our relief. Our Quartermaster was shot outside the pocket on the spot where, in his fatal weakness, he had hoped to find the door to freedom and life.

That evening of farewell which a small group of us spent with the Commanding General was like a wake. The shadow of the final catastrophe lay darkly and depressingly upon us. In a short speech, our General pointed out the desperate seriousness of our condition and the continual dissolution of our corps. In view of the unavoidable downfall, he thanked us in moving words of farewell for our comradeship and past contributions.

He had just returned from the Commander-in-Chief and was still emotionally disturbed by the sorry impressions he had formed there at the central command post. We learned that the final efforts by Army to obtain help from outside had finally failed. All requests to fly in reinforcements to the strength of several battalions, all insistent demands for an effective increase in the deployment of aircraft, had been in vain. The indignation at Army Staff about the Luftwaffe's broken promises seemed to have reached its height. They felt betrayed and abandoned.

Shortly before the turn of the year, Colonel General Paulus had sent an officer out of the pocket armed with special powers of authority. This had been the senior Quartermaster of the army who knew best the worries and needs of the encircled forces. At Army Group he was to pursue an increase of the air lift with the most extreme insistence. The Divisional Commander of the Flak forces encircled with us had also been ordered out on the same mission. In mid January the last delegate from the pocket, the Army Chief Orderly, had flown directly to Führer Headquarters with the request for a clear decision whether effective help could be counted upon and with ultimate demands, or so it went, for the salvation of the army. We had heard about this mission earlier. That it had been entrusted to the young, dashing captain and bearer of the Knight's Cross had filled us with satisfaction. Hope had hardly kindled, but we could at least be sure that our case would be laid before the responsible 'Supreme War Lord' without fear or mincing of words. What we were hoping was that the truth about Stalingrad would become known at home.

The officers and messengers from our army had not returned to the pocket. The air lift had again deteriorated catastrophically. Small wonder! The German eastern front had pulled back from us by about 300 kilometres. The air bases that remained for our supply, Salsk, Novocherkassk, Rostov and Taganrog, lay from 320 to 400 kilometres away. Without fighter cover, flights were normally possible only at night and therefore at best only fifty to seventy tonnes of supplies per day now reached our pocket. And the emergency landing strip could be lost from one day to the next.

A renewed request for freedom of action and permission to surrender had again been denied our army by Hitler. The situation and information briefing with Colonel General Paulus about the condition of the army and the alternatives remaining to it must have been shattering. Our Commanding General spoke openly of the impending collapse. Accusingly and with bitterness and secret anger, he pointed out that it was not our fault that we had got into this devilish situation of catastrophe from which there was no longer a means of escape. But he left no doubt that together we still had a task to perform, namely to fulfil our soldierly duty to the last moment. In obedience to the orders from above we would defend our perimeter fighting shoulder to shoulder with our carbines to the last bullet. From his words we could surmise that he was staunchly determined to go down like a captain with his ship and not survive the downfall of his troops. Unequivocally, he pointed out that the commandments of the traditional ethical code of the soldier now demanded our ultimate sacrifice without demur.

Coming from our General, who had served in the army for almost half a century, this position that my secret personal convictions were opposed to, appeared understandable and consistent. There he sat with his energetic lined face, with his medals and badges of honour, and was probably reviewing in his mind his long and eventful career as a soldier which was now to come to an abrupt and sorry end. With his almost sixty-five years, he was probably the oldest commanding general on any front, obviously no longer up for promotion, even though he had been the Commander-in-Chief of an army in France. Maybe his plain speaking and down-to-earth comments, arising from his common sense, had made him, the former President of the *Reichskriegsgericht* (Supreme Military Court of the Reich), uncomfortable for the high personages and offices he reported to. Spread around his bunker lay various keepsakes and presents that we had given him on his fifth anniversary as Commanding General.

As a captain, he had witnessed the fall of the Kaiserreich and the catastrophe of the First World War. From his stories and always entertainingly recounted anecdotes we knew many details of his subsequent career. He had experienced many exciting things. But what was happening now was something incomparably more terrible. The General did not comment further on the underlying reasons for our catastrophe, but he could hardly have been in doubt about the fact that the thing he had loyally served for decades had been compromised to a fatal degree by the supreme authority. Now in this forlorn position, so he intimated, there was quite naturally nothing left but the required military obedience that had been taught and practised a thousand times. For him too, however, it was not easy to face what had happened. Too many facts and measures taken by the leadership in the recent past had gone against his instincts as a soldier. And as he told us about the fate of General Heim, whom he personally regarded very highly, a rage mounted in him that he could barely conceal.

At the beginning of the encircling battle, this general with his inadequately equipped, inexperienced and not yet fully combat-ready tank corps, had been given the task of recovering the catastrophic situation on the bend of the Don. At that time the order was impossible to carry out. Disaster had taken its course. Hitler had made General Heim the scape-goat. He was reduced to the rank of private, thrown out of the army and put in jail. In a directive issued as a warning, all officers had been informed about the happenings. Our Commander spoke of this with bitterness. But otherwise not a word of criticism or accusation against the Supreme Command crossed his lips.

And yet a noticeable change had taken place in our General. When talk turned to the Quartermaster who had deserted, his eyes still flashed in outrage and anger under their thick, bushy brows. The fact that it had been an officer of his staff that had run from the colours, had almost made him lose his equilibrium. But on this evening his usually gruff, almost rough, demeanour and his abrupt, often biting manner, were transformed. Something inside him seemed to have been shattered. His human side, formerly mostly hidden, came to the fore. He showed himself open and soft and for a long time the conversation ran on sentimentally about old memories. It seemed to me as if inside him a secret, deep pity for the hopeless, tormenting sacrifice of a complete army was making itself felt.

On that sad evening of farewell, I believe it was on 24 January, I had my last encounter with my General before the final downfall. Only two days later Russian tanks split the pocket and dispersed our corps staff. I briefly saw my erstwhile Commander once again in captivity. He had not gone down with the sinking ship. Himself promoted to colonel general, he had survived the men sent to their deaths up to the very last moment in pitiless obedience to the orders of destruction from above. Caught up in the all too human tragedy, he was fated to wander through dark depths until an incurable illness took him away. Later in a prisoner-of-war camp near Moscow, I often looked through the barbed wire to the spot where the Russians had long ago levelled his grave.

The dying Army floods into the ruins of Stalingrad

While our staff in the ravine near Gorodishche was still trying to lead our increasingly dissolving corps and prepare the perimeter defence, the ruins of the beaten forces were flowing in an unending march of misery on the road of retreat via Gumrak air base towards the northern and western suburbs of Stalingrad.

I was sent into this desolate flood on a difficult assignment that seemed to me to be a suicide mission. I was supposed to reconnoitre the completely confused conditions north of the already highly endangered air base and the situation of the division from Vienna which was under our command and still fighting somewhere in the area. All communications had been lost and the last reports had talked of strong Russian tank attacks that had caused confusion and an unholy mess-up.

I had been given the assignment by the Chief of Staff and the Ia. I noticed with surprise that these General Staff officers, who were perplexedly and anxiously staring at the arrows of enemy attacks, the holes and question marks entered on the maps, had both been promoted. No one had been informed about these promotions that formerly would have been an important event for the staff. My congratulations had been received with bitter smiles.

In freezing cold and wild snow flurries I rode across the desolate battle field on a motor cycle together with a sergeant of the military police. We soon reached the road of catastrophe arising dark grey against the backdrop of the snow-bound steppe, marked by all kinds of abandoned rubbish, half-covered cadavers of horses and wrecked vehicles, scattered pieces of equipment, crates, destroyed weapons.

In the zone of horror at Gumrak, dead chimneys, walls and stumps of buildings rose eerily from the snow. In the grounds of the railway station stood the long, wide rows of box-cars that I knew to be filled to overflowing, as were the neighbouring cellars, holes and bunkers, with wounded, sick and dying. These were the places where suffering, misery and desperation were horribly concentrated. And over all this misery lay a heavy artillery and mortar bombardment that had dirtily stained the snow-covered earth all around.

At the edge of the air base and farther to the north where the sounds of battle grew ever louder, the retreat of the troops had turned into an unholy shambles. The general wave of destruction was relentlessly driving them back, singly, in groups, in columns. The dispersed, the starving, the freezing, the sick, but also those still fit for fighting, had only one objective to which they were attaching their last glimmerings of hope; and this objective was Stalingrad. In the protective walls and cellars of the ruins they might still be able to find some warmth, food, rest, sleep and salvation.

And so they streamed by, the remains of the shattered and decimated formations, trains and rear echelon services, with vehicles that were being slowly dragged and pushed by wounded, sick and frost-bitten men. There were emaciated figures among them, muffled in coats, rags; pitiful wrecks, painfully dragging themselves forward, leaning on sticks and hobbling along on frozen feet, wrapped in wisps of straw and strips of blankets. Drifting along through the snowstorm, this was the wreck of Sixth Army that had advanced to the Volga during the summer, so confident of victory! Men from all over Germany, doomed to destruction in a far-off land, mutely enduring their suffering, tottered in pitiful droves through the murderous eastern winter. They were the same soldiers who had formerly marched through large parts of Europe as proud conquerors. Now the enemy was at their backs and death lurked everywhere.

Here the same fate was being re-enacted that 130 years ago had destroyed a mighty army of which too the impossible had been demanded. The snow whirling in the wind hid many a detail in the general picture of misery and continued to weave the boundless white shroud that was being laid over the mass grave in the steppe of Stalingrad.

Against expectations I was able to complete my mission quickly. Parts of the Vienna division, flooding back in dissolution and flight, came my way. Soon I was able to locate their staff and from flight control at Gumrak, where they were just trying to organise a final deployment of the Flak as artillery, I was able to report by phone to my corps, giving them various information as to the situation. With this some of the gaps on the Chief of Staff's map could be filled and a clearer but more menacing picture of the approaching collapse obtained.

The air base at Gumrak could no longer be held. It appeared as if the general movement of flight towards Stalingrad was creating a momentum which none of the units could withstand any longer.

In contradiction to all the measures taken so far to prepare our perimeter defence, we too suddenly received the order to pull back to Stalingrad. We were only permitted to take the most urgently needed baggage; all the Ic files, papers and secret documents were to be destroyed. With heavy hearts we carried out the sad action of burning our working material and files. This was a measure only taken by a staff in a situation of the most extreme hopelessness and signified the official ending of its existence.

I consigned a number of personal papers to the flames. Included among them was a comprehensive work of military history that I had already written after the campaign in France. After its completion I had felt myself closely involved with the fate of our army corps which, having originally come from Silesia, had by now bled itself dry on all the sectors of the eastern front. Also included were private notes I had kept as a documentation of this catastrophic phase of the war, which was truly sad but also richly filled with experiences and events. Now all this and the other things I threw into the fire, appeared as just so much unnecessary rubbish. And yet it was not easy for me to do away with certain things. All kinds of favourite books and small objects tied up in my baggage had served to the last to create for me the remnant of a private sphere and to give me a piece of home even on the distant eastern front. Now all that I needed besides my pistol, were my knapsack, my clothing bag and my map case.

We spent the sleepless night somewhere on the run. Sitting freezing in our car, but still with a protecting roof above my head, I again had time to think about what had happened. The tormenting pictures of dissolution and ruin continued to plague me. The impressions of my drive over the terrible battlefield were having an after-effect. I suddenly had to think about the shattering descriptions of the participants in the campaign of 1812. What I had formerly read with secret horror by Ségur and Caulaincourt, we were now experiencing here ourselves. The dark apprehensions and feelings of unease that had befallen me on that bright summer night in 1941 at the beginning of the fateful Russian campaign, and that had later recurred again and again in the eerie depth of the endless Russian space, were now being terribly confirmed.

Already during the early months of the war in the east the reminders of the downfall of the *Grande Armée* of 1812 had weighed upon me like a nightmare. We were then advancing on Moscow almost on the exact route of march of Napoleon. My division crossed the Beresina at the identical spot where the desperate battle of retreat had been fought so long ago. There by the hamlet Studyenka, not far from Borissov, our engineers found the traces of Napoleon's bridge and one of his eagles in a swamp. As liaison officer between my division and the army corps, I often had to drive long distances through no man's land. Repeatedly lost and alone with my driver, I was in places where no German soldier had ever set foot. On such occasions I felt particularly fearful of the vastness of the eastern landscape with all its lurking dangers, that was swallowing us up. Inspired by the historic reminders that were continually being nourished by our advance over the Beresina via Smolensk to Borodino, I felt compelled to write a longer treatise on Napoleon's catastrophe, using some old historical source material I had with me. In my representation of the downfall of the *Grande Armée*, I tried to bring out the human elements that had then also played so important a part, both fundamentally and because of the under-estimation of the factors of space and weather.

In the region of Smolensk, where after the first powerful surprise attack, our victorious advance ground to a halt when our division hit upon a new and vicious Bolshevik resistance and began to bleed to death, I handed my treatise over to our General Staff officers. They showed themselves to be impressed. Even the general asked me to report to him and paid me his respects. At the same time he forbade the copying of the paper or letting it get into the hands of the soldiers. Only one younger major of the General Staff, one of those optimistic officers so confident of victory who were unconditionally loyal to the political regime, expressed dissatisfaction that I had not drawn any conclusions and parallels with our time. According to his opinion that would have given the sorrowful report a final chapter full of confidence, so positive and flattering for us. He was adamantly convinced that the mistakes of 1812 could not repeat themselves. Modern motorisation and advanced technology, the dependably organised supply of the troops and the genius of our 'Supreme Commander' were obvious guarantees of this fact.

Such memories became very vivid during that night on the run, while in the midst of the ruins of our army flooding into Stalingrad, we felt a terrible end approaching. The events of 1812 seemed to be repeating themselves after all. Once again the uncanny Russian space was swallowing many tens of thousands of human beings. Despite Napoleon's experience, the basic elements of geography and meteorology had again been ignored to a frightening degree. On top of that the modern superstition, that with the help of machines and motors the impossible could be accomplished and the dangers of space overcome, had also contributed to our downfall. And in a fatal pact with the over-estimation of the mechanised means of war had stood the misapprehension of the limits of human strength and possibilities.

I was reinforced in this conclusion during our continuing flight by the pictures of horror and the events. Around us lay the machines, motors and pieces of the gigantic army machine, broken and scattered over the entire battlefield. The columns of still serviceable vehicles began to congest the roads. Soon they would become the prey of the advancing Russian tanks. And the men, for the most part exhausted, apathetic and at the end of their tether, were still tied to this mechanism without hope of redemption. Like interchangeable spare parts of a soulless gear box, these beings of flesh and blood were used up and crushed without pity.

With the stream of fleeing men flowing slowly forward, we drifted past a broad zone filled with uncounted rows of grey wooden crosses. This glimpse of the vast cemeteries from last summer and autumn, on the outskirts of the Stalingrad suburbs, was like a sombre sermon that touched each of us deep in his heart.

Soon the seemingly endless columns of vehicles were no longer able to move forward. Some more manoeuvrable *Kübelwagen* and tractors had extricated themselves from the entanglement and driven away in time carrying our Commanding General and the members of his immediate entourage. Quickly the terrifying news spread that Russian tanks had broken through up ahead. The rattle and iron thrumming of tracks, now becoming more menacing, could even be heard in our heavy command bus where we were hastily gathering our last vital baggage and hand guns. A grey-white row of the dreaded T34 tanks came rolling along the side of our petrified column, but their cannon and machine-guns did not fire. They obviously expected no further resistance and were probably coming to gather up the rich spoils awaiting them. Their hatches were open. A Soviet soldier in a white fur coat, maybe a commissar, sat on the leading tank, waving to us and calling in broken German, 'German soldier, come, come! Hitler kaputt!'

Suddenly the Russian rolled forward over the body of the tank, mortally hit by a bullet. From somewhere, someone threw a bottle filled with inflammable liquid that the soldiers called a 'Molotov Cocktail' and set the leading tank on fire. Now our fate had been set in motion. The hatches slammed shut, the tanks rattled back a pace and then opened a murderous fire on our column and on us. The short bark of the cannon, the tacking of the machine-guns and the zipping and whistling of the rounds, surrounded us like music from hell while we sought cover in the holes and slits of the roadbed and tremblingly waited to be crushed under one of the monsters.

But nightfall soon came and saved us once again. Through the darkness we could hear the cries for help and the screams of our wounded. Here and there flames eerily rose against the sky and illuminated the gigantic, deserted snake of our vehicle column. Under the cover of darkness our decimated ranks continued their flight on foot. Death had once again passed us by.

Next day, despite great dangers, he spared us again. An hour's long march had taken us many kilometres over the snow steppe, on which, as so often before, millions of ice crystals glittered in the pitiless frost, and a penetrating east wind played its evil game from over the Volga. Russian aircraft chased through the clear, pale blue winter air in which the sun stood cold and weak. The Soviet stars on their glittering wings were clearly recognisable. Suddenly, a whole flight dived down, selecting our helpless little group of human beings as their target. Like rabbits caught in the fire from a *battue*, we scattered over the completely coverless fields of snow and then threw ourselves down with thundering hearts to burrow deeply into the snow. The hunt was repeated and once again the bullets whistled to the ground all around me.

Together with several wounded we dragged ourselves onwards until, exhausted and shattered, we finally reached the ruins and rubble of the northern Stalingrad city area. What travails did fate still hold in store for us? Death, whom I had faced more often and closely in recent days than ever before, was still refusing me. But his trusted companion for many weeks, hunger, was tormenting me with tenacious power, slowly making me ripe for the end. And frost, the third murderer in the trio, had also bitten me by now, as the constant, stabbing pains in some of my limbs warned me.

Separated from our staff, our group of officers found shelter in a dark, dirty cellar while our men went to ground in a neighbouring pile of rubble. This was to be the end of our flight and our last quarters.

The death agony is prolonged

At the beginning of the last week in January the Russians had not only increased pressure against the western and north-western perimeter of the already closely compressed Stalingrad pocket, but had also begun a new attack from the south-west in the Peschanka and Voroponovo area. There his tanks overran and ground up weapons and men who had not stopped firing to surrender in time. But even now the exhausted troops still offered resistance in several places and near Voroponovo they even succeeded in repulsing the enemy for a short while. But nothing could stop the fate that was rushing upon us.

From the Tartar Wall a wedge of tanks had driven forward towards the Volga, broken through the ruins of the beaten forces and columns of vehicles and split our pocket into a northern and a southern half. That had taken place on 26 January. I myself had witnessed this advance and the unholy confusion it caused. Segment by segment from south to north the Russians were now calmly proceeding to destroy this almost 20-kilometre-long sack hanging along the banks of the Volga filled with still resisting men, with sickness and death. Only two days after the tanks broke through from the west, they had cut the southern part of the pocket in half again and thereby again severed many nerve fibres of the army.

No official order put an end to the dissolution, mounting chaos and mass dying. Before the general flight into Stalingrad proper had begun, on an inquiry from Army the staffs had once again seriously discussed a desperate break-out plan. After so many momentous mistakes one was apparently still playing with the idea of acting on one's own responsibility. But it was now far too late. The remaining pocket was to be broken open from inside by the still combat-worthy units breaking out in all directions. The objective was the re-unification with the southern and western German front. And if this was not to be achieved, causing confusion in the enemy's rear still made military sense, or so one apparently believed. A lunatic plan of self-dissolution and self-destruction that ignored many of the sorry realities, that ignored the condition of the troops and paid no regard to the vast army of sick and wounded that would be left behind! Consequently it had been met with general refusal and indignation in the corps.

Army had once again addressed itself to OKH and pointing adamantly to the catastrophic situation, had asked for immediate permission to surrender, which might possibly still prevent complete dissolution and total disaster. Hitler's answer had been a steely 'No!'

And even now the Commander-in-Chief of the army, Paulus, was still obeying the orders and directives of Führer Headquarters, despite the fact that for a long time there could have been no further doubt that his trust in the measures of the OKH and Hitler's promises of quick, effective help from outside had been most cruelly disappointed. Maybe the incoming radio messages had convinced him that his army had to be sacrificed for operational reasons, to secure the withdrawal of the forces in the Caucasus or to generally relieve the pressure on the fronts of the other army groups which were all tottering.

'Forbid surrender!', Hitler had radioed into the pocket on 25 January. 'The army will hold its position to the last man and bullet!' This order that explicitly spoke of an 'unforgettable contribution to the establishment of a defensive front' and later still, in invocatory pathos, of 'the salvation of the Occident', remained the guide-line of their actions for our Army Command.

The military duty of obedience to orders and the 'Führer principle' appeared to be the deciding factor in all considerations, doubts and misgivings. To discontinue the battle for humane reasons was therefore out of the question. Colonel General Paulus and his Chief of Staff, whose fanatical will to hold out was well known among the staffs, relentlessly held to their fatal decision. On their part, many generals and their staffs remained the executioners of the orders of destruction. Under these sorry circumstances the fighting, suffering and dying continued. Torturingly and terribly, after the splitting of the pocket, the death agony of the army continued for a further week.

Two sets of circumstances sharpened our realisation of the total extent of the desperation of our situation, the state of our dispersion and the cessation of regular supply by air. Not only had our old community which had given us comradely security been split apart. The Russian tank attack through the middle of Stalingrad had hopelessly disrupted the chains of command, separated troops from their staffs and speeded up the dissolution. Central command came to a halt, lines of communication no longer worked properly and large parts of the organism of the army were paralysed.

The last supply aircraft filled to overflowing with wounded had taken off from the emergency air strip at Stalingradski on 23 January. After the loss of Pitomnik in the middle of the month, the exhausted men of the rear echelon services had made an effort of self-sacrifice to prepare this strip in great haste.

Since the beginning of the pocket battle our utterly fearless pilots had brought out a total of about 25,000 wounded men and specialists. A splendid achievement! With the Russians already pressing close, terrible scenes of panic had been enacted on the runway here at Stalingradski, just as when the last planes had taken off at Pitomnik. Desperate human beings had clung to under-carriages and fuselages in the insane hope of thereby being able to escape their doom.

The air lift had long ceased to function properly. An organised distribution of the supplies flown in was no longer possible. Since further landings had become impossible, in the end only canisters of food could be dropped at night on zones marked by flags and illuminated by spot-lights. But the approach was extremely difficult. After a long and dangerous flight of more than 300 kilometres, the aircraft had to daringly break through the ring of Russian anti-aircraft fire. In the choice of their drop zones they were dependent on the weather and the dispositions of the enemy. Seen overall, the help brought in so bravely by our tireless, courageous supply pilots was hardly noticeable any more. In addition, the canisters were increasingly being taken in on the spot by individual units. In the general dissolution and catastrophe it was every man for himself.

On all sides the Russians had pressed forward to the edge of the Stalingrad suburbs. The iron ring of destruction tightened ever closer around the place where the horrible fate of the doomed army was drawing to a close. The stage set of its downfall was eerie and ghostly. It was the gigantic pile of ruins and debris of Stalingrad that stretched for more than twenty kilometres along the high right bank of the Volga. A desolate city that had bled and died from a thousand wounds. For half a year destruction and death had celebrated orgies here and hardly left anything save the torn stumps of houses, naked rows of walls, chimneys sticking up from vast piles of rubble, gutted factories, formless hunks of concrete, torn up asphalt, twisted tram tracks lying on wrecked cars, piled up iron scrap, splintered tree trunks in the former parks with the remains of Soviet plaster statues, traces of fire and decay.

Under this uncanny waste of the skeletons of buildings stretched the subterranean ghostly expanse of cellar ruins, bunkers, fox-holes and communications trenches. These were places where life had crept away to hide, darkly overshadowed by ever present death. These were the places of terrible suffering and dying of many thousands of unhappy, abandoned, helpless human beings. Every hole, every bunker, every cellar, every space offering shelter was filled to overflowing.

Over the entire ruins of Stalingrad fell an almost unceasing barrage of artillery and mortar fire. This, together with the repeated air attacks, continued to cause new casualties among the human masses of the dying army which had flooded together in the city centre and were experiencing hell on earth during the last days of January.

The army of sick and wounded rapidly assumed horrifying dimensions. After the Russians had advanced to the region of Gumrak and the general flight towards Stalingrad had reached its height, Army had rescinded its former order to the contrary and directed that the wounded were to be left behind, but without doctors or medical orderlies – which was a terrible cruelty. The collection points for wounded, the dressing-stations and hospitals in the city, had long been overcrowded anyway. Now they could no longer contain the masses of men needing help. Well-nigh more than half of the survivors, in other words, about 50,000 men, were sick or wounded. Thousands of them received no treatment or care at all, because there were no dressings, medicine, morphine – or room. Many men doomed to die vainly begged for medicine to kill their pain or end their suffering. The doctors, orderlies and grave-diggers could no longer cope with the tide of misery flooding over their heads.

And so they lay about in their thousands, crammed together in the cellars of the railway station, in those around the Square of the Fallen, in the corn silo, in the cellar of the theatre, in the former city *Kommandantura*, and in many other cellars, caves and holes in the ruins of Stalingrad, moaning, whimpering, freezing, wracked with fever, praying, but mostly apathetic and resigned to their suffering. The emaciated bodies were no longer able to resist even minor sicknesses, let alone spotted fever, dysentery, jaundice or other serious illnesses for which strain, hunger and frost had worked so tragically to prepare the ground. The many dead could no longer be buried in the stonily frozen ground. The bodies were simply covered with snow or stacked in some corner. They were also no longer registered and no one was concerned about collecting their dog-tags any longer.

Innumerable helplessly suffering and immobilised wounded found a horrible end in the cellars and ruins that caught fire or collapsed under the rain of shells and bombs. The multi-storey building of the Stalingrad Centre *Kommandantura*, which had become a hospital crammed to overflowing, went up in flames caused by artillery fire. After scenes of indescribable panic and despair, a sea of flames soon consumed the whole heap of stacked-up misery.

It is small wonder that, after almost seventy days of indescribable strain, deprivation and battle, the physical and moral decline of the troops was everywhere now leading to sorry signs of dissolution and creating scenes that had formerly been unheard of. More and more, order and discipline broke down. Here and there in the cellars, the still ablebodied and combat-worthy hid among the sick and wounded. Cases of uncomradely conduct, theft of provisions, refusal to obey orders, and open mutiny mounted. Wandering about through the labyrinth of the ruins roamed soldiers who had left their posts without permission, stragglers from the various divisions, looters and foragers who, acting on their own behalf, searched for food or hid out of fear of being sent back to the lines.

These men knew that the canisters of food were not only being dropped on the marked zones. In other spots in the ruined city, in the rubble of buildings and dark courtyards, on the paths leading through the ruins and in the trenches, one could sometimes find something worth taking. Occasionally, instead of shells, whole packages of smoked sausage, hard-tack wrapped in cellophane and Schoka-Kola packs that had simply been thrown out of the aircraft rained down. The elementary drive of self-preservation no longer allowed the question of right or wrong to be raised. And in the same way that the differences between front line and rear echelon were being erased, so also were the differences in rank and position.

In the final days, summary law was imposed in Stalingrad with drastic punishments for any crime. Looters were to be shot within twenty-four hours. Patrols of officers were set up and the patrolling military police with their blinking tin badges on their chests had orders to take drastic action without compunction. Hundreds of German soldiers who had become weak in their misery thus became the victims of German bullets. In spite of this, one could not claim that the troops had become totally demoralised. The general suffering was too great and with it, the total apathy.

For the same reasons one could no longer generally speak of courageous fighting and heroic resistance. Certainly here and there individual deeds of courage, personal initiative and noble self-sacrifice were still being performed. But by and large only a mute submission to the inescapable fate remained to the bitter end. It was rather the silent heroism of acceptance, of suffering and submitting. There was hardly any longer a true soldier's death to be sought, but only a final desperate resistance out of self-preservation or the slow dying of long since exhausted, fought out, tortured human beings.

And with this mass of men, emaciated by hunger, bitten by frost and marked by death, the senseless resistance was continued. The commanding staffs still gave out their battle assignments. Counter-attacks were ordered and intended local capitulations or actions on their own initiative by individual units strictly forbidden. And replacements for the lines were still being taken care of. This sorry job was assigned to the 'hero-catching gangs', who had to comb the cellars, bunkers and cave-like emergency shelters for able-bodied men. And the men that were pulled out of the stinking, smoky underground rooms and holes looked no different from the figures of misery in the collection points for the dispersed or the exhausted soldiers wandering about outside with their dirty, bearded, hollow-cheeked faces, insufficient winter clothing, often hobbling along on half-frozen feet. These were the 'reinforcements' that were scraped together, given a thin soup and stringy horse meat at the field kitchens and thus pepped-up for further resistance to the last bullet. These were no longer soldiers but pitiful human wrecks that were being thrown against the enemy one more time, in order to hold 'Fortress Stalingrad' and to postpone for a little while longer by their self-sacrifice, expected as a matter of course, the final catastrophe.

Even if individual commanders on the lines no longer obeyed the orders from above out of compassion for the suffering men no longer able to fight, the vast general dying went on. The order by Army to fight to the last man remained in force. The sacrificial procession that was destroying all human dignity marched on without pity.

We listen to our own Funeral Oration

All the shelters, holes, bunkers and cellars in the vast mass grave of Stalingrad were crammed with human beings. The cellar in which we had found shelter could be closed by a trapdoor and protected from the creeping cold. At first in our area a row of houses were still standing fairly upright. They were part of the northern city district of Spartakovka. Not far from us General Strecker, the Commander of the split-off northern pocket, sat in the rubble piles of the tractor factory with his grenadiers, determinedly prepared to fight to the last.

Our small group of officers that had been separated from the rest of the corps staff, came directly under the command of his staff. We formed the central collection point for dispersed soldiers for the northern pocket. Our adjutant, an elderly colonel who carried a family name of old Prussian military tradition, led us with bustling activity. This feverish activity appeared to be a mixture of a sense of duty and a need for distraction.

Occasional assignments that led me to various command posts, and patrols through the desolate ruins, filled me with horror. The pictures I saw outside regularly haunted me for some time, and left me no peace in the dark cellar vault where we were so comfortably warm as we sat around our iron stove at meal-times eating with slow solemnity our meagre portion of self-cooked charred horse meat and daily ration of 50 grams of bread.

Our good comradeship was comforting and helped over many a hardship that would have been scarcely bearable alone. As officers of a completely scattered staff and also, for a long time, burdened more than others with the knowledge of the true state of things, we felt especially hopelessly uprooted and infinitely abandoned.

It was part of my duty to collect as much information as possible on the situation. For this reason I maintained close contact with the staff of a Swabian division that had formerly long been under our command and who had dug themselves in in a labyrinth of bunkers nearby. There I was a regular guest of my old acquaintances of their Ic department. Despite all the destruction of equipment, they had managed to save an army radio receiver that now stood us in good stead.

On the morning of 30 January the usual funereal atmosphere reigned in the Ic bunker. The department head, a short captain who had always been a pessimist, was sunk within himself even more gloomily than usual and his tall orderly, suffering severely from hunger and visibly aged, was chewing on his customary grains of corn which he always kept with him in a carefully guarded satchel. The room was full of officers of the staff and from neighbouring cellars. Like myself they had come to listen to Göring's speech which had been announced. No one had any particular expectations, since there was no longer anything to hope for. Would Germany today hear the unveiled truth about our catastrophe here on the Volga? Maybe we could at least glean some small consolation from this speech for our absent comrades!

The festive marching music from the Berlin Air Ministry that ushered in the tenth anniversary of the Third Reich and sounded out of the loudspeaker in the bunker in the ruins of Stalingrad formed a curious contrast to the atmosphere of doom all around.

Soon Göring's voice rang out. During the long speech it was drowned out occasionally by nearby explosions of bombs and shells that made our bunker shake. The Reichsmarschall glorified the Führer and his Herculean efforts and the new granite-hard ideology that could achieve the impossible even in the hard eastern war. Then he switched from the enemy and the gigantic struggle to the 'fortress' of Stalingrad where the Russians were making a last, desperate effort despite the fact that they were at the end of their tether. The enemy had been forced to send their last hope of half-grown children and tired old men into the front-line formations. This undernourished, freezing human material needed to be cowed by whip and gun and driven to death by the machine-guns of the commissars. Against the savagery of the Bolshevik hordes, the most heroic battle in German history was being fought on the Volga from generals down to the lowest man.

He compared the indescribable heroism and the immortal honour of the warriors of Stalingrad with the battles and honour of the *Nibelungen* who, in their hall full of smoke and flames, had quenched their thirst with their own blood, who had stood to the last man and then gone down. Even after a thousand years, with a holy shiver every German would speak in awe of this battle and remember that, in spite of everything, here German victory had been decided.

With over-exaggerated, feverish pathos, the speaker recalled the heroic example of the last of the Goths and in the end the historically so famous sacrifice of the Spartan heroes at Thermopylae, who had not faltered or given ground until the last fighter had fallen. And so it was at Stalingrad, and just like Leonidas and his loyal men in the Greek defile, so would the German heroes lie on the Volga, as the law of honour and conduct in war commanded them to do for Germany.

During this speech, full of empty phrases and lies that outdid itself in hysterical glorifications and praises, the demeanour of the deeply disillusioned and incensed audience became more and more hostile. The glances, gestures and words all around unmistakably showed the rage that was growing in people's souls. Whoever might still have trusted in the promise of help from outside now had to recognise with growing horror that at home, where relatives still hoped for a reunion, the warriors of Stalingrad had been finally written off. We all felt that we had heard our funeral oration before its time.

On this, the tenth anniversary of the Third Reich, we men of Stalingrad were supposed to offer a new epic of heroism as a sort of present. Beyond any doubt the intention was simply to gain political capital from our catastrophic military defeat, for which the 'Supreme Commander', and in part Göring himself with his unredeemable, carelessly boastful promise of supply by air were to blame. The disgusting adulation of the torturous dying of our army and the deceitful glorification of conditions that were against all the laws of humanity filled me with indignation and revulsion. During the speech I was constantly seized by the mass of terrible pictures of the dissolution, chaos and death agony of many tens of thousands of human beings suffering indescribably, pictures which, when I did not see them immediately around me, haunted my soul like a nightmare.

Must not Göring's words have pierced the hearts of our loved ones at home like daggers and robbed them of all hope now that they had been thrown into the most anxious fears for our lives? At home we had been declared dead!

The heroisation and mythical glorification of our Stalingrad army was supposed to conceal the sad truth. For a long time now, the heroic tale of the German soldier on the Volga had become an irresponsible mass dying ordered from on high. The pathetic propaganda of glorification was obviously intended to distract from the catastrophic consequences of a criminal-amateurish leadership of the war and to prevent the question of blame from even arising.

Written-off and declared dead at home! That was the shattering impression that Göring's speech in Berlin made on us, the men still alive in the hell of Stalingrad. It was a final, cynical appeal and order that we be Spartan heroes to the end.

While I was going back to our cellar through the bursting mortar fire, Hitler's speeches from last autumn came to mind and I knew for certain why our Stalingrad army had been denied time and again every breakout and retreat, any thought of freedom of action and surrender. Political and military prestige demanded that we go under. From this necessity followed the senseless orders to hold on which Führer Headquarters cynically reiterated after any effective help for us had become impossible and the conditions for fighting on with human dignity had disappeared.

The cutting voice of the Reichsmarschall rang in my ears for a long time. Time and again I thought back with revulsion to the misuse of the historic example of the Spartan heroes at Thermopylae and to the other monstrosities with which the speech had been filled. I felt instinctively that here a crime was being dressed up with heroics and glossed over with national honour. Had any people, betrayed in their trust and loyalty, ever before had to suffer the discrepancy between bombastic mouthings and horrifying reality as terribly as we were suffering it now?

In those days I had the burning wish that some day many survivors of the battle would reach home in order to give witness to the whole truth about Stalingrad and to oppose any uncalled-for soldierly or national legend-mongering.

Particularly tormenting for me was the realisation that for a long time all the command posts and staffs in the pocket had had only one aim: to ensure that the desired heroic stance in the midst of the vast dying be maintained and to guarantee the dramatic final curtain of the tragedy.

An inglorious end

On 1 February the news spread among us that Paulus had capitulated with his staff and the two southern segments of the pocket and gone into captivity. At the last moment he had been promoted to Field Marshal. This promotion in the hour of the final catastrophe was grotesque. It was simultaneously a gesture of thanks from above and a goodbye. But the unhappy Field Marshal did not set the example of heroism expected of him from the top. The German papers and broadcasts later tried to spread the impression, in the style of Göring's speech, that in the face of overwhelming superiority, the Field Marshal had burned his secret papers and that the generals, lying behind their machine-guns, had fought to the end. Furthermore, after the catastrophe German magazines lied to the German people with faked pictures showing such heroic scenes. But the truth of the matter was quite something else. We calculated that more than fifteen generals and their staffs had gone into captivity from the southern and central pockets. Soon the Moscow radio gave details of numbers and names. I was only to learn later that some of these generals had gone into captivity with neatly packed suitcases and plentiful baggage.

The Field Marshal's interpreter, a Baltic captain of special forces, later gave me details about the unofficial manner in which the capitulation of Army Staff had come about. After having made contact with enemy storm troops, the surrender took place in the cellar of the department store on Red Square! The Commander-in-Chief, sunk in total apathy, had left the initiative completely to his Chief of Staff. General Schmidt, who had been the very soul of resistance to the last, now did everything in his power to prevent further fighting in his command post and to initiate the surrender that had been so strictly forbidden until now. There were hardly any negotiations and nothing was signed. They simply stopped fighting and gave themselves up to the victor, without any further consideration for the fate of the remaining battle groups. The last request of the Field Marshal had been that the Russians should treat him as a private citizen. With this he had resigned the official role he had formerly played in the military-political interests of the Supreme Command and, a broken man, laid down his marshalship. He was driven away in a closed car and no longer needed to see the appalling misery of his sacrificed army.

For days now the Army Command had, for all practical purposes, ceased to lead. One of the last spasmodic orders to reach us had said that we were to fight for every square metre of ground and that the command posts were also to be defended. And while the senseless spilling of blood was still going on here, in the southern Stalingrad pocket the battle had been abandoned against Hitler's will and in defiance of all orders previously issued.

With the news of this surrender all the secret misgivings, doubts and sorrowful feelings that had been constantly plaguing me during the recent long weeks vividly surged up again. Deep down I had increasingly begun to oppose certain military concepts of obedience, honour and discipline, like those that had been manifesting themselves to the end in the measures taken by our Army Command. Now my feelings of outrage as a human being and the painful realisation that there was still nothing I myself could do to change the situation became almost unbearable.

Was this only the revolt of my selfish instinct for self-preservation? Was it only an unsoldierly stance, fear or cowardice at a time when things had become bitterly serious? Precisely at this point I again remembered the awkward, deeply boring thoughts and feelings with which I had asked myself at the beginning of the war, why and for whom must you make this sacrifice? The same questions that had never really taken root rose again before me, gigantically and applicable to the whole army. Was there really a noble, high, holy objective at stake here in Stalingrad and in our battle, an ethically justified goal which could be served by the ultimate human test of giving one's life? Did soldierly honour and obedience to orders really justify this demand so casually made of us, that we hold out for this lost cause, this excess of suffering and dying? Was this immeasurable sacrifice really decisive for the outcome of the war and could it serve our country and our people? Was it not from the outset far too high a price to be paid for the operational objectives that the Supreme Command might be pursuing?

A foreboding I had long held grew into a terrible certainty. What was happening here in Stalingrad was a tragic, senseless self-sacrifice, a scarcely credible betrayal of the final commitment and devotion of brave soldiers. Our innocent trust had been misused in the most despicable manner by those responsible for the catastrophe. We had been betrayed, led astray and condemned. The men of Stalingrad were dying in betrayed belief and in betrayed trust. In my heart the bitter feeling of '... and all for nothing' became ever more torturing.

In my soul arose again the whole abysmal disaster of the war itself. More clearly than ever before I appreciated the full measure of misery and wretchedness of the other countries in Europe to which German soldiers and German arms had brought boundless misfortune. Had not we, so far the victors, been all too prone to close our eyes and our hearts and to forget that always and everywhere, the issues were living human beings, their possessions and their happiness?

Probably only a few among us had entertained the thought that the suffering and dying being caused by our sorry profession of war would one day be inflicted upon us. We had carried our total war into one region of Europe after another and thereby destructively interfered in the destinies of foreign nations. Far too little had we asked the reason why, the necessities and the justifications for what was happening or reflected on the immeasurability of our political responsibility that these entailed. Misery and death had been initiated by us and now they were inexorably coming home to roost. The steppe on the Don and the Volga had drunk streams of precious human blood. Here in their hundreds of thousands had Germans, Roumanians, Italians, Russians and members of other Soviet peoples found their common grave.

The Russians were certainly also making cruelly high blood sacrifices in the murderous battle of Stalingrad. But they, who were defending their country against a foreign aggressor, knew better than we why they were risking their lives.

Several thousand Red Army prisoners suffering hunger and misery behind barbed wire at Voroponovo and doomed to share our downfall were particularly to be pitied. In my broodings which constantly haunted and tortured me, I began to realise just how much our feelings had atrophied towards the continual boundless disregard and violation of human dignity and human life. At the same time my horror and revul-

112

sion of the Moloch of war, to whom ethical-religious conscience had stood in irreconcilable opposition from the very beginning, grew.

And so as the last days of our army were drawing to a close, a deep moral misery gnawed at the hearts of the men helplessly doomed to destruction. Added to their indescribable external suffering were the violent internal conflicts caused by the voice of conscience, and not only with regard to the question of the unconditional duty to obey. Wherever I went and observed I saw the same picture. And what I learned about the matter later on only confirmed the impressions I had gained. Whoever was still unclear about the contexts and reasons for the catastrophe sensed them in dark despair.

Many officers and commanders now began to oppose the insane orders emanating from Führer Headquarters and being passed on by Army Command. By this they began to reject the long eroded military concepts of honour and discipline to which the Army leadership had clung until the end. In the unconditional obedience, such as was fatally being upheld here at Stalingrad, they no longer saw a soldierly stance but rather a lack of responsibility.

Despite the fact that until 20 January 'Führer Headquarters' had at least been sent regular reports by a staff officer seconded to the pocket as its special delegate, from 2,000 kilometres away it could not sensibly evaluate the extent of our perilous predicament. Here the purely military relationships of command and obedience must of necessity mean the elimination of personal freedom of decision based on ethical considerations and possibly even of conscience. With this, at least, the human obligations of the soldier had been shunted aside. The order to resist to the last man and bullet was never rescinded. Officially, freedom of action by the individual soldier or whole groups remained forbidden and a break-out on one's own was prohibited as being desertion. Seen from a political-moral point of view, it was interesting to note that everywhere, despite the orders, the thought of acting on one's own initiative was uppermost. We knew that plans for break-outs were being seriously discussed and prepared, all the way up to the Army Staff, and some were even attempted.

This was open mutiny. In contrast to official orders the opinion began to spread that in a situation of complete hopelessness, an attempt to break out and fight one's way through was permissible. As the end approached, many staffs and units began to consider freedom of decision and action to be completely natural. Many a small group packed their knapsacks or backpacks in great haste and plunged into an insane adventure that, inevitably, could only lead to death.

Since there were no more orders from the centre, towards the end many responsible commanders and unit leaders on the line acted on their own initiative in an endeavour to stop the senseless shedding of blood. In the Stalingrad city outskirts, initially in the south, individual groups simply stopped fighting or surrendered. There a complete division, by now however melted down to a sorry little troop, surrendered in an orderly manner with its general at its head. In other places surrender took place in chaotic confusion while shooting was still going on.

Many desperate Stalingrad warriors in the end sought a way out by suicide or by a voluntary soldier's death. We learned of two generals whose extreme resolution had been shattering. One, the commander of a division from Dresden, had shot himself after having ordered his son, a young lieutenant, to report to him to say farewell. The other, the commander of a division from Lower Saxony whose tactical emblem was a four-leaf clover and was known therefore as the 'lucky' division, who did not want to survive the downfall of his men, had been killed on the front line while standing erect and firing his weapon.

Such contradictory opinions and actions made the rounds. On the one hand it was held to be dishonourable to turn one's weapon against oneself, to violate the military duty to obey by the slightest degree, to surrender or to let oneself be taken prisoner. On the other hand the claim was soon made that in view of such a brave fight in such a hopeless situation for which we were not to blame, the exact opposite of all of these things was permissible.

And so it came about that alongside staunch resistance, the desperate upholding of a soldierly stance and unremitting discipline, lives were ended in desperation, mutiny and surrender occurred, and Germans fired on Germans who had let themselves be taken prisoner. But for the most part people behaved with dumb fatalism, or no longer acted at all and just suffered and died. True soldiery and its values had long become hatefully contorted. Basically, uprightness and heroics only existed any longer as a *beau geste* of desperation. What was lacking to the end was the redeeming decision from above and the dignified ending of the untenable situation.

When Paulus surrendered in the small hours of the morning on 31 January, he had long lost the initiative. The fight had been ended only for his staff and his immediate entourage. The newly created Field Marshal had abdicated and gone into captivity without issuing a final order, without a word of farewell or thanks to his troops who had fought and suffered beyond human endurance. An inglorious end!

Fortunately we were spared the knowledge of the radio message which, before the end, our Commander-in-Chief had personally sent to Hitler in the name of Sixth Army on the occasion of the tenth anniversary of the National Socialist seizure of power. This telegram of congratulations, which spoke of the swastika flag flying over Stalingrad and of the non-capitulation setting an example for the country and for coming generations, was bound to prove useful to the political and military leadership for their propaganda slogans and legend-mongering. Had we known of it our group of comrades would not have understood, would have rejected with outrage this contrived gesture obviously born out of the confusion of desperation. And so many of the warriors of Stalingrad would have shared these feelings with us!

What would happen to us now? That was the disquieting question that now occupied us in the northern pocket. The answer could not be far off. Why had the Field Marshal not included the rest of his army in his surrender and ended the whole senseless battle by an orderly hand-over into captivity? It should have been possible to prepare the appropriate steps in time. And when he and his staff left the military stage in the end, why had he not at least rescinded the order to hold out and granted freedom of action? The Russians would probably now throw their full might against us and perhaps also take their revenge on us for the continuing resistance. We felt lonely and full of despair, abandoned by our country and our own army, on the threshold between life and death. And so we waited in numb expectation for what was to come.

The glimpse of the abyss

Crammed together in our dark cellar vault we waited for the end in tormenting inactivity and despair. Shells or bombs could bring it to us at any time even before the victors themselves appeared. Immediately following the elimination of the southern pocket the Russians had regrouped their heavy weapons and, in wild determination, opened up a murderous fire on our northern sector of Stalingrad.

The last pockets of resistance, what was left of about six shattered divisions and the remnant of other formations that had meanwhile been left to their fate by the resignation of the Army Command, now had to bear the whole burden of the concentrated air attacks, artillery and mortar fire. Time and again our vaults rang and shook to their seams and thick clouds of sand and dust descended anew on the men filled with the fear of death. The dragging march of time was unbearable. It seemed to stand still or rather slowly to sink down into a bottomless sea of suffering.

It was not only the fear of the coming end, the hunger clawing at my intestines and the pain from my frozen limbs that turned the last, seemingly endless hours in the Stalingrad pocket into the tortures of hell for me. Despite my physical exhaustion I was in a state of over-alertness, which allowed me to stare with sharpened perception into the abyss of our misfortune, into the horrible, guilt-laden depth of our catastrophe. The proximity of death tore the last obscuring veils from my eyes and brought the fruits of long years of individual experiences, observations, tormenting feelings and thoughts to an instant maturity. Now on the very edge of being, war in its for us most terrible form became the inexorable revealer of all things. Its ethical questionability and senselessness, but also more than that, the whole fatal aberration in the larger sense which had logically led to the hell of Stalingrad, came to my awareness with a shattering certainty. I felt myself to be culpably enmeshed in the pitiless Witches' Sabbath all around. This realisation now pressed down upon me like a lead weight and burdened my heart and my conscience.

In my mind's eye the horrible experiences and pictures of destruction that would not leave me in peace by day or night were strung together in a bloody chain. Experiences and impressions stretching far into the past that suddenly awoke in my sharpened memory, I discovered to be logically connected links of this fatal chain. What had formerly always caused me to have nasty premonitions and apprehensions, what had always disquieted me, I now suddenly had to recognise as having been the warning excrescences of a fatal fundamental evil, the dimensions of which I had not thought possible.

Göring's speech of 30 January, with its all too transparent, calculated heroic pathos, with its plenitude of lying, hollow phrases, had contributed to my final sobering up and made the scales fall from my eyes. Like a flash of lightning the events leading up to our tragedy on the Volga revealed themselves to me in all their coherence. Behind this speech appeared the horrible face of a world of lies, hatred, violence and injustice, a world of inhumanity that I too had served as a soldier in error and in weakness, for which I too was now compelled to atone in this murderous battle. We had sown the wind and now we had to reap the whirlwind.

Suddenly I vividly remembered the embarrassingly ambiguous feelings with which I had reluctantly obeyed my being called to arms during the first days of September 1939. I had not been the least bit enthusiastic, nor did I believe in the unconditional justice and victory of our cause. And how many irreconcilable contradictions of beliefs and duties had I then felt during the course of the war, even in my very humble area of responsibility! I had to think back to the time of the campaign in France, that so fatal, great Pyrrhic victory, when many officers and soldiers together with the masses at home, had wallowed in the apogee of certainty of victory and self-confidence under the intoxicating spell of success. At the time I had just chanced upon Rauschning's book on his talks with Hitler and the revelations it contained about the monstrous foreign policy objectives of the National Socialists and the insane 'new order' for Europe. This had had an almost shattering effect on me, and later disturbed me even more when my insights behind the scenes of occupation policies in the west showed me to my dismay, that the intentions and plans Rauschning had published as a warning were being executed step by step.

This impression had been strengthened by my experiences in the east. Once more I had to think back to the eerie feeling of apprehension and evil foreboding that had filled us all on that exciting night in June when dangerous adventure and death-bringing fate had launched us into the vastness of Russian space. Had not this evil 'preventive war' against Russia, begun with the breach of a treaty, clearly shown to what a questionable degree the old, traditional concepts of right and humanity that had always held the forms of politics and war in check, were simply being shunted aside by the German leadership?

How shocked had we been then at the very outset of the eastern campaign, about two inhuman orders of the day that had been in open breach of international law and of true, decent German soldiery itself! These were the unethical 'commissar order' that required the physical extermination of the regulators of the Bolshevik ideology in the Red Army, and the 'Barbarossa order' dealing with military tribunals, that abolished mandatory prosecution of crimes by German soldiers against civilians in the eastern theatre. Even if these orders had only been acknowledged by our staffs on the front and evaded as far as possible, was it not guilt enough to have accepted and tolerated them in silence like so much else?

And what had gone on in the rear of the fighting troops? Many an ugly rumour had come to one's ears, many an ugly picture had come before one's eyes. I had heard of brutal acts of retribution which had struck the innocent with the guilty. On a drive through the occupied area I had on one occasion seen in Minsk, with its dozens of public gallows, scenes of shameful inhumanity. Were all these excesses and evils not bound to rebound on us sooner or later?

That unpleasant phenomena could get out of hand within the circumstances and among men of the Wehrmacht, showed the degree to which those old forces and ethical ties had declined, that had formerly guaranteed the values and inner discipline of true soldiery. Were those noble attributes that had previously characterised the old General Staff, with its great tradition running from Clausewitz, through Moltke to Schlieffen and Beck, a conservative-Christian basic position, a deep ethos and a broad educational and cultural background that went far beyond professional knowledge and ability, still alive in the mass of the senior officers?

Numerous encounters, above all among the staffs, had given me many opportunities to make my own observations about this. Certainly, many personalities there had appeared to me to be exemplary soldiers who deserved respect. These were mostly representatives of the old school. Among them had been our former Chief of Staff, whose leaving we now lamented. He had left us shortly before the encirclement to take command of a division and, having been wounded as a general, flown out of the pocket long ago. His personality had radiated a humane atmosphere that we had sorely missed of late. It had shaped our community and been good for it.

Among the up and coming younger men, things were often different. Here the questionable results of the all too rapid growth of the national socialist Wehrmacht appeared, together with the influences of a questionable political indoctrination and ideology. I had had to work together with many candidates for the General Staff, mostly young captains who had been on temporary assignment to our department as part of their practical and theoretical training. They were physically and mentally well selected men, splendid comrades, brave officers full of initiative and commitment. However, these unproblematic characters were often lacking a profounder education and culture, ties and maturity. Not infrequently I hit upon sensitive gaps in elementary geographic–historical knowledge, and the perceptions that lurked in their minds, particularly about the world outside Germany and about our opponents in the war, were often frighteningly naïve. Devoid of a sound political instinct and trained in unconditional soldierly obedience, self-confident, trusting blindly in their own ability and in the promises of success in their promotion up the ladder of the military hierarchy, they often fell prey to a carefree optimism. However, such an optimism, which incidentally infected most of the Ic departments that were responsible for the evaluation of the enemy, was bound to have fatal consequences.

And in addition I had been forced to encounter much in the way of incompetence, human frailty and weakness, ambition and ridiculous pride everywhere, even in the most senior positions and among the highest ranks. And in the final hours of the catastrophe, yes, even in captivity, at a time when the only real issue was deep human suffering, questions of promotion and decorations played a role that was beyond my comprehension.

Among the higher staffs, most of the General Staff officers maintained their stance to the bitter end, in other words, with their subordinates they conscientiously tried to perform the duties assigned to them as experts. As virtuosi of their trade, they 'led' until the end. Bent over their maps on which the abstract pictures of the situation with their lines and numbers resembled the constantly changing reality less and less and often no longer at all, they kept the command structure functioning as was demanded from above. And so it happened in the sectors under their control that troops or weapons which no longer existed were regrouped, or numbers were juggled with that only represented shadows but hardly any longer even the trace of a combat-worthy substance.

Where the ethos of the old General Staff still survived, particularly religious ties and the concept rooted in the classic German idealism of the freedom of ethical decision and responsible action based on one's own personality, it was only occasionally able to manifest itself within the smallest circle and bring good to the people below.

The news of the capitulation of the Army leadership had made me particularly painfully aware of the contrast that had suddenly appeared between the front-line troops and the higher staffs and which grew ever sharper towards the end. There, indescribable suffering and natural sacrifice until death; here, only the ordering of such suffering and sacrifice, without the ultimate personal commitment and consequence also expected from above.

.I felt embarrassed by this contrast. Was I myself not a member of a higher staff that had only discarded its over-blown train and superfluous ballast very late in the day and whose members had still enjoyed many a comfort and privilege for a long time?

Now, faced with the imminently impending final catastrophe, the question about the sense of what was happening that had plagued me so often during the war seized me again with cruel force. Hundreds of thousands of flowering human lives were suddenly being senselessly snuffed out here in Stalingrad. What an immeasurable wealth of human happiness, human plans, hopes, talents, fertile possibilities for the future were thereby being destroyed for ever! The criminal insanity of an irresponsible war management with its superstitious belief in technology and its utter lack of feeling for the life, value and dignity of man, had here prepared a hell on earth for us. Of what importance was the individual in his uniqueness and distinctiveness? He felt himself as if extinguished and used up as raw material in a demonic machine of destruction. Here war showed itself in its unmasked brutality. Stalingrad appeared to me as an unsurpassed violation and degeneration of the human essence. I felt myself to be locked into a gigantic, inhuman mechanism that was running on with deadly precision to its own dissolution and destruction.

The view into the abyss of cruel reality would probably have been enough to make me sink helplessly into the night of hopelessness and despair, had there not also been the look upwards to Him, who alone knows of the sense behind events, who is not only the Lord of Battles but also holds the fate of every individual human being in His hands.

We go into captivity

On the afternoon of 1 February we felt that our final hour had irrevocably arrived. Unremitting heavy artillery and mortar fire drummed down on Stalingrad north and finally there was an air attack of murderous intensity on the miserable remains of our city district. Cowering in our constantly shaking cellar vault where whirling dust and sand made breathing difficult, we listened to the hellish noise of the death and destruction being caused all around us outside. Any minute was bound to bring about our own end. But, incredibly, we survived. Soon after the end of the attack we crawled out through the trapdoor above, eager to drink in great draughts of the clean, fresh winter air.

The darkness of night had mercifully closed upon the scenes of horror. Our formerly so familiar field of ruins was hardly recognisable; drastic alterations had taken place everywhere. Whole rows of damaged houses had disappeared completely, the streets were ripped open everywhere, and where formerly there had been open spaces, now stark piles of debris and stones bulged up. What had happened to all the people who had found shelter in this world of ruins? Here and there the remains of buildings burned brightly, and further in the background, the sight tore at my throat, flames were rising from the exact spot where there had been a hospital crammed with sick and wounded.

Only a few days before I had been there and, surrounded by a helpless horde of overjoyed Italians, had delivered a wounded lieutenant who was the leader of their group. On this occasion I had once again had to look deeply into the misery of the overflowing dressing-stations and hospitals. Having been denied entry at every door, we had unsuccessfully gone on from place to place with our sad burden until finally a merciful doctor had taken pity on the wounded man and made the virtually impossible happen. Incidentally, there had been about thirty Italians with a large convoy of vehicles sent to Stalingrad in November to forage for wood for their army in the bend of the Don. Fate had caught up with them here. In the hell of ice and snow I felt a special pity for these sons of the sunny south. Trapped in the battle far from their unit, they had probably had to suffer additional misery. They could hardly make themselves understood and no one really wanted to feel responsible for them at a time of extreme need when it was every man for himself.

The eerie silence reigning outside over the hauntingly transformed landscape, no longer disturbed by any of the sounds of war, pursued us back to our cellar. Here we discussed our fate. Our group, which
had been taciturn during the past few days, was suddenly seized by a
strange, almost hectic activity. The younger comrades among us were in
particularly desperate revolt against events. Something had to be done.
The calm before the storm demanded it. No one could bear to stay any
longer in our cellar, which would assuredly be our burial vault after the
next attack. It was an upsurging of the will to live in the midst of all of
the holding out and suffering we all felt to be senseless. How could the
long eroded concepts of honour, duty, obedience, soldierly heroism figure any longer in our feelings, thoughts and actions! To stay alive, to be
reunited once again with our loved ones at home, this burning desire was
now the drive behind all thoughts and actions. Everywhere I had been
recently I had encountered an identical stance and atmosphere. And in
this chaos, even long-serving professional officers now dismissed the
notion of fighting to the last bullet and seeking death in combat.

Some days earlier, a regular captain and candidate for the General
Staff had left our circle against operative orders and we had accepted this
as being quite normal. After extended, secret preparations, he had
appeared one last time to say goodbye. He had been dressed in a white
camouflage suit and accompanied by several Russian auxiliaries. He
planned to break through the enemy lines on his own and try to link up
with the German front somewhere.

Now two more comrades were going to follow his example: a
young captain of the military police and our special forces interpreter
whom I had learned to respect as a man during our long association.
Their resolve had gradually ripened over time and recently been decisively reinforced by their fear of captivity and possible merciless prosecution by the NKVD. Nothing could dissuade them from their venture.
I tried in vain to convince them of the hopelessness of the planned
attempt.

The problem was not only breaking through the deadly enemy
ring of encirclement, but crossing more than 300 kilometres of mostly
bare freezing steppe without adequate equipment, sufficient food and in
the biting cold. Not even a fraction of the stamina required to achieve
this could be demanded of a body weakened by hunger. I did not see the

slightest chance for such a desperate adventure. But the interpreter, who had been sent to us at the beginning of the Russian campaign, having just graduated from university, and with whom over the years I had often discussed our secret fears in many a confidential conversation, was no longer susceptible to reason. Something was driving him away from our group of comrades, from the cellar, from the hell of Stalingrad. He no longer wished passively to watch death coming for him, but preferred to rush actively into his arms. And so we said farewell for ever.

Of those that stayed behind, each of us pursued his own private thoughts, desires, hopes and fears. No one was able to share the others' burden, but even so our comradeship and the common fate to which we were all sentenced helped to make the crushing weight of those hours more bearable. In my mind's eye, I can still see the pale, bearded faces marked by fear and deprivation. We all looked run-down, dirty and worn-out. How long had it been since we had been able to change our clothes! All joking and any gallows humour had long died out in our small group.

Even the captain of reserves, always so cheerful and full of the joys of life, who in civilian life had been the lord mayor of a city in central Silesia, had withdrawn into himself, obviously deeply shattered by the events and full of despair. He was an upright National Socialist, a glowing idealist through and through, prepared to live and die for his ideology. Now he wanted to end his life. Being taken prisoner by the Russians, so he had always maintained, was out of the question for him. Had he not been a prisoner of war once before in the west at the end of the First World War and suffered from the physical and mental miseries of captivity? As an officer in intelligence he feared, probably quite rightly, particularly harsh treatment by the Russians. He was firmly resolved to die. I vainly tried to make him change his mind. Even references to his family at home, to his children of whom I had often been shown snapshots, could not make him give up the resolve he had reached. Only in the final moment, when the firing pin of his pistol failed, were we able to convince him that fate had given him a sign.

Then there was the executive officer of our corps headquarters, a captain of reserves and president of a court in Westphalia. I secretly envied him, because he alone still had a meaningful assignment which he performed conscientiously and unselfishly until the final hour. It was his job to care for the remainder of our troops who were quartered in a ruin nearby, as well as for our small group of officers in the cellar. Admittedly, there had not been much bread for a long time. In the final days we were only issued thirty-eight grams per head, and the iron rations had long ago been eaten up. But time and again he had succeeded in scrounging some horse meat for us. Now that the end of the catastrophe was in sight, a small store of tins that had been saved up was distributed to fortify us for what was probably going to be the hardest journey of our lives.

Gradually we had accustomed ourselves to the idea of surrendering at the first opportunity and going into Russian captivity. Our elderly adjutant, who was in contact with the staff of General Strecker in the tractor factory, first hinted at this alternative and soon spoke about it openly.

Recently, the thought of captivity and the sufferings it entailed had slowly begun to lose the terror it had initially held for me. It appeared to me to be the lesser evil, an escape and a redemption from the hell of Stalingrad that had become unbearable. In the dark future, this road possibly held the promise of a way home and a reunion with our loved ones to whom so many private thoughts, longings and hopes turned unceasingly in the most fearful hours. In the end I basically had only one wish, to stay alive and healthy and to go into captivity unwounded.

On the morning of 2 February the news spread that the Russian were approaching with tanks and that people were surrendering everywhere without offering resistance. In our district the word was that there was to be no firing, but the troops were no longer resisting anyway. Just as one wipes away exhausted, half-dead flies in the autumn, the masses of tired human beings, worn out by their suffering and apathetically resigned to their fate, were being gathered in by the Russians and herded away. As far as they could still stand on their feet, they welled up out of the ruins, shelters and cellars and formed long lines of misery and helplessness in the streets. Our small surviving group had soon also become a speck somewhere within this formless mass.

In the early minutes of captivity I felt an easing of tension and relief. In the end, the insecurity of our situation between life and death had weighed down on all of us like lead. Was the road we were now going down not the way out of horror and fear? And did not the light and sweetness of a life in freedom possibly beckon at its end, admittedly in a far distant, veiled future? However, the transformation that suddenly took place within and around us was in some ways numbing and confusing.

The original deadening effect was gradually pushed aside by the approach of a world that was unknown to us. What first attracted my attention was the fresh, healthy appearance of the victors, their simple, enviable winter clothing and good weapons. Submachine-guns everywhere and the uniform picture of sheepskins, padded jackets, felt boots and fur caps with broad ear muffs swinging up and down.

The warmly bundled-up, well-nourished and splendidly equipped men of the Red Army, with their chunky, mostly red-cheeked faces, formed a stark contrast to our deathly pale, filthy, bearded and freezing figures of misery who hung exhausted and sick in their makeshift winter clothing, consisting of all kinds of furs, blankets, scarves, field-grey headgear, woollens and inadequate foot wear. This sudden meeting and comparison at once showed me how low we had sunk and how little we had been prepared for this murderous battle.

As if in a trance, I experienced the events and all the new impressions and feelings flooding down on me. I saw the muzzle of the cocked submachine-gun a Red Army soldier was aiming at my chest, who, searching impatiently, first grabbed my watch and then my pistol. I heard the calming words of a captain of the guard, who promised us life, safety and our personal property and then proudly accompanied the tired mass of his prisoners to the rear.

But such protection was not enough to spare us the initial bitter humiliations by the hate-filled victors. Malicious calls of 'Fascist!', 'Fritzi!', 'Hitler kaputt!' alternated with threats, obviously dreadful curses and contemptuous spit. Like raging wolves, vengeful soldiers from the rear echelons fell on the helpless victims time and again to steal personal baggage and to vent their spleen. First my fur coat, an old family heirloom that had stood me in inestimable good stead in the east, was torn from my body. However, far more painful for me was the loss later on of all the things I had packed before going into captivity or carefully hidden on my person; a few small books and letters from home. With them and my wedding ring, the last tie that still visibly bound me to all I held dear and precious was torn from me. Nothing was left to me that outwardly reminded me of my former life. And my heart could only surrender them in bloody torment.

During the first sleepless night of my captivity this new misery remorselessly flooded over me in all its magnitude. I had been pulled out from among my comrades and fellow prisoners sitting crammed together in a farm house and initially taken to a guard house for interrogation. There I sat alone and deeply depressed among a group of joyfully noisy Red Army soldiers who first watched me with a mixture of curiosity and suspicion and soon left me to my own devices in the farthest corner of the room. While an endless fireworks display of captured German tracer ammunition was being explosively fired into the air outside in the triumph of victory, inside our guardroom gramophone music sounded for most of the night.

Wild dance rhythms rang out and time and again they were accompanied by the dank stamping of a row of felt boots that moved over the wooden floorboards with astonishing speed. The guards, who included slant-eyed Mongolians, looked strange enough. Some had decorated themselves in the most remarkable manner with captured German rings, watches, weapons and other objects. On their Red Army uniforms they wore German officers' daggers they had found and they had hung their pistols on the long chains of the German rifle-cleaning equipment.

Besides the dances, gramophone records of folk songs, Soviet choirs and marches were played incessantly. The same music was played over and over again, sometimes sad, sometimes filled with restrained emotions, sometimes with wild outbursts of feeling, all in a minor key and often of a strangeness of character that frightened me. Under a different set of circumstances this strange music could have intrigued me strongly. Now it only depressed and tormented me.

All the noise and exuberance surrounding me formed a shrieking contrast to the inner and outer state in which I found myself. Torn from the circle of my comrades, left to myself and my emotions, in the midst of the joyfully dancing and singing victors with whom no contact could be established, in my inner heart I felt abandoned and without hope, totally depressed, uprooted, cut off from home, sunk far away, subjugated to a foreign will, pitilessly thrown to the mercy of unknown powers. To be dependent on the whim of the victor, constantly watched, menacingly surrounded by barbed wire and guns, forced to relinquish any kind of external freedom, captivity meant a hitherto unknown form of human submission and humiliation.

In the hopelessness of an existence without any apparent sense, would I be able to succeed in arming myself with the necessary patience and developing the inner forces of resistance which alone could combat the danger of abandoning myself to destruction?

Thoughts such as these tortured me during the slowly creeping hours, as did the tormenting worries about home and my loved ones to whom a great, unmerciful fate, now to be sensed for the first time, was sending its dark harbingers.

The tragedy of Stalingrad is not over

On 2 February 1943 the last battle groups of Sixth Army surrendered in the northern pocket of Stalingrad. Shortly before, their Commander, General Strecker, who in clear appreciation of the approaching catastrophe had previously repeatedly objected to the measures of the Supreme Command without mincing matters, had received a radio message from Hitler demanding obedience to duty to the extreme on behalf of the German nation. It spoke of the example set by the southern pocket and of the establishment of a new German defensive front to which every hour of continuing resistance would contribute. The general was obviously prepared to obey the order to hold out until the end. His conduct reflected the desperate helplessness and hopelessness of the situation. Only after the northern Stalingrad pocket had begun to shrink in many areas without further resistance, did he finally accede to the urgings of his subordinate commanders and stop the senseless blood-letting. A number of radio messages sent out no longer reflected the true picture of the situation. They were but a convulsive echo of the heroic mouthings that were reaching the dying army from outside.

But one of the last signs of life that the remnant of Sixth Army radioed to the OKH very likely expressed the feelings and desires of all of the warriors of Stalingrad. It read, 'Premature funeral orations unwelcome!' and was an answer from the sacrificed troops to the graveside speech by the Reichsmarschall, glorifying their death. His last message sent to the Volga, of which we were admittedly not informed, still spoke of Sixth Army's being able to count the saving of the Occident to its immortal honour.

The pocket battle that had lasted for seventy-six days and been one of the bloodiest and most murderous battles ever fought was over. But the tragedy of the German survivors continued in a new cruel manner. Because of the repeated rejections of the Russian capitulation proposals and the obvious resistance of Sixth Army to the last man, the Russian leadership had not thought it necessary to make serious preparations for the care of larger numbers of prisoners. For tens of thousands of fought-out, exhausted human beings, the able as well as the sick, this meant a further terrible catastrophe and sure death.

While the miserable columns of prisoners were being led away from the scene of the battle, mostly in hunger marches for days on end, and were painfully dragging themselves to the reception camps, the German war radio gave a summary of the battle of Stalingrad in a special broadcast full of bombastic phrases. This dressed-up report spoke of the 'disadvantages of the conditions', painted a mendaciously heroic picture of the terminal fighting and created the impression that all the participants had sacrificed themselves for National Socialist Germany in a heroic epic beyond compare.

Among other things it said: 'The surrender twice demanded by the enemy was proudly rejected. The final battle took place under the swastika flag, hoisted on the highest ruin of Stalingrad and visible for a great distance. Generals, officers, non-commissioned officers and soldiers from the ranks, fought shoulder to shoulder to the last bullet. They died, that Germany might live! Their example will have repercussions to the most distant future, in defiance of all the lying Soviet propaganda ...'

With lies such as these, the betrayal of the warriors of Stalingrad was covered up and the second greatest military catastrophe in German history turned into an heroic legend. In reality, 91,000 men of the army that had been declared dead went into Russian captivity together with 2,500 officers, including a Field Marshal and twenty-three generals.

In the late afternoon of 3 February I was suddenly put aboard a truck with a select group of companions in misery. We were to be taken to a higher staff. We sat tightly packed together under a half-open tarpaulin and warmed one another in the biting cold. The composition of our group, and the initial interrogations we had had, with their entrapping questions and threats, boded ill for us. We were all mainly officers of the General Staff and from the departments of Ic, military court, special assignment and interpreters. Present were also the interpreter of the General Field Marshal, who had helped initiate the surrender of the Army Staff, and the long-time Ic and Chief of Counter Intelligence of Sixth Army, who was soon abruptly pulled out of our group to disappear into the darkness for many years.

Our ride first took us over the vast theatre of the lost battle. Once again I had to see the scene on which thousands of ghastly traces recalled the tragedy that had been enacted here. All life had fled from the many ravines and expanses of snow. All the more ghostly did the scattered wreckage of the huge mass of weapons, vehicles and equipment that had served the men in their deadly trade appear. I saw the shot-up column of our own plundered and half-burned cars. I recognised the all too familiar tactical insignia of a dozen shattered divisions whose *matériel* lay strewn about and here and there filled the narrow snow gullies to the brim.

On both sides of the road the eye constantly caught new pictures of horror; the sorrowful remains of the march of the columns of prisoners. Often mercifully drifted over by the snow, lying there were the stiff bodies of many unrecorded German soldiers who had not been able to keep up with their comrades in misery and had dropped out in exhaustion. A bullet in the back of the neck had ended their sufferings.

As darkness was falling, we drove through the burned-out, eerie battlefield, through the landscape of ruins that was Stalingrad. As our truck rolled down a steep incline and turned north on the snow-covered ice of the mighty Volga, the last bright colours of the cloudless evening winter sky sank into darkness over the crushed city.

Our ride took us about fifty kilometres up-stream to the town of Dubovka. It took us from the zone of horror and death of the battle into the peaceful back country, untouched by war. Our roadbed was the ice shield of the majestic river, whose name was to remain linked to our fate forever. We were embraced by an overwhelmingly beautiful winter night with a dome of light, the like of which I had never seen more grandly. Improbably close and huge, almost like flaming disks, twinkled the familiar and yet strange-seeming constellations. They moved me and for a time made me forget the bottomless misery of the reality I had lived through. My thoughts wandered back into the past.

A long submerged picture rose in my memory. I again saw myself driving into the boundless eastern expanses on the ice of a mighty Russian river. That had been almost exactly one year ago. Coming from France and having been ordered to join Sixth Army in the region of Kharkov with our staff that was following behind, I had then crossed the Dnieper on a mighty bridge of ice. Behind me towered proud Kiev, and the many fantastic domes and onion towers of the convent of Lavra, which stood up from the steep river bank, sparkled in the morning sun. It had been like a gesture of farewell from the West and its culture. And when I then looked eastward into the monotonous snowscape, out of whose seemingly endless plains an icy wind blew towards me, it was as if the blood ran cold in my veins and I secretly asked myself whether I was likely ever again to return across the Dnieper. It was all too understandable that such memories and depressing feelings should now come to life again. To what sad fate was this drive on the Volga going to lead me?

It is a bounty for us human beings that a merciful hand covers the future from our eyes with an impenetrable veil. Had I known then that I was destined for more than seven comfortless years devoid of love and filled with previously unknown mental and physical tortures and fearful uncertainties on the borderline of life, I would never have found the strength to stand the sufferings of the initial hard months of captivity.

It was not only the fear for my personal well-being that filled me on that night in February. With sudden might, my anxiety about the terrible fate that I saw inescapably approaching my people and my country crushed down upon me. Time and again my thoughts circled around the experience of the tragedy of Stalingrad and in this catastrophe I recognised its exemplary importance for what was to come.

Once again I remembered the overbearing words with which Hitler in his speeches in 1942 had announced to the world that the German soldier stood on the Volga and would never again leave. Stalingrad was bound to fall, so he had declared, but it was to be cautiously taken by patrols so as to spare our blood and prevent a second Verdun. Now an entire army had been sacrificed on the Volga and not the least reason had been prestige.

During the last weeks of the senseless battle, innumerable men had recognised and felt this. In the end they had withdrawn all trust from the 'Supreme Commander' and Head of State. The saving way out had not been taken and a second Verdun had had to be the result. The terrible sacrifice of more than a quarter of a million men had struck the German nation directly throughout all its provinces. This was no longer merely a military affair. It was something far more encompassing and I had the impression that a huge slice of humanity had also sunk into the mass grave of Stalingrad. Only a political-ethical decision could have mastered the situation and prevented the worst. But the great war leader was lacking, one who would have dared to burst the bonds of purely military obedience and, obedient only to the eternal law of ethics, by acting on his own initiative out of a sense of soldierly responsibility, disobeyed the order to behave inhumanly.

In the sad events on the Volga I saw not only the military turning-point of the war. In the experiences behind me I felt and apprehended something else as well; the anticipation of the final catastrophe towards which the whole nation was reeling. In my mind's eye I suddenly saw a second Stalingrad, a repetition of the tragedy just lived through, but of much greater, more terrible proportions. It was a vast pocket battle on German soil with the whole German nation fighting for life or death inside. And were the issues not the same as those of the final months of our Sixth Army? In the sacrifice thus already ordained, would insight, the power of decision and the strength either to break out or to surrender be able to mature?

In our helpless abandonment, to feel our own fate and destruction breaking in on our country, was a crushing mental burden that was to become virtually unbearable in the times ahead.

Time and again I was soothingly distracted from my tormenting thoughts and dark visions by the wonders of the brightly shining star-filled winter sky that appeared to be so close to the touch. It constantly drew my eyes upwards as if by magical force. What had so far appeared to me as the downfall of a world come loose at the seams and a catastrophe without bounds, suddenly took on measurable dimensions. I regained my equilibrium and found my way back to myself. Where I had felt earlier that chaos was swallowing me up, now calm and peace was flowing into my disquieted heart. This reconciling effect came from the vast order and harmony that the sparkling mass of bright stars with their eternal laws of the universe brought back to my attention anew. The consolation that the stars sank into my soul was strange and hardly to be grasped by the intellect. It seemed to me as if my personal fate within the framework of events on earth was secretly included within the vast, all-embracing order of the cosmos.

For the mass of the survivors who had escaped from the hell of Stalingrad, the aftermath of the tragedy lasted for only a short while. They died in their tens of thousands during the early months of captivity. Hunger and deprivation, frost and sickness, had already made them a sure prey for death even before the fighting stopped. With the columns of prisoners death also came to the various camps of reception, to Beketovka, Krassno-Armeisk and Frolov, where terrible epidemics raged everywhere. An exact accounting of the victims of Stalingrad according to numbers, dates and individual fates will never be made.

The few that were allowed to begin a new life at home and in freedom after long years of captivity will always have to ask themselves, how they can justify the deaths of the others by their own existence, how they can uphold and fulfil the legacy of their dead comrades. But all Germany must also loyally remember its many, many sons that lie at rest in the distant Russian steppe and try, today and in the future, to understand their unforgettable sacrifice. The innumerable mounds of soldiers' graves in Stalingrad have long disappeared. The cemeteries were levelled soon after the battle and partially converted to soccer pitches. Nothing is left of the army of simple grey crosses. But it is as if a great invisible cross were rising there on the Volga, casting its shadow over our nation and addressing penetrating, admonishing words to all our hearts.

PART II

CRITICAL ASSESSMENTS
AFTER FIFTY YEARS

1. FIELD MARSHAL VON MANSTEIN

In his war memoirs, in which Field Marshal von Manstein describes and deplores his 'Lost Victories', an extensive chapter is dedicated to the tragedy of Stalingrad. When this book was published in 1955 it caused quite a sensation because of the generally high standard of reporting as well as its importance as a source for the history of the Second World War.

For the first time the existing varied literature on Stalingrad was enriched by the memoirs of a commander recognised as an authority, whose name was closely associated with the fatal battle on the Volga and particularly with the desperate winter offensive in the Don steppe which was undertaken to relieve the army encircled at Stalingrad.

Von Manstein therefore proffered the first comprehensive picture of the over-all context of the military operations as seen from the top. He himself characterised his account as follows. 'As my former position demands it, I will attempt to describe the fate of Sixth Army within the frame-work of the larger set of events, of which Stalingrad was only a part, even if it was the most tragic. The reader must therefore make allowances if he is not to be led into the din of battle, on to the snow fields of the steppe around Stalingrad or into the maze of the fight for ravines and blocks of buildings, but rather into the regions of higher command. He will not be surrounded by the heat of battle or the deathly cold of the steppe, but by an atmosphere of considerations and responsibility.'[1]

What a personality of the military rank of von Manstein had to say on this subject was bound to command the most keen attention from the beginning. After the operational mistakes of the Supreme Command had allowed the encirclement of Sixth Army between the Volga and the Don and the whole southern wing of the eastern front had become endangered, this strategically outstanding senior commander had self-confidently taken over command of the newly formed Army Group Don. Given the available forces and reserves, the achievement of his assignment to recover the situation on the Don–Volga front was actually impossible. In his capacity as Commander-in-Chief of the army group to which the unhappy Sixth Army was subordinated, he became co-responsible for the subsequent catastrophic events at Stalingrad.

In his book, von Manstein purports to be describing the course of the tragedy factually and without emotions. However, in his introduction to *Lost Victories* he makes a qualifying admission: 'Even if I have tried to view events, people and their decisions objectively, the evaluation by a participant must ever remain subjective.'

This admission emphasises a fact that is all too familiar to a trained historian and one which must always be taken into consideration, since it is rooted in human nature. In the final analysis, memoirs serve to justify their author! Should this surprise us in a person like von Manstein who was enmeshed in so many ways in the tragic spider's web of guilt and the consequence of military obedience to orders, of political inadequacy, of strategic self-assurance and human failure? We must investigate what von Manstein's objective and subjective statements can contribute to our understanding of the tragedy of Stalingrad, in particular to its manifold problems and to the lessons to be learned from it.

The serious literature on Stalingrad published since 1955, particularly the documents and statements by the military leaders of the army sacrificed on the Volga that have become available in the meantime, force us to examine von Manstein's account from a critical distance. But first we should hear the Field Marshal's own opinions, as they were expressed in the effectively and suggestively written eighty-page chapter on Stalingrad in his *Lost Victories*.

Hitler's basic mistake and General Field Marshal Paulus' submission

After an introductory glorification of the heroism of the German soldiers on the Volga, von Manstein begins with an astute analysis and evaluation of the operations, which from the summer offensive of 1942 on had led to the encirclement of Sixth Army and to the catastrophe in late autumn, and also of the situation as he found it on taking over command of Army Group Don.

He sees the principal mistake made by Hitler and the Supreme Command to be that of allowing the German offensive in southern Russia to fall into two major directions of advance, namely towards Stalingrad and towards the Caucasus, objectives that were mainly dictated by considerations of war economics. In the end there yawned a 300-kilometre gap between the two army groups in the Kalmyk steppe, in which only one motorised division was deployed to provide inadequate security.

The attempt to hold the vastly over-extended front for a longer time span was bound to have fatal consequences, particularly since the forces available were insufficient and there were no strategic reserves. Two of the most powerful armies were bogged down in Stalingrad and were left there in an exposed position while the inadequate protection of the deep and partially open flanks was entrusted to the insufficiently equipped and less combat-worthy Roumanian, Italian and Hungarian forces. Von Manstein is of the opinion, and quite rightly, that the Supreme Command should then have drawn the necessary conclusions from the fact that the German offensive had bogged down without having forced a final decision. It was a fatal mistake to nail the most powerful forces on the whole southern wing of the eastern front to Stalingrad, with their rearward communications inefficient and their flanks ill defended.

Before the advent of the Russian winter, the risk entailed in recovering operational flexibility between the Caucasus and the Don should definitely have been taken by withdrawing the all too dangerously advanced front, so as not to leave the initiative to the enemy. Since this was not done, the enemy was virtually invited to seize the opportunity for an encircling offensive that was offered to him. Von Manstein declares the actual reason for the downfall of Sixth Army to be the fanatical pig-headedness of Hitler, who refused until the end to give up Stalingrad voluntarily. With regard to this mentality of Hitler, who had tied his military prestige to the name of Stalingrad, von Manstein regards it as a psychological mistake on the part of General Paulus even to have asked Hitler for permission to break out during the initial, decisive days of the pocket battle before the enemy ring of encirclement was complete. The Army Commander, who knew Hitler's point of view from his former job at the OKH, should have seized the only chance existing at the time and simply presented Hitler with the accomplished fact of the disengagement of the army from Stalingrad, especially when the Supreme Command let a day and a half go by before it answered and forbade the break-out. Von Manstein mainly attributes it to the loyalty of the Army Commander that such an unauthorised action was not taken.[2]

In his dramatic description of his attempts to relieve Sixth Army, von Manstein treats in great detail the various reasons why the operation was ultimately doomed to fail.

He again sees Hitler, who disregarded the urgent operational demands of Army Group, clung tenaciously to his issues of prestige against all common sense and pig-headedly opposed any withdrawal from the Stalingrad pocket, as the principal culprit. But he also accuses the leaders of Sixth Army of having rejected his order to break out at the decisive hour. He talks of the weighty mistake made by General Paulus during the days immediately after 18 December 1942 when, with the relieving forces within about fifty kilometres of the pocket, the last chance to save the army was not taken. Von Manstein reports the discouraging result of the mission of Major Eismann, one of his General Staff officers, who was sent into the pocket in order to agree the views of Army Group Command with those of Army Command in respect of the break-out. Under the influence of his Chief of Staff Schmidt, who energetically held to the Führer order, rejected any 'catastrophe solution' and even maintained that Sixth Army could hold its position until Easter if adequately supplied, Paulus finally proved, as von Manstein explains, to have been averse to the terrible risk of a break-out.

The first act of the operation was the offensive 'Winter Storm', which had already been announced at the beginning of December. Fourth Panzer Army was to fight its way through to a link-up and enable the arranged convoy of supplies to be delivered.

The second act of the break-through, which would automatically result from the first, was to be initiated by the code signal 'Thunderclap' and had as its objective the evacuation of the Stalingrad area sector by sector. Von Manstein reserved the right to send this signal himself. By this measure, as he suggests, he wanted to absolve the leadership of the encircled army of the responsibility for the risky adventure and for disobeying Hitler's express order to hold Stalingrad at all costs, and by so doing motivate them to act.

For his part, however, General Paulus could not see his way clear to giving the conclusive order to attack. Von Manstein attempts to do justice to the extremely difficult position the Commander of Sixth Army was in, by explaining the pros and cons in detail, rejecting the phrase 'blind obedience' and explaining the failure as the result of a grave conflict of conscience. If Paulus refused to risk the venture and seize the last chance, this was assuredly due to the feeling of responsibility that weighed on him, a '... responsibility that the Commander of

Army Group was trying to relieve him of by his order, but which he himself believed he could not lay down, neither before Hitler nor before himself'.[3]

Von Manstein's account gives the impression that Army Group had actually given the decisive order to abandon Stalingrad against Hitler's will, whereas Paulus had denied himself out of over-conscientious obedience to the Supreme Military Command.

Paulus' responsibility is further underlined by von Manstein suggestion that the subordination of Sixth Army under Army Group Don was more or less a fiction, particularly because of the position of direct command that Hitler maintained over Sixth Army through his own liaison officers.

Von Manstein's relief operation

Only with the greatest sympathy will former Stalingrad fighters be able to read the passages full of suspense in which von Manstein describes the relief offensive directed towards Stalingrad with all its obstacles, difficulties, efforts, hopes and bitter disappointments. He portrays his nerve-wracking and ultimately futile battles with OKH and Hitler in which he attempted to obtain the decisions necessary to withdraw Sixth Army from Stalingrad and to recover operational flexibility.

The issues were the constant demands for an increase in the supply fleets and a reinforcement of the insufficient relief forces. Since taking over command on 27 November, the commitments made by OKH in this context formed the indispensable pre-conditions for all von Manstein's decisions and measures. In the firm conviction that the 'Supreme War Lord', who alone disposed of all possibilities and reserves, would make the greatest efforts and mobilise means to relieve the endangered army, von Manstein had considered the risk of waiting to be justified and concentrated his own efforts entirely on preparation of the operation to reach the encircled army. Admittedly, however, the Field Marshal had to recognise more clearly and anxiously from week to week that the conditions for the job he was to do were not being met, particularly since the operation had had insufficient forces from the outset.

The relief operation, during which the greatest risks had to be taken in order to open the way to freedom for the encircled comrades, appears in von Manstein's description as a 'race against life and death'.

This battle is also simultaneously described in its close context to recurring new dangers that threatened to destroy the whole southern wing of the German eastern front at the time. One gains the impression that '... the last man that could be made available, the last shell ...' was actually committed, even that the fate of the entire Army Group was thrown into the scales to bring the relief operation to a successful conclusion and get Sixth Army out. The desperate operational situation at the time, with all its undeniable necessities, is clearly demonstrated by the fact that von Manstein was forced at the last moment to weaken the already too weak relief forces of Fourth Panzer Army, which was fighting in front of the Stalingrad pocket in the Myshkova sector, by withdrawing the strongest of the three divisions that were already engaged in bitter defensive fighting there.

He was forced to do this in order to counter the highly critical threat that had developed on the left wing of the Army Group. He only saw his way clear to taking this unavoidable decision when it became evident that action by the encircled army and thereby a corresponding relief of the hard-pressed relieving forces could no longer be hoped for. From then on the enemy was in a position to seize the initiative even to the east of the Don and to bring about the complete failure of the relief operation.

It is interesting to learn from von Manstein's memoirs that he even considered preparing a new relief operation as a final effort. In the last week of December, he adamantly demanded that three divisions of First Panzer Army, which was part of Army Group A, be immediately put at his disposal for this purpose. According to his conviction, which he explains in detail, the release of these units would have been possible at the time. But Hitler refused. With this, the fate of Sixth Army was finally sealed.

Von Manstein calls Hitler's plan to relieve the encircled army at a later date by means of an SS panzer corps that was to be collected in the Kharkov area and was to advance 550 kilometres to the Volga in the spring, a 'utopian dream'.[4]

He speaks with factual sobriety and without mincing words of what took place in the Stalingrad pocket at about Christmas time after the failure of the relief offensive and then continues: 'In view of the other part of its assignment, preventing destruction of the whole southern wing of the eastern front, it was only in the last phase of the battle that, by proposing surrender, Army Group was able to justify making an attempt to shorten this in order to reduce the losses and sufferings of the Army.'[5]

Von Manstein justifies the deliberately demanded sacrifice of Sixth Army. In the final paragraph of his chapter on Stalingrad, he answers the question of the sense of the holding on and ultimate bleeding to death of what at the time were still about 200,000 human beings, from the point of view of the larger picture. In those days of January 1943 he saw the strategic function that Sixth Army fulfilled in holding on as being decisive for the war. For weeks it tied down the strong enemy forces facing it. Had these forces been available elsewhere they would probably have destroyed the entire southern wing of the eastern front and thereby decided the fate of the eastern front as a whole. The holding on and dying of Sixth Army, in its position of hopelessness, created the conditions under which such a threatening catastrophe could be prevented.

Von Manstein's great strategic ability therefore succeeded in gloriously fulfilling the larger assignments of his army group; keeping a corridor of retreat open for Army Group A coming up from the Caucasus and holding open the rearward communications of the southern German wing in the Don–Donetz area which was threatened with being cut off. At the end of the crisis-filled winter campaign, the Field Marshal again brought off a virtuoso success, the victorious counter-blow at Kharkov, struck from out of a flexibly conducted fighting retreat.

Gaps and questions in von Manstein's account

Von Manstein's portrayal of the tragedy of Stalingrad paints a well-rounded picture that does not appear to contain any gaps or serious ambiguities. All the evaluations, considerations and measures are logically joined together within the parameters of the catastrophic situation created by the 'Supreme War Lord'. In the sphere of command of the Field Marshal, everything that is necessary in the interests of the strategic situation and can in any way be accomplished with the limited forces available is done. The professional virtuosity with which the solution of the difficult assignment is attempted once it has been taken on, hardly seems to permit any criticism of the individual links in the chain of events which in its inescapable consequence ultimately requires the sacrifice of an entire army for the success of other important operations. When reading it, one gains the impression that in this specific phase of the war, one is dealing with a grandiose military game of chess, requiring the most daring ploys and huge sacrifices such as are demanded by the 'system of support' willy-nilly.

Why then do von Manstein's statements and observations, in which all the equations appear to be solved cleanly, still leave many critical readers, particularly the survivors of the battle of Stalingrad, with a deep concern? This is certainly not due to the fact that the Field Marshal treats the catastrophe on the Volga and his own responsible participation in the events exclusively from the standpoint of the higher command and predominantly from the point of view held at the time. That is his right, yes even his obligation, and makes his memoirs a valuable source for the historian. His memoirs are not only important for the history of war and as information on the operations of an exceptionally gifted strategist, they also provide insight into the intellect, the manner of thinking and the psychology of a senior commander in the fatal situation of those times.

But the fact that von Manstein believes he need only portray and explain the catastrophe of Stalingrad from the point of view of strategy and that in this context he refrains, despite his high position, from asking the ultimate questions regarding political and ethical responsibility, must make one wary.

It is not only the former Stalingrad warriors who will meet his attempts to find a sense of purpose in the tragedy with even more decidedly critical reservations. This is best demonstrated by the Thermopylae quotation. Selected more for a purpose than from insight, it heads the chapter on Stalingrad, is then deliberately taken up again at the end, and the tenor of the presentation, particularly all the dressing-up, is attuned to it. Here one gets the impression that in 1955 von Manstein is still maintaining his former standpoint based on the knowledge and considerations held then, as if the problematical conditions under which the sacrifice of several hundred thousands of human beings was demanded and made at the time are still valid and strategically or otherwise morally and politically justifiable in retrospect.

A purely, or predominantly, military character and an almost exclusively operational point of view, in no way do justice to the phenomenon of Stalingrad, particularly in the sphere of the higher leadership. Within the frame-work of his manner of portrayal, it is only to be expected that von Manstein touches on the human side of the tragedy but very incidentally, although not the slightest doubt should be entertained when he says that he and his staff, who all struggled to the utmost to save Sixth Army, daily and hourly lived and suffered the indescribable agonies of the doomed men.

However, for the Commander of Army Group the issue had to be something different and greater than pity and emotional involvement. It is disappointing, even crushing, that in the 'atmosphere of considerations and responsibility' into which the Field Marshal promises to take the reader, the great ethical and political ramifications of events which caused so many of the warriors of Stalingrad such acute qualms until the end, hardly assume any importance at all.

The fact that in January 1943, after having lost one-third of its original complement, Sixth Army still numbered approximately 200,000 human beings, for whom the increasingly necessary surrender was being categorically refused by Hitler, and thereby were being ordered to set out on an atrocious march into death, exemplifies the uniqueness and monstrosity of the situation. Whoever had to live through it from beginning to end, be it as an officer or as a soldier in the ranks, was simply not able to handle it mentally. And even today, those who wish to understand the nature of the catastrophe can no more accept the attempt to justify the gigantic human sacrifice of this strategic sentence of death than can the survivors. The voice of humanity and conscience simply cannot let itself be stifled by purely military arguments.

The day of decision

As already mentioned, von Manstein attributes the lack of an independent decision by Paulus during the initial days of the pocket battle to his loyalty to Hitler.

But in this Paulus was no different from all the other commanders on the Don and the Volga including von Manstein himself. They all still wanted to win the war and to conduct it successfully '*lege artis militaris*' (according to the art of war). Until then, not one of them had shown any fundamental political or moral reserves towards the Führer or towards National Socialism. They were all only concerned with purely military, operational decisions, with final victory. Even Count Schenk von Stauffenberg had only seen through Hitler's criminal nature and that of the whole war during the course of 1942.[6]

Paulus acted out of loyalty to military principles that were beyond question for him, and actually are beyond question under normal circumstances. The night of 22/23 November would have been the earliest point at which he could have ordered a break-out, but several days of preparation and regrouping inside the pocket would have been necessary for its execution. Above all, the Luftwaffe would have had to top up Sixth Army's fuel supply beforehand. Therefore, Hitler could not have been presented with an accomplished fact, as von Manstein claims.[7] Furthermore, a break-out without prior co-ordination with Army Group and the Luftwaffe would hardly have been in accordance with the art of war. And even then it would not have been a responsible action, if absolute certainty had existed that Hitler would forbid it, because it could only have been enforceable if all the other commanders and superiors involved would have backed Paulus to a man and covered for him. In that case, however, it would not have been necessary to offend these men by such an uncoordinated action. An action agreed with Army Group and the Chief of the General Staff would have made much more sense.

On the evening of 22 November Paulus had conferred with General von Seydlitz on the most appropriate action to be taken. The new Commander of Army Group (appointed on 20 November), Field Marshal von Manstein, joined von Weichs at Starobelsk at about 0900 hours on 24 November after a 3-day train ride from Vitebsk. He should have arrived on the 21st, but the weather made flying impossible. An experience that seems not to have worried von Manstein very much, as we shall see later.

From 0930 hours on, he had himself briefed on the situation. As Colonel i.G (= im Generalstab = member of the General Staff) Winter, who was on von Weichs' staff, reported decades later, von Manstein and his staff went into this meeting with an attitude of, 'OK, you old codgers, just leave things to us'. Von Manstein's arrogance and the injurious manner in which he rejected von Weichs' arguments in favour of withdrawing Sixth Army created a very frosty and reserved atmosphere.

In vain von Weichs and his staff, General von Sodenstern and Colonel Winter, cited the opinion given by Generals of the Luftwaffe von Richthofen and Fiebig, that supplying Sixth Army by air was impossible. The reports by the Quartermasters of Sixth Army and of Army Group, that the supply stock of the army was virtually nil and that it would need 400 tonnes per day in addition to food and ammunition, were also in vain.

Von Manstein was not impressed. At 1300 hours he radioed Paulus: 'Am taking over command of Army Group Don effective 26.11. We will do everything to get you out. In the meantime everything depends on the army holding the Volga and north front according to Führer Order while providing strong forces as quickly as possible to be able to break open a temporary corridor of supply to the sw if necessary.'

In his excellent documentation of the battle, Manfred Kehrig comments on this. 'Von Manstein's agreement with the Führer's decision taken that morning could not have been demonstrated more clearly.'[8]

At 1315 hours von Manstein then reported to the OKH that a break-out by Sixth Army was still possible and would be the safest course (for its salvation). With regard to the ammunition and fuel situation, holding on (to Stalingrad) was an extreme risk. Adequate munitions supply was decisive. Recovery of the situation must start by the beginning of December. Even in four weeks, further divisions would not be too late.[9] This indicates that von Manstein clearly supported Hitler's opinion that holding on to Stalingrad, supplying the army by air, its relief, and even the recovery of the former situation, were all still possible. Like Hitler, he was prepared and determined to risk the extreme. There is no room for doubt that a possible order to break out would have been rescinded by Hitler under these circumstances and Paulus would have been relieved of his command. Hitler was now able to cite the evaluation of the situation given by the recognised highest strategic authority in the German army.

Would von Manstein have decided differently if Paulus had given the order to break out the day before? Or, on the contrary, would not the extremely self-assured Field Marshal have taken it as an enormous provocation, if Paulus had bypassed and committed him, his new superior, in such a fashion?

Admittedly, von Manstein's telex message also said that despite his evaluation, a break-out by Sixth Army to the south-west could still become necessary as an ultimate way out, particularly if heavy pressure by the enemy were to prevent the deployment of the new forces. But for the time being, and this judgement is shared by Manfred Kehrig, he had split the unified front of the commanders Paulus, von Weichs, von Richthofen (and Zeitzler, one must add).[10] With this the rug had been pulled from under the feet of any opposition to Hitler.

It is significant that in his portrayal of events von Manstein makes no mention of the fact that with his evaluation of the situation, he had stabbed all the other commanders in the back. Instead, he stresses the fact that both the General Staff officers under his command had agreed with him.[11]

What would have happened if instead of splitting this unified front, von Manstein had placed himself at its head? If he had done exactly what Paulus, according to his own later judgement, should have done barely twenty-four hours earlier, namely acted on his own authority and presented Hitler with an accomplished fact? He could simply have informed OKH: recovery of the situation completely impossible; supply by air ditto; insufficient forces available for a successful relief operation; immediate break-out by Sixth Army only way to save it; have therefore issued the order in agreement with former OB. of Hgr.(= Oberbefehlshaber der Heeresgruppe = Commander-in-Chief of Army Group) and Paulus; Luftwaffe to make greater effort to fly in urgently needed fuel; will advance towards Sixth Army with all forces still available as soon as possible!

Paulus would have been easy to replace. But von Manstein? Whom would Hitler have had up his sleeve if the Field Marshal he had just sent to this most critical sector of the whole eastern front as the saviour in time of need had, with a closed phalanx of like-minded commanders behind him, taken the initiative away from him in such a fashion?

Nobody! In any case, von Manstein would have been in a far stronger position professionally and psychologically than Paulus was in the pocket on the day before. If anybody could have changed the fate of Sixth Army, it was von Manstein at midday on 24 November.

Even less than von Manstein's decision, could Paulus have foreseen what was to take place at Führer Headquarters on the evening of the same day. There the Chief of Staff, General Zeitzler, was still arguing vehemently for giving up Stalingrad despite von Manstein's evaluation of the situation. A violent confrontation between him and Göring took place in the presence of Hitler. When the Reichsmarschall, right arm raised in the Nazi Salute, solemnly promised Hitler to supply Sixth Army by air, Zeitzler asked him if he had any inkling of the daily tonnage required. The embarrassed Göring had to admit that he didn't and could only refer to his staff. But now Zeitzler himself, quite incomprehensibly, gave a figure that was totally unrealistic, 300 tonnes per day, more likely 500 tonnes per flying day, because as he knew from experience, aircraft could not fly on every day during the Russian winter. Confronted with this figure, far too low, but still considerably exceeding the capabilities of the Luftwaffe, Göring regained his composure and declared, 'I can do that!' The outraged Zeitzler exclaimed, 'My Führer, that is a lie!' But it was too late. The astonished and confused Hitler glanced from one to the other and then declared that he had no recourse but to believe Göring. His original decision would remain valid.[12]

The supply situation

Zeitzler had asked Hitler to be allowed a daily report on the tonnage flown in. Apparently this was not done. On 26 or 28 November, an officer of the General Staff of the Luftwaffe, Lieutenant-Colonel Christian, did present grave reservations against Göring's commitment to Hitler and Jodl once again. He was not far from the truth when he declared that even under the most advantageous weather conditions, the maximum amount that could be flown in daily was 50 tonnes.[13] But after all, who would listen to a mere lieutenant-colonel?

In actual fact, during the next two weeks the average daily tonnage flown in did not reach 60 tonnes. In the following week it only reached 100 tonnes, so that the average for the three weeks was a meagre 70 tonnes.[14] What these figures represented in reality can be seen from a memorandum of 25 November from LI Corps under von Seydlitz. It lists the daily requirements by division:

Ammunition   50–100 t, depending on how heavy the fighting is.
Fuel   10 cbm, under extreme economies.
Food   10 t of soft food at half-rations: 6.5 t of durable food.

Under the most advantageous conditions (only 50 tonnes' consumption of ammunition) this totalled 600 tonnes for LI Corps alone and 1,500 tonnes for the whole army. These were absolutely realistic figures, proven in eighteen months of experience of war in Russia. Even after the war they were never questioned, despite the fact that many historians do not mention this part of the memorandum at all.[15]

How these figures could have shrunk to 300 tonnes on their way from LI Corps via Army to Zeitzler is past understanding. The quartermasters had stated that 400 tonnes were required in addition to ammunition and food. Even if one calculates only 1 kg of food per man per day, the total lies between 250 and 300 tonnes. Even if one again halves the ammunition requirement calculated by von Seydlitz for the whole army, one is still left with 550 tonnes of ammunition, in other words 1,200 tonnes in total. And that was now really the minimum with which the army could have survived for a short time and maintained its ability to break out.

In a telex message, von Manstein had mentioned 400 tonnes of ammunition and fuel alone as being the minimum requirement.[16] If one adds food, this still reaches 700 tonnes. Hitler was told, however, that the army only required 300 tonnes. In order to fly in von Manstein's 700 tonnes, 350 Ju 52 aircraft would have had to land in the pocket each day; one landing and take-off around the clock almost every four minutes, during the short winter day and the long winter night! If fog, icing, snowstorms, snow drifts at Pitomnik or one of the take-off bases, or enemy interference, were to lead to a reduction in time by only one third, a flight movement would have had to take place at Pitomnik almost every minute. Even if the Luftwaffe had disposed of the required number of Ju 52 aircraft, it would still have been virtually impossible. Up to 18 December, when von Manstein had to break off his relief offensive, there were to be only two days on which more than 100 aircraft landed in the pocket.

During the first three weeks of the air lift the daily average flown in was 70 tonnes: 6 tonnes of food (20 grams per man per day!) and 64 tonnes of ammunition and fuel on average, in other words, 10 per cent of the minimum total amount required by von Manstein, 16 per cent of the tonnage of ammunition and fuel that he had declared to be imperative.

As von Manstein wrote, it may well be that Hitler superstitiously over-estimated numbers and technology.[17] Why then were these figures not explained to him? For von Manstein, the figures appear not to have existed at all. Sixth Army was starving, running out of ammunition and becoming increasingly less mobile. Its ability to break out was lessening dramatically day by day. But von Manstein stuck to his timing and plan of operations as if everything were proceeding according to his wishes.

Maybe Sixth Army might have been able to escape from the pocket if it had been ready to break out and had actually jumped off on the day LVII Panzer Corps was able to launch its attack. That could have created the possibility, as von Seydlitz writes in his memorandum, of 'destroying the southern arm of the encircling pincers, pulling a large part of the army and its arms out of the catastrophe and saving it for the continuation of operations'.[18]

Maybe!

But the complete disaster of the air lift, about which no one could harbour any further illusions, left no other choice. Neither Paulus nor von Manstein could see their way clear to a corresponding decision.

It is possible that Paulus could not imagine how erroneously the Field Marshal was judging the overall situation. And what about von Manstein?

Von Manstein's area of responsibility

The critical reader of the chapter that von Manstein dedicated to the tragedy of Stalingrad in his book *Lost Victories*, will recognise that the portrayal constructed with such compelling logic is but a self-justification, intended to serve as a veil for the inadequacies of the relief operation carried out by Army Group and finally also, for the question of responsibility within the mutual relationship between the Commanders of the Army Group and of the Army.

By his impressive analysis of Hitler as a 'Supreme Commander', which he places ahead of it, von Manstein makes an effective psychological preparation for his portrayal of the catastrophe of Stalingrad. Enter the military dictator with his fatal characteristics: his suggestive manner, his superstitious over-estimation of technology and statistics, his belief in the omnipotence of his own will, his doggedness, his lack of self-control, his boundlessness. Hitler's fanatical clinging to the concept of rigid defence, his timidity when faced by an operational risk or far-reaching directives, his postponing of uncomfortable decisions. Above all, his constant interference in the details of command, that restricted and even paralysed the initiative and willingness to take decisions of lower and higher commanders at the front, normally led to catastrophic results. Here von Manstein has hinted at the inevitable conflict that must invariably have had to take place between himself and the 'Supreme Commander of the Armed Forces'.

The fact that this conflict did not result in a solution in the fatal weeks before and during the relief offensive is certainly described quite openly. But the degree to which the Field Marshal himself was also enmeshed in the responsibility for the catastrophic military events which inevitably led to the failure of the relief operation and the sacrifice of the encircled army, is not made clear.

At the end of the Stalingrad chapter he does raise the question of responsibility, but he makes the answer too easy on himself when he simply lets Hitler, to whom he was ordered to report on 6 February 1943, in other words immediately after the end of the battle, speak. Von Manstein writes: 'He who wishes to pursue the question of the responsibility for the tragedy of Sixth Army, has been given a clear answer by Hitler himself ... Hitler opened the meeting with the words, "I alone bear the responsibility for Stalingrad! Maybe I could say that Göring painted me an inaccurate picture of the possibilities of the air lift by the Luftwaffe and thereby shunt at least a part of the responsibility off on him. But he is my successor whom I myself have selected and I cannot burden him with the responsibility for Stalingrad."'[19]

Von Manstein respectfully emphasises that Hitler accepted the responsibility for the tragedy of Stalingrad unequivocally. He calls this stance 'soldierly decent'. All the more embarrassing, therefore, that the Field Marshal strongly accuses his subordinate and comrade at the time, General Paulus, and blames him for the fatal failure of the relief operation. Had von Manstein then been totally relieved of any responsibility within the framework of his allegedly infallible strategic conduct?

With regard to his powers of command and his rights of disposition over Sixth Army, it was first of all up to him to do, or to leave alone, whatever he believed to be necessary for the discharge of his assignment. It was his duty to enforce the decisions that the situation required, both upwards and downwards. His claim that the encircled army had been under the direct command of OHK for all practical purposes and that its subordination under Army Group was more or less fictitious, has been refuted by the sources just as clearly as has his opinion that Hitler's liaison officer in the Stalingrad pocket had played a fatal role and by his reports directly to Führer Headquarters had contributed to the top level disagreement about withdrawal from Stalingrad. Sixth Army actually was under the command of Army Group! This is made clear by the orders issued by von Manstein, and even more so by the papers bequeathed by Field Marshal Paulus, the extant official war diary of Sixth Army and many other documents. That Hitler occasionally directly addressed himself to individual army commanders and repeatedly issued directives directly to Stalingrad, does not contradict this fact.[20]

In any case, Sixth Army did not receive a single order directly from Hitler during the entire course of the relief operation. General Paulus and his staff not only felt themselves to be totally under the command of Army Group, but on top of that placed an extraordinarily high degree of trust in Field Marshal von Manstein, who was revered as a strategic authority. 'Permit me to report', wrote the Commander of the encircled army on 26 November 1942, 'that in your leadership, Field Marshal, I see the guarantee that everything will be done to aid Sixth Army.'[21]

After the war, Colonel General Zeitzler, Army Chief of Staff, again expressly confirmed in a letter to General Doerr, author of the first military history on Stalingrad, that there could be no question about the reporting relationship between Sixth Army and Army Group Don at the time.[22]

Contrary to von Manstein's claim, the Supreme Command's liaison officer in the Stalingrad pocket did not have a function that interfered with or restricted the powers of command by Army Group. Nor had he been sent by Hitler personally, but by General Zeitzler, who wanted, probably because of his continual conflict with the pig-headed dictator, to be directly informed about occurrences at Sixth Army as quickly as possible.[23]

We can assume without question that von Manstein was firmly resolved to free the encircled army and, if necessary, withdraw it from Stalingrad against Hitler's orders.

But, did he, as he wishes us to gather from his memoirs, actually issue the decisive order for the start of Operation 'Thunderclap', in other words for giving up the 'corner pillar on the Volga', thereby relieving General Paulus from the responsibility of acting on his own authority against the orders of the Supreme Command? From the estate of Field Marshal Paulus and other existing documents it can clearly be seen that Sixth Army never received this order. When, on 23 December 1942, the critical point in time of the last chance for a break-out, Paulus again pressed for the start of Operation Thunderclap in an exchange of telex messages, von Manstein put him off by declaring that he could not yet give him the authorisation.[24]

Since the order to evacuate Stalingrad that the Commander of Sixth Army had repeatedly asked for was not forthcoming, Army Group in fact did not take on the responsibility for an unauthorised action against the will of Hitler, despite the order of 19 December which demanded a break-through to the relieving forces, but only spoke of the evacuation of the 'fortress' as a possibility. In any case, von Manstein's ultimate objectives were not clear to Sixth Army Command. And even the documents from the time contradict the later portrayal in *Lost Victories* in many respects and bathe the leadership of Army Group in those tragic days immediately before Christmas 1942 in a problematical light.

For this reason, von Manstein decided to issue a critical statement against Walter Görlitz's book *I Stand Here Under Orders*, even before its publication,[25] declaring that the portrayal of the key problem of a breakout by Sixth Army in the days of December to be a 'one-sidedly coloured picture'.

He tries again to reinforce the point of view developed in his memoirs and, in particular, to state more precisely the intentions of his orders at the time. Von Manstein explains that he was prepared to camouflage Operation 'Thunderclap' from Hitler, who would not have permitted giving up the Volga at any price. Army Group could not have ordered the final break-out and the evacuation of Stalingrad from the outset, because the dictator would have countermanded such an order immediately. However, if initially Operation 'Thunderclap', designed to break through to the relieving forces and form a corridor for re-supply, had gone ahead as ordered, a withdrawal of the rest of the front within the pocket would automatically have become necessary and Hitler would have had to submit to that imperative.

From this one can deduce that von Manstein had obviously only intended to accept the responsibility for the evacuation of the 'fortress', after Paulus had taken the lead by an unauthorised action. But the staff of Sixth Army, poorly informed on the overall situation and burdened by many cares, could not divine the intentions of the Field Marshal. Neither the order of 19 December nor later telex messages reveal that von Manstein wished to induce Sixth Army into a camouflaged withdrawal from Stalingrad.

This is obviously a grave omission. If Army Group had really intended to carry out Operation 'Thunderclap' in a camouflaged version and been prepared to accept the responsibility for ordering the final break-out against Hitler's orders, the cards should have been laid on the table for Paulus unconditionally. In view of such grave and momentous decisions, a personal exchange between the two commanders would most certainly have been called for.

Field Marshal von Manstein could have flown into the pocket for this purpose and informed the Commander of Sixth Army about his plans and thoughts, frankly and without holding anything back. If he did not wish to fly in himself, he should at least have sent a senior officer to Paulus, preferably his Chief of Staff. This would certainly have been possible without further ado.

A young officer of the General Staff who worked in the quartermaster department of the encircled army and whose heart beat feverishly in anticipation of the longed-for break-out, had occasion to listen-in to several of the short telephone conversations that took place between the two commanders in those critical days. He was astonished about how 'empty' and 'colourless' they were and that 'much was left unsaid ...': 'Von Manstein answered Paulus' precise questions on the situation in general and on the air lift in particular, with prevarications. I had expected that such questions by our commander would receive precise answers by von Manstein, in other words with firm dates on which help could be expected. This was not the case.'[26]

Many statements bear witness to the fact that despite Major Eismann's mission, Sixth Army was poorly informed about the situation at Army Group at the time, particularly about the progress of the relief operation. Von Manstein obviously refrained from making the alternatives clear to the Commander of the encircled army with the necessary directness and urgency; last possible chance for a break-out or assured destruction. He knew the character of General Paulus to be that of a thoroughly evaluating, meticulously checking General Staff man, who was not at all prone to act with decisive audacity and who could not easily take the step from judging to jumping.

Under these circumstances, an exceptionally firm and unambiguous leadership of Army by Army Group would have been all the more important. And von Manstein's orders on the critical factors of timing and manner of execution of the break-out should not have left any questions unanswered. However, since this was not the case, the process of decision by the staff of Sixth Army was inhibited and influenced in a negative manner.

Von Manstein would certainly not have been lacking in the arguments, will-power and authority required to convince the staff of the Stalingrad army of the necessity of his decisions and measures. That he did not bring these to bear and also refrained from imposing his orders, remains a characteristic of his ambiguous leadership at the time.

He is not convincing when he explains that Army Group had been 'powerless', because it was not able to impose a solution that Paulus considered to be impossible, particularly in view of Hitler's refusal to permit a break-out, never mind the reports from Sixth Army itself, whose prepared attack forces were restricted in mobility and pinned to the defence by the Russian attacks.

Many causes probably contributed to von Manstein's unsure and indecisive conduct at this time. Among them were certainly his grinding worry about the extremely critical overall situation of Army Group, his recognition of the insufficiency of the relief offensive whose impending failure made the possible success of a break-out appear doubtful, and his secret unease that Army Group had not succeeded in obtaining freedom of action for the Stalingrad army from Hitler.

Shortcomings and failures

As the Commander of Army Group Don, von Manstein found himself caught in a tragic dilemma. Within the parameters of a catastrophic starting situation for which Hitler was to blame, he had undertaken an assignment in the fullness of his impressive self-assurance, one which probably also flattered his ambition, that had to be mastered under specific conditions that did not depend on his will alone.

It was his foremost duty to bend all his energies to ensuring an operational leadership that held out the promise of success. He clear-sightedly analysed the military situation with all its extraordinary difficulties and dangers. He appreciated, warned, predicted and reported time and again. As absolute conditions for accepting the risk of not having the Stalingrad army break out immediately and for the success of his planned relief operation in general, he had demanded sufficient supply of the encircled forces by air, the immediate urgent deployment of strong relief forces and their constant reinforcement, and the withdrawal of Sixth Army from Stalingrad as well.

Not one of these conditions was met, however. A satisfactory supply by air proved to be impossible from the outset. The local Luftwaffe commanders had left no doubt about this beforehand, pointing out the lack of cargo space and the difficulties caused by the weather. The bringing in of new divisions, and these mainly from the Caucasus, was greatly delayed. And so far as the strength of the relief forces was concerned, the demands of Army Group could in no way be met. Furthermore, Hitler's reactions to von Manstein's repeated insistent requests and evaluations of the situation showed only too clearly that the Supreme Commander had no intention of giving up Stalingrad.

The Field Marshal fought a vain battle for the necessary decisions. The circumstances favouring his actions deteriorated from week to week. The scope of his operational freedom was dangerously restricted by the dilettantism and recklessness of the Supreme Command. Even if he did energetically and purposefully try, as he claims to have done, to do all that was conceivably possible within his remaining power of command and action, he was not able to avert the disaster. Over his decisions and measures hangs the doom-laden 'inadequate' and 'too late'. This has also been underlined by Soviet military critics.[27]

Only begun on 12 December, with forces that were far too weak, and aiming northwards from Kotelnikovo, the relief offensive by the Panzer Army under Colonel General Hoth stood under an unlucky star from the outset. Jumping off for its hazardous advance across the snowy Kalmyk steppe towards the Stalingrad pocket 150 kilometres away, the army actually consisted of a weak panzer corps, of two panzer divisions, only one of which was fresh and well-equipped for battle, and a weak flank protection provided by two Roumanian corps. This was all that was eventually made available of the eleven divisions on which von Manstein had originally counted. The so-called Army Detachment Hollidt that was to advance on Kalach from the middle Chir, in other words from a westerly direction, was soon involved in heavy defensive fighting and its already badly depleted forces were therefore no longer available for the relief operation.

What the Field Marshal calls 'the greatest risk' that had to be run if Sixth Army were to be saved, was basically an act of desperation that contained the germs of failure from the outset, ultimately also because of the strength and proven operational flexibility of the enemy. Nevertheless von Manstein felt that he could accept the responsibility for this questionable venture. Probably this was still a sort of after-effect of the self-assurance and feeling of superiority of the German leadership, that came from years of becoming accustomed to victory. But one must also ask whether a fatal under-estimation of the enemy were not also playing a role, despite all the correct theoretical evaluations.

Let us listen to how a sharply observing and soberly evaluating Panzer general describes the relief offensive, in which he played a leading role. Frido von Senger und Etterlin, Commander of 17th Panzer Division, which having been brought in too late and then idiotically held at the wrong place for days by Hitler, could only intervene in the final phase of the relief offensive, writes the following in his war memoirs.

'In my last comfortable quarters on the march, I experienced an internal conflict between my strategic conscience and my tactical assignment. It was remarkable that the attempt to relieve Stalingrad was to be undertaken with forces that were insufficient. A bit further on and still ninety kilometres distant from the encircled Stalingrad army, two divisions were engaged in battle. Of these, Sixth Panzer Division was one of the lucky ones that had just been completely brought up to strength in France. The other, 23rd Panzer Division, was alleged to be in an even worse *matériel* condition than my own 17th. One full and one half-strength division were supposed to push through an approximately 100-kilometres-deep advance to Stalingrad! The initial so-called surprise was already gone. For two weeks the two divisions had already been bogged down in front of stronger enemy forces. But even if surprise had been on their side, they could not have maintained themselves in the depth of the space that needed to be overcome. No one could assume that the enemy would do less than his utmost with all the forces at his command to prevent the relief of the encircled Sixth Army, in order to let his great victory mature. The weakness of the offensive forces permitted me to conclude that we had no more reserves available.'[28]

The impressive report by Horst Scheibert on the relieving attack by Sixth Panzer Division, which had to bear the brunt of the fighting, also leaves no room for doubt that in the final analysis the praiseworthy efforts of the bravely attacking troops, the tactical art of leadership in all its details and all the willingness for self-sacrifice demonstrated during unremitting fighting by day and by night, only served a task that had been impossible from the outset.[29]

When, after very heavy fighting and losses, the German Panzer spearheads had temporarily forced a weak bridgehead in the Myshkova sector about fifty kilometres from the Stalingrad pocket and were threatened on all sides, the exhausted corps had already gone over to the defensive and the superior enemy forces had gained the initiative. The relief operation had failed. In the meantime the crisis-fraught situation had again climaxed as a consequence of new, successful enemy offensives on the Chir and in the big bend of the Don. And this in turn meant that the operational possibilities for a successful break-out by Sixth Army were highly dubious, even before von Manstein saw himself forced to withdraw the capable Sixth Panzer Division and deploy it in the bend of the Don as protection against the deadly threat to the left flank of Army Group.

On this, von Senger und Etterlin writes: 'The defeat was total. The enemy had obviously provided strong forces. What I had feared at the beginning of the relief attempt had come to pass ... I had experienced the situation at the spearheads of the advance and was forced to reject as too optimistic the opinion that it was still possible at the time for Sixth Army to break out opposite Fourth Panzer Army, an effort for which, according to its own reports, it only had fuel for thirty kilometres.'[30]

In the portrayal of his operations at the time and of the continual crises under which they were carried out, von Manstein repeatedly proves the Soviet Command to have made mistakes and missed opportunities. Mainly, it missed the chance of cutting the lifeline of the entire German southern wing by a daring advance on Rostov, thereby taking a decisive step towards final victory.

But what the Russian forces had achieved in the Don–Volga area by Christmas of 1942 was no mean thing. The defensive front of Army

Group Don had been dangerously torn apart and driven far back. After they had succeeded in beating off von Manstein's relief offensive, the Russians could now regard the army encircled in Stalingrad as sure prey. This time, Soviet action had caused the Field Marshal's art of war to fail and the sensitive defeat was bound to have serious repercussions on the entire Army Group.

As becomes evident in von Manstein's portrayal, the contradiction between correct insight in theory and inadequate action in practice, for the success of which the repeatedly demanded conditions were lacking, shows us the tragic dilemma in which the Field Marshal was caught and in which ultimately he had no recourse but to give in and act against his own better insight and conscience.

In view of the dangers of the initial overall situation, which von Manstein so clearly recognised, and the disappointments very early on in his futile conflicts with the Supreme Command, we must ask ourselves whether under the pressure of the gigantic responsibility weighing on him, the Field Marshal in fact really did do everything within his power to impose on Hitler the mandatory conditions for a sensible operation.

He was certainly not remiss in making detailed, serious reports and urgent presentations filled with sharp-eyed analyses of the situation and its requirements. But what did he achieve in practice? Among other things, the issues were to obtain agreement to a timely abandonment of Stalingrad and to make the dictator, who did not want to leave the Volga at any price for reasons of prestige, really understand the magnitude of the fatal risk and consequences of leaving Sixth Army in Stalingrad.

For such a purpose, factual reports written in the normal manner of the General Staff probably lacked the power to convince. This can best be demonstrated by the example of the detailed situation report of 9 December 1942, in which von Manstein used poor psychology and added grist to the dictator's mill by his weighing of the pros and cons. 'If we were to leave the army in the fortress area, it is within the realm of possibility that the Russians will also sink their teeth in here and slowly but surely bleed themselves to death in useless attacks, so that Stalingrad may therefore become the graveyard of his offensive power.'[31] To do justice to the particular situation of grave anxiety in which Army Group found itself, an extraordinarily insistent and unambiguous tone and a sharp wording beyond the norm was called for.

Faced with the constant danger of the downfall of a large army and the destruction of two army groups lurking in the background, why did the Field Marshal in his negotiations with the Supreme Military Command not throw the whole weight of the authority of his person into the scales? He knew that Hitler respected him particularly highly as one of his most able strategists and as the author of the plan of operations for the campaign in the West. When he realised in the first weeks of December that only a fraction of the formations he had demanded would be made available so that the outcome of the relief operation was doubtful from the start, it was high time to fly to Führer Headquarters, present his demands in the form of an ultimatum and insist on effective measures as a condition for retaining the command of Army Group. On such an occasion, von Manstein would have been able to lend Chief of Staff Zeitzler useful support in his continual bitter battle with Hitler over vital decisions.

At the time, the whole fate of the southern front depended on a sensible and timely resolution of the decisive issues: improvement of the inadequate air lift for Sixth Army, abandonment of Stalingrad and, in close context with the problems of the relief operation, withdrawal of Army Group A from the Caucasus. As soon as Sixth Army was surrounded by the massive Soviet encircling offensive on 21 November, forces from Army Group A in the Caucasus should have been sent off to its relief. From there, von Manstein later received only one depleted panzer division. Why did he submit to such an insufficient allotment of forces from the neighbouring Army Group which could not hold its position in the long run in any case, unless the Don front were re-stabilised?

Only after the relief operation had failed on 27/28 December and it was much too late, did he insist on the immediate allotment of a panzer corps from the Caucasus in order to strengthen the depleted Fourth Panzer Army after its defeat and to plan a new advance towards Stalingrad. Would it not already have been possible in early December for von Manstein, supported by the Chief of the General Staff, whose opinions he knew to be the same as his own, to have decisively demanded of Hitler that the forces in the Caucasus be withdrawn immediately? If the situation on the Don were to be recovered at all, OKH had to be persuaded as early as possible to initiate operational movements in the Kalmyk steppe with Army Group A and to bring up its forces for use in the relief of Stalingrad. Had this been done, the worst of the tragedy could have been prevented.

That the Chief of the General Staff was looking for support from von Manstein's personal intervention with Hitler can be seen from the following report by Kunrat von Hammerstein. 'General Zeitzler, at that time Chief of Staff, hoped that as a responsible Commander-in-Chief von Manstein could disabuse Hitler of the notion of holding on to Stalingrad. Von Manstein did not wish to come, claiming to be indispensable where he was. He only came after he had been ordered to do so and went directly to Hitler. Zeitzler, who had wanted to talk to von Manstein beforehand, missed him at the airport. When he asked him after the meeting with Hitler what he had achieved, the answer was: "I can't make headway against that flood of words."'[32]

At high points in the various crises of his futile battle with the Supreme Command for sensible measures during the tragedy of Stalingrad, von Manstein repeatedly considered resigning command of Army Group. According to his statements, he refrained from doing so at the time from a sense of responsibility towards his soldiers. In this connection we must ask the question whether it was not an omission, at the beginning of the catastrophic development he foresaw, not to have used the threat of resignation as an effective weapon against the dictator. Maybe such an unbending stance in the interest of the whole, would have served to force the pig-headed Supreme Commander of the Armed Forces to give in on crucial decisions, he being particularly dependent on the abilities of his Field Marshal at this critical time. Von Manstein did not do this. Thereby he not only lost complete sovereignty on his home ground of strategy, he also lost an essential part of his personality. He bowed to the pressure of obeying despite superior insight, and resigned himself to becoming the executive organ of a dilettante leadership that refused to recognise the foreseeable. With this, he took on a far greater measure of responsibility than did his unhappy subordinate General Paulus, because he had the broader overview and saw more clearly what the game was and what needed to be done.

The bitter sentence that Colonel General Freiherr von Richthofen, chief of the air fleet that was co-operating with Army Group Don for the salvation of the encircled army during those critical weeks, temperamentally noted down in his diary without mincing words, apply to von Manstein as well, '... seen operationally, the way things are now one is but a highly paid sergeant ...'[33]

In his memoirs the Field Marshal admits that in view of the varying statements made by Sixth Army itself, Army Group was not able to obtain the accurate number of the men trapped in the pocket. But his argument that 'the number of between 200,000 and 220,000 men in the pocket is probably quite accurate despite the strong allotments of army artillery and engineers' is not convincing. We have sufficient documentation available today to enable the question to be answered with a high degree of certainty, if not with complete accuracy.

In October 1942, about one month before the Russian encircling offensive began, Sixth Army's registered number of mouths to be fed was 334,000. This made it the strongest formation in its Army Group. Up to 19 November it suffered about 17,000 casualties. The losses caused by the Russian penetrations in the days following are estimated at 34,000 men. Added to that, there were 39,000 men, mainly from the rear echelon services and trains, who were deployed on the Chir front.

The mass of Sixth Army remaining in the pocket was augmented by the strong formations of Fourth Panzer Army (two corps), substantial units of the Luftwaffe and the remnant of two Roumanian divisions, none of which were formerly included. The data compiled by H. Schröter on the basis of official documentation is highly credible, since it corresponds to the calculations made at the time by experts of Sixth Army and can also be reconciled with the figures officially published by the Soviets.[34] According to this, the number of men in the pocket after the encirclement lay between 270,000 and 280,000.

In the initial phase of the battle the number of approximately 300,000 was repeatedly mentioned among our staff at VIII Corps, which was in close contact with the supply staffs at Pitomnik air base for many long weeks. During the fighting it was possible to fly out about 25,000 sick, wounded and specialists. The concluding official Russian report spoke of 91,000 officers and men taken prisoner, but only from 10 January 1943 on, and of 147,200 'registered and interred' dead.[35]

Incidentally, the Chief Quartermaster of Sixth Army, Major von Kunowski, calculated the total number of encircled forces remaining at the start of the final Russian offensive on 10 January to have been

195,000 men. Von Manstein is no doubt correct when he states that a claimed number in excess of 300,000 men encircled from the beginning is an exaggeration.

But his own estimate seems to me to be too low by 60,000 human beings – a number, by the way, that equates to the total mass of men in a full-strength German army corps. Finally, in his letter of 26 November 1942 addressed to the Field Marshal, which von Manstein quotes in another context and which he includes in his memoirs as appendix no. 9, General Paulus speaks in earnest responsibility of the '... at least 300,000 men I have been entrusted with'.[36]

In his accounting report the Chief Quartermaster of the Stalingrad army, who was responsible for supply, initially in the pocket and later on at Army Group, and who was bound to know best about the worries and needs of the forces, gives a figure of 270,000 for the beginning and 250,000 for the middle of December, the time span during which he was learning his duties as Quartermaster.[37] General Fiebig, Commander of VIII Air Corps and responsible for the air lift, was also given the number of '270,000 men within the fortress ring' when he oriented himself on the situation personally during a visit to Paulus and his Chief of Staff on 11 December.[38]

In appendix no. 5 of Manfred Kehrig's documentation on Stalingrad, figures appear that on the one hand have probably given rise to the continuing controversy about the actual number of soldiers in the pocket and on the other hand have not received the recognition they deserve, neither in the German nor in the Soviet literature on Stalingrad.[39]

This appendix shows that in mid November there were more than 50,000 *Hilfswillige* (voluntary helpers) and so-called *zugeteilte Personen* (assigned persons), in other words Russian prisoners of war, who had been forced into working for the Wehrmacht in breach of international law, with only sixteen of the twenty divisions plus the anti-aircraft division, that were later encircled. If one assumes the same ratio for the remaining divisions, there were approximately 60,000 Russian prisoners of war with Sixth Army, most of whom had to have been inside the pocket.

The original orders read that these 'Hiwis' and 'Zugeteilte' were not to be fed from army stocks but exclusively from the resources of the occupied territories, 'off of the land'. Therefore, they do not appear in the personnel and *matériel* statistics of Sixth Army under the heading of mouths to be fed, but are listed separately.

On 6 January 1943, Doctor General Renoldi, the head of medical services for Sixth Army, stated that from the beginning of December 1942 the army was conducting an experiment in starvation on a large scale. The daily rations amounted to barely half of what a working person needed in calories per day.[40] Given the circumstances, the feeding arrangements for these prisoners can be imagined. Within the pocket, they could no longer be fed 'off of the land'. All available sources are mute as to how many of them survived the battle. Many of the survivors of Stalingrad were witnesses to the fact that after the surrender the Red Army shot some of these unfortunates on the spot. Did the Russian Supreme Command include these people in the 100,000 prisoners it reported?

The rejection of the Soviet surrender proposal of 8 January 1943, and the outright refusal of the Army leadership to negotiate an orderly capitulation at all then or at a later date, led to terrible consequences. It cost the lives of the 20,000 men that Manfred Kehrig calculated to have fallen on the battlefield itself during subsequent combat. It also cost the lives of the estimated 30,000 to 40,000 wounded who lay in the remaining field hospitals or in the cellars of the ruins of Stalingrad virtually unattended. It cost the lives of almost 90,000 men who were taken prisoner in such a state of starvation, exhaustion and sickness that they had no chance of surviving the initial hardships, sufferings and deprivations of captivity.

There are certainly many reasons for questioning whether the German prisoners would have been very much better off if an orderly capitulation had been negotiated in time, than they were under the conditions of chaos and lack of leadership that prevailed at the time the fighting died down at the end of January and the beginning of February. But it would have been the natural obligation of the Army leadership, arising from loyalty to the soldiers entrusted to it, of whom almost 200,000 remained on 10 January, to negotiate an orderly capitulation. This would have put the obligation on the Russians to ensure those conditions they themselves had named in their proposal for a surrender: strict adherence to international law and the laws of war, adequate care and shelter for survival, medical care and repatriation immediately after the end of the war.

To have submitted to the inhumane order forbidding surrender is the worst accusation that one can make against the Army leadership. It cannot absolve itself from this by any alleged military necessities, be they ever so contrived. There is a point beyond which one cannot demand of any soldier that he suffer more bitterly, more cruelly, more horribly still, for the mistakes, total lack of responsibility and boundless arrogance of his leaders.

This 'loyalty' to Hitler which, on top of everything else, the Army leadership expressed in a series of insufferable radio messages reeking with Nazi phrases, is a stigma that will cling to it for ever.

In his memoirs, von Manstein erroneously places the final capitulation one day ahead. It took place on 2 February 1943. After Paulus, who had been promoted to Field Marshal in the final hour, acting against his own order to hold on that was never rescinded, had already capitulated with his immediate entourage in the early morning of 31 January, leaving his troops to fight on without him, the senseless resistance under General Strecker continued in the northern pocket and only finally ended on the afternoon of 2 February. I stress this here, because every single day was important then. Each successive day cost thousands of human lives.

Stalingrad was no ordinary defeat

So far as the 'recovery of the situation' of which von Manstein speaks is concerned, this term should not literally be taken to mean the recovery of the positions lost to the Russian offensive, something which, however, the Supreme Command actually did expect at the beginning. The issue was rather 'to bring the defeat to heel', if we may cite this quotation from von Schlieffen which von Manstein frequently uses, or to put it more clearly, to reorganise and stabilise the front after the successful withdrawal of the forces pressed so hard by the enemy. After the loss of Sixth Army, the Field Marshal brilliantly succeeded in accomplishing this in the midst of a continuing grave threat from a vastly superior enemy.

But no operational leadership, no matter how virtuous, could compensate or eradicate from the memory the horror that had taken place in Stalingrad. No strategic calculations, no matter how clever, could banish the manifold moral and political repercussions to the world that resulted from the catastrophic German defeat on the Volga. It was not only the loss of one of the best and strongest German armies; not only the doom of some 200,000 men, in itself tragedy enough and affecting close to one million families throughout the provinces of Germany and Austria.

The catastrophe on the Volga caused by Hitler triggered off an avalanche of Russian offensives in the course of which two Roumanian armies, an Italian army and a Hungarian army were destroyed. Within a short period of time, the total mass of our allies deployed in the Russian theatre was wiped out. If one also takes into consideration the huge sacrifices that were made in connection with the relief offensive, plus the defensive fighting , the battle of Stalingrad and the associated events cost the lives of several hundred thousand human beings. The vast, 1,000-kilometres-long sector of the front between the Terek and Voronezh had been rent apart and more than sixty divisions and an entire air fleet had been engulfed.

This was not only a catastrophe in terms of loss of fighting power. The moral after-effects on the troops and civilian population were soon apparent, as was the increased self-confidence and will to fight of the enemy who had now seized the initiative. And the repercussions on domestic and foreign politics were not long delayed.[41] If one takes into account the fact that we were engaged in a total war in which psychological factors are bound to play a decisive role, then the battle of Stalingrad was something the like of which had never been heard of before, something that went beyond the boundaries of all previous experience. It was obviously the turning-point of the war.[42]

In a letter to General Olbricht of 17 May 1943, Goerdeler expressed what uncounted Germans deeply felt at the time and what was later confirmed by the verdict of history. 'Stalingrad and Tunisia are such heavy defeats as have not been recorded in German history since Jena and Auerstedt. In both cases the German people were told that overriding reasons had demanded the sacrifice of armies. We know that this is not true. Soldiers and politicians can only justify such sacrifices as being necessary that guarantee a success in some other area which outweighs the sacrifice. In actual fact, what we are dealing with is an incompetent leadership devoid of conscience ...'[43]

Is a 'death sentence' as at Stalingrad a legitimate decision?

The deep humane and ethical problems that plunged so many of us at Stalingrad into despair when the final agony of our bled-out and no longer adequately supplied army had run its course during January 1943 without being curtailed by orders from above, can be summarised by the following questions – questions which torment me just as violently now, after having read von Manstein's book, as they did then. Are human beings allowed to order and demand from other human beings such a terrible measure of unspeakable suffering, such a drawn-out horrible death agony, such an increasing violation of human dignity itself? Was not the order for the death of almost 200,000 human beings incompatible with the code of ethics from the very beginning? Was it not mandatory that such an unheard-of sacrifice be linked with a result that was truly decisive for the war? Should not the fate of an entire army have depended on a far deeper and more encompassing sense of responsibility? Was it permissible, and could such a gigantic sacrifice actually serve to re-establish a strategic balance – one that in the long run was perhaps illusory? Could not being a soldier and being a human being, military thinking and humane-ethical feeling, have been brought into harmony with each other? Was there no one among those responsible who was prepared to act bravely and effectively from better insight to avert the approaching disaster in time, or to shorten it after it had become unavoidable?

For me, what happened in Stalingrad no longer appears to be comparable to one of those sad sacrifices that are demanded from time to time by the harsh rules of war. The Way of the Cross of our army, particularly because of the slow, helpless dying of so many tens of thousands under circumstances that mocked traditional foundations of soldierly duty and honour, seemed to reduce anything that happened before to insignificance. A part of the vital substance of the German nation was condemned to destruction here. In the final analysis what was demanded and allowed to happen was a humiliation and violation of the human essence beyond measure. At the close of the battle I felt that a large portion of humanity had also sunk into the mass grave of Stalingrad.

By the second week of January, when the first surrender demand by the Russians was rejected, the combat power of Sixth Army had already become marginal. The troops were exhausted by long weeks of hardship. They no longer had enouigh to eat; ammunition was sunning short; the few remaining heavy weapons were mostly immobilised by lack of fuel and now provided hardly any support; there was no adequete protection against the heavy frost; and soon even the most primitive means and and conditions for the medical care of the sick and wounded, slowly increasing in number to become a horrific mass, were lacking. Even today I think back with horror to the daily casualty reports from the divisions of our VIII Corps who began to report sudden deaths without enemy action shortly after Christmas, which were a shattering balance sheet of death.

During the last week in December the German OKH had already sent an outstanding pathologist from Berlin into the pocket, who had the secret assignment to perform autopsies in order to discover why so many soldiers were suddenly dying from causes other than combat. The result of autopsies performed on many thawed-out bodies read. 'Under the skin and surrounding the inner organs, hardly a trace of fat; in the mesentery a watery-gelatinous mass; the organs very pale; instead of red and yellow bone marrow, a glassy, wobbly jelly; the liver congested; the heart small and brown; the right ventricle and atrium greatly enlarged.'

Hans Diebold reports on these examinations in his touching notes. As the Austrian doctor said at the time in a presentation to his assembled colleagues in Stalingrad, hunger, exhaustion and loss of body heat were the prime reasons for the enlargement of the right ventricle and were '... the cause for the sudden death of the used-up bodies gone senile of what had been German soldiers'.[44]

Admittedly, these already exhausted forces had initially still tied down strong enemy forces and for a number of days again offered desperate resistance, when the last Russian offensive broke loose with destructive power on 10 January. But after the enemy had finally shattered the western and northern perimeter of the pocket and had taken Pitomnik air base on the 16th, the heart of the army, the combat power of the troops was largely broken. The already insufficient air lift came to almost a complete stop on the auxiliary air bases used later.

Now was the time when, for humane reasons, the Commander-in-Chief should have ended a resistance that was becoming more and more senseless from day to day, and begun negotiations for a surrender against orders. All the vital conditions and soldierly circumstances for a continuation of the battle had ceased to exist.

Von Manstein's page-long, emotionally presented strategic justification of the final sacrifice demanded of Sixth Army for the withdrawal of the forces in the Caucasus and the establishment of a new front, a line of argument that smacks of the former self-serving official propaganda, appears in a dubious light under the circumstances described here.

In Stalingrad the troops knew nothing of the alleged reasons for the sacrifice they were being called upon to make. They were only ordered to fight to the last man and bullet. They were no longer being informed about the radio messages coming in to Army staff, in which there was talk of their heroic contribution to the salvation of the Army Group, of the whole eastern front, yes, even of the Western world. In the written justifications of the generals, the controversy today is about whether 16, 20 or 24 January 1943 had been the acceptable dates to end the fighting. In contrast to this, let us simply state that from mid January onwards the order for the continuing death march of the unhappy army was irresponsible and no longer in accordance with the code of ethics. Chief of Staff Zeitzler, who was best able to judge the overall situation and its requirements, makes no mention at all of the military reasons for the allegedly absolute necessity to sacrifice the Stalingrad army. On the contrary! When the first Russian surrender proposal was received on 8 January, he immediately addressed himself to Hitler in support of Paulus' request for freedom of action and suggested a surrender to be appropriate, without giving any consideration to the claim that the army was tying down enemy forces and keeping them away from other sectors of the front.[45]

At the beginning of the last week in January, the Chief Quartermaster of Sixth Army estimated the number of wounded and sick that could no longer be cared for to be in excess of 50,000.[46] Signs of dissolution began to appear and 364 death sentences that were executed are part of the tale of horror that was not being brought to an end by the high command. How could true soldiery survive under such conditions? Its healthy foundations and ethical principles had been eroded. In Stalingrad it was replaced in the end by a soulless militarism with a misunderstood and abused sense of duty and a mechanistic concept of honour.

General Hans Doerr's verdict on Stalingrad and the sacrifice of Sixth Army shows a greater sense of responsibility than does von Manstein's. 'I am not sure whether telling those who lived through Stalingrad and the relatives of the dead and still missing that the downfall of Sixth Army was a necessary sacrifice for military reasons, will be a consolation or a satisfaction for them. According to generally accepted humane and religious concepts, the term "sacrifice" contains a positive core. The death of the Saviour on the Cross was a sacrifice for all mankind. Primitive cultures made sacrifices in order to obtain the grace of some god. We know of innumerable cases in which a human being sacrificed his life in order to save someone else. None of this applies to Sixth Army. The more clearly the subsequent course of the war and its catastrophic ending demonstrated that nothing had been gained by the downfall of this army, the more it became apparent that the term "sacrifice" was inappropriate... Out of our responsibility before history, from which future generations should learn a lesson, we must reject the claim of the sacrifice of a complete army for military reasons as being factually incorrect and ethically untenable.'[47]

Von Manstein wants surrender but does not give the order

There can be no further question that on 22 January, when Field Marshal von Manstein, together with the Commander of Sixth Army, also felt that it was time urgently to request permission to surrender, the limits of what could reasonably be expected from a humane and ethical standpoint had already been exceeded. Von Manstein no longer believed that he could accept the responsibility for the death agony of Sixth Army, even though the dying troops were allegedly still pinning down superior enemy forces and thereby keeping them from being used against other parts of the menaced Army Group. On top of that we cannot even assume that by the second half of January all the ninety Russian formations of which von Manstein speaks in his rather summary statements on the enemy situation, were all still facing the shrinking perimeter of the pocket in their entirety.

The Russians had gradually been offered the opportunity to draw off forces no longer required and to reorganise their lines of supply. They certainly made use of this soon after mid January. When we marched into captivity the mass of their forces had long left the scene of the battle. Only the higher staffs and rear echelon services were still left. There can be no doubt that the Russians took their time to destroy the remaining pocket. After the capture of Pitomnik air base it took them two more weeks to end the battle, in other words, they advanced only about one to two kilometres per day.

In several German portrayals and interpretations, including for example that of Toepke, who could only judge the matter from hearsay, however, this is one-sidedly, and therefore falsely, attributed solely to the heroic fighting spirit and tenacious will to resist of the German defenders. We do not wish to decry in any way the bravery of German soldiers still being proven in individual cases, but for the main part the fighting spirit of the already shattered army was long gone. The Russians, who were aware of Hitler's refusal to permit a break-out, dictated the course of action and in the end no longer needed to run any risk, because the ripe fruit was bound to fall their way soon anyway. They could spare their own forces and take their time.[48]

Von Manstein castigates Hitler's fanaticism, who abhorred any thought of surrender if only for reasons of prestige and who had no humane considerations at all. But he does not unequivocally reject all the explanations and arguments with which Hitler attempted to support his unrelenting stance at the time. One of these was the claim made then that '... surrender would be useless, since the Russian would not feel himself bound by any agreements anyway'.

Von Manstein states that Hitler was '... proven to have been correct, not literally but in the sense of his claim ...', because due to Russian omissions, in the end only a few thousand of the 90,000 prisoners that fell into their hands survived.[49] Within the frame-work of his portrayal, such a statement is embarrassing. At the time it was not permissible for ethical reasons to lay such opinions and assumptions about how the enemy would treat the mass of prisoners in the scales of deliberation and decision, because no one could know with absolute certainty what would happen to the survivors of the battle. When von Manstein points out that the death rate in this instance exceeded all former bounds and attributes this primarily to a lack of goodwill on the part of the enemy, then for the sake of the truth the following facts must also be stated, and not with any intention to uncritically excuse what generally happened to German prisoners of war in Russia. When the totally exhausted, sick and emaciated surviving soldiers of Sixth Army went into captivity in the last days of January and the first days of February, most of them were already marked by death. With them the lice, the carriers of yellow fever, came to the various initial reception camps, to Beketovka, Krasnoarmeisk and Frolov and soon terrible epidemics raged everywhere. For the greater mass of the survivors, the aftermath of the tragedy lasted only a short time. In Beketovka alone, 40,000 human beings died during the early months of spring.

However, the Russian leadership had apparently not believed that it was necessary to make preparations for the adequate care of larger masses of prisoners, mainly because of the repeated firm rejection of its surrender proposals and the obvious intention of Sixth Army to fight to the last man and bullet. Later on, the will to help and improve conditions that von Manstein under-estimates was always there and noticeable, despite all the organisational transportation problems, despite the sufferings of the Russian civilian population and despite other inadequacies. And in this context it needs to be forcefully pointed out that Russian nurses and Jewish doctors sacrificed themselves in an unselfish labour of love for German prisoners from Stalingrad and themselves died of spotted fever.[50]

By not having ended the suffering of its soldiers from above and taken up official negotiations for a timely surrender, the leadership of Sixth Army prolonged the catastrophe for the survivors of the battle in an irresponsible manner and reduced their chances of surviving the initial hard period of captivity. The soldiers in the northern pocket were particularly badly off, because after the surrender of Field Marshal Paulus they had to go on resisting for a further two days and afterwards to bear the full brunt of the Russians' bitterness.

Field Marshal von Manstein did not utter one word of criticism against the fatal crime of omission by the Army Commander-in-Chief, who passively let things slide. The reason behind this lies in the fact that he himself was caught in a dilemma, to which he gave in against his better insight and conscience and did not push through the surrender that had become necessary but which Hitler had forbidden. Caught up in a heavy internal conflict and after having vainly tried for a long time to force Hitler into permitting the surrender, von Manstein took a decision. And if he refrained from 'throwing his command at Hitler's feet' it was because, and we may believe him in this, he had a sense of responsibility for the fate of his threatened Army Group and loyalty to his soldiers, who were also engaged in a battle of life and death outside the Stalingrad pocket. But the fact that he had got himself into this terrible situation at all, in which he had to sacrifice hundreds of thousands to the bitter end for strategic reasons, shows us the whole tragedy of this outstanding commander who, despite his occasional courageous criticism of Hitler's actions, had placed his great talents at the service of a dictatorial war leadership that was increasingly eroding the sound foundations and values of true soldiery and eliminating, for all practical purposes, the ethical conscience of many co-responsible senior commanders. Consequently matters reached the point where one of von Manstein's closest associates told the Chief Engineer of Sixth Army towards the end of December 1942, '... on the staff of Army Group, we too are mere recipients of orders'.[51]

Soldiering and resistance

The words with which von Manstein attempts to justify the sacrifice of Sixth Army in January 1943, from the point of view he held at the time, are revealing as to his opinions, acts and omissions, and bring us to the final problem of the tragedy of Stalingrad.

At one point where von Manstein speaks of the continued resistance by the Stalingrad warriors as having been, in his opinion, almost decisive for the outcome of the war, he writes: 'Let no one say afterwards that the war was lost anyway, that its earlier termination would have spared untold suffering. That is the wisdom of hindsight. In those days it was still far from certain that Germany had to lose the war militarily. A military draw that could perhaps have led to a political draw as well, was still within the realm of possibility, provided that we succeeded in somehow stabilising the situation on the southern wing of the eastern front, which in fact we finally did.'[52]

Every word here provokes a contradiction and not only from the point of view of hindsight. That the Field Marshal did not consider the war to be already lost and believed the desired ideal of a military or even a political draw was still achievable is not in question. But he has not convincingly explained in detail how he believed such a development could have come about, given the overall political situation and all that had happened in Europe under Hitler. It is certainly also hard to believe that a personality in such a high position and on such a high intellectual level should still not have recognised the extent of the political and military disaster. The conscience of many a responsible commander in those days was already long burdened by the leaden weight of his recognition that a favourable end to the war had become impossible. In the forces under von Manstein's command, and not least of all in the Stalingrad army, many a senior commander and soldier believed for well-considered reasons that the war was lost. But above all, in those days there were many far-sighted men with a deep sense of responsibility in the German resistance movement, particularly also among the soldiers, who wished with burning hearts to end the hopeless war as quickly as possible and spare the German nation the prospect of terrible sacrifices in blood and wealth. First and foremost among them ranked the man whose total thinking, willing and acting embodied the best of the tradition of German soldiery and of the German General Staff: Colonel General Beck.

Out of a deep anxiety about the further development of a war clearly leading into the abyss, this man, whom the historian Friedrich Meinecke calls, 'one of those senior officers, of which there are unhappily not very many, who rank as a true heir of Scharnhorst, not only as a taut and energetic soldier, but also as a highly educated and cultured, far-sighted patriot',[53] tried to win von Manstein over to his convictions. The attempt, however, was unsuccessful. One of Beck's confidants reports that the answer received, 'a war is not lost as long as one does not admit it to be lost' was 'just as servile an answer as it was an inner falsehood, when coming from a Field Marshal of von Manstein's strategic talent'.[54]

We must deplore the fact that in his memoirs von Manstein did not discuss this exchange of letters with Beck. He is just as mute about an hours-long conversation with Count Stauffenberg who, having been sent by Chief of Staff Zeitzler, visited him in Taganrog in January 1943, and must certainly have used the opportunity to bring up grave and decisive questions of responsibility.[55] If he carefully avoids any political discussion in connection with the tragedy of Stalingrad and the war, he is demonstrating that he had not given the actual core problem of political morality, so stirringly being felt by many at the time, and not only by those of the calibre of a Beck, any real consideration or, to put it more directly, that he had believed this question to be outside his scope of competence.

We should recall at this point that with the help of several field marshals, leading members of the resistance movement wanted to use the military catastrophe of Stalingrad, which incidentally, Beck had foreseen in all its details, to push Hitler out of his role as Supreme Commander of the eastern front. However, the condition for being able to attempt this was that Paulus act on his own authority to save his army, or by issuing a proclamation to the army and the nation, in the end at least use the catastrophe Hitler had caused his soldiers to light a torch while stepping down from the military stage.[56]

When nothing happened, when no signal was given and the responsible senior commanders went on fighting for Hitler even after the tragedy on the Volga that should finally have opened their eyes to the abyss into which the military road was leading, the men of the resistance were seized by deep despair and bitterness, but also by the determined will to end the hopeless war by extreme means. Beck is alleged to have declared that after Hitler's downfall, he would have Paulus court-martialled for his omission.[57] This bitterness probably also explains the harsh judgement rendered on von Manstein by many men of the resistance. They accuse him of having totally lost sight of military-historic events because of his highly intriguing operational assignments.[58]

One thing is certain in any case. The conviction of an inescapable catastrophic end to the war, which was really Hitler's war, and the conclusion that the overall military situation at the time of the tragedy of Stalingrad had become hopeless, are not the 'wisdom of hindsight' as von Manstein claims. During his trial in Hamburg incidentally, when asked by his chivalrous English defence counsel at what point he had concluded that the war was lost, the Field Marshal declared, 'it became clear to me in the winter of 1942 that we could not win. At that time our front in Russia was torn so far apart that it was impossible for us to hold it. I knew that the Russians would crush us bit by bit with their reserves of man-power'.[59]

Following this, however, von Manstein then spoke of his conviction, also stated in the chapter on Stalingrad in his war memoirs, that a military draw and thereby the conditions for a political draw were still possible at the time. His own operations would have held out the promise of such a chance. After Hitler rejected them, defeat then became inevitable.

These opinions held by von Manstein doubtlessly bespeak both an over-estimation of pure strategy such as no longer applies to the totality of modern war, and even more, a complete misapprehension of the psychological and political factors tied to the person of Hitler. The Field Marshal regarded the battlefield as an autonomous area in which the virtuoso handling of the instruments of war was of decisive importance.

In contrast to such an exaggeration of purely military categories and strategic considerations, let us recall some words here that Colonel General Beck wrote as early as 1938. 'The opinion still to be heard in many circles today that a major war can only be won by the victory of arms is wrong and disastrous, and at a time when the whole world talks about so-called "total war", virtually impossible to understand.'[60]

Results of an inordinate and immoral war policy

It was cheap for von Manstein repeatedly to assert that the ethical value of the futile sacrifice of the army destroyed in Stalingrad has not in any way been cancelled out by the outcome of the war, and for his insistence that the memory of the soldierly virtues of courage, loyalty and obedience to duty upheld on the Volga are a shining example that will outlast time.

These fulsome words of appreciation couched in the superlative, with which the Field Marshal sings the song of praise of German soldiery in the context of his portrayal of the tragedy of Stalingrad and where he speaks of 'a heroism that is surely beyond compare', are problematical in more ways than one.

First of all, what is called 'heroism beyond compare' and 'a most loyal obedience to duty' could be claimed as a virtue by many a German and non-German soldier in many a situation. Take as an example the excellent Russian 62nd Army. In the city on the Volga become hell on earth, it tenaciously defended two small bridgeheads against a crushing German superiority for many long months from the autumn of 1942 on and thereby created the conditions for the ultimately victorious conclusion of the battle.

It should not be denied that for many weeks up to mid January 1943, with regard to courage and comradeship, Stalingrad exemplified the best of German soldiery. What came later, after the conditions for continuing resistance had disappeared together with the last physical and moral reserves, has nothing in common with this. Certainly here and there acts of personal bravery and noble self-sacrifice were still being performed. But by and large during the final phase of the battle, and this was terribly long, the only heroism was the mute heroism of resigned acceptance, suffering and submission. Among the exhausted, dying human beings, there reigned only silent submission to an inevitable fate or, in the midst of the general lethargy, maybe a final desperate resistance stemming from the drive of self-preservation.

The orders to hold on and the blind obedience demanded no longer bear witness to a soldierly stance, but only to a lack of responsibility. Towards the end of the battle, when the ties of discipline began to loosen, at one and the same time, a 'soldierly stance' was convulsively maintained in combat, obedience was relentlessly upheld, lives were ended in desperation, Hitler and the whole senior command were cursed, hope was clung to against all reason, men surrendered and Germans fired on Germans who gave themselves up. True soldiery and its values had long been evilly distorted.

In an evaluation of the events of the battle of Stalingrad, it would be more appropriate and correct first to speak of the despicable abuse of soldierly virtues there. This abuse touched everyone, from the lowest soldier in the ranks all the way up to the Field Marshal. How much excellence, courage, commitment and obedience to duty were squandered for nothing! Whoever does not forcefully bring the weight of his considerations and evaluations to bear on the fact that our German Stalingrad warriors had to die in the name of a betrayed belief, a betrayed loyalty, and a false concept of obedience, and that basically we are dealing here with an ethically indefensible misuse of ultimate human self-sacrifice for a highly questionable objective, runs the risk of ignoring the soldierly virtues and the concept of soldierly honour in an unpermissible, fatal manner.

When reading von Manstein's war memoirs, in particular the chapter on Stalingrad, one cannot escape the impression that such an attempt to ignore was made here. Was the issue at Stalingrad, and in our war at all, really a noble, holy cause, an ethically justified objective, that soldierly honour and the extreme human test of self-sacrifice could serve? The author of these lines, and with him uncounted warriors of Stalingrad, felt the whole abysmal depth of the disaster. They were not convinced that the sacrifice ordered served vital German interests, or that it was of value to the people and the country.

The tragedy opened their eyes inwards and outwards to a more wholesome sobriety and insight. From out of a more or less sombre uncertainty grew for many the clear recognition that the military catastrophe had a demonic political background, that it was the result of an inordinate and basically immoral war policy. Hitler and the senior military leadership that served his interests were cursed by innumerable soldiers at the time. Given his position, his intelligence and his comprehensive insight into the circumstances and background of the Stalingrad tragedy, Field Marshal von Manstein should actually have been one of the first to draw the political conclusions and to object. That he refused to join the resistance, we have already seen. In his war memoirs he writes that at the time, and he means in 1944 (!), he was not able to detect the backsliding of the regime into evil and the true nature of Hitler to the necessary degree.[61] But he had experienced at first hand how the 'Greatest War Lord of all Times' by his careless dilettantism together with his, the Field Marshal's, innocent support, had brought about a military catastrophe the like of which had never been experienced before.

His sense of responsibility still remained untroubled, due to the same political indifference and casualness of heart, that had earlier permitted him to sign an evil army order that stood in crass contradiction to the Prussian-German traditions of the soldier.[62] And even if von Manstein accepted the war policy of Hitler, the Head of State, could the 'Supreme Statesman' be separated from the 'Supreme War Lord' who constantly interfered in his trade so disastrously? How deeply he was caught up in error and self-delusion at the time, and on how steep a slippery slope his fated army found itself to be, has been expressed by Bodo Scheurig with the following words: 'The cancer also appeared on von Manstein's own home ground! As elsewhere, here too the diagnosis had to be "decay". Here the foremost soldier was called upon to resist, if for no other reason then because a state leadership without conscience was ultimately trying to break the "soldier" on whom von Manstein bases his so frequently underlined sense of responsibility. What would ultimately happen to Germany, if in a process without noticeable retardation, Hitler was to destroy the Wehrmacht, which was the decisive factor and not only in the Field Marshal's opinion? If we assume this to be a criterion for von Manstein's self-awareness, then the only possible conclusion is that his soldiery too was already morally decayed and that, leaving aside the bonds of irrevocably sworn commitments, he no longer even understood the foundations on which it had grown.'[63]

A completely false and intolerable comparison

Today there can hardly be any doubt that Stalingrad was a sort of anticipated political, mental and moral downfall of National Socialism. This makes it all the less understandable how in his war memoirs, von Manstein could put the age-old, proud words of the warriors of Thermopylae at the head of his chapter on Stalingrad, 'traveller if you come to Sparta, tell them there that you saw us lying here as the law ordained'. Schiller quite rightly called the famous inscription on the tomb of King Leonidas and his three hundred Spartans who fell with him, 'the most beautiful of its kind and the most noble monument to political virtue'. But applied to the events of Stalingrad these words are a regrettable misuse of the lines from antique history. At the same time they are a dangerous attempt at heroics, suitable for veiling the true picture of the tragedy of Stalingrad and hiding the lessons deriving from it. Where is the law that commanded the German soldiers to die on the Volga?

I recall the lying 'funeral oration' full of empty phrases on 30 January 1943, with which Göring, speaking of the laws of war and the honour of the German nation, glorified the death agony of Sixth Army as a heroic deed beyond compare, and the revulsion with which his pathetic propaganda of glorification was received by my circle of comrades.

The attempt to excuse the irresponsible 'Supreme War Leadership' and to cover the horrible reality with a mantle of national honour appeared to us to be altogether contrived. And when the example of the Spartan heroes of Thermopylae was evoked, the comparison filled us with disgust. How inappropriate and internally mendacious von Manstein's disastrous attempt to create a soldierly legend is, is shown by the simply and correctly stated words with which General Doerr characterised the events on the Volga. 'Stalingrad was not a sacrifice such as that of Leonidas and his Spartans at Thermopylae, not a self-sacrifice like that of the Spaniards in Numantia. Stalingrad should go down in history as the greatest military mistake that any war leader ever made and as the greatest abuse of the vital forces of a nation that a political leadership was ever guilty of.'[64]

After von Manstein's war memoirs appeared, an old friend and comrade in suffering from the time of the Stalingrad tragedy wrote to me in fearful anxiety. 'Von Manstein is making the basically hopeless attempt, maybe unwittingly so, to continue to build the monument that the busy Nazis had already begun to build on the graves of the dead.' This is certainly a bitter statement. It is harsh when made against a soldier who was not really a Nazi general and the courage of whose convictions deserves to be underlined. But von Manstein's opposition to Hitler was first and foremost that of the superior military expert to the dilettante, and it was mainly based on the point of view of his military position and not primarily on higher ethical motives. The Field Marshal has portrayed the catastrophe of Stalingrad and the role he himself played in it in a manner remarkably lacking in political context, and has not raised the ultimate questions of the sense of the event nor of his co-responsibility for it. The military success of the big operation, in which he was a past master, was obviously closer to his heart than any anxiety about the priority of political morality. Even if out of loyalty to his soldiers he held the honest conviction that he was only serving the German nation, he was and remains, and this is his tragedy, what he has not unjustly been called, 'the devil's most uncomfortable general'.[65]

Von Manstein's virtuosic strategic abilities in the end probably contributed to prolonging the disaster hanging over Germany. It was one of the most bitter disappointments of former Chief of Staff Ludwig Beck that even the catastrophic events of Stalingrad were not enough to open the eyes of the most able senior commander to the portents of the threatening downfall of Germany. In his military legacy, written as early as 1938 in the face of the disaster approaching Germany, he set the yardstick against which the actions and omissions of the commander who was co-responsible for Stalingrad must be measured. 'It is a lack of stature and recognition of one's task, if in times such as these, a soldier in a high position only defines his duties and tasks in terms of the limited framework of his military assignments, without becoming aware of the highest responsibility he carries towards the whole nation. Exceptional times require exceptional actions!'

2. FIELD MARSHAL PAULUS

The tragedy of Stalingrad, which will retain its symbolic value as a portent in the memories of the living and of posterity, will forever be closely linked to the name of the Commander-in-Chief of the army sacrificed on the Volga.

Because of the historical role with which fate burdened him, Friedrich Paulus became one of the key figures in that tragedy and beyond that, in the downfall of Germany as a whole. His conduct during the battle, where unconditional obedience governed his deeds and omissions, and in captivity, where a long-delayed insight caused him to rebel against Hitler the destroyer, is still the subject of critical discussions and frequently enough has come under the shadowy light of assumptions and suspicions. There has been no lack of severe verdicts and grave accusations. Occasionally these have gone to the point of personal disparagement and ostracism of the unhappy army commander who has been all too readily accused of acting without honour or conscience, of servility towards Hitler to the point of blind obedience, of military incompetence and lack of character.

Historians and publishers, literary portrayals, yes, even films, have tried to throw light on the problem of Stalingrad. They have answered questions and propounded theories about the guilt and failures of the military leaders, about the senselessness and uselessness of the sacrifice of Sixth Army. Did Paulus deliberately act against better insight and conscience? Was he only a General Staff man caught up in theory, who failed in practice? Was he alone responsible for the tragedy on the Volga? Was he a ditherer, who did not dare venture the brave decision and the risk? Could he not rebel against Hitler's orders and save his men by an unauthorised break-out? Should he not have surrendered in time? These are the questions that are constantly being asked anew.

During his lifetime, Paulus did not intervene in this discussion in which the fundamentals of soldierly obedience were always the key issue. It was three years after his death before his testimony was made public by the publisher Walter Görlitz in 1960. With this, the key witness of the battle of Stalingrad, the man who was directly responsible for the life and death of hundreds of thousands of soldiers, finally took the stand.

Until then there had been no lack of evidence from survivors and officers of lower staffs and units. Besides numerous personal memoirs, there had been weighty portrayals that illuminated the fatal occurrence of Stalingrad and its background within the larger contexts from the point of view of the senior command authorities. These were primarily the writings of Field Marshal von Manstein, Commander-in-Chief of Army Group Don, and of General Zeitzler, Chief of the General Staff. Now for the first time, the comments of the highly controversial Army Commander himself were made known together with revealing new documents.

What Paulus had to say about the possibilities and motives of his decisions and measures as Commander of his Stalingrad army, was bound to throw a new light on the pros and cons of his conduct. It was also reasonable to expect the answers to many a question that had remained open.

It is therefore understandable that many read the book *Here I Stand Under Orders*, in which the publisher combined valuable, and mainly unknown source material from the effects of the Army Commander, with great expectations. On the one hand the already vivid interest in the book was heightened by the attempt Field Marshal von Manstein made in a polemic article even before its publication, to undermine the credibility of several of its theses. It was further increased by the publicity with which the editor and publisher tried to advertise it as 'the long-missing contribution to the historical truth, eagerly awaited by researchers of contemporary history' and by describing it as a 'critically balanced commentary' and 'a sober portrayal of the facts'.[1]

The words that Ernst Alexander Paulus, the son of the Field Marshal, wrote as an introduction to the book also reflect the convictions and intentions of the publisher. According to these, the intention was to provide new insights, since the previous literature had mainly consisted of legends and sensation reports, in other words fiction and not history, or had falsified historical facts by writing from hindsight.

Precisely how valuable are these documents of Paulus' and their accompanying text? Do they really give us a more truthful historical picture of Stalingrad then the wealth of previous literature? What are the new insights that the publisher claimed we should gain? An answer to these questions will be attempted by a series of critical examinations and factual evaluations of the contents of the book.

Extent and quality of the source material

The book compiled by Walter Görlitz consists of factually sober reports on Paulus' work and experiences as Deputy Chief of the Army General Staff and as Commander-in-Chief of Sixth Army. The portrayal of the preparations of Operation 'England' (also known as Operation 'Sea Lion') lies outside the topical scope of this book. In many ways more revealing and interesting, particularly for military experts and staff officers, are the extensive notes on the large planning exercise 'Barbarossa' in preparation for the Russian campaign, in which Paulus was decisively involved in 1940. This is followed by observations and situation evaluations with regard to the course of the war in the east, and then by the very important 'fundamental observations on the operations of Sixth Army in Stalingrad', in which Paulus comments on the questions of leadership and responsibility during individual phases of the battle on the Volga. Added to this are about two dozen letters mainly sent to him during the war years of 1941 and 1942, notes for speeches during his time in Dresden after 1953, and information from conversations with his son.

When one examines this fragmentary literary testament, one is first disappointed by how meagre and unsatisfying the actual core substance is. Furthermore, the few existing hand-written notes by the Field Marshal are very impersonal and highly condensed. If one excepts a few letters, the excerpts from which are innocuous and do not reveal anything important about the feelings and opinions of their author with regard to the events, there are no contemporary documents written at the front. We are dealing mainly with memoirs and observations written later, in other words *post festum*, that only conditionally reflect the impressions and thoughts the Army Commander had at the time. Some of the reports were reconstructed by Paulus from memory or patched together by his son from various undated drafts and notes for speeches.

For the most part, the notes were written from 1945 to 1948 during the years of captivity, in other words behind Russian barbed wire, and are often based on Russian questionnaires and interrogations. Many of these may not have been written totally without reservations and with complete candour; some may have been noted for a purpose or under personal or political restraints. It is therefore occasionally necessary to read between the lines and always to bear in mind the special conditions under which they were written. The Field Marshal has failed to give us an answer to many questions that press themselves upon us.

We are therefore not dealing with memoirs in the true sense. Paulus was not very communicative. He did not keep a diary and did not like making notes of a personal nature or writing letters. He expressly avoided making any personal comments on the great events and encounters of his life and career. It must be deplored that he did not leave us any candidly written memoirs. One particularly misses any discussion of the serious literature on Stalingrad, which must have become known to the former Commander of Sixth Army after his release from Soviet captivity.

From the introduction to his 'fundamental observations' we can gather that it was his intention further to elaborate on his notes on the Stalingrad operations and to put them into a larger framework, in order to make a contribution to the elucidation of the war and its course.[2] A months-long, cruel illness that led to his early death in 1957 prevented his carrying out this intention. But the question remains: why did this meticulous and conscientious former General Staff officer not use the years of life remaining to him after the catastrophe to elaborate on the thoughts about the problems of the battle of Stalingrad that he had noted down in Russia, to modify their summary character and to collect the necessary documentary proofs for his portrayal?

This would have been all the more pressing, because numerous inaccuracies and lapses of memory crept into the notes made without the aid of supporting documents. The inadequacy of the material can also be seen from the many critical references and corrections by the publisher, whose footnotes frequently speak of errors, chronological inaccuracies, hindsight and gaps.

What these documents, in particular the 'fundamental observations on Stalingrad' which in some ways contain the self-appreciation of the Field Marshal, his justification for his obedience and his strategy of holding on, provide us with in the way of new insights, where they are questionable, and where they must be disputed, will be treated in detail later on. In view of this fragmentary and meagre contribution, the publisher attempted to fill out the book by collecting additional source material on the history of the battle of Stalingrad.

For the most part these latter are documents that were published for the first time. With their strict contemporary perspective they provide not only a useful addition to the notes of Army Commander Paulus, but also the possibilities of critical elaboration. Of particular importance in this respect are the telex exchanges between Army Group Don and the Commander of the encircled army, which throw a new light on the questions of command and decision as well as on the responsibility of Field Marshal von Manstein in those tragic days of December 1942. The rich excerpts from the diary of Field Marshal von Bock refer to events during the battle of Kharkov in the spring of 1942. The lesson learned from this experience, namely the tight control by OKH which at that time imposed its operational decisions on front-line commanders, had a lasting effect on General Paulus' mental and psychological conduct.

So far as the catastrophe of Stalingrad is concerned, various documents from archives on the history of the air war provide a valuable addition to the overall picture. These are mainly excerpts from the diaries of the Commander-in-Chief and other senior commanders of the Luftwaffe who were engaged in the battle. Here the temperamental and subjectively evaluating notes of Colonel General von Richthofen predominantly stand out, who at the time repeatedly attempted to gain influence with the Supreme Command of the Wehrmacht with regard to overall operations on the gravely menaced southern wing of the eastern front. Although many of his remarks about the unhappy Sixth Army may be one-sided and unjust, his diaries are filled with the living breath of that tragedy. The files of the German Army Mission in Roumania also contain true contemporary and local colour. The reports selected from them throw light on the situation of the neighbouring Roumanian armies and on their co-operation with the senior German staffs, in particular on events in the big bend of the Don, where the four divisions of 'Group Lascar' suffered a 'Stalingrad' in miniature in the pocket of Raspopinskaya. That was where the storm of the major Russian offensive broke loose. And on the second day of the attack, the catastrophe had also taken its course with the Roumanian forces south of Stalingrad after weeks of warnings, suggestions and appeals from the Roumanian Joint General Staff to all the German command authorities had been to no avail.

In his attempt to complement Paulus' testament with other source material, Walter Görlitz was supported by numerous personalities, many of whom had been responsibly involved in the Stalingrad battle. Mention must be made of General Hollidt, whose army detachment was to take part in von Manstein's relief operation in December 1942 by attacking from the Chir, but who was soon engaged in heavy defensive fighting in retreat; Lieutenant-General Heim, Paulus' former Chief of Staff, whom Hitler demoted and made the scapegoat at the end of November 1942 for not having succeeded with his weak panzer corps in his impossible assignment to stop the offensive by the Soviet attacking armies in the bend of the Don; Lieutenant-Colonel von Zitzewitz, OKH's liaison officer with the staff of the Stalingrad army, on whose death march he conscientiously reported without being able to help; General Hoth, Commander-in-Chief of Fourth Panzer Army and leader of the doomed relief operation. They all answered questions and provided useful material.

In conclusion, one key witness of the tragedy of Sixth Army, whose weighty writings were first evaluated by Walter Görlitz, should be particularly stressed: Lieutenant-General Arthur Schmidt, the former Chief of Staff of the Stalingrad army. As Paulus' chief adviser and closest associate, he was the main actor in the drama. And today he is an indispensable authority on any questions that deal with the leadership of Sixth Army and the story of its downfall. His memoirs and notes form the most natural complement to the Paulus testament. There are sound reasons to assume that the accompanying remarks and critical comments made by the publisher of the book are largely based on them.

The wealth of material presented by Görlitz certainly serves to enhance the previously held picture of the battle of Stalingrad and the events leading up to it, and adds many interesting details, new aspects and nuances. The question is: does it also provide a convincing foundation for a re-evaluation of the tragic events and for a deeper understanding of the problems connected with them?

Görlitz, a defender of Paulus?

Professional critics have accused Walter Görlitz of a lack of understanding of operational planning and its processes as well as of many mistakes and inadequacies in his portrayal.[3]

What is far more serious, however, is the fact that this publisher was hardly willing to consider the total body of sources and literature on Stalingrad in an unprejudiced manner. Therefore he was unable to give a well-balanced historical commentary, with the necessary detachment and sovereignty, on this material which he published far too hurriedly.

Even though he diligently collected much useful information, he did not consider it necessary directly to tap one of the most important, readily available sources, namely General von Seydlitz. In him Görlitz obviously saw only a military rebel and mutineer or an unimportant commander with a narrow horizon, whose opinion could be deliberately ignored. For reasons of objectivity and fairness it would have been appropriate to obtain the views of this commanding general, who was one of the main actors in the battle and one of the most effective and proven commanders. However, Görlitz chose to record his role in Stalingrad in accordance with the biased story circulated in the literature of the subject, and on top of that, commented on it in derogatory terms. In this he was served by an obviously highly welcomed, dubious and basically derogatory characterisation of the general's personality, which he found in an older work by Hermann Teske and which he published in his Stalingrad chapter of *Decisive Battles of the Second World War*, even though it is misplaced there.[4]

In just such a prejudiced point of view by the publisher of the Paulus testament lies the explanation for his totally inappropriate portrayal of the initial decisive phase of the battle in particular and of the undignified final phase, that so heavily indicts the Army leadership. Here the testimony of General von Seydlitz would have been particularly revealing and, without question, have been of great help to the work of an editor applying the probe of historic critique.

Incidentally, the book does not lack all sorts of references to details of the Stalingrad literature and biographical information mainly concerned with the military careers of the senior officers mentioned. But this hardly says anything important about the history of the tragedy of Stalingrad, nor about the profound problems connected with it. These are only superficially portrayed. One misses a serious intellectual appraisal of the existing literature which already demonstrates clearly enough that Stalingrad cannot be understood and interpreted from a purely strategic-military point of view, as has frequently been attempted, not least in Görlitz's limited perspective.

Görlitz himself has greatly complicated his way to a deeper appreciation of the basic problem of Stalingrad by his un-historic approach to the subject, namely by his repeatedly expressed disdain for the available reports of participants and the 'subjective memoir literature'. What could have motivated him simply to shunt aside in self-assurance, as he also does with other documents, this group of important statements by eye-witnesses? Despite the errors it may contain and even though it requires a careful historical-critical testing, the memoir literature is also a noteworthy source, and not only by reason of the contemporary and local colour recaptured, and the revealing individual experiences. Before summarily rejecting it, Görlitz would have been well advised first to make an attempt to take it seriously. The historian may gain useful information even from the errors and subjective colorations of this category of document. The publisher of the Paulus testament ignored it, and one may rightly ask whether he was at all able to approach the testimony of his key witnesses, namely Field Marshal Paulus himself and his Chief of Staff Schmidt, with sufficient critical appreciation and the necessary reservations.

The extent to which Görlitz's evaluation of the various critical phases of the battle of Stalingrad do not do justice to the full historic truth will be shown in detail later on. Here I would like to interject some basic comments on the lopsidedness and inadequacies of his historical approach. He is certainly correct in his claim that the military, or better soldierly, decisions during the course of the battle cannot only be interpreted from the perspective of the resistance. We must agree with him when he writes, 'one cannot only evaluate the history of the last war from the point of view of what each one did to end it'.[5]

But he fails to recognise the special character and requirements of the unusual strategic situation of Sixth Army in Stalingrad. The issue then was not that the responsible Commander-in-Chief and other senior commanders become rebels, but simply that correct soldierly and humane decisions be taken. At the time, General von Seydlitz never alluded to the example of a Yorck, but he did frequently refer to the audacious break-out at Brczeziny during the great autumn battle of 1914 in Poland.[6] Colonel Selle actually did think of Yorck and it is also a fact that the resistance group around Ambassador von Hassel, Colonel General Beck and Carl Goerdeler were disappointed at the time that the Army Commander at Stalingrad did not display '... a spirit in the spirit of Yorck'.[7] With this they naturally meant an independent action out of a free decision of conscience. It is therefore mistaken here to speak of a 'legend', as Görlitz does, who goes on to prove, completely unnecessarily, that a historic comparison between Stalingrad and Tauroggen is not valid in any way. That Paulus obviously knew nothing of these expectations and thoughts of the resistance at home is another matter entirely.[8]

In any case, Görlitz makes it far too easy on himself when he regards what at the time actually were correct insights and demands, even in the Stalingrad pocket, only as, and I will use here the evil phrase which he so enjoys using, 'post-catastrophe insights'.

The men who in those days thought and wanted something different from what the Army Command did are not taken seriously or even disparaged. The attempts to belittle the opinions held then by several representatives of the resistance movement or to bridge contradictions of conviction at the expense of the truth are embarrassing. A comparison between General Beck and General Paulus is as unfortunate as it is ridiculous. It shows Görlitz's objectives and mode of thinking particularly clearly, when he ignores the deep gulf that separated these two men, particularly as regards those fundamental points of view that were so important then. On the one side, the paramount soldierly personality, Germany's last true Chief of the General Staff, who out of a profound ethical idealism bravely combats the national catastrophe he had warned about and who sacrifices his position for a conviction, the universality of which unites the military aspects with an encompassing political sense of responsibility and true historic insight. On the other, the personally unconditionally honourable soldier-only, who sees his duties and obligations purely from within the limited framework of his military assignments, who initially actually holds the opinion that the Russian campaign, which he considers to be necessary, may possibly lead to the Bolshevik empire falling down like a house of cards and who, as emphasised in his radio messages, remains loyal to Hitler, at least as far as outward appearances are concerned, until the bitter end at Stalingrad.[9]

Görlitz's comments and the life story of Paulus that he projects are not only devoted to a historic understanding. They are not only intended to explain and fathom, but are filled with a pronounced apologetic tendency that seems to culminate in the desire to demonstrate, far too self-assuredly, that within the framework of the emergency situation culpably created by Hitler and the huge machine of leadership, there was no other course of action; that in the final analysis Sixth Army acted correctly in the given situation and that the sacrifice of the army for strategic reasons was necessary, and even made sense. Critical experts from abroad are particularly sensitive towards such attempts at rehabilitation *vis-à-vis* the errors of the National Socialist political and war leadership. The *Allgemeine Schweizerische Militärzeitschrift* (General Swiss Military Magazine) therefore clearly stated that Görlitz's book demonstrably serves the purpose of justifying the conduct and decisions of the Commander-in-Chief of Sixth Army before posterity.[10] With the exception of the last week in January 1942, of course, the publisher of the Paulus testament unwaveringly adopts the point of view of the Army Command and its decisions at the time, naturally after having condemned the erroneous planning and the initial offensive of the summer of 1942 with its presumptuous ultimate objectives.

He decisively rejects any thought that a different course of action would have been possible or necessary. 'It was not within the authority of an individual army commander', he states, 'to try to put a spanner into the works of this strangely run, gigantic machine'.[11] This was demonstrably true. Elsewhere he declares that in war, what is theoretically correct is not always correct or achievable in practice, without however being able to present convincing proof of this statement.

With sentences such as these and similar general statements that echo many self-justifying arguments in the Paulus testament, Görlitz by his very nature is unable to do justice to the difficult problem of Stalingrad. He has not been able to grasp to its full depth the question of responsibility which at that time was simply no longer permitted to be restricted to purely military thought and ability.

The fact that history agreed with the few, even in Stalingrad, who inwardly and outwardly rebelled out of recognition of the unique, extraordinary situation, should have given him access to more valid yardsticks for the measurement of the personalities and conduct of those who were enmeshed in the tragedy. That Görlitz tries to justify where one need only to understand and that he deliberately ignores or just pays insufficient attention to the exceptional nature of the situation, remains his error and one reason for an inappropriate portrayal. In a book that lays claim to be a work of history, the effects of such a lopsided historical analysis must be deplored.

On the character of the Field Marshal

If one leaves aside the critical remarks made above and some cheap journalistic tricks used for effect, one must gladly concede that Görlitz deserves credit for his biography of Paulus as a soldier and a man. About eighty pages of the book are devoted to this portrayal of his life, using many sources and previously unpublished family documents.

Unfortunately, the biography only deals with a part of a life. Since it ends with the Field Marshal going into captivity, it is somewhat fragmentary and unfinished. It leaves the reader with the impression that Paulus had set off down this stark road unbowed and without feelings of guilt, filled only with the conviction of having discharged his duty towards the nation and the Reich in a desperate situation, whereas gnawing doubts and questions must already have filled his breast at the time. The subsequent perceptions and insights that the unhappy commander gained in his feeling of complicity after the catastrophe, while being alluded to briefly, deserve to have been taken into account and fathomed more deeply.

Walter Görlitz's endeavour to show human compassion for the senior commander who was so harshly tested and cruelly struck by fate, to illuminate the motives of his conduct, to defend him against unjust accusations, and to protect him from subsequent ostracism, is as legitimate as it is praiseworthy.

In the portrait of the life and character he draws, the publisher places the accents more correctly than had been the case in the majority of prior portrayals. It is to his credit adamantly and credibly to have pointed out how one-sided and wrong it would be to regard the conduct and measures of the former Commander-in-Chief of Sixth Army in too much isolation or even to burden him alone with the total responsibility for the events. Happily, he cleans up many a premature prejudice. In doing so, however, he bangs on many an open door. In the serious literature on Stalingrad the claim has scarcely been made that Paulus had simply failed in unreflecting, blind obedience, had flatly suppressed his conscience, or had not found the courage for the saving action from a lack of willingness to make a personal sacrifice. There can be no quibbling with the integrity of his character. This is not contradicted by the fact that the Army Commander lacked those traits, abilities and experiences of a superior commander that could have enabled him to master the outrageously unique military situation of Stalingrad. As his biography clearly shows, these gifts were just not given to Paulus.

From the portrait of his life and character we can now summarise. Paulus was the prototype of the personally honourable German professional soldier in the mould of a Seeckt, highly qualified tactically and operationally, certainly more of a theorist than a front-line soldier, outstanding as an instructor at the military academy and in his assignments on the General Staff, a career which fitted him like a glove, thanks among other things to his great talent, his carefully evaluating thoroughness and his social graces marked by agility and adaptability.

Coming from a humble middle-class background, but having risen socially by his early marriage to a woman from the most distinguished Roumanian aristocracy, he securely and determinedly climbed the ladder of the military hierarchy, thanks to his personal competence, and particularly rapidly during the build-up of the National Socialist Wehrmacht, to whose new panzer arm he greatly contributed.

When the negative and fatal aspects of the developments in Germany must have forced themselves upon him, he never jeopardised his career by voicing outspoken criticism or by taking a stand. We do not know what he thought about such things as the Röhm affair, the Fritsch crisis, the dismissal of Chief of Staff Beck or the invasion of Czechoslovakia. He was a completely apolitical soldier-only, totally concentrated on the scope of his duties within his military assignments, having that same loyalty towards the political leadership that characterised the mass of German officers who regarded obedience as being the supreme inviolable law. He was not a part of that minority of critically thinking, sceptical and politically alert soldiers who recognised with growing apprehension the fatal degree to which the military world under the dictator was being alienated from its old traditions of sobriety, rectitude and ethical responsibility. Paulus was repeatedly in close contact with senior officers who belonged to the secret military opposition. Not one of them found it appropriate to take him into their confidence or to try to win him over to the cause that was legitimised by the authority of conscience.

Görlitz succeeds impressively in describing the emasculation of the generals and the decay of German methods of leadership as a fatal outcome of Hitler's exercising the supreme military command. By continually reducing their horizons, their powers of command and their freedom of decision, the 'Supreme War Lord' had succeeded in degrading them to mere functionaries. From the first winter of the war in Russia, every change in the front line required his agreement, as did the deployment of reserves. Time and again, making unrestricted use of the technical means of communication, Hitler interfered, not only in the operational leadership, but also in minor local tactical deployments within the armies. His stringent directives on secrecy, which forbade briefing even senior staffs and commanders about the overall situation, also served the purpose of incapacitating the generals whom he viewed with suspicion and in binding them to him in blind obedience. 'There were now no longer any commanders, but only senior managers within a functionally controlled gear-box, a gigantic system of wheels within wheels.'[12]

In his subsequent notations, Paulus himself repeatedly speaks of the fact that he, together with all the senior commanders, stood '... under the paralysing effect ...' of certain orders by Hitler that made independent thought and action difficult, if not impossible from the beginning.[13] These are sober statements of fact and we have not one piece of evidence that he was secretly indignant about such a fatal curtailment of his personal scope of responsibility and freedom of action, or that he rebelled against it. He was not a staunch character and the 'higher form of disobedience' was completely foreign to him. For the most part his conduct is determined by his thinking in categories of professional competence, the reporting relationship and his innocent trust in the 'Supreme Commander' whom he seems not to have believed to be capable of any carelessness or false decisions. Several measures that Paulus initiated immediately after having assumed Command of Sixth Army speak of the honesty of his convictions and his personal rectitude. He not only decided that the infamous 'Commissar Order' was not to be obeyed, but in contrast to von Manstein also rescinded the unethical 'Severity Order' of 10 October 1941 on the 'conduct of the troops in the eastern theatre' issued by von Reichenau, which spoke of the 'necessity for a stringent but just atonement by the Jewish sub-humanity', of the destruction of the deceitful Bolshevik creed and the ' extermination of alien malice'.[14]

The Command of Sixth Army with which Paulus was entrusted at the beginning of January 1942 was to become his tragic fate. Before then he had never independently commanded either a regiment, a division or a corps. His last active command had been that of an armoured recon-naissance detachment in 1934. During the campaigns in Poland and the west he had distinguished himself as a conscientious and effective Chief of Staff next to the dashing, quite National Socialist minded von Reichenau, Commander-in-Chief of that very same Sixth Army. There followed a year and a half as Chief Quartermaster and Deputy Chief of Staff of the Army. In this senior position, as a collaborator and disciple of Colonel General Halder, in which he worked on the deployment and operational plan against the Soviet Union, he remained, as Görlitz underlines, '... only one of the bureaucratic senior executive organs of operational leadership methods, as one might say'.[15] The Command of Sixth Army was to give him a relative independence for the first time.

.Paulus' personality and soldierly character had been lastingly moulded by his long years of service on the staff. This staff officer, with his outstanding professional competence and remarkable talent for oper-ational assignments, who thought things through so thoroughly and weighed his arguments so carefully, was lacking the wealth of experience at the front, the hardness, the decisive audacity and the willingness to take decisions of a proven line commander. General Heim, the first Chief of Staff of the new Commander-in-Chief, knew him well and respected him highly as a man. The more devastating is his verdict on Paulus, of whom he says that he was more of a desk man than a man of action. That he was entrusted with an army in the eastern theatre, Heim calls an 'inexcusable mistake in personnel policy'.[16]

The degree to which Paulus was overtaxed as an Army Comman-der did not become evident in the initial, fairly normal situation during the first months, nor during the summer campaign, in which he proved himself in several ways. But it certainly did during the course of the monstrously unique battle of Stalingrad which, admittedly, made extra-ordinary demands. In his erstwhile Chief of Staff, General Schmidt, the Commander-in-Chief unfortunately did not have the adviser to hand who could have effectively counter-weighed his one-sidedness and weak-nesses.

General Doerr, author of the book *The Campaign to Stalingrad*, gave a characterisation of the two fateful personalities at the head of Sixth Army, that was based on his personal knowledge and has been con-firmed by many witnesses to the battle.

'The relationship between Paulus and Schmidt was formally correct but without human warmth. Paulus, intelligent, operationally gifted, generous, but very sensitive and highly impressionable, was not a strong personality. His Chief of Staff was a bachelor, an aesthete, intelligent, energetic, an outstanding tactician, hard to the point of rigidity. The dissimilar traits of the Commander-in-Chief and his Chief of Staff could have complemented each other well, but Schmidt was the stronger personality and he dominated. However, one can not speak of disharmony in the leadership of Sixth Army. It was also not the differences in character or the formality in the relationship of the two personalities that fatally effected the leadership of the army in those critical days. The fatality lay in exactly those things that both had in common; their belief in Hitler's luck and their trust in his moral qualities, a trust they shared with many others and that would not even let the thought enter their minds, that by giving them mendacious descriptions of the situation, their "Supreme Commander" was solemnly making promises he could not keep.'[17]

In many ways, the biography of Paulus drawn by Görlitz can be taken as a comprehensive comment on the conduct of the Commander-in-Chief of Sixth Army in Stalingrad. In his portrayal of both the biography as well as the general military-historical process, despite his exaggerated tendencies to justify, he succeeds impressively in describing why everything had to come about and run its course as it did within the framework of the 'functionally controlled gear-box' in which there were no longer any true commanders, but only senior executives who held on to a degenerated concept of obedience until the end and, being dedicated soldiers-only, ignored the demands of conscience. The title of the book is: *I Stand Here Under Orders!* This sentence, taken from the last letter the unhappy Marshal sent from Stalingrad, is completely appropriate. It encompasses the dilemma in which Paulus was caught, the whole tragedy of the Commander-in-Chief and his sacrificed army.

The motives behind Paulus' conduct

To evaluate the motives from which the leadership of Sixth Army took its decisions in Stalingrad seriously, strictly objectively and not carelessly or superficially, is an imperative demanded by justice and historical objectivity.

In his subsequently written 'Fundamental statements on the operations of Sixth Army in Stalingrad' and in the attachments thereto, Paulus has described his considerations and measures of the time. What can clearly be gathered from them in the first instance is, that the worried Army Commander had been in active discussion with the Command of his superior Army Group B long before the Russian encircling offensive began, particularly with regard to the dangers of the constantly extending and weakly protected northern flank and about his own low-combat power in the direction of his advance. At Führer Headquarters in Vinniza as early as mid September 1942, he adamantly pointed out the weaknesses of the front and demanded appropriate support. Since then he had not tired of constantly sending the higher authorities reports and warnings in order to get them to increase combat power, effectively protect the flanks and secure and augment supply. With the same objective he warned important persons who came to visit the army from higher authorities: General Blumentritt, Deputy Chief of Staff of the Army; General Ochsner from OKH, Chief of the Fog Units; the Chief of Military Communications, General Fellgiebel; the Adjutant of the Wehrmacht to Hitler, General Schmundt.

He even took an unusual route and contacted the Supreme Command of the Roumanian Third Army, in order to get support for the under-equipped Roumanian forces and German reserves via Marshal Antonescu, who had influence with Hitler. He requested three fresh infantry divisions for the final conquest of Stalingrad, and towards the end of October permission to stop the depleting battle of attrition in the metropolis on the Volga. On the success of his endeavours Paulus reports as follows. 'To all my requests, suggestions, calculations, cartographic presentations and explanations with regard to reinforcements, flank protection and supply ... the reaction by the higher authorities was totally insufficient.'[18]

However, in a radio message in mid November that ignored the major dangers to Sixth Army, Hitler again demanded a final effort to take Stalingrad and thereby secure 'the defence of this corner pillar on the Volga'.[19]

In the context of his 'futile discussions' Paulus goes on to mention the alarming reports concerning the highly menacing preparations of a major enemy offensive that were constantly passed upwards by Army but which, as he believes, were not taken sufficiently seriously by the higher command. Only in the final hour did they realise the full implications of the approaching dangers. Despite this, an order by Chief of Staff Zeitzler came in immediately before the Russian offensive began, in which he advises that the enemy had no further reserves worth mentioning and was therefore no longer capable of undertaking major operations.[20] In this context Paulus also recalls various belated measures of regrouping within his own sphere of command and responsibility, which, however, had to be modest, due to the very limited possibilities. They were supposed to serve to repulse the expected attack. He stresses that all his considerations and decisions at the time affected 'the more far-reaching overview and areas of responsibility of the Army Group Command and even of the Supreme Command'.

The historical viewer will have to ask the question here, whether his situation reports and demands at the time were couched in terms that were as extraordinarily convincing, sharp and uncompromising, as the extraordinary gravity of the situation required?[21]

Caught up in conflicting duties

During the initial days of the Russian encircling offensive the fatal issue was – break out or relief from outside? On 21 November Paulus' recommendation to the superior Army Group was to withdraw the gravely endangered army to an arc on the Don and the Chir. Army Group agreed with the operational intentions of the Army Commander. But on the evening of the same day it passed on without comment an order by OKH which said that Sixth Army was to hold Stalingrad and the line on the Volga at all costs and that counter-measures were being initiated on a large scale. Later directives by Hitler demanded digging-in and waiting.

The issue now was to obtain freedom of action in order to save the forces threatened by a deadly embrace. Together with all the Commanding Generals, the two senior men of the army, the Commander-in-Chief and the Chief of Staff, were convinced that the only thing feasible was to break out to the south-west. Pointing therefore to the increasingly more critical overall situation, Paulus repeatedly demanded immediate operational freedom, finally even in a radio message addressed directly to Hitler.[22]

The responsible Commander of Army Group, General Freiherr von Weichs, shared his point of view completely and energetically supported the requests by Army, for the last time in an extensive report to OKH on 23 November in which he said, among other things, that supplying twenty divisions by air was impossible.[23]

From 24 November on, after Hitler had refused the army the freedom of action it had requested and even proscribed the lines on which it was to dig-in and await its relief, von Weichs no longer undertook anything in favour of the break-out that he had so recently considered to be absolutely necessary and for which he had been determined to give the order on his own authority. He gave in, because he did not want to plunge his subordinate Army Commander into a grave conflict of conscience. But thereby he also avoided taking a decision of his own and shied away from shouldering the personal responsibility that the historic hour demanded.

For his part, Paulus has carefully listed the reasons that now kept him from taking the unauthorised action that General von Seydlitz demanded so forcefully. He believed that he was not entitled to break out of Stalingrad with his army against orders without having information on the overall situation, without knowing what reserves OKH had available for the announced early relief and without knowing the consequences of an independent action. The 'Supreme Military Command', or so he believed, must have weighty reasons based on its superior knowledge of the overall contexts, for unconditionally holding on to 'the corner pillar on the Volga' in the interest of the whole. He trusted in Hitler's promises that everything would be done adequately to supply the encircled forces and also considered the conditions for a timely relief to be well enough secured.

'In this situation, my acting against orders, particularly since I could not responsibly oversee the overall situation, would have pulled the operational foundation from under the 'Supreme Command'. Elevated to a system, such an action against the plans of the overall leadership leads to anarchy in the command structure.'[24] These words, however, bear witness to a complete misapprehension of the uniqueness of the situation, which was not a model case, but rather an extreme from which one cannot deduce any generally applicable rules of normal conduct. Paulus must needs have felt himself reinforced in the purely military reasons that governed his conduct as Army Commander at the time, by the fact that the superior Army Group accepted the new situation without fuss. The role that General von Weichs played in this has been characterised by General Paul Mahlmann with harsh, but appropriate words. With regard to Hitler's order to hold on he says: 'This order, that contradicted his own convictions, must have plunged von Weichs into a situation of conflict. Acting against all military and moral principles he did not resolve it, but pushed it off on to his subordinate Paulus by simply passing on OKH's assignment.'[25]

At the time, the decision to act independently should indeed have been taken by Army Group. It oversaw the general situation and was better informed than Army. Incidentally, even before his officially taking over command, Field Marshal von Manstein sent a radio message to Paulus on 24 November in which he indicated the Führer Order just received and declared that holding on to the Volga and the northern front must have top priority.

In his process of decision the Commander-in-Chief may have been influenced by several experiences in recent months, for example, memories of the battle of Kharkov where holding on in a catastrophic situation had also been the issue and where the OKH imposed the correct operational concept against the opinions of the local senior commanders, or the deterring example of the punishment and dismissal of individual rebelling generals by Hitler.

Finally there may also have been the after-effect, and that is humanly-psychologically understandable, of the confidence in one's own strength and military superiority which so far had always succeeded in mastering sudden crises and handling no matter how difficult a situation.

So far as Paulus' line of argument may be removed from the oversimplified conceptions of rigid obedience, so do they also not do justice to the monstrosity of the situation and the responsibility attaching to it, nor to the questionable trust in the measures promised by the 'Supreme Command'. Could the order by Hitler really invalidate at one blow all the carefully considered reasons with which the Commander-in-Chief had formerly pleaded for the freedom of action he had recognised as being necessary? Had not Paulus himself experienced too many disappointments that should have made him suspicious? He had been informed about the difficulties of winter supply in a memorandum by the Chief Quartermaster of Army Group, General Weinknecht, who had already recommended in October to withdraw Sixth Army to an arc position on the Don–Donetz.[26] Because of his sceptical opinions in which he had declared all means and support to be used up, Weinknecht had been relieved, as had been the commanding general of IV Corps, General von Schwedler, who had unequivocally spoken out against leaving Sixth Army in its endangered position in Stalingrad.

He could also not have been unaware of the reasons behind the dismissal of the revered General Halder, the Chief of Staff of the Army, with whom Paulus had been so closely associated. The lack of result of all of his requests, warnings and presentations and the non-appearance of any reserves should also have made him even more sceptical. So far as the future supply of the pocket by air was concerned, he was informed of the well-founded pessimistic opinions of the local Luftwaffe generals. Had he not himself been present at a conversation in which General Fiebig had told Chief of Staff Schmidt. 'Supplying a whole army by air? Impossible! Our cargo aircraft are heavily engaged in Africa and on other fronts. I warn you against entertaining exaggerated expectations!'[27]

Walter Görlitz, who tries to justify the decision by the Army leadership from the professional military perspective of the Army Staff in Stalingrad, claims that Paulus could simply not conceive of the 'Supreme War Lord' issuing careless directives, and furthermore felt himself to be 'sheltered in Hitler's leadership'.[28] That such a judgement is correct is highly questionable, if only because of the experiences described above, which must at least have given the sensitive general food for thought. But Paulus was also intimately aware of a careless action on the part of Hitler that had occurred at the beginning of the Russian campaign. The difficulties of a winter campaign presented by Paulus himself had been cast to the winds by Hitler in a manner that was both emotional and devoid of conscience: 'I do not wish to hear ... any more of this blather ... There will be no winter campaign. You can safely leave that to my diplomatic skills. The army need only hit the Russian a few heavy blows ... Then you will see that the Russian colossus is standing on feet of clay. I hereby expressly forbid talk of a winter campaign in my presence.'[29] It is difficult to conceive that Paulus, who had been an instructor in military history and tactics for many years, was not able fully to recognise the uniqueness and impossibility of the strategic situation into which his army had been manoeuvred by the dilettante and careless 'Supreme Commander'.

He had to know that he was taking an enormous risk by obeying an order that took the military initiative and freedom to manœuvre away from an army of more than 250,000 soldiers and thereby contradicted all the traditional rules of strategy. What the 'Supreme Commander' was demanding contained the danger of delivering the troops to the enemy on a silver platter with their hands tied behind their backs. Since the winter of 1941 he was also aware of Hitler's ideas about how to fight the war in the east, in which rigidly holding on at all cost appeared to be the answer to everything. According to von Manstein, Paulus should have taken the decision to break out of Stalingrad on his own during the initial days of the encirclement. 'The only possibility would have been to present Hitler with the accomplished fact of the army having withdrawn from Stalingrad, particularly after the "Supreme Command" had wrapped itself in silence for thirty-six hours.'[30] That was precisely what General von Seydlitz had unerringly recognised and demanded. On top of that, von Seydlitz also believed that such an unauthorised action for the continuation of operations, born of the imperatives of the changing situation, would actually not even have been taken for deliberate disobedience. His memorandum even suggested the wording for a subsequent report on the accomplished fact: 'A public explanation is possible that will prevent any serious damage to morale; after having completely destroyed the Soviet arms centre of Stalingrad, the army withdrew from the Volga while simultaneously destroying a group of enemy forces'.[31]

Paulus could have known from at least one example that it need not be beyond consideration and hopeless from the start to act against orders from the top. Had not his former Commander-in-Chief, Field Marshal von Reichenau, withdrawn Army Group South of which he had just taken over command, from Rostov to the Mius line for reasons of strategic necessity in December 1941, something that Hitler had strictly forbidden? He had then simply reported the accomplished fact by stating he believed himself to have acted according to the intentions of the Führer.

As part of an army group, Sixth Army could naturally not have acted entirely independently. As General Röhricht quite rightly points out, the decision to break out against the express order of the highest authority would have had to have been agreed with the Command of

Army Group,[32] in order to allow preparations for its success to be made outside the encircling ring. That such an initiative would not have been hopeless can be seen from the decisiveness with which Army Group had initially agreed with the Stalingrad army's plans of operation. The telex message which General von Weichs sent to OKH on 23 November said: 'From a break-out by Sixth Army towards the south-west I expect a relieving of pressure on the overall situation. After the complete loss of the Roumanian Third Army, the army is the only force left with which I can inflict damage on the enemy ... Finally, the remaining combat power of Sixth Army represents an indispensable addition to the defence that must be established and for the preparation of counter-offensives.'[33]

In the midst of the unique situation at Stalingrad, very grave decisions were called for, and these would affect not only OKH but also the areas of responsibility of the senior men of the superior Army Group, a fact that has often been overlooked. The dilemma in which Paulus found himself should not be under-estimated, nor should his honest intentions. In the conflict of duties in which the Army Commander was caught, things were more difficult for him than for his subordinates and critics, who did not have to carry the direct responsibility for the whole. But in this context we must raise the question as to whether at the time it would not have been appropriate for the leading personalities of Sixth Army to bring a far greater professional expertise to bear and to exercise a deeper sense of responsibility beyond the purely military-strategic. The gap between their theoretically correct insights and practical conduct, noticeable both before and after Hitler's order to hold on was received, tends to bear this out. [In obviously following the opinion expressed by the army's Chief of Staff Schmidt, Görlitz continues to insist that anyone claiming later that different decisions and actions were called for, is arguing from 'post-catastrophe hindsight', or if he held this conviction at the time, would have been demanding a deliberate reaction based on political opposition.] A special chapter of this book is devoted to the discussion of this non-historic point of view.[34]

The last chance

The second critical high-point in the fate of Sixth Army came about in the days immediately before Christmas 1942, when the spearheads of the relieving forces of LVII Panzer Corps had fought their way to within about fifty kilometres of the pocket. Once again there was a chance for a break-out. Again Paulus was faced with the question of an independent decision and an unauthorised action.

In the chapter devoted to von Manstein, we have comprehensively treated the two inter-connected operations 'Winter Storm, which aimed at opening up a supply corridor with active support by Sixth Army while maintaining the positions on the Volga, and the break-out Operation 'Thunderclap', which aimed at shrinking the pocket and giving up Stalingrad. We must now again bring out the motives behind the process of decision and the passive conduct of the encircled army.

There could be no doubt that the forces in Stalingrad, who were already eating their horses, had lost combat power to an ominous degree, mainly because of the totally inadequate air lift that was only able to deliver one-tenth of their requirements. The losses incurred in the heavy defensive fighting had not been replaced. There was a lack of ammunition and fuel. In short, the army was already desperately immobile and its fighting capacity was hopelessly reduced. Despite this, it had prepared for a break-out on its southern front and concentrated the remaining approximately eighty tanks into an attack force under General Hube. These, it is alleged, only had fuel for between twenty and thirty kilometres and so could only make a short advance out of the pocket.

After the relief offensive had fought bitterly to reach the Myshkova sector, von Manstein ordered Sixth Army to begin the 'Winter Storm' attack as quickly as possible and, if necessary, to establish contact with the relieving forces in order to pass through the prepared convoy. The second phase of the operation, 'Thunderclap', was to be ready to take place immediately afterwards, but not until 'express orders' were given.[35]

Hitler, who only thought in terms of a supply corridor and was fanatically determined to leave the army in Stalingrad, opposed von Manstein's operational intentions, who for his part, did not wish to give Paulus the expected order to break out unilaterally. The Command of Sixth Army believed it to be impossible to jump off for the partial break-out 'Winter Storm' so long as it was required to hold the front on the Volga. It set up a number of conditions: prior supply of reinforcements and fuel and a time-span of six days for preparations. Paulus and Schmidt were convinced that unless their advance into the corridor developed into an all-out evacuation of the pocket, they would be unable to withdraw sufficient forces from other sectors to achieve and secure the corridor. To hold the pocket and the corridor simultaneously was beyond the capabilities of the no longer fully combat-worthy and heavily depleted army.

That is why Paulus insisted on a rapid execution of the complete break-out, namely operation 'Thunderclap'. But in an exchange by telex on 23 December , at a time incidentally when it had already been decided to break off the relief operation, von Manstein told Paulus '... not able to give authority today. Hope for decision tomorrow'.[36] However, the authority was never given. With this von Manstein left his subordinate Army Commander in a situation of grievous inner conflict.

Paulus was faced with an uncommonly difficult decision. The planned operation was terribly risky, given the limited operational strength of his by now largely immobile army, and the forces selected for the break-out were largely being pinned down by enemy attacks. The Army Command was handicapped by insufficient information from Army Group and the ambiguities in von Manstein's orders. In any case it felt that a jump-off would only be possible when Army Group Hoth had advanced to within thirty kilometres.

In an obvius misapprehension of the ultimate gravity of the situation, and in the midst of unending doubts, Paulus and Schmidt conld not see their way clear in time to taking the decision to break out. The enormity of the risk made them hold back because in the event of a break-out, which would in any case have been an act of desperation, the army would have succumbed after finding itself without cover in the winter steppe and under attack from all sides by a superior enemy.

There can be no doubt that after a careful weighing of the limited technical possibilities against the chances of success, Paulus felt that he could not take the responsibility for the venture, but contrary to von Manstein's claims, Hitler's orders to hold on were obviously not looming large in his calculations. Paulus trusted completely and absolutely in Army Group and his revered superior, Field Marshal von Manstein. It was from him that he expected the decisive order to give up Stalingrad, and at the time he seems not even to have given serious thought to having to act without, or against, von Manstein.

In the last years of his life, Paulus was bitterly dismayed that in his memoirs von Manstein belatedly accused him of servility towards Hitler and laid the major part of the blame for the failure of the relief operation at his door. In his talks with his son, he repeatedly came back to this. He declared that the orders from OKH were always passed on by von Manstein 'without any reservations' and that he had no grounds whatsoever for believing that they were not approved by Army Group. He stressed that he was never, in any phase of the battle, given approval, let alone an express order, to break out, and that von Manstein never even gave him as much as a hint that he disapproved of or condemned the 'Führer Orders': 'He who felt at the time that he could not give me the order or the approval for a break-out, does not have the right today to write that he desired me to break out and would have covered for me.'[37]

Paulus only speaks about events and conditions in those fatal days from 19 to 23 December in a very summary and insufficient manner. Much of the tactical and strategic context and possibilities remains unclear for the time being. The condition of the source material does not yet permit an exact determination of how many tanks and what reserves of fuel the army actually disposed of for a break-out. Although the true situation during this phase of the battle will always be difficult to assess, the historian of the future may hope for new, illuminating information from further publications, war diaries and official documents, and last though not least, from the notations of the army's Chief of Staff. In his portrayal, Görlitz probably followed these to a great extent when he listed all the negative and inhibiting factors that governed the process of decision by the Commander and his Chief of Staff; the ambiguous orders from Army Group, lack of fuel, insufficient combat power, difficulties of re-grouping within the pocket, enemy counter-measures and ignorance of the overall situation.

In contrast to this manner of thinking only in terms of doubts and risks, the question must be asked whether the Army Command actually evaluated correctly the terrible alternatives. These were either a last attempt at salvation by breaking out or unavoidable downfall. The failure of the air lift and the impossibility of holding the 'corner pillar on the Volga' left as little room for doubt as to the gravity of the situation, as did the information from Army Group, which had sent Major Eismann into the pocket for a briefing on 19 December. There is enough evidence that the mostly secret *matériel* and psychological preparation of the army for the break-out were not carried out with extreme and uncompromisingly decisiveness. In his description of parts of a conversation his Chief of Staff had with General Schmidt on 21 December, von Manstein has characterised the state of mind of the Army Command in relation to the vital questions. He says: 'The Commander-in-Chief, who had made the flying-in of reinforcements (which was impossible) a condition for a break-out attempt said, "If there is no hope of bringing in reinforcements, then it would be advisable not to attempt the break-out, but rather to fly in sufficient supplies so that the men in the fortress can regain combat power and the weapons have enough ammunition to hold out. We believe we can then hold out for a longer period, even without reinforcements ... In summary, we are of the opinion that 'Thunderclap' is a catastrophe solution, that should be avoided if at all possible!"'[38]

The historical viewer will have to raise the question time and again whether Paulus should not have acted decisively in those days of crisis without any regard for the inhibiting orders and doubts.

That the break-out failed to materialise caused bitter disappointment, not only inside the pocket, but also among the relief forces and Army Group Don. General Hoth, Commander of Fourth Panzer Army, who was in charge of the relief operation, could not understand why Sixth Army did not attack in his direction after his relieving forces had reached the Myshkova sector. 'The issue is not how far one can go, but to break the encircling ring apart.'[39] The fact that important enemy forces were being tied down by LVII Panzer Corps would have been an advantage. A timely break-out could also have created the possibility of setting the advance of the relieving forces, who were bogged down in heavy fighting on the Myshkova, in motion again. Von Manstein is also of the opinion that the salvation of Sixth Army could not be expected without the willingness to take a big risk. 'One was bound to accept having to live from hand to mouth, in other words, to jump off with what was available, including the amount of fuel that could still be flown in during the days of deployment of the army.'[40] He did not under-estimate the gravity of the risk. 'If nothing else, however, the hope of regaining their freedom, of escaping death or captivity, would probably have enabled the men to make the seemingly impossible happen!'[41]

We can safely assume that the break-out would have galvanised the troops who were well aware of the gravity of their situation. In any case, at this time the Russians were fearful of getting themselves between hammer and anvil, when the German relief offensive forced him to withdraw forces clandestinely from the encircling perimeter, before their 2nd Guards Army attacked.[42]

With its total weight and the courage of despair concentrated on a single point of penetration, the closed-up mass of about twenty divisions would most likely have enabled the majority to escape destruction. Hoth's forces would most certainly have been relieved of pressure by such an initiative, and in such an extreme situation of need secretly hoarded reserves of fuel and ammunition might well have come to light among the troops in the pocket. But there was certainly no hope of success without very heavy sacrifices, particularly in view of the already highly endangered relief operation that was being pushed forward with forces that were far too weak. The army would have had to leave most of its heavy weapons, equipment and vehicles, as well as its wounded and sick, behind.

If Paulus was not able to see his way clear to a decision in favour of such a desperate attempt at salvation, this was not due to blind obedience to Hitler. That he did not take the last chance the immense risk actually held for his army was due, and we may believe him here, to the sense of responsibility weighing on him. At that time no one could relieve him of this. In such a situation a commander of the calibre of a Blücher, a von Reichenau or a Rommel would most likely have acted in autonomous sovereignty without too many meticulous qualms or considerations.

Self-sacrifice and sacrifice on demand

In other chapters of this book we have discussed under various aspects the final phase of the battle of Stalingrad with its endless suffering and dying of the soldiers that were sacrificed. The documents in the appendix also reveal a shattering picture of the downfall of Sixth Army, the tragic blindness, the betrayed loyalties, soldierly error and inhumanity.

In his later notations Paulus rendered an accounting of his conduct for which, in line with the character of the Army Commander, his ironclad clinging to a decision only reached after long and tortured deliberations was characteristic.

After the last chance of an early release from the deadly embrace had disappeared at about Christmas of 1942, he decided that a tenacious holding-on without compromise must be the supreme law governing his leadership. For the time being he clung to the vague hope, constantly being nourished from above, of a new relief operation by strong panzer forces from all the other fronts. Hitler's New Year's radio message declared that Sixth Army should have 'the rock-solid trust' that 'the Führer would not abandon the heroic warriors on the Volga'.[43]

As Paulus underlines, the intentions and promises of the 'Supreme Command' that General Hube reported after his visit to Hitler, decisively contributed to the rejection of the Russian surrender proposal of 8 January 1943. According to them, the air lift was to be put on a new, extended footing and an SS panzer corps was to be brought in for relief. The counter-offensive was to take effect during the second half of February and would turn Stalingrad into a great victory. The condition for this was the stabilisation of the southern wing of the front and the withdrawal of the armies from the Caucasus.[44]

Paulus has remained mute on the question of whether or not he still actually believed in the possibility of a timely relief, given his knowledge of the progressively worsening condition of his forces and the situation on the spot. But he was certainly convinced that the unconditional continuation of resistance and holding-on for strategic reasons was required in the interests of the whole.

And he was constantly being reinforced in his opinions by the superior command authorities. 'The statements made by General Hube,' he writes, 'and the remarks in the same sense made by the Commander-in-Chief of Army Group, bound me to the obligation of holding on, unless I was willing to shoulder the responsibility for the breakdown of the southern sector and by this, of the whole eastern front, not only before the 'Supreme Command', but before the whole German nation.'[45]

In this context we should not overlook von Manstein's message of early January 1943, with which he wanted to take the load off his subordinate Army Commander and in which he answered pressing questions about a break-out. According to Paulus' report, it read something like this: '... I understand and share your thoughts and worries about your army. However, your superior authorities have a better overview of the situation and the necessities arising therefrom and they carry the responsibility. It is your job to execute your orders with all your might.

You are not responsible for whatever may happen thereafter.'[46] And, Paulus adds, 'The fact that when talking to me, the Commander of Army Group agreed with the orders from OKH until the very end, also influenced my conduct. Field Marshal von Manstein had the reputation of being a particularly qualified operational brain and of a man who stood up to Hitler.'[47]

After the pocket broke apart under the final Russian attack, and from mid January the death agony of the encircled army ran its course attended by indescribable suffering, Paulus maintained the standpoint that had constantly been drummed into his head by the highest authority until the end; by its sacrifice, the army was pinning down enemy forces and thereby making the re-establishment, or even the salvation, of the other fronts possible. And he persisted in this belief even after his two requests for permission to surrender, which he finally realised had become necessary, were rejected by the 'Supreme War Lord'. He speaks of the indescribable sufferings of his men without restraint, but then his notes go on to say: 'The knowledge of the sufferings of my men and officers, which went beyond the bounds of anything that had been conceivable before, weighed heavily on my decisions. In the conflict between the obedience that was demanded of me with the strictest referral to the fact that every hour counted, and the humane considerations for my soldiers, I believed that I had to give priority to obedience.'[48]

In another part of his notes Paulus elaborates on these beliefs in a sort of summary, which carries the flavour of a reflection after the fact. There he speaks of the heavy burden of conflict between the constant stringent orders to hold on and the motives of humanity that prompted him to suggest that the battle be terminated. Considerations for the overall situation had required 'holding out to the extreme' and his sacrifice had been necessary in order to avoid even greater sacrifices on other fronts and prevent the general military collapse in the east. At the time, there had been no valid reasons, or so Paulus claims, for disobedience in the face of the enemy, because the subjective recognition of the hopelessness of the situation and the prospect of death or captivity did not entitle the responsible commander to disobey. At the time, neither the Wehrmacht nor the nation would have understood an unauthorised action, since in effect it would have been 'a revolutionary, political act against Hitler'. Paulus goes on to say in closing that giving up the position at Stalingrad against orders would have played the arguments into Hitler's hands, and permitted him to lay all the blame for the already discernible military defeat on the generals and thereby prepare the ground for a new 'stab in the back' legend. He himself had had no political aspirations at all. 'I was a soldier and believed that I was serving my country by obeying.'[49]

The subjective honesty and innocent trust of these statements should not be questioned. But the theoretical discussion that repeatedly ties normal rules of conduct to a unique situation of monstrous dimensions, the true nature of which was not understood, demonstrates to what a frightening degree the Army Commander as a prototype of the soldier-only thinking exclusively in military terms, misjudged the situation and the demands of the historic hour.

What would have been required in the second half of January was not so much a political act, as a humane-ethical decision, because the death agony of the army was already destined to dissolve all soldierly order by offending against the ethical code. And so far as the statement about a new 'stab in the back' legend is concerned, the question tied to it could have been answered a different way, as the men of the resistance movement demonstrated.

As one of the greatest experts on the battle of Stalingrad has claimed, when the Russian ultimatum was rejected in the second week of January, the army, depleted mainly by hunger, sickness and frost, already found itself in a situation in which according to traditional concepts, an honourable surrender could have taken place despite its remaining limited combat power.[50]

On 10 January, when the big Russian attack began, the war diary of OKW noted: 'The daily issue of rations for Sixth Army at the moment consists of 75 g of bread, 200 g of horse meat including bones, 12 g of fat, 11 g of sugar and 1 cigarette. By 20 January, all the horses will have been butchered.'[51]

The Army Commander should have weighed conscientiously the sense and benefit of the sacrifice of tens of thousands, of which he approved, against the value of the human lives that were at stake. Neither his lack of information on the overall situation nor orders from above could relieve him of this responsibility.

On 23 January, the war diary of the Command Staff of the Wehrmacht reports the following fatal event with sober brevity. 'The question General Zeitzler raised yesterday evening, whether Sixth Army could now be given permission to surrender, was answered in the negative by the Führer. The army should fight on to the last man, in order to gain time. To a radio message sent to Sixth Army by the Führer in this context, General Paulus replied, "... your orders will be carried out. Long live Germany!"[52]

That the Army Commander again made a request to the 'Supreme Authority' during the final phase of the tragedy culpably caused by Hitler, there being no doubt possible on the basis of all previous experience as to the answer, and that he expressly affirms his obedience, basically remains beyond comprehension. General Doerr has condemned this step with due severity. 'That the Commander-in-Chief responsible for his men asked the "Supreme Commander" who was 2,000 kilometres behind the front for permission to surrender in such a situation, instead of acting himself, was not in accordance with the German tradition of soldiery. On 24 January there was already such convincing evidence of the horrible forms and dimensions of the impending downfall, that on the basis of any and all soldierly concepts and traditions, General Paulus was both entitled and required to put his responsibility for the lives of more than 200,000 human beings ahead of a combat assignment that had become empty of meaning ... To date, history has never conceded the right to any commander to sacrifice the lives of his soldiers after they are no longer able to fight!'[53]

In the final days of the tragedy of Stalingrad the Army leadership was characterised by an inner schism. It clung to the inhumane orders to hold on until the bitter end, but permitted desperate break-out attempts by various groups. It demanded that its soldiers fight to the last, in a situation beyond compare, but itself took no further part in the business. Shortly after having sworn to the Führer an oath of loyalty and declared non-capitulation to be a soldierly ideal in a heroically worded radio message on the tenth anniversary of the National Socialist seizure of power, it began negotiations with the Russians and surrendered, together with the security forces around it, without including the forces fighting on in the northern pocket. [54] The newly promoted Field Marshal Paulus, who in the end no longer held the reigns of command firmly in his hands, went into captivity as a sick man. He wished to be regarded as a 'private citizen', something the Russian sources confirm, and most obstinately refused the senior Soviet generals any assistance in the capitulation of the remaining parts of his army.[55]

His conduct not only outraged the Führer who had expected that Paulus would commit suicide. During the situation briefing on 1 February Hitler uttered evil curses against the unhappy Commander-in-Chief, whom he called a coward and said that by his going into captivity, he had erased the heroism of his soldiers.[56] None of the senior officers present, including Zeitzler, dared to contradict the enraged dictator or to inject a single word of compassion for or in defence of Paulus. Hitler had obviously intended that the suicide of the Army Commander, whom he had just distinguished with the highest military rank for his obedient loyalty, would contribute to distracting public attention from the actual culprit responsible for the devastating defeat. The circles of the resistance movement were also deeply disappointed, but for a totally different reason. They had vainly hoped that Paulus would act against the insane orders in time or at least object vigorously. 'In Beck's circle, his weakness of character was known. But it would have meant much if immediately before his army went under, he had at least decided to issue a flaming indictment to the German people against the madness of this leadership in war and government of the state and thereby tear apart the thick fog of propaganda with which the truth about Stalingrad was being hidden from the eyes of the nation.'[57]

In his comments and portrayal of the battle of Stalingrad, publisher Walter Görlitz repeatedly deplores that contemporary German authors 'are far more attracted by the boundless suffering that was connected with the downfall of the army than by the fact that in this hopeless situation, in bitterness and despair, tens of thousands still knew how to die honourably; generals, officers and soldiers'.[58]

What took place during the final act of the tragedy of Stalingrad was not an honourable series of events, but rather a violation of soldierly virtues, the final catastrophic outcome of a functionalised obedience gone astray. To examine and portray this seems to me to be far more wholesome than to attempt to abstract the soldierly concept of honour that was misused at the time for questionable objectives, because the courage to make the sacrifice must needs become invalid when the reason for the sacrifice no longer exists. Karl Jaspers has correctly characterised this situation. 'The whole thing became a mere mechanism of obedience and discipline without the freedom of the soldierly ethic, a total inhumanity, dressed up in words that had become hollow ... Where there is no sacrifice rendered, but only obedience born out of the fear for one's life, to place a halo of heroism on the affair is mendacious.'[59]

It remains the tragedy of Sixth Army, that it was sacrificed completely senselessly and for no military benefit.[60] This is not altered by the fact that for a short time it tied down important enemy forces and kept them away from other fronts. That this was not decisive for the fate of the southern wing of the eastern front at the time, has been confirmed by Zeitzler in his memoirs, in which he states that this view of the alleged historic task of Sixth Army was but an argument deliberately propagated by Hitler for reasons of self-justification and propaganda.[61] Görlitz also tends to exaggerate the strategic value of the Stalingrad army holding out as ordered. In any event, General Doerr's words remain valid: 'If the argument propagated at the time by Hitler that "the sacrifice of Sixth Army" had been necessary for military reasons is still being repeated in all seriousness in contemporary literature on Stalingrad, then we must take this as a complete lack of understanding of the art of war, not to mention the inhumanity of such a point of view.'[62]

In a closing paragraph of his biography of Paulus which is as short as it is ill-considered, Görlitz calls the 'massive crisis of trust' that was connected to the defeat on the Volga and the 'dissolution of the soldierly concept of loyalty', the 'heaviest mortgage that Stalingrad left us with'.[63] He makes the exaggerated claim that this 'psychological devastation' had caused all of the yardsticks for any sort of leadership and the basic soldierly concepts of honour, obedience, orderliness, manliness, commitment and sacrifice, to lose their foundations. He appears to believe that the healthy insights that the thinking soldiers reached then and afterwards, and the necessary discussion about the sense of the sacrifice and the ethical foundations of military obedience, to be something disastrous. With his hasty and, moreover, ambiguous comments he is not able in the slightest to do justice to the deeper problem of Stalingrad.

One is the more disappointed in this context that his portrayal, which makes the claim that it will destroy legends, is not able to enrich our historic picture in any important way. Our distance from the events and the status of the source material certainly permit us to reach certain basic insights today, and give urgency to the questions that the tragedy of Stalingrad has left to us: exactly wherein does the value of the event lie, and how it can be conserved as a living value. Walter Görlitz still owes us an answer to this.

In closing let us return once more to the character of the unhappy Field Marshal Paulus. Only rarely in history has a senior commander been plunged so abruptly from the pinnacle of a career rich in success and fame into the depths of such a military and human catastrophe. During the battle of Stalingrad an unbearable load of responsibility lay on his shoulders. It remains the personal tragedy of this army commander of unblemished character, who found himself overtaxed by a uniquely terrible situation, that a degenerated concept of obedience paralysed his resolve to act independently. His claim that an unauthorised break-out would have led to anarchy in the leadership structure, and his apologist's claim that not to hold on would have been the same as 'mutiny' appear to be exaggerated and unjustified. 'If with a clear realisation of the situation of the catastrophe of Sixth Army, Hitler and the OKH did not draw the required operational conclusions, it was not required of the Army Commander to demand the impossible from his men.'[64]

If one leaves aside the final phase of the battle, his failure, certainly also influenced by physical suffering and nervous exhaustion, where the right to decide had to lie with Paulus alone, then the question of overall responsibility can only be considered in the broader context of the situation and of the reporting relationships. In this book I have endeavoured to show in all clarity the degree to which the commanders of the Army Group that was superior to Sixth Army were involved in the responsibility, and how they decisively influenced the process of decision by the Army Commander.

Paulus must be seen as an exemplar of the officer caste, of his generation and of his times. For better or worse he was the product of his education and environment. His mental mode, like that of the others, was determined by the (by now only theoretical) fixed soldierly traditions and strict concepts of honour that had been eroded step by step by Hitler. As an apolitical soldier-only he was interested solely in the tactical-strategic concerns of the war. The 'Supreme Commander', however, had transposed these to a totally different sphere, namely the political-psychological-military. Like most of the other senior officers Paulus was completely helpless in the face of the basically inconceivable perfidy of the dictator. He also shared that far too simple a view of command and obedience that must become a problem in times of a dictatorship and of a criminal regime. But it was foreign to his nature to question the legitimacy of the supreme leadership.

As both a loyal executive organ and at the same time a victim of Hitler, Paulus becomes a symbol for the many, the far too many, who also should or could have acted differently.

In one important point however, he is different from the majority of his fellow generals, not least of all from Field Marshal von Manstein, his superior Commander-in-Chief of Army Group. He admits his responsibility unequivocally.[65] He also felt it was appropriate to voice his belated insights and his recognition of the road of error that was being trod. 'The generals', he declares, 'were the product of their environment and training and saw it as their job to place their "professional skill" at the disposal of the Head of State and thereby, according to their subjectively honest belief, at the disposal of the German nation. Some of the manifestations of National Socialism which bothered them, they opposed. Other weighty ones, they ignored. The roots, they did not recognise. Subjectively they believed they were serving their nation. Objectively they became pillars of a system they themselves rejected and which spelled disaster for our people. In any case, the outcome was an institutionalised irresponsibility that led to devastating results in the area of command. I too shared this error at the time and I do not hesitate to admit it.'[66]

3. GENERAL VON SEYDLITZ

Among the senior commanders of the Stalingrad army was a man who carried a famous name and who embodied the best of Prussian-German soldierly tradition – General of Artillery Walther von Seydlitz-Kurzbach. Because of his proven military ability this commander of LI Corps had been earmarked at the highest level for larger, more responsible assignments. It was intended that he replace Paulus as Commander-in-Chief of Sixth Army. General Schmundt, Hitler's senior adjutant and Chief of Army Personnel, had informed Paulus of this decision when he visited the staff of Sixth Army at the end of October 1942.[1]

Paulus, we know today, had been chosen to become Chief of the Executive Staff of the Wehrmacht, in other words to succeed General Jodl, an assignment for which he appeared to be particularly well qualified given his former performance and experiences on the Army General Staff, and probably also because of his political loyalty.[2]

The Russian offensive intervened and the intended change of command did not come about. We may ask what might the fate of the hundreds of thousands of German soldiers at Stalingrad have been if instead of the carefully evaluating General Paulus, filled with doubts and obeying with too much trust, the reins had been in the hands of von Seydlitz, a man with front-line experience and one prepared to take decisions.

The character of General von Seydlitz is as controversial as that of Field Marshal Paulus, among other things because both men, under the constraints of captivity, issued appeals for the removal of Hitler, their former 'Supreme War Lord' to whom they had sworn allegiance and whom they now recognised to be the destroyer of their country.

The problematical political role which von Seydlitz played as a leading member of the 'A Free Germany' movement, has been validly commented upon by historians in the meantime.

Bodo Scheurig's profound analysis has accurately explained this attempt by German prisoners of war – unsuccessful but noteworthy none the less – to take part in the resistance against Hitler in co-operation with Communist emigrants, as being the political-psychological consequence of the monstrously unique situation of Sixth Army being sacrificed on the Volga and the criminal nature of the National Socialist regime that was revealed thereby.

But in the evaluation of the personality of General von Seydlitz, many summary utterances of condemnation and malicious simplifications continue to have their effect. Many Germans, in particular colleagues of his caste, to whom the gift was not given intellectually and politically to assimilate the unhappy past in which they were all culpably involved, believe they have the right to vilify him. They are neither able nor willing to forgive the fact that the General who was twice sentenced to death, by Hitler and by the Soviets, took a different path from them through the disaster that was so abundant in error, self-deception and suffering for all of us.

Within the framework of our considerations of the problems of Stalingrad, we shall not discuss further the conduct of General von Seydlitz during his captivity. It would also be an error simply to project this conduct back in time to the battle on the Volga, as has occasionally been done. In any case, the role he played at Stalingrad has frequently been dramatised, distorted and portrayed one-sidedly in the literature on Stalingrad. There has also been no lack of defamation and attempts to ridicule what the general intended and actually did at the time. The result has been an indistinct and equivocal picture. Sometimes von Seydlitz emerges as a worried admonisher in favour of a break-out or a timely surrender, and thereby as a counter-player to Paulus and a disciple of Yorck, and sometimes as a short-sighted strategist with no comprehension of the larger operations, a disobeyer of orders and breaker of discipline, a political rebel and mutineer.

Before going further, it is necessary to correct this colourful plenitude of mostly questionable conceptions and to bring things back to their correct dimensions. We will therefore let the decisive phases of the battle pass in review once again and concentrate ourselves mainly on the conduct of General von Seydlitz. Such a critical assessment will serve to deepen our understanding of the soldierly, political and human lessons tied to Stalingrad and to destroy new legends in the interest of historical knowledge.

Attrition in the city on the Volga

Among the few noteworthy documents that portray responsible soldierly thinking and intentions that have come down to us from the fatal days at the beginning of the battle of Stalingrad, we must unequivocally include that 'evaluation of the situation' of 25 November 1942, in which General von Seydlitz again presents the whole monstrosity of the encircled army's situation and requests Commander-in-Chief Paulus to act against the orders given by Hitler unless they were rescinded.

This memorandum and its daring conclusions was the result of a long series of worried observations and experiences, insights and perceptions, inner conflicts and tortures, that had not permitted the general to relax since the very beginning of the battle. The memorandum therefore has a pre-history without knowledge of which its true importance cannot be appreciated. Consequently, we must first put it into the context of the events. In doing so, the soldierly concepts and the conduct of General von Seydlitz during the struggle for Stalingrad and at the beginning of the Russian counter-offensive will be the focal point of our considerations.

From the moment when the leadership of Sixth Army had given the order, on 19 August 1942, for the attack on the city proper, LI Corps, commanded by General von Seydlitz, had for the most part been engaged in the thick of the fighting. In September, while the enemy tried time and again with massive attacks by hundreds of tanks to penetrate the northern front of the army between the Don and the Volga and take the attacking infantry divisions in rear, the heaviest part of the fighting for the tenaciously and bitterly defended city centre fell on LI Corps.

The corps advanced step by step in costly street fighting, house by house, overcame the Soviet defence system around the Gumrak railway station and occupied the neighbouring heights. Against ever stiffening resistance they pushed forward for some kilometres, deep into the centre of the city, through the wilderness of devastated factory buildings, barracks, railway terminals, until they reached the banks of the Volga at the Tsaritsa (Red Square) and the tractor plant. Next came weeks of exhausting attritional fighting which called to mind the bloody struggle for Verdun during the First World War. Finally, the concentrated German advance dissolved into costly individual actions, in which the opponents were fighting hand to hand. It had become evident as early as the second half of October, that the exhausted troops no longer had the strength to eliminate the remaining pockets of resistance and bridgeheads that were still being bitterly defended in the city centre. The heart of the city and the ferry across the Volga remained in enemy hands, and the attempt to take it by a pincer attack by Sixth Army and Fourth Panzer Army had to be admitted as having been a failure.

The progress of the fighting that appeared to be becoming more and more senseless was observed by General von Seydlitz with anxiety and growing unrest. Nine divisions had been assigned to his corps in those difficult weeks of October and November. The burden of responsibility for so many men weighed the more heavily on him, as he was being forced to abandon his long-proven principles of leadership. Hitherto he had always prided himself in sparing his men unnecessary losses in the combat to which they were assigned. The effectiveness and circumspection with which he had led his brave Mecklenburg 12th Division at the beginning of the Russian campaign, advancing from East Prussia to the sources of the Volga and the Waldai Heights, had already earned him the high distinction of the oak leaf cluster to the Knight's Cross at the close of 1941. During the relief of the Demjansk pocket, his forceful objection had succeeded in obtaining the cancellation of a disastrous, interfering order by Hitler that would have squandered his troops uselessly in bloody losses.[4]

General von Seydlitz felt that what was taking place in Stalingrad was a futile sacrifice of his divisions. These had been engaged in continuous combat for more than two months and had come to the end of their resources. The average combat strength of the companies was down to little more than thirty to forty men. The casualty reports were frightening. The losses in men and *matériel* no longer bore any reasonable relationship to the meagre tactical gains. And the consequences had to be all the more disastrous, because there were no longer any more replacements.

The sorry state of LI Corps was shared by the other formations of Sixth Army that had also endured boundless hardships and achieved astonishing results since the beginning of the summer offensive in June, in other words, well before the actual attack on the city began to take its pitiless toll.

The divisions were burned out and it was high time for them to be pulled out for rest and recuperation. And although the morale and sense of superiority of the men remained unbroken, the combat power had been alarmingly weakened, and operational manoeuvrability was highly restricted thanks to the serious supply situation.

Heedful of his exhausted divisions, the exposed position of the army and the approach of the dreaded Russian winter, General von Seydlitz sent a closely reasoned request to Army Command at the end of October 1942.

He requested the immediate termination of the fruitless attacks in the city proper, particularly on the 'Red October' steel plant, in order to spare the troops and to prepare them for the onset of winter. He suggested withdrawing his 14th and 24th Panzer Divisions from the line, replenishing them as a mobile reserve and deploying them in defence against the expected Russian winter attacks.

These requests were denied by Army Command. And to make matters worse, following the example set by XIV Panzer Corps, the order was even given to use the tank drivers as riflemen![5]

This was a bitter experience for von Seydlitz and his disappointment increased when in mid November, despite signs of preparation of a major Russian offensive that had been clearly recognisable for weeks, the Commander-in-Chief ordered the continuation of the exhausting attacks on the inner city and the banks of the Volga. This was in response to an order by Hitler which appealed to 'the proven Command of Sixth Army and its generals' as well as to 'the bravery of its men that has been demonstrated so often'.[6] But the troops were no longer able to meet the demands made of them. After temporary initial gains, all their attacks failed with appalling losses, despite the fact that five engineer battalions had been specially flown in from home and other sectors of the front for the attack on the steel plant which in the meantime had been converted to a veritable fortress. XIV Panzer Corps, which had simultaneously received the assignment to eliminate the Russian bridgehead north of the tractor plant near Rynok and Spartakovka, fared no better. 'And so the divisions continued to bleed to death, and the armoured forces were not rested and replenished, but were deeply enmeshed in street fighting, when the major Russian offensive began on 19 November 1942.'[7]

With this, fate overwhelmed Sixth Army.

Independent action in the initial stages of the battle of encirclement

General von Seydlitz was well aware that Army Command recognised the danger of the overall situation during those fatal autumn weeks of the bitter struggle for Stalingrad, and that it was issuing warnings, making reports, submitting well-founded requests and raising objections. What he did not understand was, why it so obviously did not oppose and rebel forcefully against a development which it too believed to be fraught with disaster.[8] Neither von Seydlitz nor his Chief of Staff Colonel Clausius had the slightest illusions about the monstrosity of the strategic situation in which Sixth Army found itself even before it was encircled. Having regard to the clearly recognisable deployment operations of the Russians south of Stalingrad and on the northern bend of the Don, against which only totally inadequate measures were being taken, and in anxious expectation of the dangerous eastern winter, both officers felt themselves, as did many of their comrades, to be caught in a trap against which their instincts and their will rebelled. What they had experienced in recent months went against their soldierly and strategic concepts. More and more it was beginning to shake their trust in the 'Supreme Command'.

There was a chain of logically connected circumstances and facts, the true meaning of which was beginning to reveal itself in the light of the approaching catastrophe: limitless horizons so far as operational planning and objectives were concerned; insufficient forces; a complete lack of reserves; ceaseless over-taxation of the troops; disregard of the human-psychological factors; supply crises; deceptive self-confidence and under-estimation of the enemy. Two armies had sunk their teeth into the labyrinth of ruins called Stalingrad and were pinned down in a battle of attrition by an enemy who was constantly growing stronger. The initiative had already gone over to the other side. And did not Hitler's recent political speeches show that a sober military-strategic evaluation of the situation was being pushed aside by fanatical expressions of will, by dangerous considerations of prestige and for reasons of propaganda?

With the start of the Russian counter-offensive, which everyone had seen coming but which still struck Sixth Army virtually unprepared, General von Seydlitz clearly recognised that the deep penetrations on both flanks of the army was the crisis point. After all that had gone before, there could not be the slightest doubt about the gravity of the situation. For him there was only one solution: regain operational freedom of action by an immediate withdrawal or a break-out from the developing pocket. At that point, Army Command and the superior Army Group wanted nothing else than that, though they were unable to assist because they had no reserves. So it was in the spirit of the directive received from them, according to which the break-out planned for 25 November was to be prepared for by burning all superfluous *matériel* and by other measures, that General von Seydlitz briefed the General Staff officers of his eight divisions. He reminded them of the historic pocket battle of Lodz in 1914 and of the famous break-out at Brczeziny in which he had taken part as a young lieutenant exactly twenty-eight years before. Convinced that Sixth Army must get itself out of the fatal embrace of the enemy as quickly as possible, he told them that the only choice was between a 'Brczeziny' or a 'Cannae'.[9]

Firmly trusting in the impending break-out and in further decisions in connection with it by Army Command, whose staff for the moment was still on the west bank of the Don, von Seydlitz ordered the withdrawal of a particularly endangered bulge which projected towards the Volga in the north-eastern angle of his front. His reasons for this measure were purely military. After the mass of XIV Panzer Corps had been withdrawn from the same area (much too late!) to secure the most seriously menaced northern flank of the army, LI Corps had been given the additional assignment of taking over the denuded, approximately thirty kilometre-wide sector from Spartakovka to the Kotluban area. This practically doubled the length of the previous defensive line The gap could not be effectively sealed by the depleted divisions moving in; the only available troops being 60th Infantry Division (motorised) and the heavily decimated 94th Infantry Division. So the inner wings of these two formations, who would not have been able to hold the extended and exposed front anyway, were withdrawn to a shorter arc line, thereby shortening the sector to be held by about fifteen kilometres.

This was certainly an unauthorised deployment. But during the initial days of the enemy's storming advance von Seydlitz, out of immediate touch with Army staff – far off and itself over-taxed – felt that he could accept the responsibility for it, particularly in view of the expected order to break out. He was convinced that the withdrawal of the front he had initiated would also serve in the interest of the impending big decisions. 'During these early days I believed myself entitled and obliged to act independently in order to relieve Army, but naturally acting according to their intentions, in other words, in the sense of the only possible solution to this major crisis they too most emphatically favoured, an immediate break-through to the south-west in the direction of Kotelnikovo.'[10]

It was not his fault that the break-out did not take place and that his unilateral action, enforced by circumstances, was to have negative repercussions on the men by robbing them of part of their fortified winter positions. The no longer combat-worthy infantry units of 94th Division were destroyed by the hard-pressing Russians. Despite this, the new positions on the shortened front were held, something which the Deputy Chief of Staff of the division, Günter Toepke, who witnessed the events at first hand and has described them impressively, confirms in his memoirs.[11]

Also, in his belated report to Army command, Colonel Clausius is alleged to have declared that the withdrawal of the front sector at Yersovka had been done in order to make the decision to break out easier for Army Command to take.[12] For General von Seydlitz, however, other motives took precedence. He saw the shortening of the front as a prime tactical necessity.

Soon after this unauthorised action by the corps commander, Army in turn saw itself forced to shorten the front in other sectors in order to save men. And this took place under the same difficult conditions, because there were no prepared positions or fortified points of support anywhere.[13]

In his 'fundamental statements' on the operations in Stalingrad, Paulus incidentally makes no mention at all of the tactical deployments General von Seydlitz was forced to take and which were of no real consequence to the larger events. When the OKH issued a sharply worded demand for a justification of the unauthorised shortening of the northern front, he supported the action.

We have treated these events in such detail here because in the literature on Stalingrad they are mostly falsely described, dramatised or exaggerated. For example, the circumstances of fact and timing are incorrectly portrayed by Toepke and Schröter. Even General Doerr is in error here when he speaks of a 'breach of discipline by a Commanding General in the face of the enemy and at the height of a crisis'.[14] He later regretted having made this accusation and promised to correct it in a next edition of his book.[15] His otherwise excellent study of the battle of Stalingrad shows some weaknesses, specifically with regard to the phase of encirclement, because the testimonies of the leading personalities of Sixth Army were not yet available. Had Walter Görlitz been more conscientious in his portrayal, he could easily have better informed himself. But he did not do this and therefore had the presumption to make claims with regard to the conduct of the Commanding General of LI Corps that are just as incomprehensible as they are absurd. 'This was mutiny in *praxis*' he claims, and 'had General Paulus not been such a kindly-disposed man, von Seydlitz would have been assured of a court-martial.[16]

Görlitz has also treated the responsible role that von Seydlitz played with regard to the question of a break-out from the pocket in a totally distorted and inadequate manner. We must next throw some illumination on this.

Von Seydlitz's assessment of the situation

Acting on orders from above, Paulus and his immediate staff had flown back into the pocket on 22 November from Nizhne-Chirskaya, where they had been up to that date, and had set up a new command post near the Gumrak railway station. Until now Army had received a number of orders, either directly from OKH or via the superior Army Group. These said that Stalingrad and the front on the Volga were to be held at all costs, countermeasures on a large scale were being initiated and Sixth Army was to hold on and await further orders. In the meantime, the situation had continued to become more menacing and it had already been necessary to withdraw against orders those elements of the army engaged in heavy defensive fighting to the west of the Don because they could no longer hold their positions.

Hitler's last radio message of 22 November had not mentioned the repeated requests for freedom of action by the Commander-in-Chief at all, but had demanded that the army dig-in and await relief from outside. Paulus and his Chief of Staff, however, were determined to take the only possible course and break out with the army to the south-west.

To this end a final decisive request was to be sent to the 'Supreme Commander'. Before sending it the opinion of all of the commanding generals was to be solicited. General von Seydlitz arrived quickly, his command post being not far from that of Army. His report on this noteworthy meeting reads as follows: 'On the evening of 22 November Paulus called me and my Chief of Staff, Colonel Clausius, to a meeting in his bunker in which, besides the three of us, the Army Chief of Staff, General Schmidt, also took part. The purpose of the meeting was jointly to draft a radio message to Hitler in which Paulus was to declare Hitler's order of 22 November to dig-in and await relief as being impossible to carry out, and to demand freedom of action. I can still recall this portentous exchange in detail. Today my ears still ring with the constant questions Paulus and Schmidt asked on every sentence that was drafted; "Is that not too strong? Can one say that?" On the other side Clausius and I constantly proposed succinct words and phrases that would not permit any other conclusion in this exceptional situation than the immediate break-out, that had already been initiated. Our suggestions were made all the more readily as the four of us were in complete agreement that an immediate break-out was the only solution to this catastrophic crisis. To believe that the order to stand and hold was impossible to execute, would not have been deliberate disobedience. The fact that digging-in for all-round defence was later successful does not contradict this; our success was only due to the hesitant manner in which the Russians advanced. Therefore I had no particular reason on this occasion to call upon Paulus deliberately to disobey Hitler. If we were again going to ask Hitler at all, then we would logically have to await his decision. The question of deliberate disobedience could only present itself in case of a negative decision.'[17]

In other words, von Seydlitz and Clausius proposed that Hitler not be asked to permit freedom of action, but merely to be informed that digging-in for all-round defence as ordered was impossible and outdated by the tumultuously moving events. They recommended that it should be categorically reported that in view of the completely altered situation, the only conceivable solution to the crisis was a break-out to the southwest which had been initiated immediately. But Paulus refused. He did not wish to act without prior approval by Hitler. It becoming very late, General von Seydlitz and his Chief of Staff did not stay to see the final version of the radio message that evening. They considered sharp, unmistakable words and phrases to be necessary. Von Seydlitz characterised this important message as follows: 'Can one say that the wording corresponded to the catastrophic exceptional situation? In my opinion not. Sound, factual, sober general staff work! But in such a situation, a true commander speaks a totally different language.'[18]

No reply was received to this radio message other than Hitler's notorious order on the morning of 24 November, by which Sixth Army was irrevocably nailed down in Stalingrad and condemned to stay put and hold-on. Simultaneously a further order came in from the very top, according to which General von Seydlitz was to be given unified command of the northern and eastern fronts of the pocket and was to be personally responsible to the Führer for their defence.[19] There have been occasional speculations in the literature about the motives behind this unusual measure. The claim that Hitler thereby intended to counteract von Seydlitz's tendencies towards independence is mistaken any way you look at it.

At OKH no one was aware of such tendencies. The order much more likely suggested a certain degree of mistrust towards Paulus, which had probably grown in Hitler because of the former's repeated requests for freedom of action. Von Seydlitz on the other hand was seen, as Heusinger has confirmed in his memoirs on the situation briefings at Führer Headquarters, to be the 'toughest man' in Stalingrad in whom one believed one could place a special trust, all the more so because of his experience in the pocket of Demjansk.[20] What an irony and tragedy of fate these orders had to be for the one commanding general among all the Stalingrad commanders whose instinct had most surely recognised the dilettantism of the 'Supreme War Lord' and who most forcefully of all favoured a break-out.

When the Army Commander personally brought these two orders from Hitler to his command post shortly after they had been received, General von Seydlitz was stunned. Paulus too was deeply depressed, but obviously prepared to give in and submit to the apparently unalterable. The assignment to be personally responsible to Hitler for the defence of the eastern and northern fronts of the pocket, completely nonplussed von Seydlitz. On this he writes: 'This peculiar order took me so much by surprise, its effect in connection with the further development of things in general remained so obscure for the time being, that all I could say at first was, "there is naturally nothing I can do about this either".'[21]

This statement by von Seydlitz has often been cited in an attempt to question his own determination to act independently. But that is a highly prejudiced view. Only the whole army could and should have broken out. The only one who could act was the commander of the 'fortress', Paulus, supported by the unanimous opinion of all his commanding generals. The claim that von Seydlitz could have acted on his own now that he reported directly to Hitler is simply absurd. How was he supposed to break out alone to the south-west with his army corps, which was holding the Volga and north fronts? In his writings Paulus also mentioned the private conversation that the two men, caught in bitter conflicts of conscience, had in a friendly atmosphere. He stresses that von Seydlitz submitted in soldierly obedience, but later on, 'constantly advised me to act independently without regard to the orders from above'.[22]

The Commander-in-Chief of the army trusted in the decisions taken at the very top. Von Seydlitz, however, was not prepared to accept them. His reaction was not long delayed. He was painfully aware that his own hands were tied. Their despair and outrage about the Hitler order that simply ignored all the arguments by Army and Army Group just would not let von Seydlitz and his Chief of Staff rest. All the appalling experiences of recent weeks and months came flooding back; all the futile requests and demands by Army for adequate flank protection, deployment of reserves, fresh replacements and sufficient supply.

Why had the strongest army on the German eastern front not received timely help in its dangerously exposed position and strategically so important function? There were obviously no reserves available worth mentioning or they would have been provided in time for the final capture of Stalingrad. Now that the foreseeable disaster had arrived simultaneously with the advent of winter, could one suddenly trust the 'Supreme Command', whose irresponsible mistakes were to blame for the monstrous emergency affecting twenty-two divisions and who now demanded something that spurned the strategic principles and lessons tested and proven for generations? Could one assume that now suddenly and all at once supply and air lift would be able to achieve the extraordinary at a time when heavy crises were developing in other distant theatres: the major British offensive against Rommel's Panzer Army in North Africa and the landing of British–American forces in Morocco?

The specific experiences that General von Seydlitz had gained during the relief of the pocket of Demjansk in March and April 1942 filled him with particularly heavy anxieties and scepticism with regard to Hitler's orders to hold-on, and in his talk with Paulus he had not left

Army in any doubt about this. During that event there had also been disastrous interference by the 'Supreme Commander' who was unable correctly to evaluate the difficult situation because he wasn't on the spot. At Demjansk an air lift had just been still barely possible, because only six divisions had been encircled and the short flight distances and heavily wooded terrain had favoured the operation. But at Stalingrad and the steppe between the Don and the Volga, the overall situation made a relief operation a gigantic military venture, a game of hazard with the lives of a quarter of a million German soldiers at stake.

In clear appreciation of the threatening disaster, von Seydlitz and Clausius were prepared to risk the extreme. 'We were totally in agreement in our evaluation of the situation of Sixth Army,' the General explains. 'We were convinced that the pocket meant the downfall of the army because a relief, if such were conceivable at all for lack of sufficient reserves being brought in time, would only be possible after the army had starved to death or shot itself out of ammunition, as a result of the totally inadequate air lift.'[23]

The detailed evaluation of the situation sent to Paulus on 25 November again summarised all the arguments against the Stalingrad army digging-in and in favour of an immediate break-out from the encirclement which had not yet been fully stabilised. The initiative for this important memorandum and its daring conclusions came from Colonel Clausius who also drafted the text in a most close exchange of ideas with his commander. Von Seydlitz had no hesitation whatsoever in accepting the responsibility for it by his signature, regardless of what the consequences might be.[24]

This written evaluation of the situation, set down 'in appreciation of the gravity of the situation', declared the two decisive conditions on which the fate of the army depended: an adequate air lift and the timely approach of relief. An adequate supply by air was already questionable with regard to their own corps alone and was completely impossible for the whole of the encircled forces. 'To attach hopes to this, means grasping at a straw. Where the large number of Ju required for the supply of the army are to come from, is nowhere to be seen. If they are available at all, the machines must first be flown in from all over Europe and North Africa. Given the vast distances that must be covered, their own fuel requirements would be so enormous that in view of past experiences with the fuel situation, its satisfaction appears to be highly questionable, let alone the operational effects this effort would have on the overall conduct of the war.'

With regard to the well-known lack of reserves, the vast distances, the rigours of the weather, the short hours of daylight and the presumable actions of the enemy, 'for whom victory in a classic battle of destruction beckons', the memorandum declared itself to be particularly sceptical as far as its trust in a rapid and successful advance by a relieving army was concerned. 'The possibility of speeding up the deployment of relief forces by employing a larger number of motorised columns cannot be reckoned with. Neither the columns nor the fuel can be available, because otherwise they would have had to be provided much earlier for a much smaller cargo capacity requirement, in order to build up the supply reserves of the so highly exposed Stalingrad front.'

An emphatic warning was given against 'dangerously false conclusions' to which a comparison with the Demjansk pocket of the previous spring could lead. 'Despite the short distance to the German front then, the creation of a very narrow entry into the pocket had taken weeks of heavy winter fighting.' Von Seydlitz was not far wrong in fearing that Army Command would cling to the precedent of the 'corridor' of Demjansk. And he saw no reason for watering down his dark pessimism in the analysis of their own situation.

The conclusions were inescapable. 'In the time permitted by the supply situation, the expectation of being able to obey the order by OKH to hold the position until help arrives, obviously rests on unrealistic foundations. It is therefore not executable and will inevitably lead to catastrophe for the army. If the army is to be preserved, it must immediately obtain a different order or immediately take a different decision on its own. With regard to its operational, political and moral effects, the idea of deliberately sacrificing the army should be beyond any consideration.' The paper closed with the noteworthy sentences: 'If OKH does not immediately rescind the order to hold-on in the position, then one's own conscience dictates the imperative duty towards the army and the German nation to seize the freedom of action denied by the existing orders and to make use of the still existing possibility of averting catastrophe by attacking on one's own. The complete destruction of two hundred thousand fighting men and all their equipment is at stake. There is no other choice.'

There are mainly three things that make this memorandum differ from similar documents, messages and situation reports. On the basis of the circumstances of his own corps, General von Seydlitz assumes the role of spokesman for the whole army. The temperamental, unmistakable and sharp wording goes far beyond the normal, routine language of General Staff documents and does reflect the monstrosity of the existing, strategically extraordinary situation. However, what was finally most unusual and daring in the paper, was the appeal to conscience in demanding that a sense of responsibility deemed it necessary to disregard disastrous orders from on high, and if necessary act against them. In this, the opinions of von Seydlitz and Clausius were now irreconcilably at odds with those held by Army Command and the other commanding generals. These had shared in the basic assessment of the situation until Hitler's shattering order had arrived. Now they believed they had to obey.[25]

Historic events have shown the main contents of the memorandum to have been completely correct, have agreed with the two far-sighted soldiers who wrote them and proved that von Seydlitz and Clausius recognised the imperative of the hour. Compared to that it is of no importance that some of their judgements, particularly with regard to the conduct of the enemy and the time calculation of the supply question, were wrong and too pessimistic. In actual fact, the army, pinned down by its own 'Supreme Command' and robbed of its operational freedom, held on not for just a few days but for long weeks, but from mid December on, only under such appalling conditions that its final downfall was inevitable. Because by that time, as the memorandum had correctly predicted, it had lost its ability to break out. What von Seydlitz and Clausius desired and desperately tried to bring about in those days fraught with decisions had nothing to do with deliberate political rebellion or even mutiny. Their motives were purely military. In the midst of an extraordinarily catastrophic situation, their issues were exclusively the correct soldierly and humane decision. This however, presupposed a deep political-moral sense of responsibility.

At the time von Seydlitz could not know that 2,000 kilometres away, at the headquarters of the 'Supreme Commander of the Armed Forces', General Zeitzler, Army Chief of Staff, was using the same arguments in an endeavour to get the pig-headed dictator, who was only thinking in terms of his own prestige, to back off from the order by which the Stalingrad army was being denied the saving freedom of action. Finally, Zeitzler declared in the sharpest words that 'it would be a crime to leave Sixth Army there where it stands. We can neither relieve it nor supply it. We would only be sacrificing it to no avail'.[26]

This corresponded exactly with von Seydlitz's opinion. His indignation about the order that was unique in military history and contradicted any healthy soldierly instinct, was set down in his assessment of the situation.

The memorandum was first published in Hans-Adolf Jacobsen's *Documents on the Second World War* without, however, including the important attachment on the 'supply situation of LI A.K.' (A.K. = Army Corps), on which the evaluation was based. It is also unfortunate that Jacobsen did not include the note with which General Schmidt, Chief of Staff of Sixth Army, passed the paper on. This remark also deserves to be recorded for history, because it shows the reaction of Paulus' responsible adviser. It reads: 'We are not to wrack the Führer's brains for him and neither is General von Seydlitz those of the O.B.' (O.B. = Commander-in-Chief).[27] This curt rejection of a document in which the question of the fate of the army had been treated with a deep sense of responsibility demonstrates the low degree of sovereignty, in fact the servility, in the stance of the Chief of Staff towards the 'Supreme Commander' whom he obviously trusted uncritically. Paulus himself did not endorse the paper. Did he not wish to grasp the hot potato? But he did pass it on to Army Group by air courier, while simultaneously reminding them of his own situation report and again requesting permission for the break-out to the Don.[28]

The memorandum had reached von Manstein's desk by 28 November. According to the report by his orderly, First Lieutenant Alexander Stahlberg, when von Manstein read it he grew highly emotional. 'General von Seydlitz has gone and written a memorandum that I do not approve of. The sort of thing this Seydlitz is sticking his nose into is unbelievable.' Von Manstein kept the memorandum under lock and key and would not even let Stahlberg, from whom he normally had no secrets, read it.[29] He did not mention it in his memoirs either, obviously because it refuted with telling arguments his own evaluation of the situation next day.

In passing on the memorandum, did Paulus do so with decisive energy and the full unremitting force of his personality? According to his own line of argument and the marginal note by his Chief of Staff, we can hardly assume that he did. In any event the memorandum had no effect. For us and for posterity it remains a historic testimony, that provides a shattering insight into an absolute border-line situation of soldiery and shows the tragedy of the events of the time.

Interestingly enough, Paulus' Chief of Staff, General Arthur Schmidt, stated in 1972 that Paulus had initially not wanted to pass the memorandum on to von Manstein at all. He, Schmidt, had insisted on it, his reason being that he felt it was necessary that Army Group learn what kind of a man had been given command of the northern front.[30]

The semi-official work *Decisive Battles of the Second World War* makes no mention of von Seydlitz's memorandum in its detailed portrayal of the battle of Stalingrad. The author, Walter Görlitz, thought it unnecessary even to mention it. Had he taken seriously the statements in this document, originating directly from those days in November 1942 that decided the fate of Sixth Army, and critically evaluated the pros and cons of the arguments made then, he would have spared himself many inadequacies in his observations and many a false judgement.

Görlitz simply declares the necessity for an immediate unauthorised break-out of the Stalingrad army at the beginning of the encirclement, to be an easy and comfortable judgement in retrospect, a wisdom of hindsight and a political speculation. He shows no compunction about speaking of a 'legend'. 'Let us leave the legend aside,' he says. 'Let us rather ask anew and soberly, what Generals Paulus and Schmidt could have know in those days in November, what the conditions were under which their process of decision must have taken place?'[31] We have already shown elsewhere the military reasons and the unshakeable loyalty to obedience that governed their conduct. But I believe that to the question Görlitz raises, General von Seydlitz's memorandum, taken as the sum of bitter experience and worried observations as well as a sovereign expression of true soldierly feeling, gives a clear and convincing answer.

The road to ruin

From the time when the Army Command had decided to abstain from the break-out that had initially been considered to be necessary, and to passively hold-on and await the relief announced from above, General von Seydlitz found himself in a painful conflict of duties.

He could not understand why Paulus, who was himself disappointed and dismayed by Hitler's decisions, abruptly stopped fighting for freedom of action and did not make a final decisive attempt to convince Army Group of what needed to be done immediately. He was convinced that considerations for the operational intentions of the 'Supreme Command' and for the situation of the neighbouring armies whose fronts had become shaky everywhere, could not possibly demand the loss of the vital fighting power of a quarter of a million soldiers. Since every day of waiting must reduce the combat power of the army and give the enemy further opportunities to take the initiative, he saw a growing danger for the other sectors of the southern wing of the eastern front if the army remained pinned down.

Von Seydlitz declares the words of justification in the Paulus testimony to be 'a boundless exaggeration', when it says that 'any independent emergence from the overall framework' or deliberate action against the orders received, would have meant accepting the responsibility, initially for the fate of the neighbours and in case of an early termination of resistance, in the further course of events for the fate of the whole eastern front, maybe even for the cause of the loss of the war. He goes on to say, 'In my opinion the exact opposite is the case. Particularly at the beginning, a break-out by Sixth Army would have strongly reinforced the neighbours, namely the remnant of Fourth Panzer Army and the remnant of the Roumanians who had fallen back to the north and northwest of them all the way to the Chir. I would have preferred an army of twenty-two divisions that was mobile and able to operate outside the pocket, even if it had suffered not inconsiderable losses during a break-out, a thousand times more than the same army paralysed and incapable of operations inside the pocket... I am absolutely sure that a break-out, initiated at the beginning of the encirclement by the enemy, would have been successful. The first question asked by General Chuikov, the first Russian general to whom we were brought after having been captured, was, "Why didn't you break out soon after the beginning of the encirclement? We were very worried."'[32]

With his written protest of 25 November 1942, General von Seydlitz had dared the extreme. It could have cost him and his Chief of Staff their heads. Now all he could do was to submit to the orders from Army in soldierly obedience and t do his duty, which was bitter enough. In recalling those dark weeks of uncertainty, he says: 'After Hitler's final order of 24 November 1942 to dig-in and await relief, all those in the know were seized by a curious fatalism and a mute subjugation to a fate that seemed to be inescapable. The dumb feeling of approaching doom was reinforced by the sudden extraordinarily poor orientation on the part of Army on the situation outside the pocket, particularly on the deployment of Hoth's relief forces and their advance towards Stalingrad.'[33] Hitler had radioed: 'The army may rest assured that I will do everything to supply it accordingly and to relieve it in time.'[34] Von Seydlitz's own experiences and the sober facts of the situation had filled him with justifiable scepticism and anxiety towards such promises. His warning predictions were now to be fulfilled in a cruel manner. The events of November and December confirmed his evaluation of the situation. The air lift failed and the relief offensive, the start of which had been dangerously delayed, was unsuccessful, not least of all because the army no longer had sufficient combat power and was immobilised.

The General believed it to have been disastrous that from the beginning Army Command had on the one hand assessed the supply problem too optimistically and on the other had been paralysed in its decisions with regard to the break-out, by thinking far to much in terms of the risks. 'Later on we listened-in on many a report by Army Command. We frequently had the impression of a glossed-over optimism of expediency rather than of a situation report that did justice to the whole monstrous gravity of the events.'[35]

At the beginning of December, LI Corps even felt obliged to remonstrate with the Chief of Staff because of the too favourable reporting. 'This led to a controversy between my Chief of Staff Colonel Clausius and General Schmidt. The result was that the radio code was changed, so that we could no longer listen-in.'[36]

Major von Zitzewitz, who was not a spy of the OKW but rather OKH's observant and well-disposed liaison officer in the Stalingrad pocket, had similar experiences. His radio messages had to be passed on to General Schmidt for countersigning. But one day after the Chief of Staff had modified a clearly worded message that left no doubt as to the gravity of the situation by adding the comment, that the time was not yet ripe for such a pessimistic report, Zitzewitz saw himself forced after a talk with the senior officer of the General Staff, to send the most important radio messages at his own discretion, without prior approval by the Chief of Staff.[37]

That von Seydlitz's criticism of the conduct of the Chief of Staff was justified has been confirmed by a whole series of other witnesses who were involved with General Schmidt at the time. At the beginning of the encirclement, when the local commanders of the Luftwaffe vainly tried to explain the impossibility of an adequate supply by air, he declared, 'It will just have to work! And apart from that, we can first eat all of the many horses in the pocket [!].'[38]

The representatives von Manstein sent into the Stalingrad pocket from Army Group for a briefing, his Chief of Staff, General Schulz, and his Ia Colonel Busse, both came back with the overall impression that 'Sixth Army, presupposing sufficient supply by air, does not assess its situation and possibilities of resisting in the pocket unfavourably'.[39]

In the days of decision in December, when the relief offensive was approaching the Stalingrad perimeter, General Schmidt explained to Major Eismann from the staff of Army Group Don that, given better supply, the army would 'still be holding its position at Easter', but that a break-out would be 'a catastrophic solution'.[40]

A weighty voice in this context is that of the Stalingrad Quartermaster, Captain Toepke, who at the time was not only in constant contact with the Chief Quartermaster of Sixth Army, Major Kunowski, but also with Chief of Staff Schmidt. Toepke has impressively described for us the feeling of depression that reigned at Christmas time in the Army Staff after the break-out operation he had so diligently helped to prepare for had been cancelled. He also reports on several conversations with General Schmidt whose expedient optimism specifically caught his attention. After the relief offensive had failed, the Chief of Staff said: 'We do not want to view things too darkly. A solution has always been found before and one will be found this time as well. You should remember that last winter up on the northern front, II Corps was also encircled for a long time and had to be supplied by air before relief came.'[41]

These words show how well-founded General von Seydlitz's fears and how accurate his assumption had been, that Army Command might cling to the example of the pocket of Demjansk. Based on his personal experiences he had expressly warned against this in his memorandum. Considerations were being given to this in the quartermaster department as well. These, however, were different from those of the Chief of Staff. Toepke says: 'Kunowski and I had once noted on another occasion, that Schmidt liked to take the fate of II Corps as an example. To believe in this comparison appeared to us to be more than just daring. Our situation was substantially different. To begin with, the distances to the supply bases of the air lift were much longer for us. Furthermore, relief operations begun on the ground had to start from a far greater distance and therefore required far longer time.'[42]

With regard to the relief operation and the break-out of the army in December, Toepke has given us an interesting insight into the western region of the pocket, mainly the preparations made in the sector of the 3rd (motorised) Infantry Division. The corps staffs were only sent a general orientation because Paulus did not want his intentions, particularly the timing of the break-out, to become known prematurely in order to avoid any excitement among the troops.[43]

This conduct by Army command, which clothed itself in mysterious silence, has been criticised by General von Seydlitz, whose corps was naturally not directly involved in the preparations for the break-out: 'A curious light is shed on Army by the fact that we were being remarkably poorly informed about the situation in those days in December, when the issue was whether or not "Winter Storm" was to take place. Actually, we no longer knew what the game was. One could not speak of the feverish, energetic preparation for "Winter Storm" that we had actually all expected. Especially now when the last chance for escape from the pocket was approaching, one expected communications from Army and a psychological preparation of the troops for this decisive hour.'[44]

At the time, Toepke compared the two senior personalities of the Army, the Commander-in-Chief and his Chief of Staff, with each other, and came to a characterisation that many others, including von Seydlitz, have confirmed. 'Schmidt was the motor. Without doubt he was the one who time and again had confirmed Paulus in his resolve to hold on. Any doubts about Hitler's orders did not exist for him. He was unable to conceive of the idea that we had been manoeuvred into this situation for some sort of reason of prestige or by the incompetence of the "Supreme Command". Since Paulus discussed everything with him, his views must obviously not have been without effect on the Commander-in-Chief.'[45]

Von Seydlitz speaks about a dumb waiting and a complete loss of confidence since the cruel disappointments of those anxious days of Christmas: 'I do not know of anyone who still radiated confidence by this time.' During these days, the Commander-in-Chief presented him with a high Croatian decoration on behalf of the Croat forces under the command of LI Corps. In the desperate situation, von Seydlitz regarded the decoration as being a 'poor ballroom joke'. He accepted the prevarications and empty promises coming from Führer Headquarters with secret indignation. He believes that Paulus too was no longer filled with trust in the help promised by the 'Supreme Command'. 'At the time he had already completely given up. I can still recall how he came to see me between Christmas and New Year to show me Hitler's Christmas telegram, "The army can trust me implicitly." We both agreed that this was the purest sort of derision.'[46]

At about the turn of the year, the soldiers in Stalingrad who were in the know clearly recognised that after the front with the army's supply bases had been thrown back for hundreds of kilometres and the whole Don front had fallen apart, any thought of a new relief offensive coming in time had to be a figment of the imagination. The situation at the time has been briefly and accurately described by Tippelsskirch: 'Sixth Army was cold-heartedly written off by the "Supreme Command", held off and admonished to hold-on with empty promises and verbal commitments, the unfulfillability of which nobody with insight had any doubts about.'[47]

The downfall that had been ordained cast its shadow and the disaster ran its course with implacable logic.

Conflicts of conscience in the face of catastrophe

January came and plunged not only those commanders who had a sense of responsibility, but also uncounted soldiers of other ranks, into painful conflicts of conscience.

The last act of the tragedy of Stalingrad began with the rejection of the Russian surrender proposal and the start of the enemy offensive of destruction on 10 January 1943.

General von Seydlitz was of the same mind as the other commanders about the rejection of the ultimatum: 'None of us was in doubt about the correctness of the decision, because the remaining assignment of the army, after the failure of Fourth Panzer Army's attempt at relief had failed, was to pin down enemy forces in order to relieve the other German fronts, respectively to enable the re-establishment of a new defensive position by the two southern army groups. As long as a major Russian attack had not compressed the pocket and as long as some sort of air lift was still possible, there was no immediate pressing reason to surrender.'[48] But only a few days later, after the western and southern perimeter of the pocket had broken down, disaster remorselessly overtook the army which for a long time had been dying slowly of hunger, frost and sickness.

Von Seydlitz rejects as being highly questionable von Manstein's claim that on 19 January ninety major enemy formations were still deployed opposite Sixth Army. With regard to the dimensions of the pocket, which by then was already down to about one-third of its original size, these would have had to be 'Lilliputian formations'. 'In my opinion, by 17 or 18 January the time had come when we were no longer tying down important enemy forces for the relief of the other fronts. Signs of dissolution were already visible everywhere. Supply by air was virtually nil. The already greatly shrunken pocket could be guarded by numerically reduced Russian forces, and the Russians could simply wait for its slow, sure dying and demise, without real need for further combat and attacks.'[49]

With regard to these facts and the inhuman conditions that were worsening day by day, von Seydlitz felt that action against the existing orders was called for. In his opinion sensible conditions for military obedience no longer existed. He decided to act. 'I therefore went to see Paulus on the evening of 18 January, in order to learn his assessment of the situation and his further decisions and, in view of the catastrophic condition of the men, to try to move him to end the battle for the whole army in an organised fashion... Paulus promised me to hold a further meeting with all the reachable commanding generals and divisional commanders next day, in order then to ask Hitler for freedom of action.'[50]

The meeting actually took place on the 20th and the answer to the cable sent to the 'Supreme Commander' was, as could be expected, a terse brutal No! 'Surrender out of the question!' Hitler radioed back. 'By holding out to the extreme, the army fulfils its historic role, permitting the establishment of a new front and the withdrawal of Army Group

Caucasus.'[51] A further radio message demanded that the fighting continue to the last man and bullet.[52]

Von Seydlitz was enraged by this insane order, which Army accepted obediently and only passed on to a part of the subordinate formations in an amended version. He did not understand why Paulus had even bothered to ask the Führer again, instead of simply acting independently in this catastrophic situation the full horror of which could only be grasped by those on the spot. The soldierly conditions for further fighting no longer existed. The issue now was to end the suffering and dying by responsible measures on the part of Army Command. But Paulus remained passive. He seemed not even to have assimilated Hitler's motto of 'fighting to the last man and bullet', since final rousing orders to that effect were not forthcoming.

Colonel Selle, the army's Chief Engineer, has commented on the feelings and thoughts of von Seydlitz, who was caught in deepest conflicts of conscience, and whom he encountered at the time in his corps headquarters. Both officers were old comrades from the times of peace and trusted each other without reservation. 'The General was pacing back and forth in his bunker in a state of agitation. He knew that he could speak freely. And so he opened all the locks of his heart and mind that he had kept artificially closed. With razor-sharp logic he explained to me that, given such a dilettante 'Supreme Command' that valued loyalty to party politics higher than professional military ability, the only possible outcome had to be criminal chaos.'[53]

Subsequently von Seydlitz made accusations against Army Command, particularly against the Chief of Staff whose one-sided experience on the General Staff had closed his mind to the true nature of the conditions in the front line. In the end he bitterly deplored the fact that all his efforts to bring his Demjansk experiences to bear in influencing Army had been futile. Now all was lost, and even Schmidt had come to realise it.

With his final words, von Seydlitz was obviously referring to a dramatic scene that had been enacted on 19 January at Army staff, the close of which he had witnessed.

Major Thiel, the young commander of a fighter squadron, had appeared before Paulus as the envoy of Field Marshal Milch, the man Hitler had appointed far too late as special representative for the air lift for Sixth Army, in order to gather information on all the relevant aspects of co-operation and to answer questions. Paulus and Schmidt, both in a state of extreme agitation, had heaped accusations about the failure of the Luftwaffe on this poor flying officer, in which bitter disappointment and maybe also a suppressed feeling of the guilt on the part of the senior men of the army with regard to the approaching catastrophe, suddenly found expression. At the end, the Chief of Staff had said in uncontrolled rage, that the Luftwaffe had betrayed Sixth Army and that this crime could never be atoned for.[54]

Von Seydlitz's comment on this sudden explosion of outrage was as follows. 'Their own bad conscience was obviously blowing off steam here and putting all the blame on the Luftwaffe. But had not von Richthofen and Fiebig as well as Pickert urgently and unmistakably warned that the two armies could never be supplied by air? And had not Schmidt rejected all these objections? Did he not remember this? Had not his argument at the time been, that one could first eat the horses in the pocket?'[55]

General Schmidt said goodbye to Colonel Selle, who was flown out of the pocket as a courier on 23 January, with the words: 'Tell them everywhere you feel it to be appropriate, that Sixth Army was betrayed and abandoned by the highest authorities.'[56] If this was not just a temporary expression of outrage resulting from overtaxed nerves, then von Seydlitz is correct in his statement that in the end even the Chief of Staff of the army in the pocket had come to a correct, if belated, recognition of the disaster. But in spite of all such insights and despite the knowledge of the increasing suffering of the soldiers doomed to go under, nothing was done on the part of Army Command to end it.

Humane-ethical reasons determined von Seydlitz to go one last time to Army Command with a request. This took place on 25 January after he had again been horrified by the unimaginable conditions in the cellars and hospitals, by the heaped piles of dead, the wounded and frost-bitten wandering about in search of food. 'It was simply impossible for me to see the ultimate sense of soldiery and soldierly honour in this suffering of hunger, freezing to death and dying away or in German soldiers being shot to bits by Russian tanks advancing without need of cover ... At the time, everything in me rebelled against this madness and against this leadership without a conscience.[57]

238

Von Seydlitz presented his request to Paulus and the Chief of Staff. 'Without entering into a discussion about the serious signs of dissolution of which Paulus was just as much aware as I was, I asked whether Army still intended to do anything with regard to a united surrender. If this were not done, then every single officer and soldier would be faced with the question of whether and how he should act on his own. Paulus, completely giving up, answered just as briefly, "I will do nothing." He did not give any sort of reason for this. Schmidt stood by silently. After a short consideration I reported that I would then act independently. Neither Paulus nor Schmidt made any reply to this, whereupon I took my leave. It was the last personal encounter I had with Paulus in the pocket.'[58]

Immediately on his return, Seydlitz issued his last corps order which was sent to his two remaining divisions (100th Jäger Division and 295th Infantry Division). The order said that an order by Army on the final phase of the battle was not to be expected. Army had forbidden negotiations with the enemy and rejected suicide. A further splintering of the front into small sectors and individual pockets had to be avoided under all circumstances in order to prevent further completely useless sacrifices. The regimental and battalion commanders were therefore authorised to act independently according to local circumstances, to use up the last of their ammunition and then to terminate the fighting.

This last order by General von Seydlitz in the Stalingrad pocket was a responsible act, the result of a conflict of duty from which the man and the officer had suffered bitterly. In his choice between rigid obedience to the top leadership, which in this instance meant a combat assignment become void of meaning, and his duty towards the soldiers he had been entrusted with, he decided to follow the dictates of his own conscience.

Other commanders besides von Seydlitz also acted on their own and in rebellion against the remorseless order by Army to hold out, obeying instead the higher authority of the ethical code. General von Drebber arranged for a timely and orderly termination of the fighting at the head of his 297th Infantry Division and General Schlömer, Commander of XIV Panzer Corps, prevented unnecessary further blood-letting and the worst of the confusion of dissolution by a united surrender.[59] Many regimental and battalion commanders, and even leaders of smaller units, found the redeeming freedom of decision in this border-line situation to be without precedent.

During the entire battle von Seydlitz had suffered from the fact that his hands had been tied and that independent action was denied him in the decisive phases, because he did not hold the key position. What he criticised in Army Command was its passive and resigned conduct which, together with a falsely understood concept of obedience, was again to manifest itself disastrously in the chaos of downfall.

In looking back he writes: 'As far as I can recall, from the beginning to the bitter end of this monstrous emergency situation, one actually did not have the impression of a leadership by Army that was aware, clear and taut in all its thinking, objectives and commands. Neither for a break-out at the end of November and again at the time of "Winter Storm", did Army issue orders that in their language and arguments were enlightening with regard to the terrible gravity of the situation and that called for and prepared for the extreme, nor can I remember any directives that clearly and unambiguously corresponded to the dimensions of the assignment to hold-on in a lost position. And this is even more true for the finale, with its increasing dissolution. Here indeed did the unclear, mute, ambiguous and resigned conduct of the Army Command, which could no longer find the strength or courage to act independently, triumph.[60]

The effects of such an unsure leadership that could not find the way to extricate itself from the dilemma of constantly new situations of conflict, had not only to be borne by the troops in the line, whose trust and loyalty were deliberately misused in the end. They also made themselves felt at a different level among the higher staffs, frequently thrown together hodge-podge and vegetating in the cellars and bunkers of the Stalingrad labyrinth of ruins passively to await the end, while outside the troops went to the dogs.

In his notations von Seydlitz was not afraid to paint a shattering picture of the confusion, helplessness, tension and dumb resignation of the generals and their remnants of staffs. He reports that despite its orders to defend the command posts to the last man, Army approved of the desperate break-out attempts by individual officers or groups. Among the senior officers who plunged into the adventure of trying to escape from the pocket shortly before the end and were killed while trying to pass through enemy lines, were the Army's Ia, Colonel Elchlepp and the Chief of Staff of LI Corps, Colonel Clausius, whose name will remain connected to the Seydlitz memorandum.

Von Seydlitz considered it to be completely unjustified and a betrayal of the men on the line, as these did too, that two of the commanding generals of the encircled army no longer shared the fate of their soldiers in the end, having left the pocket on orders from above. One of them, General of Panzer Forces Hube, had been given the assignment to reorganise the air lift which by now had hopelessly broken down, the other, General of Engineers Jaenecke, had been flown out because he had been lightly wounded. Incidentally, Seydlitz also reports on the little known fact that at the last moment even the Chief of Staff was obviously prepared to leave the sinking ship at whose helm he had stood together with Paulus during the long, fatal months of the Stalingrad battle. After several couriers had been sent out, what important mission could Schmidt still have been entrusted with at the time? Faced by the final downfall Schmidt, like many other officers in the catastrophic final phase of the battle, had shared in the flood of promotions that rained down from on high. Promoted to Lieutenant General, he still ended his military career in captivity. Because when he held the order to fly out in his hands on 25 January, the last aircraft had already taken-off from Stalingradski. At the time, von Seydlitz felt this was poetic justice.[61]

Von Seydlitz's capitulation order had an aftermath that was humiliating for him. Army, which had learned of it indirectly, first considered having him arrested and then simply relieved him of his command. The remnant of his divisions, which were acting in the sense of the order they had been given, were put under the command of General Heitz, the Commanding General of VIII Corps. While on the run, he had strayed into the southern pocket area with some remnants of his troops and could have been given overall command of this sector of the front anyway because of his seniority. Seydlitz quite rightly attributes this measure to General Schmidt, the unbending proponent of holding on.[62]

For this reason, he refuses to take the subsequent claim by the Chief of Staff seriously, according to which Schmidt allegedly recommended to Paulus on 22 January that he permit the surrender of the formations that were no longer able to fight, without referring the matter to Führer Headquarters.[63] If Schmidt had actually really no longer understood the continued obedience of his Commander-in-Chief and considered it to have become necessary to demand that he act on his own responsibility, then he should have clung to von Seydlitz as an ally when the Commanding General asked the Commander-in-Chief for the last time on 25 January to permit an orderly surrender.

This had not been the case. On the contrary, there are enough witnesses who are able to testify to Schmidt's will to hold on and to his obduracy to the end. When the Chief of Staff of XIV Panzer Corps, Colonel Müller, asked him to intervene with Paulus for the urgently needed surrender, he received the cynical answer that after all, the soldiers still had knives and their teeth with which to fight.[64]

In his portrayal of the battle of Stalingrad, Walter Görlitz has repeatedly over-stressed the intervention by Schmidt, who himself seems to give it great importance in connection with the question of surrender, while apparently believing he could ignore mention of the attempts made by General von Seydlitz, who first brought up the matter as early as the meeting of the generals on 20 January.[65]

In his 'fundamental statements', Paulus conscientiously records the two interventions by von Seydlitz. He has nothing to report on any differences of opinion with his Chief of Staff, and this would after all have been the first time that they would not have been of the same mind on an important matter.[66]

Beyond any doubt it was also General Schmidt who on 29 January, in other words immediately before the end, the army having been long in the process of dissolution, presented his Commander-in-Chief with that lying radio message to the Führer in which non-capitulation is lauded as an act of heroism and an example for the future. When asked about this message of servility during the Nuremberg military trials, Paulus declared: 'I regret that out of the overall situation at the time, I let this pass and did not prevent it'.[67]

The subordination of himself and the remnant of his staff under the command of VIII Corps in the last days of January, led to a further grotesque experience for General von Seydlitz. The iron General Heitz, who was resolved to defend every metre of ground and to hold-on until the bitter end, believed that faced with the dissolution of the army he himself must firmly grasp the reins. For this purpose he convened a corps order briefing on 29 January at which two commanding generals with-

out troops, three divisional commanders, three colonels and some additional officers were ordered to appear. Von Seydlitz could not imagine
what further demands could now be made of the soldiers who were
already completely exhausted, almost out of ammunition, exposed to the
icy cold and abandoned to the enemy tanks. He expected a serious order
commensurate with the tragedy of the situation and which would com-
bine a recognition of the sacrificial commitment made to date with a
rousing appeal to the men to make an ultimate effort. But something else
entirely happened. The main content of the order was a list of death
threats: 'Whoever surrenders, will be shot! Whoever shows a white flag,
will be shot! Whoever finds a loaf of bread or a sausage dropped by our
aircraft and does not hand it in immediately, will be shot!' And then
came further items, all ending with the stereotype, 'will be shot'.[68]

Two days later von Seydlitz experienced the results of such fanaticism when he set out on the harsh road of captivity in the midst of a
sorry group of captured generals, staff officers and other ranks. 'We had
to climb the narrow stairs that led upwards over the steep bank of the
balka in single file. At this moment, as a result of Heitz's order, we
received fire in the back from our own machine-guns. This caused the
death of Colonel of Engineers Schilling who had found refuge among us,
and of Captain of Cavalry Bethge from my own staff. Their bodies rolled
down the embankment and landed at the feet of the Russians who were
standing below.'[69]

This was the General's last shattering experience on the Stalingrad
front. Von Seydlitz has not forgotten to report that several days later
General Heitz, who had been thought to have fallen, and who had so
remorselessly sacrificed his men and left no doubt in his insane order of
29 January that he himself would fight to the last bullet and seek a soldier's death in the defence of his command post, joined the group of captured generals. To outward appearances he seemed to be completely
unaffected by the hardships and strains of two months of living in the
pocket and, in contrast to all the other generals, he had a wealth of personal baggage with him.

The impressions and experiences, the inadequacies and errors,
described in this chapter, belong to the overall picture of the battle of
Stalingrad. The viewer who is searching for the whole truth must tap the
totality of the available sources. It is certainly not very edifying to have

to investigate the total external and internal course of events of the tragedy on the Volga and particularly its final phase.

What has been revealed here is not only a plenitude of the symptoms of dissolution, but the clearly demonstrated ultimate result of a soldierly and human misconduct to which the course of events had to lead in fatal logic. The bitter medicine of remorseless examination is required, particularly against certain attempts and tendencies to justify, belittle and conceal by silence.

If General von Seydlitz has been moved into the centre of the examination here, this was not so as to present him as a special ideal, let alone to describe him in the role of a would-be hero. He too had his human weaknesses and inadequacies. In the bitter fulfilment of duty he too had to give in in the end and tread the path of disaster with his men against his own better judgement. Together with his fellow generals and comrades in arms, he too was enmeshed in the web of guilt and fate. Therefore it is far from his intentions to be omitted from the count among this harshly tested community. He was neither a mutineer nor a rebel intending to raise the flag of political resistance against Hitler on the Volga.

However, he was probably the most prominent representative of the thinking and seeing soldiers in Stalingrad who recognised the military-political contexts and demonic background of the events sooner and more clearly than others. Both his military experience as a commander and the unfailing soldierly instinct that lay in his blood, from the very beginning of the battle of Stalingrad on, put him into decided opposition to an Army Command that he tried to influence in favour of independent action in a monstrous and exceptional situation.

It was his personal tragedy that he was only able to attempt by criticism, remonstration and independent action within a modest framework, to fend off the disaster hanging over the heads of a quarter of a million German soldiers. Fate did not permit him to demonstrate by a deed of greatness that he was prepared and determined to risk everything in order to meet the demands of the hour. His feelings and thoughts, his intentions and actions within the limited scope of the possibilities remaining to him, were indicative, however, of the more or less conscious reactions of many of the warriors of Stalingrad to an event that had to erode the traditional concepts of honour and obedience step by step and finally to reveal, in a most terrible manner, the lack of conscience of a degenerated leadership of war and state.

General von Seydlitz's conduct in Stalingrad must call to mind the responsibility of any senior soldier towards the higher dictates of his own conscience beyond the merely military and essential ethical foundations on which the military duty to obey must be based.

Within the framework of this portrayal it was designed to remind us by proxy of the boundless psychological tortures, the unending internal strains and conflicts with which innumerable German soldiers suffering most cruelly in the battle of Stalingrad were burdened.

Stalingrad
Memories and
Reassessments

PART III

APPENDICES

THE LITERATURE ON STALINGRAD:
A CRITICAL ASSESSMENT
(For detailed source information refer to Bibliography)

Being one of the major decisive battles and the military-political turning point of the Second World War, from very early days Stalingrad provoked a wealth of diverse literature from both the German and Russian sides. The murderous struggle on the Volga, a shattering tragedy for one nation, a triumphant victory for the other, hell on earth and death for the hecatomb of soldiers of both sides, has remained a subject of lively interest. And this interest is not only concentrated on military-strategic matters, despite the fact that the advance to Stalingrad, the tenacious fighting for the metropolis on the Volga and finally the pocket battle, can teach us many tactical and operational lessons. The interest also touches on many general soldierly and human as well as political, moral and historical topics.

In addition to dramatic reports of personal experience and individual memoirs written by participants in the battle, we find memoirs and written attempts at justification by generals, sober investigations by military historians, and historical studies, portrayals in the form of fiction, and other types of literature, many of which have even been made into films. There is no lack of sensationalising trash-literature and grossly distorted legends.

We shall attempt here to provide a short inventory of the more important literature on Stalingrad.

Let us start with the notations of the responsible senior generals of Sixth Army and its superior command authorities. The testimony of Field Marshal Paulus, published in 1960 by Görlitz, who also drew on the notes of Sixth Army's Chief of Staff, General Schmidt, for his commentary, and the memoirs of Field Marshal von Manstein, already published in 1955 with the chapter on Stalingrad, so revealing in many ways, provide us with an insight into the senior command, into the way the operational decisions were reached and also attempt a self-justification of the conduct of the personages in the key positions of responsibility during the battle. We have treated these particularly important sources in detail, and their importance is in no way lessened by the ambiguities that we have pointed out.

The Chief of the General Staff of the Army, General Zeitzler, reports on the tragedy of Stalingrad from the viewpoint of the very top. His interesting commentary is hardly known in Germany, because it was published in 1956 in English as part of a report by several German generals on 'fatal decisions' made during the war.

Zeitzler's sixty-page chapter on Stalingrad takes the reader into the OKH and permits him to take part in the tenacious and brave struggle with the incorrigible and pig-headed dictator who opposed all the recommendations for saving Sixth Army made by the Chief of Staff in those critical days in November and December; who was inordinately pleased with the term 'Fortress Stalingrad' which he himself had dreamed up, who believed superstitiously in the technical miracle weapon, the new Tiger tank, and finally, while remaining completely unmoved by the tragedy on the Volga, repeatedly denied the dying army permission to surrender.

Zeitzler describes how he tried to prevent Hitler from making General Heim the scapegoat at the beginning of the Russian offensive; how he vainly suggested flying to the front with the Führer; how he outwitted him at the end of December 1942 in order to obtain the withdrawal of the armies from the Caucasus; how he refused to pass the mendacious New Year's telegram on to the betrayed troops; how he and the members of his staff voluntarily went on the starvation rations of Sixth Army in mid January as a comradely gesture; how in the end Hitler convulsively attempted to justify the senseless sacrifice of the Stalingrad forces as being the only measure possible for the salvation of the southern wing of the eastern front.

It may well be that in retrospect, Zeitzler dramatised the futile role he played in those months so full of despair for him, and that not all the words were spoken precisely as he claims. But there is much evidence to indicate that he was a robust man with a mind of his own and was not lacking in the courage of his convictions. His report proves in a most shattering manner how the General Staff had long been hopelessly deprived of power and degraded to a mere executive organ of the dictator.

Among the sources that give us a direct insight into the workings of Hitler's mind, intentions and decisions during the battle of Stalingrad, we have the memoirs of General Heusinger, Chief of Operations of the OKH. These are in literary form, but are based on extensive notes and exude the authentic atmosphere of the Staff. Then there is the official War Diary of the Wehrmacht Command written by Greiner. His strictly factual entries only illuminate the big picture but they do give us highly accurate information on important dates, facts and relationships. It is interesting to learn here that Hitler had expressed his concern about a major Russian offensive across the Don towards Rostov early on, particularly after the last week in October, but did not draw any practical conclusions from this insight.

The works of justification and the portrayals that lead us into the realm of operational considerations and decisions from the point of view of the senior command authorities are complemented by a group of important, if not always dependable testimony, without which the picture of the battle of Stalingrad would not be complete; the personal memoirs and experiences written by individual participants. That these publications stem exclusively from officers and members of the staffs is only natural. The most important and frequently cited among them are those by Selle, Toepke, Scheibert and von Senger und Etterlin. The book by Herhudt von Rohden is more a work of military history.

The viewer would be well advised to approach these more or less sub-jectively coloured accounts of personal experiences critically, since their quality varies according to the intellectual ability, experience and mental horizon of their authors. One cannot expect to find a completely accurate reporting on the strategic events in them, nor an always correct evaluation of the motives behind the measures taken by the higher command authorities. They do, however, add much life and blood, colour and atmosphere to the overall picture.

Most of these eye-witness accounts and memoirs, still reverberating with the emotions aroused by the impressions and experiences of the time, are fruit-ful for the historian by virtue of their factual information, and in addition they show an earnest attempt mentally to assimilate the experience.

The book by Schröter, *Stalingrad ... to the Last Bullet* (1953), is a colour-ful patchwork of official documents, many eye-witness reports and effectively presented journalistic articles, that repeatedly lets the former war correspondent from the propaganda unit attached to Sixth Army shine through. Shortly after the battle, Schröter was given the assignment by Göbbels to write the official history of the Stalingrad army based on the documents of the German Supreme Command. He had access to all the relevant material and used important oper-ational documents, radio messages and telexes from the various staffs, authentic reports, maps, letters and numerous personal notations by men who had fought in Stalingrad.

When the manuscript was ready, the Reichs Minister for Public Educa-tion and Propaganda forbade its publication as being 'intolerable for the Ger-man people'. Schröter was able to save his manuscript until after the war and then wrote a new version. It contains many faultlessly reproduced official doc-uments and excellent maps and pictures. But the totally unscientific presenta-tion of the documents, the many false datings, the eye-witness accounts whose sources can be neither identified nor dated, and the many fictitious events and conversations, demand that this colourful book always be approached from a critical distance and with caution.

The compilation anonymously published in 1950 as the *Last Letters from Stalingrad*, with a postscript on the history of these letters that were intercepted by the OKH and confiscated in order to learn the true feelings of the troops, evidently stems from the same author. A statistical evaluation gives a rough pic-ture of the thoughts and feelings of the soldiers, of whom 50 per cent did not trust and rejected the military leadership. The thirty-nine letters selected, whose remarkable similarity in style suggest that they were edited, are shattering documents. But they do not permit a totally satisfying examination of the psychological state of the warriors of Stalingrad. Incidentally, seven mail bags containing the last greetings from the dying troops reached Germany, but minus the names of their addressees.

In 1951 the German Communist author and former president of the National Committee for a Free Germany, Erich Weinert, published a book of notations from the front line under the title of 'Memento Stalingrad'. These had already appeared in Moscow, New York and London during the war. Weinert reports on his experiences at Stalingrad where he, together with Walter Ulbricht, Willi Bredel and a number of captured German officers, attempted by propaganda leaflets, megaphones and mobile sound units, to induce the German soldiers to stop fighting and desert. His attempts which, incidentally, he undertook in close contact with Khrushchev, at the time a member of the War Council of the Soviet Stalingrad Front, were mostly unsuccessful. The German soldiers not only rejected them as 'enemy propaganda', but above all they were fearful of falling into the hands of the Russians. The portrayal permits an insight into the minds of the Communist emigrants of the time, whose ideology made them believe that the men were bound to revolt against their officers and that discipline 'only resulted from the combination of the morality of the master with the servility of the slave'. Weinert rhapsodises on the conditions of service in the Red Army, and reports in detail on his conversations with captured German soldiers and gives the contents of documents from mailbags captured by the Russians when German aircraft were shot down.

The copious volume of illustrations of the battle of Stalingrad published in East Berlin in 1960 by Bergschicker was compiled from an insufferably propagandistic point of view and includes many false interpretations. The history and lessons of Stalingrad are made to serve as a justification of Socialism in its eastern version and for the founding of the German Democratic Republic, which is interpreted as being the fulfilment of the legacy left by the German catastrophe on the Volga. This compilation should be approached with critical reservations. None the less, many of the images in the wealth of illustrations from German and Soviet archives give an eloquent and shattering impression.

It is appropriate here to give some indicators on the nature of Marxist historiography on the other side of the iron curtain. In the portrayal of the battle of Stalingrad, this also faithfully follows its Soviet model. This form of historical assessment characterised by uniformity, systemisation, bias and ideological clichés, forces the richness of life and intellect into the Procrustean bed of dogmatic concepts. It includes the standard accusation made against any historical works from West Germany, that they all serve resurging imperialism and militarism and are only intended to prepare for a Third World War and a new Stalingrad. Current political and tactical needs govern historical writing in the East, which accuses the West German publications on Stalingrad of having reactionary and revanchist tendencies and, among other things, of the intentions of masking the genius of the Soviet military leadership at Stalingrad and of deliberately misrepresenting the decisive importance of the battle.

The crass polemics against the West are complemented by a boundless apologia for the East. And Paulus, who opted for the East and spent the final years of his life in Dresden, is excluded wherever possible from becoming the subject of a serious critical historic examination. Despite this, the copious West German researchers, whose law of life is an untiring search for the truth and a constant control of its results, will always remain receptive towards individual critical arguments that remorselessly brand certain weaknesses and restorative tendencies on our side here.

The questionability of Eastern historiography briefly discussed here is eloquently reflected in the book *The Second World War 1939–1945: Reality and Falsification*, in which a series of examinations are devoted to the topic of Stalingrad.

The accusations against us just mentioned would have to be a cause for real concern, if the book published in Heidelberg in 1956 by Lenz, *Stalingrad – the Lost Victory*, had to be taken seriously and had any importance as being representative. In a downright grotesque mixture of fiction and truth, it attempts to justify Hitler and propound the theory that the battle of Stalingrad was lost because of the incompetence of a few generals, sabotage and betrayal and, in the end, because of espionage by the 'Red Chapel'. Such Neo-fascist, or better yet, Nazi atavism, combined with malicious attacks against the resistance fighters, is an exception. But this publication also takes its place among the colourful literature on Stalingrad.

In the realm of sober military history, Doerr's *The Campaign to Stalingrad*, published in 1955, deservedly stands out. It is based on years of research as well as on personal experiences. As Chief of the German Liaison Staff with Roumanian Fourth Army and leader of German combat groups, its author was involved in the Russian penetration south of Stalingrad, the relief offensive and the break-down of the front between the Don and the Volga. This excellently documented scientific study in war by a professionally trained military expert with combat experience deals with the larger operations and the wealth of frequently inter-connected events from the end of June 1942 until the destruction of Sixth Army at the beginning of February 1943, and pays careful attention to the many strategic and fundamental soldierly lessons to be learned. There is no lack of decisive criticism and judgements, that would no doubt have been brought out in even greater detail, had the testimonies of the senior commanders of Sixth Army already been available to the author. Even though they were not, this book, which Halder ranked as a work on the professional level of the General Staff, remains of fundamental importance for future research.

In his contribution to *Decisive Battles of the Second World War*, Görlitz thoroughly evaluated the internal documents of the Command of Sixth Army, whereby his all too far-reaching tendencies to justify detract from its historic value. I have already repeatedly pointed out the reasons for the lopsidedness and inadequacies of his *Battle for Stalingrad*, which is nevertheless rich in information and based on copious source material and literature.

The multi-layered problems anent the catastrophe on the Volga are not grasped but, as we have seen already in the biography of Paulus and Görlitz's comments to the testimony of the Field Marshal, are reduced to a purely military-strategic controversy. For this reason the chapter on Stalingrad with which Scheurig begins his book *A Free Germany*, becomes a mandatory correction and complement to the overall picture painted by Görlitz. While short, it encompasses all the deeper ethical, psychological and political dimensions of the event and clearly brings out the monstrosity of the situation and its consequences.

It goes without saying that the battle of Stalingrad has received the attention it deserves in the general accounts of the history of the Second World War and the German General Staff by Görlitz, von Tippelsskirch, Erfurth and Dahms.

In our list of the literature on Stalingrad, we should not omit a short treatment of the documentary novels, because many Germans have drawn their knowledge of the tragedy on the Volga mostly from them. In first place we must list the novel *Stalingrad* by Plievier. It was written shortly after the end of the battle, was the first book on the subject after the war and familiarised the German nation with the details of the downfall of Sixth Army in a shattering fashion. Plievier, an emigrant, who was living in Moscow at the time, was never at the front himself and so did not witness the Stalingrad débâcle. He collected his copy by months-long, thorough questioning in the prisoner-of-war camps around Moscow and also received copious material from the Russian side. What he presents in the way of factual material is therefore hearsay at second or third hand. The different scenes and individual episodes in the story, however, are for the most part accurate. But the picture painted of the German soldiers of various ranks, their mode of thinking and speaking with which the emigrant was hardly familiar, mostly do not ring true. The overall atmosphere has not been correctly grasped in so far as the ending is projected to the beginning and the novel starts off with an orgy of horror, that hardly permits any intensification. What is missing, are the ups and downs of feelings reflecting the individual phases in the development of the battle. In the collage of all of the terrible facts, all the painful events and pictures of a virtually apocalyptic downfall, there are none of the brighter lights that were there in reality. His characters are hardly capable of generating true human sympathy. They appear more like germs seen through a microscope.

Plievier's mode of perception is explainable in the end by his basic ideological point of view and his materialistic spectacles, which prevented him doing full justice to the totality of the soldierly and human tragedy, particularly in the spheres of psychology and religion. His book is therefore certainly less inadequate and incorrect by what he describes, than it is by what he has left out. None the less, the positive sides of his literary effort should not be overlooked. They lie mainly in the visionary power that is not lacking in Dantesque scenes and pictures. In its unstructured form the novel has the appearance of a gigantic fresco whose main composition is most assuredly a symphony of horror. However, he was the first to bring the problems connected to Stalingrad to the attention of a wider audience, while at the same time intending to motivate his readers to reject war by means of a sort of shock therapy. Therefore, it was also a necessary book.

In contrast to Plievier's portrayal, in which the macabre scenes of destruction and death dominate, Gerlach's documentary novel, *The Betrayed Army*, published in 1957, is a testimonial of the real experience of suffering and surviving, that is as instructive as it is shattering. This is a book without prejudices and resentments, without colourings in black and white and without ideological distortions. The unconditional reality in the descriptions of the military events and localities, but above all of the human beings, their feelings and thoughts, hopes and fears, give the novel the credibility of a document.

Gerlach, who lived and suffered throughout the whole of the event as an officer on the staff of 14th Panzer Division, but also as a member of combat teams on the front line, while remaining meticulously accurate in his descriptions of the external framework of the battle, places the emphasis of his portrayal on the inner human occurrences, on the psychological situation, on the insights and transformations of the soldiers, and on their fates. These are described at three levels; that of the man in the ranks, that of the officer, and that of the higher command. The character portraits of individuals whose fates appear as symbols for all the other Stalingrad warriors and co-sufferers, remain most closely tied to the general disaster. What is particularly impressive in a portrayal that manages to organise highly complicated and almost limitless material in a clear and logical manner, is the powerful way in which individual scenes are integrated into the whole fate of a large army, even of a whole nation. This novel, which avoids any sort of glossing over, also contains scenes of apocalyptic horror that invoke the hell of despair, hopelessness and madness. Examples of these are the hopeless march of the wounded through the frost to the already long over-crowded field hospitals, the death agonies of the starving, sick and freezing in the ultimate shelters of despair, the cellar vaults reeking of excrement, blood and fever, or the pitiless fight for the last seats in the aircraft leaving the pocket, prompted by the naked drive of self-preservation.

The soldier, however, is portrayed in all his humanity, not only in his weaknesses and errors, but also in his unbelievable efforts, in his self-sacrificing will to hold on, his will to survive and in his incredible ability to suffer the most extreme hardships and strains.

A reputable Swiss military magazine was therefore able to write that this book does honour to the warriors of Stalingrad. Any other form of honouring that would attempt falsely to attribute a heroic sense to the sacrifice of Sixth Army, would be an inner lie and mendacious pathos.

A third novel that can claim some right to being a documentary statement became known not so much for its intellectual distinction and style of writing, but rather because of the film with the same title that was based on it and the publication by Schröter. This is *Dogs, Do You Want to Live Forever?* by Wöss. One criterion for the poor formal quality of this book that portrays the tragedy of Stalingrad through the eyes of a front-line officer filled with resentment and hatred of the staffs and senior command, is its colloquial language. The author was over-taxed by his subject and was unable mentally to assimilate the experiences of yesterday and put them into the appropriate form. The characteristics that make Gerlach's novel so impressive are missing here; a psychological distance from the tragedy and a humane maturity of judgement, both of which are necessary if such a book is to avoid being a mere chronology of disaster and, more importantly, a manifesto against inhumanity and a convincing appeal to humanity.

At the close of this overview, we must also briefly consider the Soviet literature on Stalingrad.

The first information about the months-long battle for the city on the Volga came from reports by the official information office and the notes of Russian war correspondents, publishers and authors, from among whom we need here only mention the well-known names of Ehrenburg, Grossman, Simonov and Tolstoi. They were mostly also translated into other languages and widely utilised by foreign publications, as for example, in the French book by Milhaud. The English publication by Seth is also mainly based on Soviet reports, even though it also leans on such conflicting works as those of Schröter and von Manstein.

Immediately after the end of the war, the 'First Authentic Reports by Russian Generals Rokossovski, Voronov, Telegin, Malinin and Russian war correspondents' appeared and was also published in German. The huge book, published in 1958 as *Stalingrad. Battle on the Volga* (*Bitva za Volgu*), contains many eye-witness accounts by participants in the battle.

Up to the mid Fifties, many Soviet publications of various kinds appeared. But during this period the personality cult made around Stalin, the withdrawal from the foreign literary scene and, in general, the inadequacies of source material, militated against the production of a serious work of military history.

Stalin's military genius was lauded to the sky. Time and again he himself appeared as the infallible, incomparable, victorious commander who by his personal intervention had brought about the fatal turning-point on the Volga. The difficulties and setbacks of the Red Army were played down or ignored entirely. One of the Soviet films that was also shown in many prisoner-of-war camps was characteristic of the boundless glorification of Stalin and his immediate colleagues. The 'Screenplay in Literary Form' by Virta about 'The Battle of Stalingrad', which appeared in 1948 in German, impressively reflects these tendencies which were to dominate all categories of Russian literature for a decade.

The XX Congress of the Communist Party in Moscow in 1956 proclaimed the revision of Soviet historical writing and a re-evaluation of the military operations of the war. After the Stalin myth had been overcome, a new point of view prevailed, according to which victory had not been won by military genius, but by the collective efforts of the Party, the Soviet government, the heroic Soviet army, its commanders and brave soldiers and the whole Soviet nation. Since then these directives have also governed the literature on the battle of Stalingrad. It profited from the fact that the official archives were slowly being made available and also, that important western publications were being translated and becoming known in the Soviet Union. Four extensive important works on the topic of Stalingrad have appeared since 1959. Their authors are two well-known Soviet historians, Samsonov and Telpushovski, both of whom had already written about the battle on the Volga some years previously, not without having paid tribute to the Stalin cult, and two Marshals of the Soviet Union who became famous as commanders, Yeremenko, the former Commander-in-Chief of the Stalingrad Front, and Chuikov, who had been entrusted with the defence of the city on the Volga with his legendary 62nd Army.

All four authors diligently obeyed the official party directives and also took part in the fight against the 'reactionary falsifications by the bourgeois writers of history and memoirs' in the West that had been demanded from above. The bases of their points of view, their reasoning, style and quotations are of a remarkable uniformity. This enables us summarily to point out some characteristics here that are valid for all the new literature on Stalingrad we have mentioned.

The victory at Stalingrad is normally seen as an incomparable triumph of the 'superior Soviet art of leadership and science of war' over the 'mistaken strategy and stereotyped tactics' of the Germans, as the logical result of the better organisational effort by an advanced, superior political and social system. In constantly recurring cliché-like statements, the authors underline, frequently in words full of pathos, the leading role played during the battle by the Party and repeatedly weave numerous acts of heroism by the Communist and Komsomol 'shining examples' into the historic portrayal.

In contrast to the 'miracles of courage and tenacity' of the Red Army, lauded by the use of superlatives, the picture of the German enemy is normally distorted, his efforts are played down, his successes attributed to mere numerical superiority, his combat strength and losses greatly exaggerated. The scope and nature of the internal problems and difficulties of the German leadership, Hitler's disastrous interventions, stirrings of opposition and the struggle of individual personalities and higher staffs for correct measures, are normally completely ignored. It is a part of the cliché-like view of Soviet-Communist historical writing, to portray Hitler, the German General Staff, the commanders and soldiers, as a united and uniform block of rapacious imperialists.

The undeniably extraordinary efforts and the triumph of the Red Army at Stalingrad are celebrated as being the sole, decisive turning-point of the whole war and also as the true reason for the downfall of National Socialism.

The events fraught with decisions on all the other fronts and the military successes of the Western allies are just as inadequately portrayed, if they are mentioned at all, as is the military supply by America, even though this also contributed to making the Soviet victory possible and to bringing about the final destruction of the Hitler regime.

Of particular interest in the Russian literature are the constantly recurring references to the great successes of the Soviet planned war economy, whose rapid reconstruction in the Ural region and in Siberia from hundreds of arms plants that had been evacuated began to make a telling effect in the winter of 1942/3 and contributed to the offensive at Stalingrad.

We learn that the whole nation, whose material resources had been mobilised to the extreme, stood behind the defenders on the Volga and was prepared to make any sacrifice. The counter-offensive in the Don–Volga area, carefully prepared in secrecy and under great difficulties, therefore enabled the concentration of a surprisingly powerful mass of forces: 17,031 guns and mortars, more than 1,140 tanks and 1,267 aircraft were concentrated in the three Soviet Fronts that were to take part in the offensive. The start of the encircling offensive on 19 November 1942 was seen as an act of liberation. Near Kletskaya, an infantry division jumped off to the rousing strains of a military orchestra of ninety musicians. In the Soviet portrayals there is no lack of numerous and varied quotations that show the degree of sympathy with which the world took part in the fight and victory of the Red Army at Stalingrad and how great the political impact of the battle was at the time.

The Eastern point of view and historiographic characteristics discussed above, are clearly demonstrated in the approximately 100-page-long chapter which the official party military historian Telpushovski devoted to Stalingrad in his history, *The Great Patriotic War of the Soviet Union* (1959). In the German translation of the work, the publishers have critically commented on the lopsidedness of the portrayal while still recognising the instructive content of the whole as well as the Soviet effort.

The more than 600-page-long book published in Moscow in 1960 by the historian Samsonov is based on many-sided source material, official Soviet documents from the State and Party archives as well as on foreign research literature.

This is the most comprehensive portrayal of the battle of Stalingrad to date and is enriched by many illustrations, helpful maps, tables, documents, indications of military formations and troop strengths. German publications have largely been taken into consideration and the Paulus testimony was also utilised. In his preface, the author provides an overview of the Soviet literature on Stalingrad. Samsonov has placed the battle, on which interesting insights into its individual phases and episodes are conveyed, into the larger military, political and economic contexts and clearly made it appear as the decisive turning-point of fate.

Among the writings by Marshal of the Soviet Union Yeremenko, the enormous book on Stalingrad published in 1961 takes first place. It combines personal memories with the historical portrayal of the operations of the Southeast and Stalingrad Fronts whose Commander-in-Chief the author was. The portrayal mostly uses official source material, eye-witness accounts by other generals and senior commanders, as well as important Russian and foreign literature, and also takes the international press into account. Yeremenko describes the events connected with the German advance to the Volga and the months-long defence of Stalingrad in detail, as well as the planning and execution of the encircling offensive in which he played a major role. A detailed chapter is devoted to the German relief offensive attempted by von Manstein and to the Russian counter-offensive which later enabled the Southern Front, newly formed under Yeremenko at the beginning of January 1943, to advance to Rostov. Like all the other newer publications on Stalingrad mentioned, this book also strongly emphasises the role played by Khrushchev, who was active in Colonel General Yeremenko's army group as a member of the war council. Also worth mentioning is the reproduced report by General Shumilov on the capture of Paulus and his staff.

Marshal Chuikov, Commander-in-Chief of the famous 62nd Army, which he subsequently led all the way to Berlin as 8th Guards Army, has also reported on the battle on the Volga in several publications. His last book, published in Moscow in 1962, bears the meaningful title *180 Days in the Fire of Battle*. His most important notations, however, had already been published in 1959 as the first volume of his war memoirs *From the Volga to the Spree*, also published in an abridged German version under the title *At the Beginning of the Road*, in East Berlin in 1961.

What makes this in many ways instructive work stand out and be so effective, is the personal colour and candour of the portrayal by an exceptionally energetic and able commander, whose personal conduct radiated courage and confidence, whose exemplary personal fearlessness, bravery and unconditional commitment, shaped the morale of his men and officers and inspired his army to praiseworthy efforts amidst grave crises.

Chuikov neither glosses over nor hides anything. He not only lauds the heroic deeds, the commitment and sacrifice of the untiring defenders of the city. He also speaks of the failures and the cowards. He criticises mistakes in leadership and personalities wherever necessary. His book is a rich historical source, not only for the military events during the battle, but also for the feelings and thoughts of the Soviet warriors, the continuous political indoctrination and the mobilisation of all the physical and moral energies with which the last islands of indomitable resistance on the banks of the Volga were defended as a symbol of the unbroken fighting power and the virtually inexhaustible reserves of an entire nation.

The reader can gain a vast amount of interesting information from the writings of the Field Marshal. Quite naturally the emphasis of the portrayal lies on the month-long bitter fighting of the 'active defence' in late summer and autumn of 1942, with all its ups and downs and desperate crises.

We learn of the shattering power of the unceasing German air and tank attacks, of the frightful Russian losses, of the almost hopeless situation Chuikov found on taking over command in mid September. The formations had been battered, reserves and heavy weapons were lacking, morale was nil, many men of the Red Army had only one desire; to escape the hell of Stalingrad by fleeing across the Volga.

The new Commander took over with iron remorselessness in order to eliminate the panic-mongers and cowards and to re-establish the spirit of combat. The Party sent the best forces available to the front. Nine thousand Party members were drafted to 62nd Army from all over the USSR. Many of its battalions consisted exclusively of Communists or Komsomols, who by their example inspired the spirit of sacrifice in the other soldiers. In October, 8,000 Komsomols of the 37th Guard Division defended the tractor plant.

We learn details of the unceasing, inspiring informational activities of the political organs, about combat orders, patriotic songs, and oaths sworn, about the services performed by women on the front line, of whom more than 1,000 in 62nd Army received awards, about the death-defying sailors of the Volga flotilla, who took care of the supply of ammunition and food at three crossing points, despite air raids and artillery fire, and who brought back more than 2,000 wounded to the left bank on many a night. From mid October until the freeze in mid December, 28,000 men, more than 3,000 tonnes of ammunition, and other supplies were transported across the Volga. After the freeze until the end of the battle, the tally was more than 18,000 vehicles, 263 tracked vehicles, 325 guns and more than 17,000 wagons. For an intermediate period of time a 270-metre-long footbridge was put into service. For more than a month, from mid November on, a war on two fronts had to be fought; against the enemy and against the ice drift on the Volga.

In tenacious defensive fighting in confined space and initially against a numerically superior enemy, Chuikov's army, frequently split into combat teams, had held an 18-kilometre defensive front in the narrow bridgehead of the ruins for many months. The command post of the Commander-in-Chief was always in close proximity to the front line, initially on the 'Mamai-Kurgan' and in the end on the bank of the Volga near the industrial plant 'Red Barricade'. On one day alone in October, when the battle for the tractor plant was raging, thirty men from the army staff fell and for days on end he was surrounded by a sea of flames running down to the Volga from burning oil tanks. The Army Commander himself had many hair-breadth escapes.

The final chapter of the book offers an interesting summary of the military-tactical lessons and experiences to be gained from the defence of Stalingrad, which Chuikov had glorified earlier in a special article about 'The Army of Mass Heroism'. The Army Commander develops new tactical methods of combat which consist of forcing the enemy into hand-to-hand combat by day and night by means of heavily armed attack teams, thereby depriving him of his major trump card; air superiority. Every individual soldier had to become a fortress and had to defend every square foot of Stalingrad terrain to the death, in obedience to the supreme law of the soldiers of 62nd Army – 'Not one step back!'.

The three outstanding Soviet books in which the battle of Stalingrad is treated as literature have been frequently translated and into German as well. The 900-page novel by Grossman, *Turning Point on the Volga*, appeared in Moscow in 1954 under the Russian title *For a Just Cause*. It contains a comprehensive picture of the events of the war during the summer and autumn of 1942, the pre-history of the battle, brilliant characterisations of people and places, and describes the fighting up to the high-point of the defence of Stalingrad by the Red Army in the second half of September against the background of Soviet life in general.

Two older, shorter novels: Simonov's *Days and Nights* and Nekrassov's *In the Trenches of Stalingrad*, first published in 1944 and 1946 respectively, also deal with the fighting in the summer and autumn during which the Soviet armies initially hastily retreated back over the Don, the hold on the Volga and the defence which clawed itself into the Stalingrad labyrinth of ruins until the beginning of the big encircling offensive. These works of literature are not only impressive because of their portrayal of the dramatic events. They make just as lasting an effect by the human content of the portrayal, that impress by their cleanliness and truthfulness and their freedom from hatred and resentment.

Important sources and literature of the last thirty years

Since the Sixties there has been a remarkable increase in the publications on the battle of Stalingrad; books and magazine articles, memoirs and studies in military history. The bulk of this literature quite naturally comes from the two German states and the Soviet Union, where the interest in this noteworthy historical event has remained very much alive into the present. The historic portrayals of the Second World War and of the Russian campaign, in which the big turning-point of the war in the winter of 1942/3 is always carefully treated, are on the increase. This increase in the literature on Stalingrad is also due in the end to the fact that sources of fundamental importance, particularly the archives of the Wehrmacht, were returned by the Americans and became more readily available in the German central archives than they had been. Other important material such as testimonies, the results of interviews, diaries, unpublished statements and studies, found their way into the Research Office for Military History in Freiburg or into the Institute for Contemporary History in Munich.

Among the printed sources, published and commented upon by outstanding experts, are Hitler's speeches, proclamations, dinner-table conversations and talks with diplomats. Particularly illuminating for the campaign to Stalingrad and the events of the battle are his directives for the conduct of the war and the fragments of the minutes of his situation briefings. Very important is the war diary of the Supreme Command of the Wehrmacht (Wehrmacht Command Staff) that has been complemented by detailed explanations by first-class historians. In close context to this, stand the very instructive personal notations and short notes of Chief of Staff Halder and other officers of the Führer Headquarters who were present at the situation briefings. These documents often dramatically reflect the continuing struggle for command decisions at the highest level, as well as the functioning and atmosphere of the OKW and the

OKH. The short daily notations in Halder's war diary, that were exemplarily edited by Jacobson, are an unfalsified source, in the end also for the process of the disempowering of the General Staff carried out step by step by Hitler. The memoirs of General Warlimont, Deputy Chief of the Wehrmacht Command Staff and one of the closest associates of Jodl, are a valuable complement to the publications from the files and documentary sources. They offer a very illuminating insight into the functions and methods of work of Führer Headquarters with its fragmentation into the various theatres of the war, its conflicts of responsibilities and personal tensions. Despite certain tendencies towards justification and subjectively coloured statements, this substantial, critically well-balanced book remains an important document for the comprehension of Hitler's leadership mechanisms and the unpreventable deterioration of German military policy in which the catastrophe of Stalingrad was rooted. In contrast to most of the military memoirs, incidentally, its introduction contains a humanely sympathetic confession by Warlimont of his co-responsibility 'with which my own conscience will not cease to struggle'.

Thanks to the increase in source material, interesting portrayals of the battle of Stalingrad also appeared in France and the Anglo-Saxon countries during the Sixties, mainly within the framework of the whole German–Russian campaign. Highly worth mentioning are the French military-historical studies (1968) by Aimé Costantini, *Echec à la Wehrmacht* (Check-mate to the Wehrmacht) that are specifically based on Soviet documents, as are those of his predecessor of 1949, General Guillaume. The American General Staff work by Earl F. Ziemek (1968) was able fully to utilise the readily available wealth of the German military files on a broad basis. This is also true of the carefully balanced and authoritative overall portrayal by the British historian Albert Seaton that was published in 1971. This is a work that not only appeals to the experts, but to a broad readership interested in historical-political matters, whose author successfully made the attempt effectively to utilise the wealth of sources available at the time in the East and the West as well as the most diverse literature, which he evaluated critically. The publisher of a shorter version of this enormous work, Andreas Hillgruber, declares that the author has made 'an intensive effort at differentiation and to do justice and be fair towards both sides in the war' and calls the book 'a convincing intermediary summary of all the insights into the German–Soviet war that have been gained by research to date'. The chapter devoted to Stalingrad is fruitful, stimulating and worth thinking about, particularly because it goes beyond the mere military-strategic analysis, which this sort of topic needs must do.

We still have some extremely meaningful and humanly moving testimony by a prominent participant in the battle of Stalingrad that has not yet been taken into consideration by the relevant literature. For this reason, it should be briefly treated here. This consists of the letters written from the front in those days by Colonel Helmuth Groscurth, Chief of Staff of XI Corps, who died in Soviet captivity in April 1943. Groscurth was an outstanding, active representative of the military opposition to Hitler. After his transfer to the front, he wrote more than twenty letters in which he paints a shattering picture of the sliding downward path into catastrophe. Six of these letters, containing detailed critical reports on the situation, already carry particular weight because of the person they are addressed to, Colonel General Beck. The soberly and strictly evaluating Groscurth sent home impressive descriptions of the situation and worried criticism from all the phases of the battle of Stalingrad, having clearly recognised the irresponsibility of the campaign that contradicted all the laws of strategy. He experienced the demise of the General Staff, the over-taxation of the troops and the leadership of his own army, which he castigates with irony. As early as 18 August 1942 he writes to Beck that, 'the General Staff is marching to its complete ruin. It is no longer an honour to be a part of it. I have received the most serious letters from headquarters about the interference by the Party ...' And on 29 August 1942 he writes, 'To do one's duty in this chaos is getting harder and harder, and in recent days I have frequently asked myself if one can still accept the responsibility of continuing to take part in this madness ...' Towards the middle of January he made a last desperate attempt. He was able to procure an order to fly out one of the officers on his staff, who was given the task of immediately making contact in Berlin and Paris with several influential members of the officer faction opposed to Hitler. In particular, he was to tell Colonel General Beck that 'only an immediate action' by the opposition could save the encircled army. At the time Beck decided to send an urgent letter to Field Marshal von Manstein in the cause of the opposition. But the attempt came to nothing.

In 1974 the long-awaited German General Staff work *Stalingrad. Analysis and Documentation of a Battle* by Manfred Kehrig appeared. It had been preceded by General Doerr's more modest but serious studies within a larger framework, as well as by those of Philippi and Heim. Kehrig's large book, rich in substance, is the fruit of an admirable diligence and extraordinary thoroughness. Despite its ambitious title it deliberately restricts itself to the portrayal and analysis of all of the ascertainable operational, tactical and logistic sequences of events as well as to the development of the relationship with the Roumanian allies, which was becoming progressively worse. The complete files on the war from the three branches of the Wehrmacht that have been preserved, a richly varied source material of war diaries, testimonies, situation evaluations, letters and other notations, as well as interviews, all enabled the author to reconstruct the larger events, frequently down to the actual hour, and also to offer a precise analysis of the decisions made at various levels of command. The work contains an astonishing wealth of documents and sources, all meticulously listed, of instructive statistics, overviews of troop formations on both sides of the front, and maps. The perfection with which the purely military-historic aspects of the catastrophe have been treated and the way the study has been substantiated by source material, are probably beyond compare. In the midst of the previous controversy of opinions and portrayals, the work aims at providing a firm foundation for all future discussions and evaluations and it will certainly be of great value for many aspects of detailed military-historical analysis. However, the book makes high demands of the reader, who grows tired of the multitude of facts that overwhelm him and who misses summarised results and clarifying evaluations in the portrayal. Highly problematical are the lopsided, inadequate analyses of the terrible final phase of the battle, and the playing down of the failure of Army Command which resigned ignominiously after having wickedly violated the virtues of the soldier. On balance, besides the mistakes and omissions by the higher command, Kehrig's interesting studies clearly demonstrate the untiring but futile attempts, in the midst of grave conflicts, to apply military intelligence and ability to a strategy of the impossible, the insufficient and the inhuman.

On the Russian side, three noteworthy novels about Stalingrad have been published: Konstantin Simonov's *Days and Nights*, Nekrassov's *In the Trenches of Stalingrad*, and, the most important, Vassili Grossman's *Life and Fate*.

Grossman's novel is only a book about Stalingrad in so far as it portrays life in the Soviet Union at the time of the battle. However, he who truly wishes to understand what Stalingrad meant for this country and the terrible conflicts into which all its people were enmeshed, will find it indispensable. The manuscript of the book and all copies that the NKVD was able to lay its hands on were confiscated. Suslov, the chief ideologist of the Party, declared that a book such as this could only be allowed to appear after 200 years. Sacharov, the great physicist and fighter for human rights, was able to save one copy and the writer Vladimir Voinovitsh smuggled it out of the country, so that Droemer Knauer was able to publish the novel in German in 1984.

BIBLIOGRAPHY

The Battle

Bergschicker, Heinz. *Stalingrad. Eine Chronik in Bildern* (*A Chronicle in Pictures*). Berlin, 1960

Bitva za Volgu. Vospominanija ucastnikov Stalingradskogo srazenija (*The Battle for the Volga. Memoirs of Participants in the Stalingrad Battle*). Stalingrad, 1958

Busse, T. *Stellungnahme zu der Kritik des GenLt. a. D. Schmidt an dem Buch des Feldmarschalls v. Manstein* 'Verlorene Siege' *und zu den Ausarbeitungen von Schmidt zum Fall 'Stalingrad'* (*Statement on the criticism of Field Marshal von Manstein's book* Lost Victories *Lt. Gen. (ret) Schmidt and to Schmidt's works on the 'Stalingrad' case*). October, 1967

Chuikov, V. I. *Armija massogo geroizma. Iz zapisok o boevom puti 62-j armii* (*The Army of Mass Heroism. From the notes on 62nd Army's role in the war*). Moscow, 1958

– *Nacalo puti* (*The Beginning of the Road*). Moscow, 1959

– *Vystojav, my pobedili* (*We Won by Tenacity*). Moscow, 1960

– *180 dnej v ogne srazenij. Is zapisok kommamdarma 62-j* (*180 Days in the Fire of Battle. From the files of the Commander-in-Chief of 62nd Army*). Moscow, 1962

Deborin, G. A. 'Stalingrad'. *O Vtoraja mirovaja vojna* ('Stalingrad', in *The Second World War*, pp. 194–224). Moscow, 1958

Dibold, Hans. *Arzt in Stalingrad. Passion einer Gefangenschaft.* Salzburg, 1949. English tr. *Doctor at Stalingrad. The Passion of a Captivity.* 1958

Doerr, Hans. *Der Feldzug nach Stalingrad. Versuch eines operativen Überblickes* (*The Campaign to Stalingrad. Essay of an Operational Overview*). Darmstadt, 1955

– 'War Stalingrad ein Opfergang?', in *Die politische Meinung. Monatshefte für Fragen der Zeit* ('Was Stalingrad a Sacrifice?', in *The Political Opinion. Monthly for Contemporary Topics*), p. 89 *et seq.*, 1958

'Dokumenti o Stalingradskoj bitve', in *Voenno-istoriceskij zurnal* ('Documents on the battle of Stalingrad', in *Military–Historical Journal.* Moscow, February, 1959

Erickson, J. *The Road to Stalingrad,* London, 1975

Filippov, N. *Severo-zapadnee Stalingrada. Zapiski armejskogo redaktora* (*To the North-West of Stalingrad. Notations of an Army Editor*). Moscow, 1952

Fischer, J. 'Über den Entschluß zur Luftversorgung Stalingrads. Ein Beitrag zur militärischen Führung im Dritten Reich' ('On the decision to supply Stalingrad by air lift. A contribution on the military leadership in the Third Reich'), in *MGM*, no. 2, 1969

Forster, J. 'Warum erfolgte der Entsatzstoß der 4. Panzerarmee in Richtung Stalingrad nicht mit zwei Panzerkorps?' ('Why was the relief attack by Fourth Panzer Army towards Stalingrad not undertaken with two Panzer Corps?'), in *MGM*, no. 2, 1969

Fretter-Pico, Max. 'Herbst- und Winterkrieg im Osten, Teil II' ('Autumn and Winter War in the East, part II'), in *Europäische Sicherheit*, 1951

Genkina, E. *Geroiceskij Stalingrad* (*Heroic Stalingrad*). Moscow, 1943

Görlitz, Walter. 'Die Schlacht um Stalingrad', in *Der Zweite Weltkrieg 1939 bis 1945* ('The Battle for Stalingrad', in *The Second World War 1939 to 1945*), vol. 1, pp. 391–417, Stuttgart, 1951

– 'Die Schlacht um Stalingrad 1942-1943', im *Entscheidungsschlachten des Zweiten Weltkrieges. Im Auftrag des Arbeitskreises für Wehrforschung, Stuttgart, hrsg. von Hans-Adolf Jacobsen und Jürgen Rohwer* ('The Battle for Stalingrad', in *Decisive Battles of the Second World War*. Comissioned by the Committee for Military Research, Stuttgart). Frankfurt, 1960, pp. 273–311

– see also Paulus

Grams, Rolf. *Die 14. Panzer-Division 1940–1945* (*14th Panzer Division 1940–1945*). Bad Nauheim, 1957, pp. 52–97

Guillaume, A. 'La Bataille de Stalingrad', in *La Guerre Germano-Soviétique*. Paris, 1949, pp. 33-60

Herhudt von Rohden, Hans-Detlef. *Die Luftwaffe ringt um Stalingrad* (*The Luftwaffe Fights for Stalingrad*). Wiesbaden, 1950

Hillgruber, A. 'So opferte Hitler die 6. deutsche Armee in Stalingrad' ('How Hitler sacrificed the German Sixth Army at Stalingrad'), in *Münchner Merkur*, 25 January 1963

Ingor, M. *Sibirijaki – geroi Stalingrada* (*The Siberians - The Heroes of Stalingrad*). Moscow, 1954

Jacobsen, H. A. 'Zur Schlacht von Stalingrad – 20 Jahre danach' ('On the Battle of Stalingrad – 20 years later'), in *ASMZ*, vol. 2, 1963

Kehrig, Manfred. *Stalingrad. Analyse und Dokumentation einer Schlacht.* (*Stalingrad. Analysis and Documentation of a Battle. Contributions to military and war history*, vol.15, Office of Military-Historical Research, Stuttgart, 1974

Kolesnik, A.D. *Velikaja bitva na Volge, 1942–1943* (*The Big Battle on the Volga, 1942–1943*). Moscow, 1958

Korfes, Otto. 'Stalingrad als militärische Planung und politische Wirkung', in *Der Zweite Weltkrieg 1939–1945: Wirklichkeit und Fälschung* ('Stalingrad in its Military Planning and Political Effect', in *The Second World War 1939-1945: Truth and Falsification.* German Section of the Commission of Historians of the GDR and the USSR, pp. 102–12, Berlin, 1959

Lenz, Friedrich. *Stalingrad – der 'verlorene' Sieg* (*Stalingrad – the 'Lost' Victory*). Heidelberg, 1956

Letzte Briefe aus Stalingrad (*Last Letters from Stalingrad*). Frankfurt and Heidelberg, 1950

Leyser, Hans-Georg. 'Stalingrad', in Lemelsen, Joachim. *29th Division*. Bad Nauheim, 1960, pp. 204–60

L'8ª Armata italiana nella Seconda Battaglia difensiva del Don (*The Italian Eighth Army in the Second Defensive Battle of the Don*). Rome, 1946

Manstein, Erich von. 'Die Tragödie von Stalingrad' in *Verlorene Siege* ('The Tragedy of Stalingrad', in *Lost Victories*, pp. 319–96). Bonn, 1955

– 'Stalingrad – war es so?' ('Stalingrad – was it like this?'), in *Welt am Sonntag*, 24 April 1960, p. 17

Mantello, H. H. 'Versammlung und Vorstoß der 6. deutschen Panzerdivision zur Befreiung von Stalingrad' ('Deployment and Advance of the German 6th Panzer Division for the Relief of Stalingrad'), in *Allgemeine Schweizerische Militär-Zeitschrift*, vols. 6–8, 1950

Mellenthin, Friedrich Wilhelm von. 'Disaster at Stalingrad', in *Panzer Battles 1939-1945*, pp. 183–97, London, 1955

Meyer, C. *Die morphologischen und klimatologischen Verhältnisse* im *Raum zwischen Don und Wolga im November/Januar und ihr Einfluß auf die Entschlußfassung der deutschen Führung im November/Januar 1942/43* (The morphological and climatological situation in the region between the Don and the Volga, and its influence on the decisions of the German Command in November 1942–January 1943), 1970

Milhaud, Gérard. Stalingrad. *Porte de la Victoire* (*Stalingrad. The Door to Victory*). Collection 'Libération', Paris, 1956

Mösch, Gerhard. *Stalingrad. Ein Erlebnis und seine Konsequenzen* (*Stalingrad. An Experience and its Consequences*). Kassel-Sondershausen, *c.* 1946

Piekalkiewicz, Janusz. *Stalingrad. Anatomie einer Schlacht* (*Stalingrad. Anatomy of a Battle*). Munich, 1977

Podewils, Clemens Graf. *Don und Wolga* (*Don and Volga*). Munich, 1952

Paulus, F. *Ich stehe hier auf Befehl!* (*I Stand Here Under Orders!*) The Life Story of General Field Marshal Friedrich Paulus. With notations from his letters and documents, publ. by Walter Görlitz). Frankfurt, 1960

Rieker, Karlheinrich. *Ein Mann verliert einen Weltkrieg. Die entscheidenden Monate des deutsch-russischen Krieges 1942/43* (*One Man Loses a World War. The Decisive Months of the German–Russian War, 1942–43*). Frankfurt, 1955, pp. 150–71

Röhricht, Edgar. 'Die Einschließungsoperation von Stalingrad (Winter 1942/43)', in *Probleme der Kesselschlacht, dargestellt an Einkreisungsoperatio-*

nen im Zweiten Weltkrieg. Mit einem Geleitwort von Franz Halder ('The encircling Operation at Stalingrad (Winter 1942/43), in *Problems of the Pocket Battle, Demonstrated by Encircling Operations of the Second World War*. With an introduction by Franz Halder), pp. 93–102, Karlsruhe, 1958

Samsonov, A. M. *Stalingradskaja bitva. Ot oborony i otstuplenji k velikoj pobede na Volge. Istoriceskij ocerk* (*The Stalingrad Battle. From Defence and Retreat to the Great Victory on the Volga. An historical sketch*). Moscow, 1960

– 'Stalingrad. The Relief', in Liddell Hart, *History of the Second World War*, vol. 3/15, London, 1967

Scheibert, Horst. 'Nach Stalingrad – 48 Kilometer! Der Entsatzvorstoß der 6. Panzer-Division / Dezember 1942. Mit 16 Kartenskizzen' ('To Stalingrad – 48 kilometres to go! The relief advance by 6th Panzer Division / December 1942. With 16 sketch maps'), in *Die Wehrmacht im Kampf*, vol. 10, Heidelberg, 1956

– 'Zwischen Don und Donez. Winter 1942/43' ('Between Don and Donetz. Winter 1942/3'), in *Die Wehrmacht im Kampf*, vol. 30, Neckargemünd, 1961

Scheurig, Bodo. 'Stalingrad', in *Freies Deutschland. Das Nationalkomitee und der Bund Deutscher Offiziere in der Sowjetunion 1943–1945* ('Stalingrad', in *A Free Germany. The National Committee and League of German Officers in the Soviet Union 1943-1945*). Munich, 1960, pp. 11–32

Schröter, Heinz. *Stalingrad '... bis zur letzten Patrone'* (*Stalingrad '... to the last bullet'*). Osnabrück, *c*. 1952

Schulz, F. *Stellungnahme zu den Ausführungen von GenLt. a. D. Schmidt, betr. Buch v. Manstein 'Verlorene Siege'* (*Comments on the statements of Lt. Gen. (ret) Schmidt in respect of von Manstein's Lost Victories*). August, 1967

Selle, Herbert. *Die Tragödie von Stalingrad. Der Untergang der 6. Armee* (*The Tragedy of Stalingrad. Downfall of Sixth Army*). 3rd rev. ed., Hanover, 1948

– 'Zwischen Steppe und Strom' ('Between the Steppe and the River'), in *Allgemeine Schweizerische Militärzeitschrift*, vol. 8, 1949

– 'Die 6. Armee auf dem Wege in die Katastrophe' ('Sixth Army on the Road to Catastrophe'), in *Allgemeine Schweizerische Militärzeitschrift*, vol. 8, pp. 579–91, 1956

– 'Die Panzerschlacht von Kalatsch' ('The Tank Battle of Kalach'), in *Allgemeine Schweizerische Militärzeitschrift*, vol. 9, pp. 420–25, 1961

Senger und Etterlin, Frido von. 'Konnte die Stalingrad-Armee entsetzt werden?' ('Was it possible to relieve the Stalingrad Army?'), in *Krieg in Europa*, pp. 72–129, Cologne and Berlin, 1960

Seth, Ronald. *Stalingrad, Point of No Return. The story of a battle, August 1942 – February 1943*. London, 1959

Seydlitz, W. von. *Stalingrad – Konflikt und Konsequenz* (*Stalingrad – Conflict and Consequence*). Oldenburg, 1977

Simonov, K. *Stalingrad.* Moscow, 1967

Stalingrad. *Die ersten authentischen Berichte der russischen Generäle Rokossowski – Woronow – Telgin – Malinin sowie russische Kriegsberichterstatter* (Stalingrad. The first authentic reports by Russian Generals Rokossovski, Voronov, Telgin, Malinin and Russian war correspondents). Zurich, 1945

Stalingrad. *Gosudarstvennyj muzej oborony Caricyna - Stalingrada. Istoriceskie mesta oborony Caricyna-Stalingrada. Putevoditel* (*The historic sites of the defence of Tzaritsa-Stalingrad. A guide*). 2nd. ed., Stalingrad, 1956

Stalingrad. *Gosudarstvennyj muzej oborony Caricyna - Stalingrada. V dni velikogo srazenija. Sbornik dokumentovi i materialov o Stalingradskoj bitve* (*In the Days of the Big Battle.* Collection of documents and material on the Battle of Stalingrad). Stalingrad, 1958

Steidel, L. *Entscheidung an der Wolga* (*Decision on the Volga*). Berlin, 1969

Stein, H. P. *Die sowjetischen Angriffsoperationen im Raum Stalingrad, 1943* (*Soviet offensive operations in the Stalingrad region in 1943*). 1971

Strategicus. *To Stalingrad and Alamein.* London, 1943

Strechnin, Ju., F. Surjadov. *Bronekatera v bojach za Stalingrad* (*Armoured Cutters in the Battle for Stalingrad*). Moscow, 1949

Streit, Kurt W. 'Der Flug aus der Hölle'. Tatsachenbericht über die beiden großen Luftbrücken-Operationen Demjansk und Stalingrad ('Flight out of Hell'. Factual account of the two major air lift operations of Demjansk and Stalingrad), in *Der Frontsoldat erzählt,* no. 17, pp. 13–74, 1953

Stupov, A., and Kokunov, V. *62-ja armija v bojach za Stalingrad* (*62nd Army in the fighting for Stalingrad*), Moscow, 1949

Talenskij, N. *Velikov srazenie pod Stalingradom* (*The Big Battle at Stalingrad*). Moscow, 1943

Telpuchovski, B. S. *Velikaja pobeda Sovetskoj Armii pod Stalingradom* (*The Big Victory of the Soviet Army at Stalingrad*). Moscow. 1953

– 'La Victoire de Stalingrad', in *Revue d'Histoire de la Deuxième Guerre Mondiale,* no. 11, pp, 3–19, 1961

Toepke, Günter. *Stalingrad – wie es wirklich war* (*Stalingrad – as it really was*). Stade, 1949

Vasilev, E. *Bitva pod Stalingradom i ee voenno-politilceskoe znacenie* (*The Battle of Stalingrad and its military-political importance*). Moscow, 1958

Vinokur, L. *7-ja Stalingradskaja gvardejskaje* (*The 7th Stalingrad Guards Division*). Stalingrad, 1958

Vodolagin, M. *Stalingrad v Velikoj Otecestvennoj vojne 1941–1943* (*Stalingrad in the Great National War, 1941–1943*). Stalingrad, 1949

– *U sten Stalingrada* (*At the Walls of Stalingrad*). Moscow, 1958

Waasen, Heinrich Maria. *Was geschah in Stalingrad? Wo sind die Schuldigen?* (*What happened at Stalingrad? Where are the Guilty?*). Zell am See and Salzburg, 1950

Weinert, Erich. *Memento Stalingrad. Ein Frontnotizbuch* (*Memento Stalingrad. A Notebook from the Front*). Berlin, 1951

Werth, Alexander. *The Year of Stalingrad*. An historical record and a study of Russian mentality, methods and policies. London, 1946

Werthen, Wolfgang. *Geschichte der 16. Panzer-Division 1939–1945* (*History of 16th Panzer Division, 1939–1945*), pp. 106–37, Bad Nauheim, 1958

Wieder, Joachim. *Die Tragödie von Stalingrad. Erinnerungen eines Überlebenden* (*The Tragedy of Stalingrad. Memories of a Survivor*). Deggendorf, 1955

– 'Welches Gesetz befahl den deutschen Soldaten, an der Wolga zu sterben?' ('Which law commanded German soldiers to die on the Volga?'), in *Frankfurter Hefte*, vol. 11, pp. 307–27, 1956

Yeremenko, A. J. *Stalingradskaja bitva. Iz vospominanij* (*The Battle of Stalingrad. From Memories*). Stalingrad, 1958

– *Stalingrad. Zapiski komandujuscego frontom* (*Notations by an Army Group Commander*). Moscow, 1961

– 'Der historische Sieg bei Stalingrad' ('The Historic Victory of Stalingrad'), in *The Second World War 1939-1945. Truth and Falsification*. German Section of the Commission of Historians of the GDR and the USSR). Berlin, 1959, pp.113–29.

Zamjatin, N. *Srazenie pod Stalingradom* (*The Battle of Stalingrad*). Moscow, 1943

Zeitzler, Kurt. 'Stalingrad', in *The Fatal Decisions*, pp. 129–89, New York and London, 1956

– 'Das Ringen um die militärischen Entscheidungen im Zweiten Weltkrieg' ('The Struggle for Military Decisions during the Second World War'), in *Wehrwissenschaftliche Rundschau 1*, vol. 8, 1958

– 'Die ersten beiden planmäßigen großen Rückzüge des deutschen Heeres an der Ostfront im Zweiten Weltkriege' ('The first two planned major retreats of the German Army in the Second World War'), in *Militärkunde 9*, vol. 3, 1960

Ziemke, E. *Stalingrad to Berlin – The German Campaign in Russia 1942–1945*, Washington DC, 1968

Documentary novels and other literary forms

Gerlach, Heinrich. *Die verratene Armee* (*The Betrayed Army*). Munich, 1957

Grossman, Wassili. *Za pravoe delo* (*For a Just Cause*)

Nekrassov, Victor. *In the Trenches of Stalingrad.*

Plievier, Theodor. *Stalingrad.* Vienna, Munich, Basle, 1948

Pötzsch, Arno. *Die Madonna von Stalingrad. Ein Gedenken vor der Weihnachts-madonna von Stalingrad. Verse von Arno Pötzsch. Zeichnungen von Kurt Reu-ber* (*The Stalingrad Madonna. A memorial to the Christmas Madonna of Stalingrad. Verses by Arno Pötzsch. Drawings by Kurt Reuber*). Hamburg, 1946

Simonov, K. *Days and Nights.* A novel with epilogue.

Wirta, N. *The Battle of Stalingrad.* A screen-play in literary form.

– *Katastrofa* (*The Catastrophe*). Moscow, 1962

Wöss, Fritz. *Hunde, wollt ihr ewig leben?* (*Dogs, do you want to live for ever?*), Hamburg, 1958

General accounts

Beck, Ludwig. *Studien, herausgegeben und eingeleitet von Hans Speidel* (Studies, published and introduced by Hans Speidel). Stuttgart, 1955

Bilanz des Zweiten Weltkrieges (*Balance Sheet of the Second World War*), Olden-burg/Hamburg, 1953

Buchheit, Gert. *Soldatentum und Rebellion. Die Tragödie der deutschen Wehrma-cht* (*Soldiery and Rebellion. The Tragedy of the Wehrmacht*). Rastatt/Baden, 1961

Bullock, Alan. *Hitler, a Study in Tyranny.* London, 1952

Dahms, Hellmuth Günther. *Der Zweite Weltkrieg* (*The Second World War*). Tübingen, 1960 and Munich, 1989

Dulles, Allan W. *Conspiracy in Germany.*

Erfurth, Waldemar. *Die Geschichte des deutschen Generalstabs von 1918 bis 1945* (*History of the German General Staff from 1918 to 1945*), 2nd rev. ed., Göt-ting, 1960

Foerster, Wolfgang. *Generaloberst Ludwig Beck. Sein Kampf gegen den Krieg. Aus nachgelassenen Papieren des Generalstabschefs* (Colonel General Ludwig Beck. His Fight Against the War. From papers of the estate of the Chief of the General Staff). Munich, 1953

Garthoff, Raymond. *Soviet Military Doctrine.*

Geschichte des Großen Vaterländischen Krieges der Sowjetunion, hrsg. vom Institute für Marxismus-Leninismus beim Zentralkomitee der Kommunistischen Party der Sowjetunion (*History of the great national war of the Soviet Union, publ. by the Institute for Marxism-Leninism of the Central Committee of the Com-munist Party of the Soviet Union*). six vols, Berlin 1962–8

Gilbert, Felix. *Hitler Directs His War.* New York, 1950

Gisevius, Hans Bernd. *Bis zum bitteren Ende. Vom Reichstagsbrand bis zum 20. Juli 1944. Vom Verfasser auf den neuesten Stand gebrachte Sonderausgabe* (*To the Bitter End. From the Fire in the Reichstag to 20 July 1944*). Special edition up-dated by the author), Hamburg, 1960

Görlitz, Walter. *Der deutsche Generalstab. Geschichte und Gestalt 1657 bis 1945* (*The German General Staff. History and Structure 1657 to 1945*). Frankfurt, 1950

Greiner, Helmuth. *Die Oberste Wehrmachtsführung 1939-1943* (*The Supreme Command of the Wehrmacht, 1939–1943*). Wiesbaden, 1951

Groscurth, H. *Tagebücher eines Abwehroffiziers 1938-1940* (*Diary of a Counter-Intelligence Officer, 1938–1940*). H. Krauskick, Stuttgart, 1970

Grossman, Vassili. *Life and Fate.*

Hassel, Ulrich von. *Vom anderen Deutschland* (*The Other Germany*). Zurich and Freiburg, i. Br., 1946

Herzfeld, Hans. 'Das Problem des deutschen Heeres 1919–1945' ('The Problem of the German Army, 1919–1954'), in *Geschichte und Politik. Eine wissenschaftliche Schriftreihe*, vol. 6, H. G. Dahms, Laupheim, 1952

Heusinger, Adolf. *Befehl im Widerstreit* (*Orders in Conflict*). Tübingen and Stuttgart, 1950

Jacobsen, Hans-Adolf. *1939/1945. Der Zweite Weltkrieg in Chronic und Dokumenten* (*1939–1945. The Second World War in Chronicles and Documents*), 5th rev. and extended ed., Darmstadt, 1961

Kriegstagebuch des Oberkommandos der Wehrmacht (Wehrmachtsführungsstab) 1940-1945, geführt von Helmuth Greiner und Percy Ernst Schramm (*The War Diary of the Supreme Command of the Wehrmacht kept by Helmuth Greiner and Percy Ernst Schramm*). P. E. Schramm in co-operation with Hans-Adolf Jacobsen, Andreas Hillgruber and Walther Hubatsch, 4 vols., Frankfurt, 1961–9

Liddell Hart, B. H. *The Other Side of the Hill*

Meinecke, Friedrich, Die deutsche Katastrophe. Wiesbaden, 1949

Morzik, F. *Die deutschen Transportflieger im Zweiten Weltkrieg* (*German Cargo Planes in the Second World War*), ed. and publ. by Gerhard Hümmelchen, Frankfurt, 1966

Picker, H. *Hitlers Tischgespräche im Führerhauptquartier 1941*-1942 (*Hitler's Table Talks at Führer Headquarters, 1941–2*), P. E. Schramm in co-operation with A. Hillgruber and M. Vogt, Stuttgart, 1965

Ritter, Gerhard. *Carl Goerdeler und die deutsche Widerstandsbewegung* (*Carl Goerdeler and the German Resistance Movement*). Stuttgart, 1955

Rohden, H. *Das deutsche Wehrmachtstransportwesen im Zweiten Weltkrieg* (*The Transport System of the Wehrmacht in the Second World War*). Stuttgart, 1971

Salvatores, U. *Bersagliere on the Don*. Bologna, 1966

Schlabrendorff, Fabian von. *Offiziere gegen Hitler* (*Officers Against Hitler*). Zurich, 1946 ·

Shukov, G. K. *Memories and Thoughts.*

Stahlberg, Alexander. *Die verdammte Pflicht. Erinnerungen 1932 bis 1945* (*Damn Bloody Duty. Memoirs 1932 to 1945*). Berlin, 1987

Telpuchovski, B. S. *Soviet History of the Great Patriotic War 1941-1945*

Tippelsskirch, Kurt von. *Geschichte des Zweiten Weltkrieges* (*History of the Second World War*). Bonn, 1951

Uhlig, H. 'Das Einwirken Hitlers auf Planung und Führung des Ostfeldzuges' ('Hitler's Influence on Planning and Command during the Campaign in the East'), in *Das Parlament*, 1960

Werth, A. Russland im Krieg 1941–1945 (*Russia at War, 1941–1945*). Munich/Zurich, 1965

Wheeler-Bennett, John W. *The Nemesis of Power. The German Army in Politics, 1918–1945*

Der Zweite Weltkrieg 1939-1945. Wirklichkeit und Fälschung (*The Second World War 1939–1945. Truth and Falsification*), German Section of the Commission of Historians of the GDR and the USSR). Berlin, 1959

NOTES

Part I. Memories of a Survivor

These 'Memories of a Survivor', written in 1950, first appeared in 1955 in a limited edition as a small brochure entitled *The Tragedy of Stalingrad* (published by Buchdruckerei Jos. Nothaft, Deggendorf). Here the former text has been used with only slight revisions. Only so far as the external framework of events was concerned did occasional minor modifications and additions appear to be advisable. The bulk of the text, based on the direct source of personal experience and dealing mainly with the psychological reactions to events, was not affected.

The following excerpts from the former introduction are intended to provide some information about the author, the origin of these memoirs of Stalingrad and the spirit in which they were written down.

The horrible tragedy on the Volga, which represented hell on earth for hundreds of thousands of troops and which was cruelly extended long after the end of the bloody 76-day battle on 2 February 1943, was one of those experiences in life that brand a human being indelibly. Such experiences lead the individual to the limits of his being, churn up the depths of the awareness of his existence, his total feeling and thinking, and open his eyes both inwardly and outwardly to a healthy sobriety and insight. Many of those that were overwhelmed by it were scarcely ever again able to free themselves from its dark spell.

And so the memories of the Stalingrad experience weigh me down. After I came home from Russia in early May 1950 after more than seven years of captivity, the need to gain a perspective and to free myself from them, forced me to take up the pen. The core of these notations is comprised of my personal experiences, observations, feelings and thoughts, which in part had already found expression in the few letters that reached home from the Stalingrad pocket. My position as an orderly officer on the staff of an army corps enabled me to gain insights into the larger set of circumstances and the problematic nature of the senior command. During my long years of captivity, many encounters with my surviving comrades from Stalingrad and companions in fate of all ranks: generals, officers of the staff, military chaplains, commanders and officers of the front-line formations from the various sectors of combat, but also non-commissioned officers and men from the ranks, gave me ample opportunity to extend and round off my knowledge and my appreciation of things. Where my memory was no longer precisely accurate, I was aided by statements of facts and dates in the few serious reports that have been published since the end of the war.

My notations are not intended to replace portrayals of the battle of Stalingrad based on official documents. These are sparse anyway, because the official files that could bear witness to the boundless efforts and sufferings of Sixth Army were mostly destroyed in the pocket. The whole unvarnished picture of the tragedy, with all its unfathomable depths of the sorrow of human experience and suffering, must be painted once again without mercy. Where I have had to criticise individuals and circumstances, it was not my intention to pretend to be an accuser or a judge. I would already be restrained from such a presumption and arrogance by my recognition that I too was enmeshed with my whole being in that web of stirrings of conscience and obedience to orders, of soldierly duty and political inadequacy, of human failure, of guilt and fate that could not be disentangled. My portrayal will restrict itself to the thoughts, needs and experiences that moved me at the time. Seen in this light, my recounting of experiences is intended to be taken as a simple human document that may also gain some importance in the annals of history and claim a place beside the military-historical portrayals or the memoirs of generals bent on self-justification. Only the full wealth of all of the testimony will reveal the total picture to contemporaries and to posterity, and thereby also reveal the density of the entanglement that had led to the indescribable sufferings of such a war and to the terrible catastrophe of Stalingrad ... The few survivors of the murderous battle, who went through hell unleashed, have the duty before all else to tear the old, false, fatal shimmer of the glory of war from soldiery for ever, and mercilessly to expose the whole horror of this peculiar trade of mankind. We will be fulfilling the bequest of the dead if we destroy its spell and anathematise war with all the strength at our command, so that something as humanly undignified as happened during the horrible battle of destruction on the Volga can never happen again. This must also include the intellectual overcoming of power and its demonic temptations. Today we must be untiringly committed to fulfilling the obligations that the fallen of all of the nations have bequeathed to us. In attempting this, the issue is to create a better order of human relationships from the start, and in mutual responsibility bridge the old friend-foe relationships between the nations. In this sense, may the memory of Stalingrad go down in our history as a memorial to the need for inner contemplation and the changing of our ways ...

My memoirs of the tragedy of Stalingrad are meant to be a belated but still valid passionate protest against such a boundless degradation, humiliation and violation of the human spirit as we were forced to experience it on the Volga, and against any violation of mankind at all, such as every totalitarian war carries in its train. The hope of being able to keep the memory of the dead and their bequest alive is what has motivated me after many years to publish these notes that were originally only intended for a smaller circle. May they contribute to the realisation, that the true, and best heroism may not be looked for in the service of destruction, but can only be fruitful and alive, when without the material or the mental weapons of murder, it is found in the works of love, peace, and humanity.

Part II. Critical assessment after fifty years
1. Field Marshal von Manstein

The core of this chapter appeared in 1956 as an essay in the *Frankfurter Hefte* (1956, vol. 5, pp. 307–27) under the title 'What Law Commanded the German Soldiers to Die on the Volga?'. The present text is a completely revised version that has been adapted to our current level of information based on the evaluation of new sources and publications.

1. Erich von Manstein, *Verlorene Siege* (*Lost Victories*), Bonn, 1955, p. 321, hereinafter referred to as 'Manstein'; Manfred Kehrig, Stalingrad. *Analysis and Documentation of a Battle*, vol. 15, Hereinafter referred to as 'Kehrig'.
2. Manstein, pp. 369, 371.
3 Ibid., pp. 335 *et seq.*
4. Ibid., pp. 367 *et seq.*
5. Ibid., p. 372.
6. Hoffmann, Peter, *Claus Schenk Graf von Stauffenberg and His Brothers*. Stuttgart, 1992, pp. 241 *et seq.*
7. Manstein, pp. 369, 371.
8. Kehrig, pp. 223 *et seq.*
9. Ibid.
10. Ibid.
11. Manstein, pp. 335 *et seq.*
12. Memorandum Zeitzler in appendix under 'Documents'.
13. Kehrig, p 264.
14. Ibid., document 22, p. 670.
15. Memorandum Zeitzler in appendix under 'Documents'.
16. Kehrig, document 22, p. 573.
17. See p. 000
18. Memorandum von Seydlitz in appendix under 'Documents'.
19. Ibid., p. 380.
20. Ibid., p. 343.
21. Paulus, Friedrich, *I Stand Here Under Orders!*, hereinafter referred to as Paulus.
22. Manstein, p. 395.
23. Only in specific critical situations did Paulus address himself directly to

Hitler; the majority of the orders and reports came and went via Army Group Command.

24. Manstein, p. 651; Paulus, pp. 218 et seq.

25. Hans Doerr, *The Campaign to Stalingrad, Essay of an Operational Overview*, Darmstadt 1955, p. 96.

26. Paulus, p. 202.

27. Yeremenko, A. J., *Protiv falsifikacy istorii vtoroj mirovoj vojny*, Moscow, 1959. Soviet Marshal Yeremenko, Commander-in-Chief of the Stalingrad Front, emphasises von Manstein's enormous responsibility and proves that he made serious mistakes. By waiting for ten precious days before attacking, he let good chances for success slip by. The initially solely available 51st Army, which was extended over a front of 100 kilometres, could not have contained a timely attack by the very powerful German 6th Panzer Division. Moreover, the Soviet lines on the pocket perimeter had to be seriously weakened to ward off the threat of the relief offensive. See also *Revue d'Histoire de la Deuxième Guerre Mondiale*, vol. 11, no. 44, 1961, p. 82.

28. Frido von Senger und Etterlin, *War in Europe*, Cologne and Berlin, 1960, p. 74.

29. Horst Scheibert, 'To Stalingrad – 48 Kilometres to Go. The Relief Attack by 6th Panzer Division, December 1942', in *The Wehrmacht in Battle*, vol. 10, Heidelberg, 1956

30. Von Senger und Etterlin, ibid., pp. 87, 91. That Zeitzler, Chief of the Army General Staff, was sceptical from the beginning and did not give the relief operation much chance for success, is testified to by General von Mellenthin (*Panzer Battles*, London, 1955, p. 166). Zeitzler's subsequent comment on the failure of the relief offensive was, 'The forces were too weak. The attack used itself up and could no longer be nourished from out of the depth. That was the end of it.' (Kurt Zeitzler, 'The Struggle for Military Decisions during the Second World War', in *Wehrwissenschaftliche Rundschau 1*, 1951, vol. 8, p. 27).

31. Manstein, p. 654.

32. Kunrat von Hammerstein, 'Manstein', in *Frankfurter Hefte* 11, 1956, p. 453.

33. Paulus, p. 227.

34. Heinz Schröter, *Stalingrad ... to the Last Bullet*, Lengerich, n.d., pp. 185 *et seq.*

35. See: *Stalingrad. The First Authentic Reports by Russian Generals ...* , Zurich, 1945; more recently, the official Russian work by A. M. Samsonov, *The Stalingrad Battle*, Moscow, 1960, pp. 546 *et seq.*; Telpushovski, *The Great Victory of the Soviet Army at Stalingrad*, Moscow, 1953, p. 109.

36. Manstein, p. 650. In his reproduction of the letter mentioned (Paulus, p. 222) Walter Görlitz simply left out this sentence.

37. Toepke, Günter. Stalingrad – wie es wirklich war, 1949, pp. 42, 52.

38. Hans-Detlef Herhudt von Rohden, *The Luftwaffe Fights for Stalingrad*, Wiesbaden, 1950, p. 35. In his 'Experience Report on the Supply of the Stalingrad Fortress by Air' of 15 March 1943, General of Panzer Forces Hube writes: 'At the beginning of its encirclement [end of November 1942] "Fortress Stalingrad" had a re-victualling count of approximately 260,000 men which had shrunk to about 250,000 men by the end of December because of deaths and wounded flown out.' This interesting report is reproduced in Hans-Adolf Jacobsen, *1939–1945. The Second World War in Chronicles and Documents*, 5th ed., Darmstadt, 1961, pp. 365 *et seq.*

39. Kehrig, p. 662.

40. Kehrig, p. 338.

41. The effects of the German defeat could be seen everywhere. The neutral powers, Turkey, Spain, Sweden and Portugal, stepped back, the fighting spirit of our allies sank to nil, the partisan movement in the occupied territories revived, the military resistance faction in the German army became stronger, as did the general resistance. The leaflet by the Munich Professor Huber, calling upon the German students to fight for their freedom, that led to the execution of the Scholl siblings and their mentor, invoked the Stalingrad dead and began with the words, 'Our nation stands shattered before the deaths of the men of Stalingrad. Three hundred and thirty thousand German men have been senselessly and irresponsibly driven to death by the brilliant strategy of the First World War corporal. Führer, we thank you!' This manifesto by the Munich resistance group 'White Rose' appealed to the students to 'take revenge and atone, as your contribution to the establishment of a new intellectual Europe'. (Reproduced in Jacobsen, ibid., pp. 619 *et seq.*).

42. The Eastern historians and the Soviet generals have begun a violent campaign against certain tendencies on the part of historians and the military in the West not to accept or to play down the decisive importance of the battle of Stalingrad. For this see the 'Overview of the Literature on Stalingrad' at the end of this book. See also B. Telpushovski, 'The Victory of Stalingrad', in *Review of the History of the Second World War*, 11, no. 43, 1961, pp. 3–19.

43. Hans Bernd Gisevius, *To the Bitter End*, Zurich, 1946, vol. 2, p. 272.

44. Hans Diebold, *Doctor in Stalingrad. Passion of a Captivity*, Salzburg, 1949, pp. 17 *et seq.*

45. Manstein, pp. 390 *et seq.*

46. Toepke, op. cit., pp. 131 *et seq.*

47. Hans Doerr, 'Was Stalingrad a Sacrifice?', in *Political Opinion*, 1958, p. 89. Report of the speech General Doerr made on 4 October 1958 at the first national reunion of men who fought at Stalingrad.

48. How the enemy assessed the German formations doomed to go under is demonstrated by an episode reported by General Chuikov, Commander of the legendary 62nd Army deployed on the Volga and at Stalingrad. Before the start of the Russian offensive, General Rokossovski, Commander-in-Chief of the Don Front charged with its execution, appeared at Chuikov's staff in order to find out whether 62nd Army would be able to throw back an enemy who under concentric pressure might attempt a desperate break-out across the Volga. Chuikov set him at ease, spoke about 'rabbits that had been herded together' and declared 'the Paulus army is no longer an army, but rather an encircled prisoner camp'. (W. I. Chuikov, *The Beginning of the Road*, Moscow 1959, p. 286).

49. Manstein, p. 391.

50. See Helmut Gollwitzer, '... *and leading where you do not want to go. Report on a Captivity*, Munich, 1951, pp. 110 *et seq.*

51. Herbert Selle, *The Tragedy of Stalingrad. The Downfall of Sixth Army*, 3rd rev. ed., Hanover, 1948, p. 6.

52. Manstein, pp. 384 *et seq.*

53. Friedrich Meinecke, *The German Catastrophe. Reflections and Memories*, Wiesbaden, 1946, p. 146.

54 Gisevius, op. cit., vol. 2, p. 271; see also Gerhard Ritter, *Carl Goerdeler and the German Resistance Movement*, Stuttgart, 1955, pp. 343 *et seq.*, 523.

55. Von Hammerstein, ibid., p. 453.

56. Gisevius, op. cit., pp. 267 *et seq.*; Ulrich von Hassell, *The Other Germany. From the Diaries 1938–1944*, Zurich and Freiburg, 1946, p. 291; Gerhard Ritter, op. cit., p. 343.

57. Allan W. Dulles, *Conspiracy in Germany*.

58. Gisevius, op. cit., p. 271.

59. R. T. Paget, *Manstein, his Campaigns and his Trial*.

60. Wolfgang Foerster, *A General Fights Against the War*. From the testimony of Chief of Staff Ludwig Beck, Munich, 1949, pp. 113 *et seq.*

61. Manstein, p. 603.

62. This was the order of 20 November 1941 which von Manstein issued as Commander-in-Chief of Eleventh Army in the Crimea and which says, among other things. '... the Jewish-Bolshevist system must be exterminated once and for all. Never again will it be permitted to interfere in our European *Lebensraum* ...' ; See also the transcripts of the International Military Court, Nuremberg, 1948, vol. XX, pp. 697 *et seq.*

63. Bodo Scheurig. 'Orders and Conscience. The Memoirs of Field Marshal von Manstein', in *Mind and Action, Monthly for Law, Freedom and Culture*, 15, 1960, p. 148.

64. Doerr, op. cit., p. 89; and *The Campaign to Stalingrad. Essay of an Operational Overview*, Darmstadt, 1955, p. 119.

65. Burghard Freudenfeld, in *Süddeutsche Zeitung*, no. 179, 31 July 1955.

66. Wolfgang Foerster, op. cit., p. 103.

2. Field Marshal Paulus

1. Paulus, F. *I Stand Here under Orders!* (Hereinafter referred to as 'Paulus'.) For the many reviews of the book see: *Allgemeine Schweizerische Militärzeitschrift*, 1960, vol. 8; *Wehrkunde 9*, 1960, vols. 7 and 9; Paul Mahlmann, 'Obedience as an Alibi', in *Stuttgarter Zeitung*, no. 120, 25 May 1960 and in Evangelischer Literaturbeobachter, vol. 6, 1960; Herbert G. Marzian, 'Passing the Buck in Stalingrad', in *Die Welt*, 22 October 1960; Bodo Scheurig, 'The Stalingrad Legend', in *Der Monat 12*, vol. 144, 1960; Christian Schuetz, 'Stalingrad and the Aftermath', in *Zeitwende*, vol. 3, 1961; Adalbert Weinstein, in *Frankfurter Allgemeine Zeitung*, 18 November 1960; Albert Wucher, in *Deutsche Zeitung*, 22 May 1960.

2. Paulus, p. 207.

3. See Friedrich Wilhelm Hauck, in *Wehrwissenschaftliche Rundschau 10*, 1960, pp. 571–3. Hans Doerr, in *Wehrkunde 9*, vol. 7, 1960, speaks of 'many ambiguities, errors, mistakes, questionable statements as well as spiteful remarks'. His erroneous opinion that no one who has not been professionally trained on the General Staff and gained experience as a commander is able to judge command decisions, in other words, that writing military history is the privilege of the generals who took part in the battles, has been quite rightly refuted. See Ernst Hermann and Graf von Brockdorff-Ahlefeldt in *Wehrkunde 9*, vol. 9, 1960, p. 489.

4. Paulus, pp. 212 note 2 *et seq.*; also Walter Görlitz, 'The Battle for Stalingrad 1942–1943', in *Decisive Battles of the Second World War*, 1960, p. 299, note 35. Teske, who was von Seydlitz's Ia during the campaign in the West, praises his 'straightforward and natural way of thinking, which often led to an astonishing correctness in the evaluation of the situation'. But von Seydlitz was allegedly a stranger to his men. 'The effect of his personality was often diminished by inhibitions due to intellect and age.' For want of a strong, active intellect of his own, he allegedly liked to believe someone else's opinion, if it were convincingly presented. By this Teske tries to explain von Seydlitz's later 'collaboration with Bolshevism', which, so he states, was otherwise completely out of character for this nobleman (Teske, *The Silver Mir-*

rors. *Staff Service Under Close Examination*, Heidelberg, 1952, pp. 68 *et seq*. As being representative of a contrary opinion on von Seydlitz as a man and a soldier, here is the characterisation by Major General (ret) Gerhard Kegler (Gießen), who commanded the 27th Infantry Regiment. under von Seydlitz in 1940–1941. After rejecting Teske's evaluation, he writes: 'General von Seydlitz was highly respected by the men. His frequent appearances at the front were well received and acclaimed by the officers as well as the ranks. Von Seydlitz kept in contact with the men. His personality radiated warmth and confidence. Under his leadership we felt ourselves protected from inhuman demands and senseless orders that came from higher authorities far away. The men felt clearly that the great results achieved with small losses were due to the professional and level-headed leadership of their divisional commander. A man like General von Seydlitz was never a stranger to his men.' (Letter of 25 June 1962 from General Kegler).

5. Paulus, pp. 91, 205.
6. See p. of this book.
7. Selle, Herbert, *The Tragedy of Stalingrad*, p. 11; von Hassel, op. cit., p. 291; see also note 56 to this chapter.
8. Paulus, pp. 80 *et seq*. In the postscript to his 'fundamental statements' Paulus writes: 'The revolutionary intention deliberately to bring about the defeat in order to remove Hitler and the National Socialist system as an obstacle to the ending of the war never entered my mind, nor was it brought to my attention in any way from within my whole command. Such thoughts were completely outside the scope of my thinking at the time. They were also foreign to my nature. I was a soldier and believed that by obeying I was rendering a special service to my country.' (p. 263). According to Gerhard Ritter (ibid., p. 523), the claim by Wheeler-Bennett, in *The Nemesis of Power*, that Beck addressed a personal appeal to Paulus via an officer of the air force, cannot be substantiated.
9. Ibid., p. 34. On Paulus' optimistic appraisal of the chances for success of the planned Russian campaign, see p. 43. That he, like Halder, quickly became disillusioned, is demonstrated by his discussion in July 1941 with General Kirchheim on matters of supply and enemy arms production (pp. 49 *et seq*.; see also p. **000 of this book**.
10. *Allgemeine Schweizerische Militärzeitschrift*, vol. 8, 1960.
11. Paulus, p. 64.
12. Ibid., p. 53.
13. Ibid., pp. 150, 218.
14. Ibid., p. 48.
15. Ibid., p. 55.

16. Ibid., p. 59. See also a remark by General von Hammerstein. 'He was a good worker on the General Staff, but it was known that he lacked the qualities for an independent command. He should therefore never have become the Commander of an army. Paulus should have broken out right at the beginning without asking Hitler, even at the risk of being court-martialled later. (Kunrat von Hammerstein, ibid., p. 425).

17. Doerr, op. cit., p. 75.

18. Paulus, p. 216.

19. Ibid., p. 216.

20. Ibid., pp. 216 *et seq.*

21. See General von Seydlitz's statements in the chapter 'Von Seydlitz's Assessment of the Situation'.

22. Paulus, p. 210. The radio message to Hitler is reproduced in the appendices to this book. The text has been taken from H.-A. Jacobsen, *1939/1945. The Second World War in Chronicles and Documents*, Darmstadt, 5th ed., 1961, p. 357. Oddly enough, in the wording provided by Jacobsen, the name of General von Seydlitz is missing. This must be due to an error in transcribing the appendices to the war diary of Sixth Army. In his notations, Paulus emphasises (p. 210) that all the Commanding Generals were listed in the message. I have therefore added the name of von Seydlitz. See also Schröter, op. cit., pp. 86 *et seq.* This text appears to be correct.

23. In this message, Army Group again summarised its evaluation of the situation, after an uninterrupted exchange of views had taken place with the Army Chief of Staff. Zeitzler and Freiherr von Weichs were completely of the same mind. Reproduction of the telex message of 23 November 1942 is in Doerr, op. cit., p. 72.

24 Paulus, p. 72.

25 Paul Mahlmann, 'Obedience as an Alibi', in *Stuttgarter Zeitung*, no. 120, 25 May 1960.

26. Paulus, p. 161.

27. H. von Rohden, op. cit., p. 20; see also Paulus, pp. 224 *et seq.*

28. Paulus, p. 52.

29. Ibid., p. 49.

30. Manstein, p. 333.

31. Von Seydlitz, Evaluation of the situation of Sixth Army in the Stalingrad pocket on 25 November 1942; see appendix under 'Documents'.

32. Edgar Röhricht, *Problems of the Pocket Battle as Demonstrated by Encircling Operations of the Second World War*, Karslruhe, 1958, p. 100.

33. See note 23.

34. See chapter 'The Role of General von Seydlitz in Stalingrad'.

35. Manstein, p. 367; and in *Welt am Sonntag*, no. 17, 24 April 1960, p. 17.

36. Paulus, p. 256.

37. Personal statement by Ernst Alexander Paulus.

38. Manstein, 'Stalingrad – was it really like this?', in *Welt am Sonntag*, no. 17, 24 April 1960, p. 17.

39. Paulus, p. 86.

40. Manstein, p. 370.

41. Ibid., p. 372.

42. Telpushovski writes: 'As soon as it became known that the enemy had begun a counter-attack from the region of Kotelnikovski with the objective of relieving the encircled army, the Soviet Command pinned the encircled 22 divisions down by active combat actions, in order to be able to withdraw a part of its forces unbeknown to the enemy and send them against the Hitler army attacking from the south.' (*The Soviet History of the Great Patriotic War*). M. Bragin writes: 'The danger was grave ... The danger would have been even graver, if Hitler's Supreme Command had taken the decision to give up Stalingrad and break out towards Rostov with the mass of the 22 divisions.' (*Stalingrad. The First Authentic Reports by the Russian Generals ...*). See also the comments by Marshal Yeremenko, II, 1 in note 27 to this chapter.

43. Paulus, p. 242.

44. Ibid., p. 242.

45. Ibid., p. 243.

46. Ibid., p. 247.

47. Ibid., p. 247.

48. Ibid., pp. 251 *et seq.*

49. Ibid., pp. 262 *et seq.*

50. Doerr, op. cit., p. 114.

51. Helmuth Greiner, *The Supreme Command of the Wehrmacht, 1939-1943*, Wiesbaden, 1951, p. 433.

52. Ibid., p. 435.

53. Doerr, op. cit., p. 118.

54. See the report by Colonel G. Ludwig (appendix).

55. Description of the surrender and capture of the Army Staff in A. M. Samsonov, *The Battle of Stalingrad*, Moscow, 1960, pp. 543 *et seq.*; Yeremenko, *Stalingrad. Notations of an Army Group Commander*, Moscow, 1961, pp. 437 *et seq.* which gives a personal report by General M. J. Shumilov, Commander-in-Chief of 64th Army.

56. *The World as History*, 10, 1950, pp. 279 *et seq.*; also Hitler's situation briefings and fragments of the minutes of his military conferences 1942–1945,

published by Helmut Hieber in *Sources and Portrayals of Contemporary History*, vol. 10, Stuttgart, 1962. At the time Hitler said, among other things: '[We have] paid too much attention to training the intellect and not enough to force of character ... In this war, no one else is going to make Field Marshal. We will leave all that until the war is over. One should not praise the day before evening comes ...' In his extensive monologue, he expressed his fear that the captured generals would come to Moscow and in that 'rat trap' would sign anything, make confessions and issue proclamations. To the Italian Ambassador he had shortly before compared Sixth Army in Stalingrad to the 300 Greeks at Thermopylae. He had declared that it would show the world the true spirit of national socialist Germany and its loyalty towards the Führer. See Alan Bullock, *Hitler. A Study in Tyranny*, p. 632.

57. Ritter, ibid., pp. 343, 523. See also Wheeler-Bennett, ibid., p. 557, where he writes, 'Would Paulus give the longed-for signal? He sent the Führer a series of messages which were duly reported to the conspirators by General Fellgiebel, Chief of Communications and a member of the conspiracy. There followed several orders of the day that admonished the forces to hold out to the last bullet. The conspirators asked themselves if this was the way a man acted who was about to give the signal to revolt, possibly as the last act of his life?'

58. Görlitz, *The Battle of Stalingrad*, p. 309.

59. Karl Jaspers, *The Atom Bomb and the Future of Mankind*, Munich 1958, p. 84.

60. See Karlheinz Rieker, *One Man Loses a World War*. Frankfurt, 1955, pp. 169 *et seq*. See also von Senger und Etterlin, p. 93; Waldemar Erfurth, *The History of the German General Staff from 1918 to 1945*, Göttingen, 1960, p. 302. After the catastrophe of Stalingrad, Ulrich von Hassel wrote in his diary, pp. 290 *et seq*.: 'The military incompetence of the 'most brilliant war lord of all times', i.e., of the insane corporal, which up to now has been hidden by a few intuitive bright spots, by lucky wagers, inadequacies on the part of the enemy and coincidences, has come to the fore. The sacrifice of precious blood for idiotic or criminal points of prestige is largely self-evident.'

61. Kurt Zeitzler, 'Stalingrad', in *The Fatal Decisions*, New York, 1956, pp. 175, 182, 188.

62. Doerr, op. cit., pp. 100 *et seq*.

63. Paulus, pp. 93 *et seq*.

64. *Allgemeine Schweizerische Militär Zeitschrift*, vol. 8, 1960.

65. Paulus, p. 263. At the end of the retrospective summary of his observations on Stalingrad he writes: 'I bear the responsibility before the men and the officers of Sixth Army and before the German nation that I carried out the

orders by the Supreme Command to hold out until the final downfall.'
66. From the notations of Field Marshal Paulus. Personal comment by Ernst Alexander Paulus.

3. General von Seydlitz

The notations of General von Seydlitz consist of unstructured personal memories, certain hitherto unpublished documents, letters and numerous written comments to questions which the author addressed to the general as an important key witness to the battle. In the sources and notes they are cited as 'Seydlitz, Notations'.

1. Paulus, p. 219.
2. Zeitzler, p. 136; Paulus, pp. 76, 219. See also Field Marshal Keitel, *Criminals or Officers?* Memoirs, letters and documents of the Chief of the OKW, publ. by Walter Görlitz, 1961, p. 308. We see from Keitel's memoirs that Hitler was determined to replace General Jodl, Chief of the Wehrmacht Command Staff, by Paulus after the end of the Stalingrad battle.
3. Bodo Scheurig, *A Free Germany. The National Committee and League of German Officers in the Soviet Union 1943–1945*, Munich, 1960.
4. Von Seydlitz, 'The Liberation of the Demjansk pocket'. Unpublished manuscript.
5. Seydlitz, Notations.
6. Paulus, p. 216.
7. Seydlitz, Notations. The histories of two divisions impressively describe this bloody fighting: Rolf Grams, *14th Panzer Division ...* , Bad Nauheim, 1957, pp. 54 *et seq.*, pp. 61 *et seq.*; Wolfgang Werthen, *History of 16th Panzer Division ...* , Bad Nauheim, 1958, pp. 113 *et seq.*
8. Seydlitz, Notations; on the measures taken by Paulus, see p. 193.
9. Ibid.
10. Ibid.
11. Toepke, pp. 45 *et seq.* In his chapter 'Seydlitz acts on his own', Toepke has given a dramatic description of the events, but portrayed General von Seydlitz's role incorrectly. The chronological contexts of his description are also mostly incorrect.
12. Paulus, p. 203. Seydlitz cannot recall this message. The line of argument did not stem from him. He does, however, consider it possible that Clausius, whose relationship with the Army Chief of Staff was strained, actually did give this reason.
13. Paulus, p. 219.
14. Doerr, op. cit., p. 74. Here Doerr's erroneous portrayal follows the unreli-

able reporting by Heinz Schröter, (ibid., pp. 92 *et seq.*) and also mentions his fictitious situation briefing of the Commanding Generals with Paulus.

15. Letters by General Doerr to Seydlitz of 2 and 29 November 1956.

16. *Decisive Battles* ... , p. 311. See also Paulus, p. 219. In contradiction to Görlitz's claim, von Seydlitz declares that Paulus never personally took him to task about 'the wrongness of his conduct'.

17. Seydlitz, Notations.

18. Ibid. For the text of the radio message see appendix under 'Documents'.

19. Paulus, pp. 212, 219. See also Manstein, p. 332. Von Manstein remonstrated with the OKH and requested that this order be rescinded, since it contained an expression of unwarranted mistrust in the Army Commander. In actual practice he rescinded it himself by a sort of counter-directive which told Paulus, that he (Paulus) reported to him alone (Paulus, p. 213).

20. Adolf Heusinger, *Orders in Conflict* , Tübingen and Stuttgart, 1950, p. 220.

21. Seydlitz, Notations.

22. Paulus, p. 212.

23. Seydlitz, Notations.

24. Ibid. Evaluation of the situation of Sixth Army in the Stalingrad pocket on 25 November 1942. The document is contained in vol. 1 of the appendices to the war diary of Army Group Don – Dep. Ia – in Washington. The author used one of the copies which Dr Friedrich Christian Stahl had made in 1954.

25. Paulus, p. 211.

26. Zeitzler, pp. 160 *et seq.*; see appendix under 'Documents'.

27. See appendix (Evaluation of the situation ... on 25 November 1942).

28. Paulus, pp. 211, 247.

29. Alexander Stahlberg, *Damn Bloody Duty! Memoirs 1932 to 1945*, Berlin, 1987.

30. Kehrig, p. 246, note 30.

31. *Decisive Battles*, p. 207.

32. Seydlitz, Notations.

33. Ibid.

34. See appendix, 'Documents on the battle of Sixth Army'.

35. Seydlitz, Notations. Doerr, (p. 70) has sharply criticised the message radioed by Sixth Army to Army Group after the encirclement, because in such a critical moment it did not emphasise with decisive forcefulness, that the only salvation lay in the break-out to the south-west. 'This thought, weakly expressed in the conditional, goes under in many details of the unimpressive message and is pushed into the background by the clearly stated intent to hold the area from Stalingrad to the Don.'

36. Seydlitz, Notations.

37. Heinz Schröter, p. 191.

38. H. von Rohden, p. 21; Paulus, pp. 223 *et seq.*

39. Manstein, p. 346.

40. Ibid., p 346.

41. Toepke, p. 77.

42. Ibid., p. 77.

43. Ibid., pp. 59 *et seq.*

44. Seydlitz, Notations.

45. Toepke, p. 78.

46. Seydlitz, Notations; see also Paulus, p. 242.

47. Kurt von Tippelsskirch, *History of the Second World War*, Bonn, 1951, p. 318.

48. Seydlitz, Notations . See also statements in chapter 'Von Manstein Desires Surrender ...'.

49. Those who wish to demonstrate how much sense the tenacious holding out by the Stalingrad army made like to refer to the ninety major enemy formations von Manstein mentions as allegedly having been pinned down by Sixth Army until the final days of the battle. Görlitz claims that up to 143 and finally still fifty to sixty such Soviet 'major formations' were pinned down (see *Decisive Battles*, p. 309). But it is not permissible to count such formations as being of equal strength on both sides. As a rule, Soviet formations had only about one-third of the manpower of the equivalent German formations. A. M. Samsonov's *The Battle of Stalingrad*, Moscow, 1960, provides illuminating information on the organisation and manpower of the formations deployed at Stalingrad. See also the report by Hermann Pörzgen on the Stalingrad memoirs of Soviet Marshal Yeremenko in *Frankfurter Allgemeine Zeitung* of 15 October 1961. In the literature on Stalingrad one finds the tendency on both sides to over-estimate the strength of the enemy's formations.

50. Seydlitz, Notations.

51. Paulus, p. 244. The wording of the message has been reproduced by Paulus from memory.

52. See Zeitzler, p. 185. The wording of this order of 25 January 1943 by Hitler, according to Schröter (p. 203) was: 'Forbid surrender. The army will hold its position to the last man and bullet. By its heroic holding out, it makes an unforgettable contribution to the establishment of the defensive front and the salvation of the Occident.'

53. Selle, p. 11.

54. H. von Rohden, pp. 88 *et seq.*; Paulus, pp. 245 *et seq.*

55. Seydlitz, Notations.
56. Selle, p. 12.
57. Seydlitz, Notations.
58. Ibid.
59. Hellmut Schlömer, 'The end of XIV Panzer Corps at Stalingrad'. Previously unpublished report from the memoirs of the General. See appendix under 'Documents'.
60. Seydlitz, Notations.
61. Ibid.
62. Ibid. The suffering during the last weeks in the pocket and the disorganisation in the conduct of the leadership is impressively described in the experience report by Lieutenant General Hans-Georg Leyser, Commander of 29th (motorised) Infantry Division in Joachim Lemelsen, *29th Division ...* , Bad Nauheim, 1960, pp. 204–60.
63. Paulus, pp. 91, 244.
64. Schlömer, op. cit. See appendix, 'The end of XIV Panzer Corps...'.
65. Paulus, p. 91; See also Görlitz, *Decisive Battles*, p. 310.
66. Paulus, pp. 247 *et seq*. Here Paulus also mentions three other generals who were in favour of surrender: General Pfeffer, Commander of IV Army Corps, Schlömer, Commander of XIV Panzer Corps and von Daniels, Commander of 376th Infantry Division.
67. Testimony by Paulus on 12 February 1946 in Nuremberg (*The Nuremberg Trials*, vol. VII, p. 318). Wording of the radio message in appendix, 'Radio messages...'.
68. Seydlitz, Notations.
69. Ibid.

DOCUMENTS

Order no. 4 to the Forces of the Stalingrad and South-west Fronts
(From A. J. Yeremenko, *Stalingrad*, Moscow, 1961, pp. 159 *et seq.*)

1 September 1942
The Army in the Field

Comrade fighters, commanders and political workers, heroic defenders of Stalingrad!

The bitter fighting for the city of Stalingrad has been raging for months. The Germans have lost hundreds of tanks and planes. Hitler's brutalised hordes are advancing towards Stalingrad and the Volga over mountains of dead bodies of their own men and officers.

Our Bolshevik Party, our nation, our great country, have given us the task not to let the enemy reach the Volga, to defend the city of Stalingrad. The defence of Stalingrad is of decisive importance for the whole Soviet front.

Without sparing our strength and with scorn for death, we shall defy the Germans the way to the Volga and not give up Stalingrad. Each one of us must bear in mind that the capture of Stalingrad by the Germans and their advance to the Volga will give our enemies new strength and weaken our own forces.

Not one step back!

The War Council expects unlimited courage, tenacity and heroism in the fight with the onrushing enemy from all the fighters, commanders and political workers, from all the defenders of Stalingrad.

The enemy must and will be smashed on the approaches to Stalingrad.

Forward against the enemy! Up into the unremitting battle, comrades, for Stalingrad, for our great country!

Death to the German invader!

Commander-in-Chief of	Member of the War Council of
Stalingrad and South-west Front	Stalingrad- and South-west Front
Colonel General A. Yeremenko	Lieutenant General N. Khrushchev

Evaluation of the Situation of Sixth Army in the Stalingrad Pocket

25 November 1942
by the Commanding General of LI Army Corps
General of Artillery von Seydlitz

The Commanding General LI A.C. O.U., 25.11.1942
No. 603/43 g. Kdos.   form. TOP SECRET

To
Commander-in-Chief, Sixth Army
Having received Army order of 24.11.1942 on the continuation of the battle, I feel obliged with a view to the gravity of the hour, to put my appreciation of the situation which has been reinforced by the reports of the last 24 hours down in writing once again.

The Army is faced with a decisive either/or; break-out to the south-west in the general direction of Kotelnikovo or destruction within a few days.

This opinion is based on a sober evaluation of the actual circumstances.

1. Since there is virtually no stock-pile of supplies at the outset of the battle, the supply situation is the key factor for any decision.

For the supply situation of LI A.C. as of the evening of 23.11. see attachment.

The numbers speak for themselves.

Even the minor defensive engagements of the past few days have noticeably depleted ammunition stocks. Should the corps be attacked on its full front, which must be expected daily, then it will shoot itself completely dry within one or two days.

It is hardly to be expected that the ammunition situation is any better with the other army corps that have already been heavily engaged for days.

From the calculations made, it is clear that an adequate supply by air lift of LI Corps alone is questionable, therefore completely impossible for the whole army. What 30 Ju (on 23.11.), or the further 100 Ju that have only been promised so far, can bring in, is only a drop. To attach hopes to this, means grasping at a straw. Where the large number of Ju required for the supply of the army is to come from, is nowhere in evidence. If they exist at all, the planes will have to be flown in from all over Europe and North Africa. Because of the distances to be covered, their own fuel requirements would be so great that coverage is highly questionable given the fuel situation as experienced so far, not to mention the operational consequences for the whole conduct of the war. Even if 500 planes were to land daily instead of the envisaged 130, they could only bring in 1000 t of supplies, which would not suffice to cover the needs of an army of approx. 200,000 men engaged in heavy combat and without stockpiles. More than the coverage of the minimum fuel requirement, a small fraction of our own ammunition types and maybe also a fraction of the required food for humans, cannot be hoped for. The horses will all have died within a few days. Tactical mobility will thereby be restricted even further, the distribution of supplies down to the lines made more difficult and on the other hand, the fuel requirement increased.

There can be no doubt that the mass of the weather-proof Russian fighters will be deployed for attacks against the incoming cargo planes and against Pitomnik and Peskovatka, the only two air bases capable of handling bulk cargo. Heavy losses are inescapable, continuous fighter cover over the long distances and for the two bases far from assured. The weather situation will also variably influence the tonnage results.

The impossibility of adequate supply thus proven, the air lift can only delay the exhaustion of supplies of the army by a few days, in the case of ammunition within 3 to 5 days, but not prevent it. Extension of the food supply lies in our own hands up to a certain degree (extension by 100% was ordered three days ago in LI Corps). Extension of fuel and ammunition stocks depends almost entirely on the enemy.

2. The probable conduct of the enemy, for whom victory in a battle of destruction of classic proportions beckons, is easy to predict. Knowing his active mode of combat it is hardly to be questioned that he will continue his attacks against the encircled Sixth Army with undiminished force. We must grant him that he recognises the need to destroy the army before German relief operations can become effective. From experience we know that he has no compunction about sacrificing human lives. Our successes in containing him, especially on 24.11. and the heavy losses we have seen him sustain at several points, should not lead us to self-deception.

The enemy is probably not totally unaware of our supply problems. The more persistently and harder he attacks, the more rapidly will we exhaust our ammunition. Even if no single attack succeeds, success will come about when the army has shot itself dry and is defenceless. To pretend that he does not recognise this would mean that we expect the enemy to act mistakenly. In the history of war such an attitude has always led to defeat. It would be a dangerous game and if it led to a catastrophe for Sixth Army, would have the most serious consequences for the course, and maybe also the result, of the war.

3. Operationally the conclusion is irrefutable; if it digs in, Sixth Army can only escape destruction if relief becomes effective within a few, i.e., within about 5 days, to such an extent that the enemy must break off his attacks. There is not a shred of evidence that this will happen. Should the relief only become effective later on, then the condition of helplessness will inevitably come about, i.e., the destruction of Sixth Army.

What measures the OKH has taken for the relief of Sixth Army, is not clear. Relief from the west can only lie at a great distance, because our own security forces only stand to the westwards of the upper Chir and from about Oblivskaya onwards on the lower Chir. Therefore the deployment of relief forces must take place at a great distance from Sixth Army. Even with the aid of the effective rail line via Millerovo, the deployment of an army powerful enough to carry out a rapid penetration while simultaneously securing its northern flank, will take weeks. To this must be added the time required for the operation itself which, due to the inclemencies of the weather and the short days at this time of the year, will be far longer than during the summer.

The deployment of 2 Panzer divisions initiated near Kotelnikovo for relief from the south and their attack must be calculated as requiring at least 10 days. The possibilities for a rapid penetration by the attack are greatly inhibited by the need to protect the flanks, particularly the eastern flank, that will grow longer with each step, leaving aside the unknown condition the divisions are in and the question whether 2 Panzer divisions are strong enough at all. One cannot count on the possibility of relief forces being deployed by means of a larger number of motorised columns. Neither the vehicles nor the fuel can be available, otherwise they would already have had to be made available earlier and at far lower cost in fuel, to supply the so greatly exposed Stalingrad front.

4. The possibility that relief will become effective within the time dictated by the supply situation is therefore nil. The OKH's order to hold the position until relief is here, is obviously based on unrealistic foundations. It is therefore impossible to execute and will invariably lead to catastrophe for the army. If the army is to be preserved, it must immediately obtain a different order, or else immediately take a different decision itself.

With regard to the operational, political and moral effects, the idea of deliberately sacrificing the army should be beyond any consideration.

5. From the comparison of the time scales based on the supply situation and the operational requirements, including the probable actions of the enemy, the conclusion is so clear that further considerations are hardly required. None the less, the following factors, all pointing in the same direction, should be listed:

(a) The western perimeter is still far from being stabilised.

(b) On the northern front, it is impossible to contain a sharply concentrated attack by opposing forces for a longer period of time, because after first having pulled out 16th Pz.Div., then 3rd Inf.Div. (mot), the front had to be withdrawn to a shorter, but almost completely unprepared line.

(c) Tense situation on the southern front.

(d) Reduced combat strength of the heavily combed-out Volga front, particularly if the ice cover on the river solidifies, which is to be expected soon, and is no longer a barrier for the attackers.

(e) Due to lack of ammunition, prevention of continuous reinforcement of the enemy bridgeheads on the Volga not possible. Enemy attacks to date have already required full commitment of all local reserves there.

(f) Condition of the divisions, heavily depleted because of the attacks in Stalingrad.

(g) The army compressed in a scanty steppe area that offers hardly any usable shelters and cover any longer, so that men and *matériel* are everywhere exposed to the weather and enemy air attacks.

(h) Expected advent of severe frost with almost complete lack of firewood on the major part of the present perimeter lines.

(i) Only insufficient support by the Luftwaffe due to lack of favourably situated bases.

In contrast to this, no anti-aircraft protection, since all anti-aircraft formations must be exclusively used for anti-tank combat.

A comparison with last year's Demjansk pocket can lead to dangerously false conclusions. The distance to the German front was several times shorter. The supply requirements of one encircled corps were far less, particularly since there were far fewer of the weapons required here in the steppe (tanks, heavy artillery, mortars) to be supplied. Despite the short distance to the German front, at the time the establishment of a very narrow corridor into the pocket required weeks of heavy winter fighting.

6. The conclusion is clear.

Either Sixth Army defends itself in the pocket until it is shot dry, i.e., defenceless. Since, given continued enemy attacks and their probable extension to sectors of the front that have been quiet so far, this condition must occur before relief can become effective, such passive conduct means the end of the army.

Or the army acts and breaks open the ring of encirclement.

This is only still possible if the army makes forces available by withdrawing them from the northern and Volga fronts, i.e., by shortening the front, and attacks with them on the southern front, and then by giving up Stalingrad, breaks out in the direction of the weakest opposition, i.e., towards Kotelnikovo. This decision requires leaving much *matériel* behind, but offers the chance of breaking the southern jaw of the pincers, withdrawing the army and its weapons from catastrophe and preserving it for further operations. By doing this, a part of the enemy forces will remain occupied for the duration, whereas if the army is destroyed in the pocket, it will cease to occupy any enemy forces at all. A public announcement of the event that will not substantially damage morale is possible. 'After having completely destroyed the Soviet armament centre of Stalingrad, the army has withdrawn from the Volga while simultaneously smashing a substantial enemy force.'

The expectation that the break-out will be successful is all the greater since the fighting to date has frequently demonstrated a poor stability of enemy infantry forces in open ground and as some of our own forces are still on the tributaries east of the Don and in the Aksai sector. As regards timing, the break-out must be initiated and carried out immediately. Any delay reduces its chances. With every delay the number of combatants and ammunition is reduced. With every delay the enemy becomes stronger on the break-out front and can bring in further forces of containment against the Kotelnikovo group. With every delay combat power is reduced because of loss of horses and therefore loss of horse-drawn weapons.

If the OKH does not immediately rescind the order to dig-in, then conscience adamantly dictates the duty towards the army and the German nation to seize the freedom of action denied by the existing orders and to take advantage of the still existing possibility of averting catastrophe by our own attack. The complete destruction of 200,000 combatants and their total *material* is at risk. There is no other choice.

sig. von Seydlitz
General of Artillery

Comment by the Chief of Staff of Sixth Army, Major General Arthur Schmidt: 'We are not to wrack the Führer's brains for him, and neither is Gen. v. Seydlitz those of the C. in C.'

For the correctness of the copy:
sig. Schatz, Lieutenant

ATTACHMENT TO 603/42 g.K.
Supply situation of LI A.C. as of 23.11. evening

1. *Ammunition* (excl. 3rd [mot], 60th [mot] and 94th Inf.Div.)

Hand-grenades	30% of complement
8cm mortar shells	20% of complement
light inf. rounds	8% of complement
heavy inf. rounds	12% of complement
light field how. 16	60% of complement
light field how. 18	30% of complement
heavy field how. 18	25% of complement
10cm guns	12% of complement

Armour-piercing ammunition approx. 30 – 40%.

Hand-grenades only meagre stocks.

Tracer and signal ammunition only very meagre stocks.

3rd Inf.Div. (mot), 60th Inf.Div (mot) and 94th Inf.Div, latter as of 22.11. stand at:

light field how.	60%
heavy field how.	50%
heavy inf. rounds	25%
light inf. rounds	40%

Daily ammunition requirements of the corps (based on defensive combat to date):

(a) 400 t in case of lighter combat (50 t per div.) = 200 Ju

(b) 800 t in case of heavy combat (100 t per div.) = 400 Ju

2. *Fuel situation*

Exact reports from the div. not obtainable.

Stocks as good as exhausted.

The most urgent driving to bring up supplies, deployment of anti-tank troops, field guns, only possible for a short while longer.

Daily requirements of the corps under extreme economies:

80cbm (10cbm per div.) = 40 Ju

3. *Food situation*

On average the div. dispose of:

   7 full days soft food
   4 full days bread
   3.5 days flour

We must assume, however, that bakery operations have ceased because the mass of the bakery company is deployed in the Karpovka valley.

Daily requirements of the corps (on half rations)

      80 t soft food   = 40 Ju

      70 t tinned food   = 35 Ju

Assuming half-rations, the supply of the corps will require in total:

(a) in case of lighter combat: 598 t of supplies = 295 Ju

(b) in case of heavy combat: 990 t of supplies = 495 Ju

F.t.c.o.t.c.

signature

General Zeitzler, Chief of Staff of the Army, struggles with Hitler for the salvation of the Stalingrad army

The dramatic discussions took place during the nights of 22/23 and 23/24 November 1942 at Führer Headquarters, the *Wolfsschanze*, near Rastenburg. Zeitzler reported on this in an article that contains his memoirs of the battle of Stalingrad and was published in book form in English in 1956 under the title *The Fatal Decisions*.

'Since the operations proposed for the relief of Sixth Army cannot be successful, it is decisive that orders for a break-out be issued. This must be done at once. The last possible moment has arrived.'

While I was speaking, Hitler was visibly growing more and more angry. He had repeatedly tried to interrupt me but I had not permitted this because I knew this to be my last chance and I could not stay silent. When I was finally finished, he screamed, 'Sixth Army will stay where it is! It is the garrison of a fortress and it is the duty of garrisons to withstand sieges. If necessary they will hold out all winter and I will relieve them by an offensive in the spring.'

This was pure fantasy. I added, 'Stalingrad is not a fortress. There is no way to supply Sixth Army.'

Hitler became even more enraged and shouted louder than ever: 'Reichsmarschall Göring has said that he can supply the army by air.' Now I too shouted 'That is crazy!'

Hitler insisted. 'I will not leave the Volga!' I said in a loud voice, 'My Führer! It would be a crime to leave Sixth Army in Stalingrad. That would mean the death or capture of a quarter of a million men. Any hope of freeing them would be in vain. The loss of this army would break the back of the eastern front.'

Hitler grew very pale, but did not say anything. He looked at me with an icy expression and pushed the bell button on his desk. When an orderly officer of the SS appeared he ordered, 'Go fetch Field Marshal Keitel and General Jodl.'

Not a word passed between us until they both appeared. They were here in a minute and had doubtlessly been waiting in the next room. If that had been the case, then they must have heard our loud exchange through the thin walls of the map room. And they would not have had any mistaken ideas about the nature of the noise. Keitel and Jodl saluted formally. Hitler remained standing with a serious expression on his face. He was still very pale but outwardly calm. He said, 'I am faced with a very difficult decision. Before I decide, I would like to hear your opinions. Should I give up Stalingrad or not? What are your thoughts on the matter?'

And then something began to unfold that one could almost call a council of war, an occurrence such as Hitler had never practised before. Keitel, who was standing at attention, said with flashing eyes, 'My Führer! Stay on the Volga!'

Jodl spoke calmly and factually. He weighed his words before saying, 'My Führer, it is indeed a difficult decision you must take. If we withdraw from the Volga, this means giving up a good part of the territories we won at such great sacrifices during the summer offensive. On the other hand, if we do not withdraw Sixth Army the situation may become grave. The operations planned for its relief may be successful, but they may also fail. Until we see the results of these operations, my opinion is that we hold out on the Volga.'

'Now it is your turn,' Hitler said to me. He was obviously hoping that the words of the other two generals had caused me to change my mind. Even though it was Hitler who took the decisions, he was anxious to obtain the agreement, if only pro forma, of his professional advisers. I now came to attention myself and said with all the formality I could muster. 'My Führer! My opinion has not changed. In my view it would be a crime to leave Sixth Army where it is. We can neither relieve it nor supply it. It would simply be sacrificed and that would be senseless.'

Outwardly Hitler remained calm and self-controlled even though he was boiling mad inside. He said to me, 'You see General that I am not alone in my opinion. It is shared by these two officers here, both of whom are senior to you. I will therefore remain with my previous decision.'

He bowed stiffly and we were dismissed.

The second discussion I would like to describe took place the following night.

Despite Hitler's harsh rejection of my reasoning, I did not want to give up my struggle for the salvation of Sixth Army under any circumstances. By experience I knew that I now had to approach the problem from a different direction. Hitler's decision, which appeared to be final and unalterable, was based on strategic considerations. There was no sense in trying to re-open the discussion on these grounds during the next few days. He would simply refuse to listen. But this did not apply to questions of supply. My thought was that where strategic arguments had failed, maybe matters of supply could carry the day. Maybe I would be able to bring him over to my way of thinking if I showed him the details of Sixth Army's supply situation and was able to prove to him on the basis of accurate facts and figures that an air lift for the army was impossible. Hitler always tended to be impressed by statistics ...

The facts were put together by my staff in easily readable tables of numbers. As soon as these were ready, I again asked for a private audience with

Hitler. He again chose a time late at night. Because of our discussion of yesterday, the reception was very cool. However, I succeeded in awakening his interest in the figures I showed him and he permitted me to finish the explanations that were required to understand the statistics. I closed with the following words. 'After I have studied the facts in detail there is only one possible conclusion; it is not possible to supply Sixth Army by air for a longer period of time.' Hitler's demeanour became icy. He said, 'The Reichsmarschall has assured me that it is possible.' I repeated, that that was not true. Hitler continued, 'Well then, let him tell you himself.'

He had the Commander-in-Chief of the Luftwaffe brought in and asked, Göring, 'Can you supply Sixth Army by air?'

Göring raised his right arm and solemnly pronounced, 'My Führer! I assure you that the Luftwaffe can supply Sixth Army.' Hitler threw me a triumphant look, but I simply said, 'The Luftwaffe can do no such thing.' The Reichsmarschall looked black and said, 'You are not in a position to presume an opinion on that.' I turned to Hitler and asked, 'My Führer, may I be permitted to ask the Reichsmarschall a question?' 'Yes, you may.'

'Does the Reichsmarschall know', I asked, 'the tonnage that must be flown in each day?' Göring grew visibly embarrassed and wrinkled his brow. He answered, 'I do not, but the officers on my staff will.' On this I continued, 'If one takes the actual stock of Sixth Army into consideration, the absolute minimum requirement, and all sorts of emergencies, then Sixth Army will need a daily delivery of 300 tonnes. But since not every day is good for flying as I know from my experiences on the front last winter, this means 500 tonnes each actual day of flying, if the average minimum is to be maintained.'

Göring answered, 'I can do that!' With this, I lost my self-control and cried, 'My Führer, that is a lie!' An icy silence descended on the three of us. Göring was white with rage. Hitler looked from one to the other and was obviously confused and astonished. Finally he said to me, 'The Reichsmarschall has made his report and I have no choice but to believe him. Therefore I will stay with my original decision.' I now said, 'I would like to make one further request.' Hitler asked, 'And what is that?' I answered, 'May I give you, my Führer, a daily report that accurately lists the supply tonnage flown in to Sixth Army during the preceding 24 hours?' Göring objected and claimed that this was none of my business. But Hitler rejected him and I was given permission to present this daily report. With that, the discussion was over.

Once again it had been to no avail. The only thing I had achieved was the enmity of the Reichsmarschall. I would like to point out here that many staff officers and commanders of the Luftwaffe shared my opinion from the beginning. A number of them put their doubts down in writing. They were not able to convince their Commander-in-Chief. He simply locked their reports away and made sure they did not reach Hitler's desk...'

Zeitzler's report on the downfall of Sixth Army ends with the following sentences: 'I had struggled for months to make Hitler see reason and take the right decisions. I had failed. I therefore drew some conclusions as to my own position as Chief of Staff. I went to Hitler and tendered my resignation. He was angry and brusquely said, 'A general does not have the right to leave his post.'

Documents on the Battle of Sixth Army

Paulus to Hitler:

23 November 1942
TOP SECRET FOR THE CHIEF
copy; Army Group B

My Führer
Since receipt of your radio message of evening 22.11. events have come thick and fast.

We have not succeeded in closing the pocket to the south-west and west. Impending enemy penetrations begin to emerge there.

Ammunition and fuel are coming to an end. Numerous batteries and tanks have shot themselves dry. A timely and adequate supply is impossible.

The army will shortly be destroyed unless a concentration of all forces succeeds in totally defeating the enemy attacking from the south and west.

For this we must immediately withdraw all forces from Stalingrad and strong detachments from the northern front. Unavoidable sequel must then be a break-out towards the south-west, since eastern and northern front can no longer be held with such weak forces.

In this case we will lose much *matériel* but the majority of the valuable combatants and at least a part of the *matériel* will be preserved.

I retain full responsibility for this message even if I add that Commanding Generals Heitz, von Seydlitz, Strecker, Hube and Jaenecke all share this evaluation of the situation.

Based on the situation, I again request freedom of action!
Heil my Führer!
signed Paulus

Führer Order
To the C. in C. Sixth Army

24.11.1942
Sixth Army has been temporarily encircled by Russian forces. I intend to concentrate the army in the area Stalingrad North - Kotluban – Hill 137 – Hill 135 – Marinovka – Zybenko – Stalingrad South. The army may rest assured that I will do everything to supply it accordingly and to relieve it in time. I know the brave Sixth Army and its Commander-in-Chief and I am sure it will do its duty.
signed: Adolf Hitler

Daily situation reports of Sixth Army to Army Group Don from 14 to 31 January 1943

By their factual wording these excerpts from the situation reports impressively demonstrate the horror of the final phase of the downfall of the Stalingrad army. They are taken from Karlheinrich Rieker's *One Man Loses a World War*, pp. 166–9, Fridericus-Verlag, Frankfurt, 1955.

January 14, morning report. 'Only half of forces now have 200 grams of bread. Ammunition so low that combating enemy masses in front of perimeter no longer possible.'

Day report. 'Parts of divisions fighting with bare steel because ammunition exhausted. Impossible to hold present positions on western perimeter due to enemy superiority, particularly in artillery. Numerous cases of frostbite and total exhaustion of the men.'

Comment to this report by Army Group. 'Army Group no longer counts on situation of army being re-established due to continuing inadequacy of supply.'

January 15, day report. 'Despite heroic resistance by 16th Panzer Division, hill three kilometres south-east of p. 139.7 lost to heavy attacks, after having been encircled on three sides for several days. Recapture of hill impossible due to lack of ammunition and men.'

January 16, day report. 'Enemy continues mass attacks against south, south-west and west perimeter; was thrown back after heavy fighting on new line of resistance. Supply situation catastrophic. Due to lack of fuel, no longer possible to bring food to front line. Many companies on west perimeter without food for two days. During whole day, men without bunkers exposed to 30 degree cold, and attacks by Russian dive-bombers with heavy bombs. Own dive-bombers, fighters and spotters either broken down or flown out.'

January 17, morning report. 'Since midnight, rolling enemy air attack on fortress, which is without fighter cover and almost without Flak protection. If increase in supply promised again not immediately forthcoming, any further holding on hopeless.'

Day report. 'Sixth Army has mostly held positions on north-east, west and north-west perimeter despite further heavy attacks. Many local crises due to lack of fuel and ammunition... Due to insufficient supply the worst must be expected in the fortress. Many soldiers dead of starvation.'

January 18, day report. 'Fuel situation caused by failure of Luftwaffe paralyses all movement, even for supply of men with food. Continuing bomb attacks. Gumrak air base fully serviceable. Only two Heinkel 111 landed all day.'

January 19, day report. 'Enemy resumed mass attack on western perimeter against left flank 76th and right flank 44th Inf. Div. but was thrown back. Supply canisters only partially found, due to snow drifts. Collection of same very difficult, due to lack of fuel.'

January 20, morning report. 'Withdrawal of right flank of 60th Inf. Div. (mot) executed according to plan; heavy weapons left behind (lack of fuel).'

Day report. 'Withdrawal of north-west perimeter initiated. Due to lack of fuel and state of exhaustion of troops, expect heavy losses in men, weapons and equipment during withdrawal.'

January 21, morning report. Since January 16 only received 36 rounds for light howitzers, used up several thousand; only 30 rounds per barrel left. Fuel and food equivalent.'

Day report. 'In unimaginably heroic and desperate fighting back and forth, the divisions on the western perimeter attempted to throw back enemy mass attacks by artillery and tanks. Several deep penetrations temporarily contained, counter-attacks by small groups stopped enemy regiments, several tanks destroyed, some in close combat. Since fall of darkness, 60th Inf. Div. (mot) and 113th and 76th Inf. Div. fighting rearwards under enemy pressure (enemy in rear!) to line Nadesha four kilometres east of Gonchara, which is to be held until 22.01. 44th Inf. Div. apparently destroyed.'

January 22, day report. 'In heavy fighting throughout the day on north, west and south-west perimeter, enemy gained deep penetration on south-west perimeter. In heroic fighting despite lack of artillery and anti-tank ammunition, strong enemy attack contained on line two kilometres north-west of Talavoi – Talavoi – two kilometres north-west of Minina. Ammunition mostly used up, partial signs of dissolution. Over 20 enemy tanks destroyed with last rounds. On western perimeter only thin garrison in pockets of resistance; here also only few heavy weapons left. 76th, 297th, 29th (mot) and 3rd (mot) Inf. Div. destroyed. Southern and Stalingrad perimeter holding against superior attacks; ammunition there also coming to an end. Ability of fortress to resist coming to an end.'

January 24, morning report. 'Horrifying conditions within city proper. Approx. 20,000 wounded uncared for seeking shelter in ruins, intermingled with about same number of starving, frost-bitten and dispersed, mostly without weapons.'

Day report. 'In the fighting in Stalingrad, formations of Roumanian 1st Cavalry Division and Roumanian 20th Infantry Division have fought outstandingly shoulder to shoulder with their German comrades to the end. Their deeds deserve to stand out in the annals of this unique battle.'

January 25, morning report. 'Swastika flag on highest house of city centre, in order to fight the last battle under this emblem.'

Day report. 'Heavy attacks by superior artillery and tanks and only weaker, hesitatingly attacking infantry. Western city edge mainly held; Suburb of Minina lost. XI A.C. fighting with only few heavy weapons, scarce ammunition and without food. Heaviest rolling enemy air attacks on whole city area. Number of wounded, starving and dispersed grows hourly.'

January 25, day report. 'Superior enemy forces took southern Stalingrad south of Tsaritsa by noon and destroyed remnant of IV A.C. Enemy forces crossing the Tsaritsa destroyed. Defence of city greatly impaired by 30,000 to 40,000 wounded and dispersed. A few energetic commanders attempt to form combat teams out of the dispersed, with which they continue resistance by fighting themselves on the front line. Food, saving few remnants, used up. In the fighting for Stalingrad, the Croat 369th Infantry Regiment together with a Croat artillery detachment have proven themselves outstandingly.'

January 28, day report. 'After heavy enemy attacks with superior artillery and launchers, Tsaritsa perimeter to the west of the railway penetrated after ammunition ran out. Food situation requires no longer feeding sick and wounded in order to maintain combatants.'

January 30, morning report. 'Night attacks against western and southern perimeter being opposed with their last remaining strength by the few remaining combat-worthy groups that still have ammunition; several tanks destroyed. Under heavy, bloody losses, enemy achieved wide and deep penetration. Final resistance will be offered by remnant of 194th Grenadier Regiment and Army Command in the high-rise building. Possible that XI A.C. in tractor plant will resist longer since enemy is weaker there.'

Day report. 'Army forming defensive perimeter with last remaining forces 300 m around Red Square. XI A.C. will hold out to the last according to orders. Despite heavy losses, conduct of troops there exemplary.'

January 31, 0745 hours. 'Russian outside the door. We are destroying.'

The following radio messages are taken from the book *The Luftwaffe Fights for Stalingrad* by Hans-Detlef Herhudt von Rohden, Wiesbaden, 1950, pp. 113, 118, 123.

To the Führer

On the anniversary of the seizure of power, Sixth Army greets its Führer. The swastika flag still flies over Stalingrad. May our fight be an example for the still living and for future generations never to surrender, even in the most hopeless situation; then Germany will win.

Heil my Führer!
Paulus, Colonel General
Stalingrad, 29. 1. 1943, noon.

30. 1. 1943
My Colonel General Paulus.

Already today the whole German nation looks towards this city with deep emotion. As has always been the case in world history, this sacrifice too shall not be in vain.
Clausewitz's 'Confession' shall be fulfilled. It is only now that the German nation realises the full gravity of this struggle and it will make the greatest sacrifices.

My thoughts are ever with you and your soldiers.
Your Adolf Hitler

30.1. 19.50 hours
VIII Air Corps to 4th Air Fleet Command.

In the cellar ruins of Red Square in Stalingrad, have heard the proclamation by our Führer through the thunder of enemy fire. It gave us courage and firmness for the last hours of battle for the ruins of the Red stronghold on the Volga. Over us flies the swastika flag. We will obey the order of our Supreme Commander until the end. We think in loyalty of home. Long live the Führer!
104th Flak Regiment, Rosenfeld, Colonel.

The following two radio messages were sent by Göring to the Stalingrad army during the final days of the battle. The third was sent by Army Group Don. (Taken from the book by Hans Schröter, *Stalingrad ... to the Last Bullet*, Lengerich, n.d.

'One day people will proudly say about the fight of Sixth Army; as to defiance of death a Langemark, as to tenacity an Alcazar, as to courage a Narvik, as to self-sacrifice a Stalingrad.'

'Sixth Army can count it as part of its undying honour to have saved the Occident.'

'In ages to come the German nation will still silently honour the heroic struggle of its sons on the frontier between Europe and Asia.'

31.1.1943
'True to its oath to the flag, Sixth Army has held its position for Führer and Fatherland to the last man and bullet, in accordance with its high and important assignment.'
Paulus.

1.2., 17.25 hours:
Army Group Don to XI A.C.
'I expect that the Stalingrad north pocket will hold to the last. Every day, every hour that is gained thereby is of decisive benefit for the rest of the front.'
Adolf Hitler.

The End of XIV Panzer Corps in Stalingrad
Notes by Lieutenant General Hellmut Schlömer

The remnant of XIV Panzer Corps reached the railway line Gumrak–Voroponovo west of the Tolevoy ravine on 19 January 1943. The retreat from Karpovka to here had been a road of horror and suffering for the troops. Close to physical exhaustion, the soldiers had stamped through the endless snowy waste in which formless mounds lay here and there; fallen or frozen comrades, destroyed and abandoned vehicles. Sometimes there had still been signs of life in the plump piles; wounded, mutilated and half-frozen human beings, crying for help and asking to be taken along.

Despite this the exhausted and over-tired formations had withstood the snowstorms, the cold and the lack of food and ammunition. Under heavy losses and almost inhuman efforts they had at least temporarily prevented an advance by the Russians on this sector of the perimeter.

Rumours and reports of actual facts about the catastrophic situation on the whole defensive front, about the tragic events at Pitomnik air base that had already been lost and the impressions left by their own personal experiences, were grinding the hard-pressed men down. As self-sacrificing as each of them may have acted despite all of this, we could not prevent the Russians from infiltrating the front in many places and causing confusion in the rear of the line.

On 22 or 23 January the Commander-in-Chief ordered the Commanding Generals to report to his command post. In his presentation he emphasised that since the overall situation did not permit giving up resistance and the Army had the order to fight on to the last bullet, surrender was out of the question.

In unmistakable terms, General von Seydlitz pointed out that in his opinion a continuation of the battle was irresponsible with regard to the troops and would only demand a useless sacrifice of human lives. I agreed with him without reservations. The other generals also shared his thoughts; however they emphasised that the order by the OKH had to be obeyed under any and all circumstances. The decision therefore was to continue the battle.

A few days later the situation required withdrawing the forces to the city limits of Stalingrad. If we had all believed some days ago that we had borne and seen the extreme of human pain and suffering, we now had to recognise that the degree of horror and despair had grown beyond any bounds. The officers and men felt they had been betrayed and abandoned by the Supreme Command and no longer believed in the promised help and relief. Terrible experiences are still clear in my mind's eye, I still feel the helplessness of human inadequacy, of not being able to help when suffering and horror became incomprehensible.

We reached the city limits under heavy losses, exhausted, over-tired, freezing, apathetic.

The staff of XIV Panzer Corps found shelter in two narrow cells of the city gaol on the northern bank of the Tsaritsa, that was overflowing with wounded and dispersed.

There could no longer be any talk of organised combat; only a few small formations, left completely on their own, were still resisting the Russians and delaying their advance. As far as this was possible, we established contact with these groups, supplied them with the bare essentials and told them what we had. It was not much. The rations in these days consisted of 50 g of bread per day for each of us, a soup made of snow water without any fat and a morsel of tinned meat, as far as there was any left. We were lacking in medicine and dressing materials but above all, in warm shelters for the wounded, sick and healthy.

Despair found its first victim. Rumours were confirmed that several officers had put an end to their lives because they could not reconcile the tragic ending of this senseless battle with their concept of soldierly honour. Others had taken off on their own to break out to the west. A hopeless endeavour. They all found a bitter end in the vast snowy steppe.

On my walks to the so-called front, on my visits to the wounded, also in many talks with doctors, officers and men from the ranks, I constantly asked myself the same question. Why this senseless dying, these sacrifices, these tortures? Cold, hunger and the constant bombardment exhausted and enervated the men more and more.

I could no longer stand this suffering and on 27 January I asked the Commander-in-Chief for permission to stop the fighting. The Field Marshal insisted on the order from OKH.

In the afternoon of the same day, however, Colonel General Paulus came to see me again. In the most emphatic manner I once again tried to convince him of the senselessness of continuing resistance. I had the impression that through his personal experiences the Army Chief had come to the same conclusion and shared my view. But despite all human pity, he gave the constantly arriving orders from OKH priority. He pointed out time and again that the overall situation required maintaining resistance as long as possible and would not permit a voluntary termination of the fighting. There was nothing left for me but to give in.

In the meantime my Chief of Staff, Colonel Müller, had approached the Army Chief of Staff, General Schmidt, and asked him to plead with the Commander-in-Chief for the termination of the fighting. He was given a strict No! Schmidt's answer must have gone something like this. 'We know the situation and the order is; you will fight on!' To Müller's despairing question, what the half-starved soldiers were still to resist with, the succinct answer was, that the soldiers still had their knives or else they could use their teeth!

That evening as we made our usual orientation rounds to the few troops we still had left, the picture was the same everywhere, exhausted, apathetically dozing men, penned together in the driving snow with dead and wounded. Here and there, a shot was still fired. The lines had interlaced, so that friend could hardly be distinguished from enemy any more.

Depressed and shattered, we returned to the city gaol. In the meantime a new load of wounded had arrived in the building that was already filled to overflowing. The sights we saw on our way through the corridors were indescribable in their horror. Colonel Müller became highly emotional, which turned to despair on learning of the suicide of our orderly officer. He ran out of the building, threatened with his pistol all who tried to stop him and then disappeared among the ruins. We never heard of him again.

That night I could find no rest despite my physical exhaustion. Conflicting emotions raged within my conscience; human pity and the sense of responsibility against soldierly obedience and the sense of duty. The questions that tortured me remained unanswered. When the morning of 28 January broke, I had still not seen my way clear to a decision.

Now the events came thick and fast. They forced me to take a clear stand.

The Russians advanced to the city centre and encircled us in the city gaol. The building complex threatened to become the mass grave for the people penned-up there. The Russian infantry did not succeed in penetrating into the blocks of houses, but the bombardment by mortars and launchers continued. Tanks drove up close to the buildings and took the entry ways under fire. We could no longer beat them back. Our only weapons were some rifles and a few pistols. The darkness of night saved us from the final combat.

I was forced to act in this chaos of destruction, unless I wanted to expose the survivors to hopeless house-to-house fighting and impose further inhuman sufferings on the wounded. I therefore took the responsibility for all the soldiers, officers and formations remaining in the gaol. I declared that I would end resistance at dawn next day and go into captivity with all those who were willing to follow me. A sigh of relief went through the ranks.

When the morning of 29 January broke, the remaining staff of XIV Panzer Corps and all those who shared my view, went into captivity.

No one knew what to expect. But we had reached the extreme limit of human endurance and resisted to the last. What could still make us afraid?

What was left to us was the chance that we might be able to serve our country again after many years.

(Original in the possession of J. Wieder)

The Surrender of the Army Staff at Stalingrad
Notes by Colonel Günther Ludwig
Commander 4th Panzer Artillery Regiment

During the final days of January 1943, I lay on the western edge of Red Square with the remnant of 14th Panzer Division. According to an order by Army, the division had been 'disbanded', the few remaining combat-worthy formations assigned to other units. With this measure, however, about 2,000 wounded and missing had become homeless and, more importantly, deprived of sustenance by the stroke of a pen. There was no legal way for them to obtain any more food. I had collected these men at Red Square in order to organise their supply (incidentally, I was not able to have these men that had been 'written-off' put back into the normal chain of supply!) and to put together new combat teams as far as this was possible.

On 30 January the defence in the Tsaritsa sector had broken down and the Russian front line was approaching Red Square from the south. By the afternoon, only the width of a single street still separated it from the square. I was occupying the row of ruins that bordered on Red Square on the south with a minimal force. The command post of Commander-in-Chief Paulus was about 100 m to the rear in the so-called 'department store'.

In this situation I received the assignment from the Chief of Staff of Sixth Army, General Schmidt, 'under all circumstances to prevent the Russians from entering Red Square and from taking out the Commander-in-Chief in his command post during the night.'

The spearheads of the Russian 69th and 29th Divisions stood on the southern edge of the square. I had about 50 men available who were still barely able to lift a rifle. The assignment was impossible. General Schmidt would not listen to my objections. The assignment remained in force.

My command post was in the corner building on the south-west corner of the square. This ruin was the key to the defence of the square. Across from me on the other side of the square was the theatre, held by Russian forces and full of hundreds of wounded. At 18.00 hours German time, three Russian tanks moved to the front of my command post. Even though they were only 5 m away, we were helpless against them, because the only defence we had were rifles and pistols. At the same time I was called upon by name from the theatre to evacuate my corner building within 10 minutes, otherwise the tanks would open fire.

Evacuation was irreconcilable with my assignment. Should the tanks open fire, this would mean the deaths of uncounted wounded who would be buried in the cellars. The only way out I could see lay in negotiating. I gave my adjutant the job of establishing contact with the occupants of the theatre under a flag of truce. This was successful but he was sent back with the directive that I would have to present my wishes in person.

In the meantime twilight had fallen. Accompanied by my adjutant and orderly, I went across to the Russian side and was taken to the command post of a battalion commander of 29th Division. Having been received correctly and pleasantly, I made the request to refrain from having the tanks open fire in the interest of the many wounded. The commander said that he was not authorised to take such a decision and offered to have me speak to his divisional commander by radio. The connection was made and I made my request. I was answered in German with deliberate politeness, but was immediately offered terms of surrender. I replied that I had not come to discuss surrender but only wished to clear up a local situation. At this point the radio link broke down and could not be re-established. With regard to my assignment, I now agreed a truce with the local Russian commander until daylight at 04.00 hours next morning. That was the only way to prevent a hopeless fight around Paulus' command post. After this agreement was reached, I went back to my command post.

Shortly thereafter, an officer with a steel helmet and heavily armed with rifle and hand-grenades, which we no longer had, appeared and said that he had been ordered by General Schmidt to conduct me to Army. A pregnant exchange of glances with my adjutant confirmed that nobody was in doubt about the reason for this. I went on ahead. However, I only needed a few quick steps to lose my escort in the darkness of the field of ruins with which I was familiar. I wanted to account for my action before my own conscience and then take the necessary decision.

In an unbelievable contrast to the noise of the last few days and nights, a deep silence lay over Red Square. Through the deep snow I again walked around my 'position' on the southern edge of the square. A few of our sentries lurked in the shadows of the ruins. They had been without a warming fire, without food, without heavy weapons for days. They were not capable of withstanding a further attack and had not been so for days.

My negotiations with the Russian side had to have been right. With a clear consciences I went to Army, prepared to accept any responsibility.

Here I was received by General Schmidt in the company of General Roske. 'You have been in radio contact with the Russians. Are you aware that this is strictly forbidden?', was the greeting. In a few short words I described the situation and the reasons for my decision. Without interrupting me, Schmidt listened to my report with a stony face, while Roske stood to one side. When I mentioned that a negotiator had called me from the theatre, I was suddenly and spontaneously interrupted under wild swinging of arms by the words, 'Negotiators come to you, why do none come to us!' It sounded like a cry for help. I was speechless, completely stunned. My answer was, 'If that is all that this is about, General, I guarantee you that a flag of truce will come to this house at 08.00 hours tomorrow.' 'Agreed!' General Schmidt was a different man. Excited, almost happy, he agreed with my decision that my officers and men would go into captivity and that I would arrange for a senior Russian officer to come to the 'department store'.

Seconds later I found myself alone and shaking my head in the badly lit cellar of Paulus' command post. So that was to be the end of a 'fight to the last bullet', that Mr. Schmidt had constantly been on about! Deeply depressed, but also with a view to the future, I slowly walked across Red Square to rejoin my comrades.

Next morning, as discussed, the tragedy of Stalingrad came to an end.

(Original in the possession of J. Wieder)

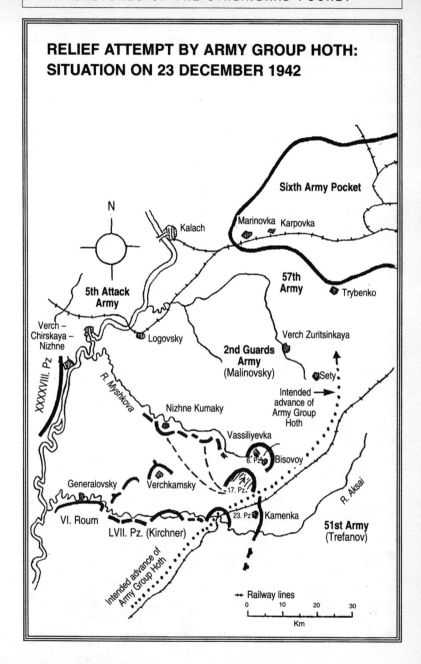

RELIEF ATTEMPT BY ARMY GROUP HOTH: SITUATION ON 23 DECEMBER 1942

N

Sixth Army Pocket

Kalach

Marinovka Karpovka

57th Army

Trybenko

5th Attack Army

Verch Zuritsinkaya

Verch – Chirskaya – Nizhne

Logovsky

2nd Guards Army (Malinovsky)

Sety

Intended advance of Army Group Hoth

XXXXVIII. Pz

R. Myshkova

Nizhne Kumaky

Vassiliyevka

6. Pz Bisovoy

Generalovsky Verchkamsky

17. Pz.

VI. Roum

LVII. Pz. (Kirchner)

23. Pz Kamenka

R. Aksai

51st Army (Trefanov)

Intended advance of Army Group Hoth

Railway lines

0   10   20   30
Km

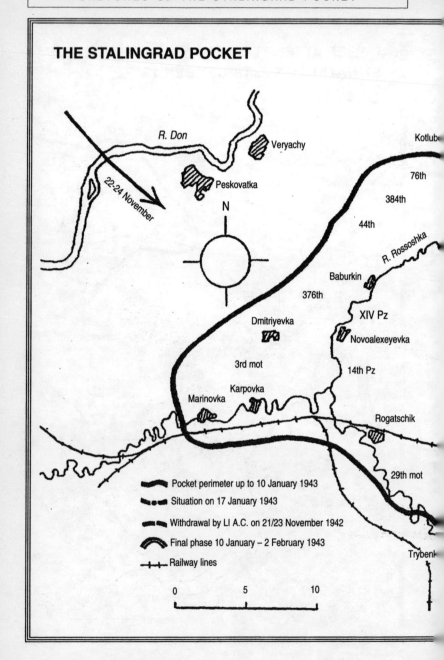

THE STALINGRAD POCKET

R. Don

Veryachy

Kotlube

Peskovatka

22-24 November

N

76th

384th

44th

R. Rossoshka

Baburkin

376th

XIV Pz

Dmitriyevka

Novoalexeyevka

3rd mot

14th Pz

Karpovka

Marinovka

Rogatschik

29th mot

Pocket perimeter up to 10 January 1943

Situation on 17 January 1943

Withdrawal by LI A.C. on 21/23 November 1942

Final phase 10 January – 2 February 1943

Railway lines

Trybenk

0   5   10

314

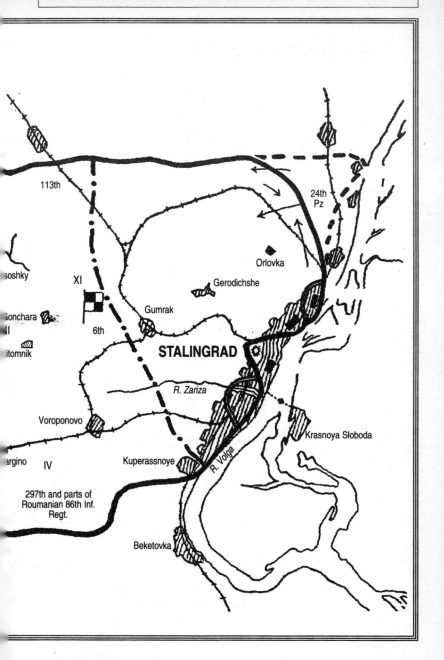

113th

24th
Pz

soshky

XI

Orlovka

Gerodichshe

Gonchara

Gumrak

6th

itomnik

STALINGRAD

R. Zariza

Voroponovo

Krasnoya Sloboda

argino   IV

Kuperassnoye

R. Volga

297th and parts of
Roumanian 86th Inf.
Regt.

Beketovka

INDEX OF PERSONAGES